GLORIES OF
THE
ROMANTIC BALLET

GLORIES OF
THE
ROMANTIC BALLET

EDWIN BINNEY 3RD

DANCE BOOKS LTD
9 CECIL COURT LONDON WC2

First published 1985 by Dance Books Ltd.,
9 Cecil Court, London WC2N 4EZ

ISBN 0 903102 82 X (cloth)
ISBN 0 903102 83 8 (paper)
Printed by BAS Printers Limited, Over Wallop, Hants

British Library Cataloguing in Publication Data

Binney, Edward
Glories of the romantic ballet.
1. Prints–19th century   2. Ballet dancers in art
I. Title
769´.42   NE962.B2/

ISBN 0 903102 82 X
ISBN 0 903102 83 8 Pbk

CONTENTS

Acknowledgements

Debts of gratitude in the form of acknowledgements are very common in modern book publications. They are frequently alphabetized to avoid 'hurt feelings'. I could do the same, conscientiously listing every print dealer who has provided material for my collection. I prefer to concentrate solely on those who have helped by overall example and specific information in making this 'Gallery of Glories' what it is. The Harvard Theatre Collection (Jeanne T. Newlin, Curator) is my 'home away from home'. There, where I have been appointed 'Curator of the Ballet Collections', I learned my craft as iconographer. My debt to Hannah Winter, equally large, is repaid by my dedication. How to thank a friend of twenty-five years, however, who has never failed to respond to my questions with information and support, is much harder. A request for a short, simple introduction to this collection elicited the present magnificent text. To him I can only repeat:

'Ivor, I owe you one!'

FOREWORD

OUR KNOWLEDGE AND UNDERSTANDING OF BALLET in the remote past would be immeasurably diminished were we to be deprived of the drawings and prints that enable us to see in our mind's eye how the dancers appeared to their contemporaries. The importance of pictorial material to the ballet historian can hardly be over-stated. To begin with, it fires his imagination. This is of vital and indeed primary importance, for history is much more than a compilation of the facts gathered by research, it is a literary art that carries the reader back in time with an insight into how things were and why. Before writing his narrative, therefore, the historian must experience his subject as deeply as his material, and his perception and interpretation of it, will allow. With such a visual art as ballet, pictorial records have a profound signifi-cance, revealing and explaining much that otherwise would be unattainable: subtle indications of a dancer's technique and style — elusive qualities in attempting to recapture an age before the advent of photography — and, to the observant eye, a host of other clues that throw light on choreographic conventions, stage production, scenery construction, costume design, stage lighting, the audience (which should never be forgotten), and countless other aspects that go to make up a complete survey.

In ferreting out this material the ballet historian is blessed with an indispensable guide in the form of the iconographer. The period of the Romantic Ballet, which flourished so gloriously in the first half of the nineteenth century, has been specially well served by scholars of this nature, and most deservedly so, for it coincided with the golden age of the lithograph. The emergence of the specialist iconographer of ballet is fairly recent, dating from the 1940s when George Chaffée's catalogues of English, French and American prints were published in the scholarly periodical, *Dance Index*. These were pioneer works and covered only part of a much wider field. More recently, another series of catalogues — covering, so

far, Italian and German and Austrian prints, but with the promise of more to come — have been compiled by Edwin Bin-ney, 3rd. I was otherwise occupied when Chaffée produced his catalogues, but Ed Binney and I have been colleagues for more than twenty years, ever since we first met in Paris when he was gathering material for his great work on Théophile Gautier and his ballets. Being both indefatigable researchers, we have shared the joys and the fruits of the hunt, and I have owed much to his erudition and unrivalled knowledge of the prints of the period in which I specialize.

My qualification for the pleasurable task of writing this fore-word is that of a major beneficiary of the iconographer's con-tribution, and Ed Binney's in particular. Better than most, I can appreciate the long and patient search and the historical erudition that have resulted in those detailed catalogues, with their identification of the subjects of the prints and the artists who drew them, and — most important — indications of where copies are to be found. I can thrill, too, to the iconographer's urge for completeness, a goal which can never quite be achieved in this imperfect world and which consequently acts as an ever-present spur to further endeavour. I introduce this book, therefore, if not as a fellow iconographer, at least as a committed iconophil. The prints that grace the pages that fol-low are the personal selection of a scholar who is also an enthu-siast of the first water. Some of the prints will be well-known, but others have never been reproduced before; many are of great and glorious stars, but others recall dancers whose names have long been forgotten. Taken together, they bring to life, in a refreshingly original way, that most nostalgic of chapters in theatrical history, the Romantic Ballet, which exerts its fascination, like a sort of terpsichorean Shangrila, long after its glamorous protagonists have all vanished from the world's stage.

IVOR GUEST

INTRODUCTION

THE 'GLORIES' OF OUR TITLE ARE TWO-FOLD. FIRST, the dancing luminaries of the Romantic Ballet at its apogee— the ballerinas of the *Pas de Quatre* (London, 1845) and Fanny Elssler who was not personally in that famous divertissement although she was included anyway, by her Viennese compatriots—as well as a few earlier pioneers, and some very famous younger contemporaries. Second, the elegant lithographs which immortalize these divinities. They constitute a corpus of the finest work by some of the finest contemporary artists, in Europe and in America, and are veritable 'keep-sakes', in the truest sense of the much-abused term.

A different aspect of the self-imposed limitations upon a selector of dance memorabilia is the previous publication of works which have already presented many of the finest prints of the period from the 1830s through the 1850s. Curiously, it was in Tsarist Russia and not in Western Europe that systematic publication of ballet iconography first appeared. N. V. Soloviev in his pioneering biography of Marie Taglioni (St. Petersburg, 1912), and S. H. Khudyekov in the third volume of his *Istoria Tantsev* (Petrograd, 1915) who reproduced hundreds of the prints he owned himself in this monumental compendium, were the first to impose obvious limitations on choice for future authors in the field.

Since World War I, many ballet historians and iconographers have published the same and additional prints. Most notable was Cyril W. Beaumont who, with Sacheverell Sitwell, produced *The Romantic Ballet in Lithographs of the Time* (London, 1938). After it, few of the great English prints had not been either reproduced or at least published.

After Beaumont came George Chaffée whose extensive catalogues of American, English and French dance prints listed about 1000 separate items, and their variants, as well as reproducing many of the little-known ones. Slightly earlier, André Levinson, along with Serge Lifar, each Russian but living in Paris, illustrated a series of books on dance history with contemporary prints.

In America, the late Lillian Moore, Parmenia Migel (Ekstrom), and the present author have continued to list and reproduce still other mementos of the *Ballet romantique*. In

Austria, the iconographic part of Pirchan's biography of Fanny Elssler (1940), although full of mistakes, is very important. From Great Britain, Ivor Guest, claiming to be no iconographer but 'only a dance historian', has enriched his histories of classical dance in both Paris and London, as well as his biographies of Cerrito and Elssler, with previously unknown or little-known prints. His catalogue of the Rambert Collection (1965) published the largest collection of dance lithographs in private hands in England. And, fortunately, he will continue with works in progress and others still only in a pre-planning stage. The Danes, Swedes and Russians have also contributed to our knowledge of an ever-widening sphere of ballet iconography. Jose Sasportes continues to present the Romantic Ballet in Portugal and Nicole Wild of the Opéra produces her very important catalogues of the separate sections of that rich repository. Works by these friends and colleagues constitute my bibliography.

To restate the criteria for inclusion in this GLORIOUS Album, the prints have been chosen for the following reasons:
1. The artistic importance of the performer or performers depicted.
2. The artistic merit of the print itself (simple possession by the compiler of a series of otherwise undistinguished prints is NOT sufficient reason for inclusion).
3. The rarity of the print and/or its status as 'not-already-overly-reproduced'. (Here, exceptions must be made to include works already well-known. With the plethora of reproductions in catalogues and other works of dance history, the slavish limitations of such a rule as this would cause veritable sterility. For example, to omit the greatest of all Romantic Ballet lithographs, *les Trois Grâces*, just because Beaumont and Sitwell published it in 1938, Chaffée discussed it at length and reproduced it again in 1944, and Lillian Moore [1938 and 1962] and Parmenia Migel [1981] have included coarse American variants of it in their works, would destroy the validity of categories 1 and 2, solely to fulfil an undesirable limitation not entirely predicated by category 3.)

INTRODUCTION

By their inclusion in this gallery, these long-vanished artists are again judged worthy of praise.

By their helpful previous works, my colleagues and friends have allowed me to grow and publish in this, our own narrow field. But one name has purposely been omitted until now. My choice of 'Glories' is respectfully and lovingly dedicated

to

The memory of Marian Hannah Winter (1910–1981) who learned her craft as iconographer with the same works as those presented here, and used that craft to embellish her marvellous works, both in this field, and also beyond it.

BIBLIOGRAPHY

Catalogues Containing Prints of the Romantic Ballet

Abbreviation

A/B — ARRIGONI, Paolo and BERTARELLI, Achille, *Ritratti di Musicisti ed Artisti di Teatro conservati nella Raccolta delle Stampe e dei Disegni* (Milano, 'Popolo d'Italia', 1934).

Amer. I — CHAFFÉE, George, 'A Chart to the American Souvenir Lithographs of the Romantic Ballet 1825–1870', *Dance Index,* vol. I, no. 2 (Feb., 1942).

Amer. II — CHAFFÉE, George, 'American Romantic Ballet Music Prints', *Dance Index*, vol. I, no. 12 (Dec., 1942).

B/S — BEAUMONT, Cyril W. and SITWELL, Sacheverell, *The Romantic Ballet in Lithographs of the Time* (London, Faber and Faber Ltd, 1938).

Eng. — CHAFFÉE, George, 'The Romantic Ballet in London 1821–1858', *Dance Index*, vol. II, nos. 9–12 (Sept.–Dec., 1943).

Fr. — CHAFFÉE, George, 'Three or Four Graces, A Centenary Salvo', *Dance Index*, vol. III, nos. 9–11 (Sept.–Nov., 1944).

Germ. — BINNEY (3rd), Edwin, 'A Century of Austro-German Dance Prints 1790–1890', *Dance Perspectives* 47 (Autumn, 1971).

HALL, Lillian Arvilla, *Catalogue of Dramatic Portraits in the Theatre Collection of the Harvard College Library*, 4 vols. (Cambridge, Harvard Univ. Press, 1930–34).

IG, *Rambert* — GUEST, Ivor, *A Gallery of Romantic Ballet* (London, New Mercury Ltd, 1965).

Ital. — BINNEY (3rd), Edwin, 'Sixty Years of Italian Dance Prints, 1815–1875', *Dance Perspectives* 53 (Spring, 1973).

LM, *C/I* — MOORE, Lillian, 'Prints on Pushcarts, The Dance Lithographs of Currier and Ives', *Dance Perspectives* 15 (1952).

Other General Works with Large Numbers of Illustrations of Iconographic Interest

Abbreviation

CBB — BEAUMONT, Cyril W., *Complete Book of Ballets* (New York, G. P. Putnam's Sons, 1938).

EB 3rd — BINNEY (3rd), Edwin, *Royal Festivals and Romantic Ballerinas* (Washington, D.C., Smithsonian Institution, 1971).

CLARK, Mary and CRISP, Clement, *Design for Ballet* (London, Studio Vista, 1978).

GREGOR, Joseph, *Kulturgeschichte des Ballets* (Wien, Gallus Verlag, 1944).

GUEST, Ivor, *The Ballet of the Second Empire, 1847–1858, 1858–1870*, 2 vols. (London, Adam and Charles Black, 1955 and 1953).

IG, *England* — GUEST, Ivor, *The Romantic Ballet in England* (London, Phoenix House Ltd, 1954).

IG, *Paris* — GUEST, Ivor, *The Romantic Ballet in Paris* (London, Sir Isaac Pitman and Sons Ltd, 1966).

HASKELL, Arnold, *Ballet Panorama*, 3rd edition (London, B. T. Batsford Ltd, 1947–48).

KHUDYEKOV, S. H., *Istoria Tantsev*, vol. III (Petrograd, 1915) (in Russian).

KIRSTEIN, Lincoln, *Movement and Metaphor Four Centuries of Ballet* (New York, Praeger Publications, 1970).

LEVINSON, Andrei, *Meister des Balletts* (Potsdam, Müller & Cie, 1925).

MIGEL, Parmenia, *The Ballerinas From the Court of Louis XIV to Pavlova* (New York, Macmillan, 1972).

Migel — MIGEL, Parmenia, *Great Ballet Prints of the Romantic Era* (New York, Dover Publications, 1981).

LM, *Artists* — MOORE, Lillian, *Artists of the Dance* (New York, Thomas Y. Crowell, 1938).

LM, *Images* — MOORE, Lillian, *Images of the Dance, Historical Treasures of the Dance 1581–1861* (New York, N.Y. Public Library, 1965).

READE, Brian, *Ballet Designs and Illustrations 1581–1940* (London, Her Majesty's Stationery Office, 1962).

9

BIBLIOGRAPHY

REUMERT, Elith, *Den Danske Ballets Historie* (København, Hjemmets Forlag, 1922).

SITWELL, Sacheverell, *The Romantic Ballet from Contemporary Prints* (London, B. T. Batsford Ltd, 1948).

MHW   WINTER, Marian Hannah, *Le Théâtre du Merveilleux* (Paris, Olivier Perrin, 1962).

(Other works whose specialty is related only to one single section of the forthcoming prints are listed at the beginning of those sections.)

PRECURSORS

AT WHAT MOMENT 'PRE-ROMANTICISM' BECAME 'Romanticism' in all of the arts is a thorny question, and nowhere more difficult to predicate than in ballet. With classical dancing it is always linked to the discovery and use of the *pointes*, the rising onto the tips of the toes as a technical feat. The names of Geneviève Gosselin, Elise Vaque-Moulin and Amalia Brugnoli (nos. 3A and 3B) are usually listed as very early exponents of this ability. Previous to 1820, however, in St. Petersburg Avdatya Ilyitchna Istomina (1799–1848) was described by a colleague Adam Glushkowski as dancing on the tips of her toes, and the poet Pushkin in *Eugène Onegin* (1823) rhapsodized over her ethereal talents in a way that suggested exactly the same opinion, as expressed by a layman. Stronger visual proof is furnished by two prints dated 1821, the first of Fanny Bias from the Paris Opéra performing in London at the King's Theatre (repr. *Eng.*, pl. III, p. 124); and the second of Angelica Mées (later Saint-Romain) in a firm arabesque (repr. Winter, *Théâtre du Merveilleux*, p. 102, lower R). And Miss Winter, in her history of *The Pre-Romantic Ballet* has traced the use of full *pointes* by *grotteschi* dancers many decades previously.

The labelling of certain themes as 'Romantic' also fails to provide a helpful specific date. Jean-Jacques Rousseau was postulating the '*moi*' as a suitable literary subject in the 1760s and 1770s; Bernardin de Saint-Pierre used the exotic wonders of the tropics for his *Paul et Virginie* in 1787; and Charles Didelot caused his dancers 'to fly' in *Flore et Zéphire* first in London in 1796.

It is equally hazardous to equate the birth of the *Ballet romantique* with the premieres of *Robert le Diable* (1831) or *la Sylphide* (1832). Each provided a stellar vehicle for Marie Taglioni (1804–84), the *première danseuse* of the Opéra. With her must begin the Romantic Ballet. Whatever was earlier must thus be labelled 'Pre-Romantic', its practitioners as precursors. With them begins our odyssey into the realm of ballet iconography.

Our earliest datable print is that of Charles Mazurier (1798–1828) in two different guises as Fritz in *la Fille soldat* (no. 4). It comes from Lyon where he was leading comic (and acro-

batic) dancer before his arrival at the Porte-Saint-Martin in Paris, and is previously unpublished. The best 'gallery' of prints of the Mazurier repertoire is found in Winter's *Théâtre du Merveilleux* (seven different roles including Jocko and Polichinelle, pp. 120–122).

At the Porte-Saint-Martin, Mazurier often appeared with Louise Pierson, a *danseuse* fated to die even younger than he: she at 24, only three years after his death at 30, in 1828. We see her as Ida, the title role in *la Laitière suisse* (1823) (no. 5), rearranged for Paris by Titus from a Vienna ballet of Filippo Taglioni two years before. In the scene below her half-length portrait is a comic *pas de deux* that the milkmaid performed with Zug, a role certainly danced by Mazurier. She later performed with the Taglioni family in both Stuttgart and Vienna, dancing a Mazurka with Filippo, a *Pas de Trois* with the young Paul Taglioni and Stiasny, and with both Marie and Paul, as well as Anton Stuhlmüller in *Schwerdt und Lanze*—all from the first year of the Stuttgart *Erinnerungen* (1826), the extremely rare series of a dozen prints which confirm their Württemberg experiments.

While the Taglioni groupe was performing in South Germany, the Hoguets: Michel-François (1793–1871) and his wife Emilie Vestris (1801–69), were appearing in Berlin. Unlike the *danseuses* of the Stuttgart company, Mme Hoguet was not yet on full *pointe* in *Nurmahal* (no. 2), an opera by Spontini (1821) which featured a *pas de deux* by the young marrieds. Another Berlin *pas de deux* was danced, somewhat later, by Mme Desargus-Lemière with Amalia Galster, soon to become the wife of Paul Taglioni. Although undated, the Polish Pas de Deux must come from the late 1820s (no. 9). It is an excellent example of a Berlin print. Its painter Eduard Gleich apparently never prepared another ballet souvenir.

Vienna also prepared fine ballet prints. Marie Taglioni's original début had taken place there in 1822, without iconographic notice. Amalia Brugnoli, however, was remembered in her first Vienna role as the Fairy in Armand Vestris' *die Fee und der Ritter* (1823) (no. 3A). Partnered by Jean Rozier, she was portrayed by 'J. S.' (Johann Josef Schindler 1777–1836) in this first depiction of a *danseur* supporting a partner on full *pointe*.

Even greater lithographic consecration was awarded Brugnoli in London. In 1832, with her husband Paolo Samengo, she appeared in four of the six *Sketches in the King's Theatre*. Number 4 showing them in the divertissement from *Masaniello* is presented here (no. 3B) because it has not previously been reproduced. In the same series, number 6, Albert partners Theresa Heberle (1806–40) in the divertissement of *Daphnis et Céphise* (no. 1A). This print has not even been catalogued before. At age 45, Albert was already exhibiting the longevity of the perfect *danseur noble*. His last appearances at the Opéra were in 1843, eleven years later. Heberle, his London partner, was almost 20 years his junior. Her original training in Vienna with Horschelt's *Kinderballet* received official consecration during several seasons at *la Scala* between 1825 and 1832, at which time she arrived at the British capital in order to appear with Albert. Number 1B gives a good sample of Italian dance lithographs, showing her surrounded by a floating shawl and appearing from clouds. Its publishers list both Florentine and Milanese addresses.

A similar Italian 'conceit' are the Roman *Primi ballerini assoluti* Adelaide Grassi and Egidio Priora (no. 6). They headed the cast at the Teatro di Apollo during Carnaval Season, 1832. Their Roman appearances may postdate our period for the beginning of the Romantic Ballet. Their costumes and coiffures certainly do not!

More pleasing to the artistic conventions of the *Ballet romantique* are a pair of charmers: *l'Adonis* and *la Fleur du Village* (nos. 7 and 8 [Colour plates I and II]). They were catalogued by Chaffée (*Eng.* 9 and 8) but have never been previously reproduced until 1971. They are atypical of English prints. First, they are aquatints, not lithographs. And their titling does not identify the dancers depicted. Chaffée would have preferred to suggest Charles Vestris and his wife Caroline Ronzi, but the dates of Jan. 1, 1827 do not support such an attribution. He therefore postulated 'Brocard and Coulon?' Regardless of less than specific identification, the prints speak for themselves. As Chaffée wrote, almost 40 years ago, 'These are the two finest English ballet prints of the 1820s known to us; that of the man is one of the most elegant items on a danseur to be found in 19th century prints.' (*Eng.*, p. 177).

With whatever is conventional—or non-conventional— the man on full *pointe*, without the ubiquitous trunks worn by male dancers until the time of Nijinski, the girl fading demurely away in contrast to her partner, we are now ready for the *Ballet romantique*.

The titles, with the names of artists, printers and publishers, as found on the prints, are listed verbatim except for addresses which are omitted and usually replaced by a line of periods. Diagonals (/) separate the lines of text. Sizes are given in centimeters, height preceding width. The height of the printed figure, including head or hat ornaments, is given first, followed, where needed, by the size of the geometric border or different coloured paper. All prints are from the author's collection.

BIBLIOGRAPHY
Winter, Marian Hannah, *The Pre-Romantic Ballet* (London, Pitman, 1974). (Abbrev.: *PRB*)

1A. (top:) Sketches in the King's Theatre No. 6/(bottom:) Monsr. Albert and Madlle. Heberlé/In the Favorite Ballet of/Daphnis et Cephise./Levasseur delt./ ///Margins trimmed but prob. read: Printed by Maguire, Lemercier & Co./London, Pub. by A. Ackermann . . . May, 1832   17.3 cm.
Eng. series B, uncat.; EB 3rd, no. 49; never repr.

1B. Teresa Heberlé/Litografia Ricordi./P. F. disegnò/Firenze. Presso Ricordi, Pozzi e C.   Milano Presso Gio. Ricordi/No. 28.   17.6 cm.
not in *Ital.*; never repr.

2. Madame und Herr/Hoguet/in der Oper: *Nurmahal*/Gez. v. J. Schoppe/Lith. Inst. v. L. Sachse & Cs./Verlag v. Gbr. Gropius i. Diorama   17.2 cm.
Germ. 124; repr. Winter, *PRB*, p. 268.

3A. Hr. Rozier und Dlle. Brugnoli/im Ballete die Fee und der Ritter./ged. im lith. Institut in Wien./(on stone:) J. S.   15.5 cm.
Germ. 17, repr.; repr. Winter, *PRB*, p. 273; Moore, *Images*, no. 39.

3B. (top:) Sketches in the King's Theatre No. 4/(bottom:) Sigr. Samingo and Madc. Brugnoli/In the Divertissement of/ Massaniello./Levasseur delt.///Margins trimmed but prob. read: Printed by Maguire, Lemercier & Co./London, Pub. by R. Ackermann . . . May, 1832   17.2 cm.
Eng. 143, unnumbered; A/B 4018; EB 3rd, no. 49; repr. Khudyekov, p. 84.

4. M. Mazurier, rôle de Fritz, dans la Fille Soldat/(Ballet en 3 Actes)/1er Acte   2e Acte/Lith. de H. Brunet à Lyon. (left:) 19.6 cm; (right:) 21.6 cm in two rects. total: 22.1 × 32 cm.
not in *Fr.*; never repr.

5. Mlle. Louise Pierson./(Rôle de la Laitière Suisse.)/Ballet Pantomime)/Thtre. de la Porte St. Martin Lith. de G. Engelmann/(on stone:) C. F. (the portrait:) 12.8 cm; (the scene:) 4.7 × 11 cm.
Fr. 85; never repr.

6. Adelaide Grassi Egidio Priora/Primi Ballerini assoluti/nel/ Nobile Teatro di Apollo nel Carnevale del 1832./(on stone:) A. Almerini dis.—Roma lit. Battistelli (she:) 18.3 cm; (he:) 18.6 cm in tinted rect.: 21.7 × 29.1 cm.

  Ital. 188 Var; A/B 1963; repr. Khudykov, p. 341.

7. [Colour plate 1] L'Adonis du Village/London Engraved and Published January 1ˢᵗ, 1827 by J. Cross . . . 22.3 cm in tinted rect. 30.2 × 24 cm.

  Eng. 9; repr. EB 3rd, no. 48A; a postal card from the coll. of Allison Delarue.

8. [Colour plate 11] La Fleur du Village/London, Engraved and Published January 1ˢᵗ, 1827 by J. Cross . . . 18.7 cm in tinted rect. 30.2 × 24 cm.

  Eng. 8; repr. EB 3rd, no. 48B.

9. Mad. Desargus-Lemière et Delle Amélie Galster/dans/le pas de deux polonais./d'après la nature par Edouard Gleich . . . Lith. de G. Edouard Müller à Berlin (the taller:) 30.1 cm.

  Germ. 59; repr. IG, *Rambert*, 53.

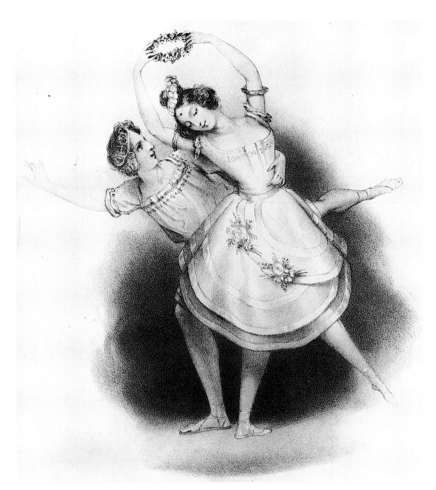

Ger. v J. Schoppe   Lith. Inst. v L. Sachse & Co.

2. Michel-François Hoguet and his wife Emilie Vestris in *Nurmahal* (Berlin, 1821)

3A. Amalia Brugnoli and Jean Rozier
in *die Fee und der Ritter* (Vienna, 1823)

3B. Amalia Brugnoli and her husband
Paolo Samengo in *Masaniello*.
Sketches in the King's Theatre, No. 4 (1832)

4. Charles Mazurier in two different roles. *la Fille soldat* (Lyon, 1818)

5. Louise Pierson in *la Laitière suisse* (Paris, Théâtre de la Porte-Saint-Martin, 1824)

6. Adelaide Grassi and Egidio Priora (Rome, 1832)

9. Mme Desargus-Lemière and Amalia Galster in *le Pas de Deux polonais* (Berlin, late 1820s)

MARIE TAGLIONI
1804–1884

THE SUPREME BALLERINA OF THE ROMANTIC BALLET was Marie Taglioni. An Italian father who was also teacher, business-manager and choreographer for her, and a Swedish mother whose parents were important Opera singers in Stockholm. An apparently unbeatable combination! If she was not beautiful, she could embody a symbol of unattainable gracefulness and ethereality. Her primacy is attested by the most extensive printed iconography of any dancer, of any period. More than 300 separate items! The largest problem for choosing a selection for this book is an embarrassment of riches. The major criterion for inclusion, for Taglioni as well as for the other great dancers of the period, is to present as many facets of her professional career as possible: (1) a portrait or portraits that show some of the emotional character of the performer; (2) a selection from the major roles she created or performed; (3) caricatures or unusual souvenirs; (4) a range of different national origins for the prints themselves—trying always for as-yet-unpublished or little-known examples.

The earliest prints of Marie are contemporary with the dancers in the first section herewith, previously labelled 'precursors'. Her appearances in seven of the dozen Stuttgart *Erinnerungen* series (1826–27) and a group of portraits, including an early Stuttgart one by Lauter (1827) and three Paris ones by different artists: Vigneron (1828), with Gigoux and Grevedon (both 1831), bridge the years until she found her 'perfect painter'—the English-based, Swiss-born Alfred Edward Chalon (1780–1860). In London, during her second season there in 1831, she sat for him for the first of many times. Although Chalon never lithographed his own works, his favoured collaborators being Richard James Lane (1800–72) and Thomas Herbert Maguire (1826–95), his artistic style as translated by the various lithographers he favoured perfectly captured Taglioni on stone. 1831 witnessed the *Flore* (no. 102, INSERT) which was often to be pirated, several times with the title 'la Sylphide', and the *Six Sketches* (*Eng.* series H). Chalon's first real Sylphide, dated 1836 (*Eng.* 111) is his least successful depiction of her. His most successful, and the print

she supposedly preferred to all others, was the *Bayadère* (*Eng.* 112). It is one of the few major English prints that does not bear a date of publication. Chaffée equates it with a souvenir for Queen Victoria's Coronation Year (1838). It must be earlier, as a variant of it had already appeared in Paris in 1835, interestingly subtitled '*la Sylphide*' (no. 15).

1835 was also the year that Lépaulle's painting of Marie with her brother Paul asleep in the armchair from the opening pose of *la Sylphide*, which is dated 1834, was engraved by Garnier and appeared at the annual Salon (*livret* no. 2392). Rather than use that famous mezzotint which figures in Beaumont and Sitwell (B/S 18, plate 15) and many other publications, we use an English reduction engraved by J. W. Huffam (*Eng.* 118) entitled . . . 'in the Mountain Sylph.' (no. 11 [colour plate III]). The hand-colouring of this copy is particularly strong and fresh.

As Lépaulle was painting his double portrait which he dedicated to Dr. Véron, Director of the Opéra, Bernard Mulrenin (1803–68) in London was designing and lithographing still another Sylphide (*Eng.* 110) which was not reproduced until 1965 when Ivor Guest presented the Rambert copy (IG, *Rambert*, no. 118). We present it here again (no. 12).

All was not perfect for Taglioni. While a possible rivalry with Fanny Elssler seemed unlikely, when based solely upon the Viennese's first two Paris ballets, but her third vehicle *le Diable boiteux*, in 1836, presented her with a perfect role, Florinde, and the most famous of character dances, *la Cachucha*. At the same time, in London, Taglioni had to endure the malicious ridicule of caricature by 'Théophile Wagstaff' (pseudonym of William M. Thackeray) in the *Flore et Zephyr Ballet Mythologique* (*Eng.* series I), the proof vignette for the title page of which we include (no. 13). More pleasant for her, probably dating from 1837, when four Taglionis performed at Drury Lane, are a series of tiny lithographs which grace a collection of flute solos—*Six Gems de Ballet*. We present two (nos. 14A and 14B) which show her with her brother Paul. The *pas de deux* from *la Sylphide* was catalogued by Chaffée (*Eng.* 120) who remarked because of its small size that it was 'apparently, a bookplate'. Obviously he did not have a complete copy of the tiny music collection. He did, however, note its re-use as a music title (*Eng.* 121). Again he had a trimmed copy! He did not realize that the music was number 3 of the series *Beauties of the Ballet*. The second of the *Pas de Deux* with Paul has never been either catalogued or reproduced.

1837 was the year Marie left the Paris Opéra and began the first of five seasons in Russia. It was also the year a curious portrait was prepared by Firmin Salabert (no. 10) and Auguste Barre sculpted the statuette of her in *la Sylphide* as pendant for another of Fanny Elssler in *la Cachucha*. Both statuettes were immediately used for prints by Achille Devéria (1800–57) who included them in his monumental *Costumes historiques* series. The Taglioni *Sylphide* has been overreproduced (B/S 17, pl. 14; Migel 12, among many others), but it is presented here yet again (no. 16A) in order to contrast it with its pendant—a late variant, with ageing face and dying rose bushes under her *grand jeté devant* (no. 16B). Chaffée, consulting only a London version of the later print, could not understand why Henri Grevedon, when recopying Devéria's lithograph after Barre's statuette, had the lithograph titled in English (*Fr.* 99, and *Eng.* 119). His dating of 1844–45 would have made this a definite *Souvenir d'Adieux* for her last six Paris performances in June, 1844. It was printed, however, in 1838.

But in the interim, her father had presented her with two 3 act ballets for her Russian seasons, each extremely successful. They are best known from English prints. *La Gitana* (St. Petersburg Dec. 5, 1838; London June 6, 1839) starred Taglioni in two London lithographs (*Eng.* 113–114) during its first summer there, shortly before Elssler brought over her own *la Gypsy* from Paris. The next winter Emma Soyer presented Taglioni in *la Gitana* again (*Eng.* 115; B/S 6, not repr; Migel 34), and Weld Taylor drew on stone, not one, but two, different depictions of Taglioni in the same ballet by Edwin Dalton Smith (b. 1806). Beaumont and Sitwell did not know them. Only one was catalogued by Chaffée (*Eng.* 116) although both had been by Soloviev in 1912 (his nos. 26 and 27). We present them as the proper pendants that they have always been (nos. 18 and 19 [Colour plates IV and V]).

The second St. Petersburg ballet to have a London, and also a Paris, sequel was *l'Ombre* (St. Petersburg Dec. 4, 1839; London June 18, 1840). The ethereal impalpability of the Romantic ballerina is suggested nowhere better than in the lithograph where Antonio Guerra remains stupefied as she balances on a rose (no. 17). How her left *pointe* must have hurt if he did not place her exactly onto her precarious floral support. For the Paris farewells in 1844, she did not appear in the complete ballet. For her benefit performance on June 29, however, she performed two scenes from the Russian work. Her *Pas de l'Ombre*, reminiscent of Cerrito's *Ondine* (no. 41A), was used for a woodcut in *l'Illustration*. More popular was the *Scène des Fleurs* from the same ballet. It was not only used as Plate 16 in Challamel's *Album de l'Opéra*, designed by Devéria (*Fr.* 532), but for three separate music titles (only one catalogued by Chaffée—*Fr.* 106). *Le Ménestrel, Journal de Musique* published still another version, this one by Janet Lange (1815–72). It has neither been catalogued nor reproduced before (no. 21A).

Two other Taglioni rarities need mention. Her foot appearing from clouds, with a poem in Russian, has been reproduced by Lincoln Kirstein (*Movement and Metaphor*, no. 244), after its initial publication by Khudyekov (p. 104). Its rarity forces its inclusion again (no. 21B). Even rarer, never catalogued nor reproduced, is a full-length caricature. Entitled *The Original Taglioni! A Fashionable Favorite*, it presents her in Bayadère costume which is almost covered by an overcoat, a handkerchief dangling from her breast pocket. On *pointes* before a pier-glass, she presents us with still another unique personality (no. 20).

The last three years of her performing life collectively become the Apotheosis of Marie Taglioni. On June 1, 1844, same day as the first of her six Paris Adieux performances, was published the supreme icon of the *Ballet romantique—les Trois Grâces* by Lejeune. She may be presented as gradually fading away to the left, but she is definitely there in still another depiction from the Barre statuette (no. 61 [Colour plate XII]).

For the *Pas de Quatre*, first performed in London on July 12, 1845, Taglioni is presented 'front and center' by Chalon, as lithographed by Maguire, in the brilliant plate published less than two months later (no. 62). *The Illustrated London News* on July 19 had meanwhile issued a woodcut which was pirated in America the following year as 'The Dance of the Fairies' (no. 64). And Brandard's treatment of a different pose from the same *Pas de Quatre* had appeared both as an easel print (no. 63) and as a music title (also in this collection).

Chalon's supreme tribute to the *danseuse* were the six plates of the *Album d'Adieux*, showing her various appearances during *la Sylphide*. There were five different lithographers, as Lane only did the first and last prints, and the others were prepared by Templeton, Morton, Lynch and Maguire (this lithographer also drew the *Pas de Quatre* on stone). The date on the cover of the group may read Sept. 15, 1845 (same date as the *Pas de Quatre*): the individual plates themselves all say Sept. 8th (nos. 22 and 23).

After 1845, only two years remained in Taglioni's performing life. But another great print was to immortalize her last appearances. The *Pas des Déesses,* a divertissement in Perrot's *Jugement de Pâris*, was premiered on July 23, 1846. Again, a woodcut appeared in *The Illustrated London News* nine days later. By the time the authoritative print had appeared on Sept.

8, Taglioni was already on tour in Plymouth and Ireland. It was not Chalon who immortalized the new spectacle. It was Jules Bouvier at his most 'Chalonesque' (no. 65 [Colour plate XIII]). The following year, without elaborate fanfare,

Taglioni appeared for the last time, on Aug. 21, 1847 in a performance of the *Pas des Déesses*. She was almost four months past her forty-third birthday.

BIBLIOGRAPHY

Soloviev, N. V., *Maria Taglioni* (St. Petersburg, 1912).

Khudyekov, S. H., vol. III, pp. 105–130.

Levinson, André, *Marie Taglioni (1804–1884)* (Paris, Félix Alcan, 1929) English translation by Cyril W. Beaumont (London, Dance Books Ltd, 1977).

Vaillat, Léandre, *La Taglioni, ou la Vie d'une danseuse* (Paris, Albin Michel, 1942).

Guest, Ivor, . . . *Paris*, pp. 73–159.

Migel, Parmenia, *The Ballerinas*, chap. 11, pp. 115–144.

Lacotte, Pierre and Binney (3rd), Edwin, *Marie Taglioni* (forthcoming) with a complete iconography by the present author.

10. Marie Taglioni (*facs. sign.*)/F. Salabert del./Lith. par Sudre/ Imp. Lith. de Thierry frères   27.7 cm.

> Soloviev, no. 55; Hall 9; A/B 4335; repr. Haskell, pl. 33.

11. [Colour plate III] Mad.lle Taglioni as La Sylphide,/in the/ "Mountain Sylph."/Painted by G. Lepaulle Engraved by J. W. Huffam. (the sleeping hero:) 17 cm in rect. 29.7 × 22.8 cm.

> *Eng.* 118; never repr.

12. Mademoiselle Taglioni/Designed & Drawn on Stone by B. Mulrenin./London, Published Sep.r, 1834 by Ackermann & C.o . . ./ and at Paris by Rittner & Goupil./Printed by C. Hullmanel. 31.8 cm.

> *Eng.* 110; Soloviev, no. 41; Hall, 57; repr. Guest, *Rambert*, 118.

13. (Proof before titling) (Title page:) Flore et Zephyr/Ballet Mythologique/dédié à/. . ./par Théophile Wagstaff (facs. sign.)/ London, Published March 1st 1836 by J. Mitchell . . ./à Paris chez Rittner & Goupil . . ./Printed by Graf & Soret. 11.2 cm.

> *Eng.* series I, not cat.; repr. Guest, "Thackeray and the Ballet", *Dancing Times*, vol. LXII, no. 737 (Jan., 1972) p. 188 top.

14. (Two *Pas de Deux* with Marie and Paul Taglioni) Six/Gems de Ballet,/Danced by/Mad.lle Taglioni/Mad.lle Fanny Elssler,/and/ Mad.lle Duvernay/Arranged expressly for the/Flute/and Illustrated with Portraits/Taken from Drawings made at/The Queen's Theatre,/During the Present Season./London:/George and Manby . . .

  A. Mad.lle Taglioni & Sig.r Paul Taglioni/Pas de deux. (on next page:) N.o 4/(W. Lake litho.) (she:) 7 cm within triple octagon   11.6 × 9.7 cm.

> not in *Eng.*; never repr.

  B. Mad.lle Taglioni & Sig.r Paul Taglioni/Pas de deux. La Sylphide (on next page:) N.o 6/(W. Lake Lith.) (she:) 7 cm within triple octagon   13.8 × 10 cm.

> *Eng.* 120; never repr.

15. M.elle Taglioni/dans la Sylphide [*sic* for la Bayadère] Lith. de Gihaut frères Editeurs . . . Lith. par F. Courtin . . . 32 cm.

> not in *Fr.* (but a Var. of *Fr.* 104); a reduction of *Eng.* 112 which is repr. B/S 1, pl. 3; *CBB*, opp. p. 75; IG, *Rambert*, no. 108.

16A. Marie Taglioni/(Sylphide.)/(on stone:) Deveria (facs. sign.)/ A. Devéria, del.   Imp. Lith. de Cattier/Paris, Goupil et Vibert . . . 26 cm in rect. 34.8 × 23.8 cm.

> *Fr.* 98; Soloviev 4; B/S 17, pl. 14; EB 3rd, 53; Migel 12.

16B. Marie Taglioni/Sylphide/A Devéria et H. Grevedon d'après A. Barre   Publié par Cattier . . .   lith. de C. Motte/Paris, chez Aumont . . . et Rittner et Goupil.   26.3 in rect. 34.7 × 23.8 cm.

> *Eng.* 119 and *Fr.* 99 (each titled in *Eng.*); Hall 36; A/B 4333; never repr.

17. Marie Taglioni (facs. sign.) and Signor Guerra (facs. sign.)/in the Celebrated Ballet/L'Ombre/London, Published by T. McLean . . . July 15th 1840/Bouvier del. (she:) 22.5 cm in rect. 37.5 × 29 cm.

> *Eng.* 117; Hall, 22; EB 3rd, 55; repr. B/S 7, pl. 6; Khudyekov, p. 125; *CBB*, opp. p. 99.

18. [Colour plate IV] (on flat feet) Marie Taglioni (facs. sign.)/La Gitana/Painted by Edwin D. Smith   Drawn on Stone by Weld Taylor. 24.4 cm.

> not in *Eng.*; Soloviev 27; A/B 4322; repr. Levinson, no. 71, p. 146.

19. [Colour plate V] (on pointes) Marie Taglioni (facs. sign.)/La Gitana./Edwin D. Smith del.   Drawn on Stone by Weld Taylor/London, Published June 12, 1840, by J. Watson . . ./ M. & N. Hanhart, Lith. Printers. 26.2 cm.

> *Eng.* 116; Soloviev 26; A/B 4321; never repr.

20. The Original Taglioni!/A Fashionable Favorite. (no artists) 24 cm in octagon 28.7 × 22 cm.

> not cat.; never repr.

21A. (top:) (Académie Royale de Musique)/Journal de Musique   Le Menéstrel/Scène des Fleurs, dansée par M.lle Taglioni (on stone:) Janet Lange (facs sign.)/Imp. Bertauts (horiz.:) 17.2 cm in rect. 16.8 × 25 cm.

> not in *Fr.* (Var of nos. 106 and 532); repr. Khudyekov, p. 127.

21B. (Her foot appearing from clouds)/(Quatrain in Russian by Kn. [Prince] P. A. Vyasemski)/Pourquoi chausser une aile?/Ris Kiel   Grav. Rait [Wright?]   3.7 cm.

> not in Soloviev; Hall 107 (as Elssler); repr. Khudyekov, p. 104; Kirstein, no. 244.

22–23. The Album d'Adieux: La Sylphide/Souvenir d'Adieu/de/Marie Taglioni/par/A. E. Chalon R.A./Artistes Lithographes/R. J. Lane A.R.A./Edward Morton,/J. S. Templeton,/J. H. Lynch,/T. H. Maguire,/Londres, Sept! 15, 1845, Publié par J. Mitchell . . ./Imprimé par M. & N. Hanhart in double octagon 41.7 × 28.7 cm (several are slightly smaller).

Eng. 177–182; Hall 30, 35, 34, 32, 33, 31; repr. Khudyekov, pp. 113, 114, 116; B/S 11–16, pls. 8–13; LM, Images, 50–55; Lacotte, Marie Taglioni la Sylphide, pls. I–III, V–VII.

22A. (Number 1) (Hovering over the chair) R. J. Lane A.R.A.

Levinson, no. 79, p. 155; CBB, opp. p. 92, lower R; Gregor 172; IG, Rambert, no. 110, not repr.

22B. (Number 2) (Standing in the window) J. S. Templeton

Soloviev 8; Levinson, no. 80, p. 156; CBB, opp. p. 92, top L; Gregor 171; IG, Rambert, no. 111, not repr.

22C. (Number 3) (on pointes in fifth position) Edward Morton

CBB, opp. p. 92, top R; IG, Rambert, no. 112, not repr.

23A. (Number 4) (with the bird's nest) J. H. Lynch

CBB, opp. p. 92, bottom L; Gregor 173; IG, Rambert, no. 113, repr.; repr. IG "Dandies and Dancers", Dance Perspectives 37, spring, 1969, p. 5.

23B. (Number 5) (wings falling) T. H. Maguire.

IG, Rambert, no. 114, repr.; Migel 13.

23C. (Number 6) (bowing) R. J. Lane A.R.A.

Soloviev, 9; IG, Rambert, no. 115, not repr.

10. Marie Taglioni. Portrait by Firmin Salabert (Paris, 1837)

MADEMOISELLE TAGLIONI.

12. Marie Taglioni in *la Sylphide* by Bernard Mulrenin (London, 1834)

13. Marie Taglioni as *Flore*. Caricature by Theophile Wagstaff (William Makepeace Thackeray) (London, 1836)

14A and B. Marie Taglioni with her brother Paul
in [A] a classical *Pas de Deux*
and [B] the *Pas de Deux* from *la Sylphide*

15. Marie Taglioni in *le Dieu et la Bayadère* but titled *la Sylphide*

16A. Marie Taglioni in *la Sylphide*
from the statuette by Barre *fils* (Paris, 1837)

16B. Marie Taglioni in *la Sylphide*
from the statuette by Barre *fils*,
with faded rosebushes (Paris, 1838)

[1] 7. l'Adonis du Village (London, 1827)

[11] 8. la Fleur du Village (London, 1827)

[III] 11. Marie Taglioni with her brother Paul. Opening pose, *la Sylphide* (Paris, 1832)

Edwin D. Smith

[IV] 18. Marie Taglioni in *la Gitana* (London, 1840)

[v] 19. Marie Taglioni in *la Gitana* (London, 1840)

[VI] 26. Fanny Elssler as Florinde in *le Diable boiteux* (Paris, 1836)

[VII] 32. Fanny Elssler in *la Cachucha* probably after Napoleon Sarony (New York, 1840)

[VIII] 35. Fanny Elssler dancing in Hamburg

17. Marie Taglioni with Antonio Guerra in *l'Ombre* (London, 1840)

20. 'The Original Taglioni. A Fashionable Favorite'

21A. Marie Taglioni in *l'Ombre* (Paris, 1844)

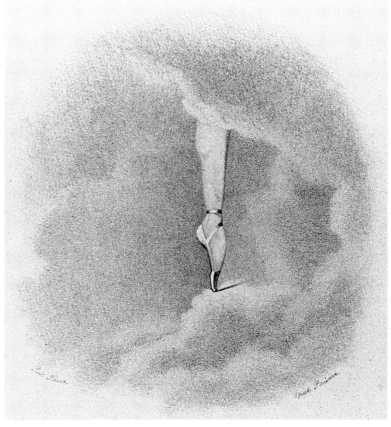

21B. Taglioni's foot appearing from clouds
(St. Petersburg, *c.* 1840)

A. Number 1   B. Number 2   C. Number 3

A. Number 4   B. Number 5   C. Number 6

23. The *Album d'Adieux* (cont.)

FANNY ELSSLER
1810–1884

THE REPUTATION OF FANNY ELSSLER HAS ALWAYS been limited by the supposed rivalry with Taglioni and her definite artistic and financial conquest of the United States. But her two years in America, which enrich her iconography by myriads of prints—in many of which her head was simply substituted for the original on any available lithograph—were only a small part of an overall career which began and ended in Vienna, her birthplace, and included 'the Germanies', Britain, France, Italy and Russia also.

The rivalry with Taglioni was not so much a shifting of popular opinion from one to the other as the expression of personal preferences by the ordinary spectator as moulded by the critics. Taglioni was older and homely. Fanny, born in 1810, was not only six years younger, but was also a supremely beautiful woman. Their styles of dancing were also diametrically opposed: Taglioni's *ballonné*, the ability to hover over the surface of the stage without appearing to need it for support, the lightness and control of her jumps, was in complete contrast to Fanny's *terre-à-terre tacqueté*, technical brilliance and speed in her *pointe* work. When Elssler finally found her perfect roles, the contrasting repertoires of the two *danseuses* embodied both aspects of the Romantic vision.

'Mlle. Taglioni is a Christian dancer . . . Fanny Elssler is a completely pagan dancer,' wrote Théophile Gautier in 1837, a few months after the older *danseuse* had left Paris for Russia. His friend Arsène Houssaye in his *Confessions* contrasted 'a religious rite, an uplifting, an ascending cloud' as compared to 'a delight for the eyes, a voluptuous pose, a challenging flight' (vol. IV, p. 341). To state it ever more simply, Elssler appealed to men while Taglioni appealed to women. Once this basic dichotomy is accepted, the rivalry assumes its proper perspective. Each might try to succeed in the specialty of the other; Elssler might appear in Taglioni's *Sylphide* and *la Fille du Danube* (each in 1838), and Taglioni might, with better claims to success, appear as a terrestrial in *la Gitana* (see nos. 18 and 19 [Colour plates IV and V]). But each was supreme in her own sphere.

During her early years at the Opéra, Fanny starred in Louis Henry's *l'Ile des Pirates* (1835). Her role of Mathilde was not very successful. But the print showing her in it is number 6 of an unknown series—*le Théâtre* (no. 25). The contrast with Florinde, the Spanish dancer of *le Diable boiteux* (1836), who revolutionized the Opéra with the Cachucha, was enormous. Barre's statuette of Fanny in the dance became her hallmark. Devéria's print from it is THE Elssler icon. It is presented here again (no. 27) in contrast to another Devéria lithograph of her in the same role, this one drawn from life (no. 26). Each one was included in the *Costumes historiques*, with the Taglioni *Sylphide* which slightly post-dated them (no. 16A).

Fanny's sister Therese (1808–78), who often partnered her, and was portrayed with her by Firmin Salabert (no. 24) who had also depicted Taglioni (no. 10), choreographed a light ballet for her Paris benefit on May 5, 1838. *La Volière* was certainly no success—only four performances in Paris and none anywhere else. But in London that summer, the very young John Deffett Francis (1815–1901) drew Fanny in her costume for the ballet and a lithograph was published there in August, although the ballet was not performed. Even more curious is a unique American copy of the English print, dated 1840, which we present here (no. 28).

A single important role was not sufficient for a *première danseuse*, and this no doubt caused Duponchel, the Director of the Opéra, to suggest Elssler's assuming the title role in Taglioni's *Sylphide* during the latter's absence in Russia. Fanny had already performed that ballet in Bordeaux in 1836, but not elsewhere. The charming little memento of her Paris *Sylphide* (no. 29A) appeared without her name. There was only one Sylphide for most of the Opéra-goers! A later Berlin lithograph, probably from 1842, is properly labelled (no. 29B).

A new ballet, *la Gypsy*, with a new character dance, *la Cracovienne* (Opéra, 1839; London, summer of the same year), again demonstrated the Elssler formula with the addition of a tragic ending where her fine dramatic gifts were stretched to their fullest extent. Iconographic consecration of the new character dance was in London, where Thomas McLean published Bouvier's depiction of her on Aug. 24, 1839 (*Eng. 56*). Our variant of the Bouvier original (no. 30) appeared, without credit to the London artists, in New York, published by Atwill, attributed to Eliphalet Brown Jr. (fl. 1843–59) who does not even merit a notice in Bénézit's *Dictionnaire*. It is much rarer than Bouvier's initial lithograph.

1840 was the beginning of Elssler's 'discovery of America' . . . each city, as it fell at her feet succumbing to '*Fannyelsslermania!*' Her opening night at the Park Theatre in New York (May 14) featured *la Tarentule*, her newest Paris (June 24, 1839) and London (March 15, 1840) success. Only a week before she sailed from Bristol on *The Great Western*, another Bouvier lithograph of her in the new role appeared in London. Although copies of this print with American artists' names would appear in both Philadelphia and New York (*Amer.* II, 42) during the first months of her American tour, it was Nathaniel Currier (1813–88) who capitalized most on her premiere ballet. He not only adapted Bouvier's lithograph (*Amer.* I, 28) but also 'invented' one of his own (no. 31) (not in *Amer.* I), using an English music title of Taglioni in *la Gitana* as his source (*Eng.* 205; *Beauties of the Ballet*, no. 13), but with an entirely different costume.

Even before she left New York, for the first time, Elssler had actually 'sat' for Henry Inman (1801–46), seated at the table in her dressing room at the Park, dressed for the bridal scene in *la Tarentule*. The portrait went back to Europe with her two years later and is now in the Haydn Museum in Eisenstadt, outside of Vienna (repr. IG, *FE*, opp. p. 128, bottom). Before she left, however, she permitted Thomas Sully (1783–1872) to copy Inman's work—the smaller Sully copy is in the Dance Collection of the New York Public Library (see Moore, *Images*, frontispiece). An American print from the Inman painting was published before she left the United States for home. Two partial examples, in fragments, remain at Harvard. A second lithograph from Munich, dated 1845, still lists Inman's name. It is reproduced here (no. 33).

Another American souvenir of Elssler's stay is a fine print of *la Cachucha*. It exists in many versions—Chaffée catalogued eight easel prints (*Amer.* I, 18–20) and at least three music

titles (*Amer.* II, 20). Many are signed or attributed to Currier or to Nathaniel Sarony (1821–96) whom Chaffée guesses to have been the original artist (*Amer.* I, p. 29). We present one of the Currier variants which lists John L. McGee as its designer (no. 32 [Colour plate VII]). It obviously shows far more 'action' than the European prints after the Barre statuette, and their American adaptations also (*Amer.* I, 21; and II, 21).

Home in Europe, richer by hundreds of thousands of dollars, even after several legal suits against her by the Opéra from which she had greatly overextended her leave of absence, Elssler continued her career. Even though she was *persona non grata* there, she still was pictured in central splendour in the Paris *Trois Grâces* (no. 61 [Colour plate XII]) in 1844. Highpoints of this later career were appearances in London in works by Jules Perrot who also partnered her in them. A fine example is *The Castilliana Bolero*, a national dance she performed with the choreographer in his *le Délire d'un Peintre* (1843). It is Bouvier at his colourful best (no. 34). Other ballets were *Giselle* and *Esmeralda*, both conceived for Carlotta Grisi but to each of which she added her own dramatic expertise. She appeared also in Russia from 1848 into the spring of 1851, in these ballets and in *Catarina* which Perrot had originally prepared for Lucile Grahn in 1846 (see nos. 60 and 103). After her last Moscow season in 1851, she returned to Vienna for her farewell performances in May and June. Her last appearance, in Perrot's *Faust* (first at la Scala in 1848), was three days before her 41st birthday.

But Fanny did not remain in Vienna. She lived for the first three years of her retirement in Hamburg. Parmenia Migel (*The Ballerinas*, pp. 166–167) writes of a possible morganatic marriage there to a Wettin (Saxe-Coburg-Gotha) prince who was later considered for the throne of Spain. Miss Migel's source misread the name of 'Eisner', who did marry the prince, with 'Elssler'. A more definite Hamburg provenance can be given to our last print of Fanny. She always loved that city in a special way. How proper for us to conclude our Elssler section with a Hamburg lithograph (no. 35 [Colour plate VII]) which, to our shame, we did not include among the 37 Elssler examples of our Austro-German catalogue in 1971. I did not find the print until 1978!

BIBLIOGRAPHY
Khudyekov, vol. III, pp. 147–170.
Pirchan, *Fanny Elssler, Eine Wienerin tanzt um die Welt* (Wien, Wilhelm Frick, 1940).
Guest, Ivor, *Paris*, chapters 6–7, pp. 131–185.

Guest, Ivor, *Fanny Elssler* (London, Adam and Charles Black, 1970).
Delarue, Allison, *Fanny Elssler in America* (New York, Dance Horizons, 1976).
Migel, *The Ballerinas*, chapter 12, pp. 145–167.

24. Therese et Fanny Elssler (facs. signs.) (no other information on this clipped copy, although it should read like the portrait of Taglioni by the same artist, Firmin Salabert. See no. 11 above). (Therese: standing:) 33.3 cm.

> repr. Pirchan, no. 25.

25. (top:) No 6/Le/Théâtre/(bottom:) Opéra/L'ile des Pirates/(on stone:) A. Lacauchie (facs. sign.)/A Collin et Cie Editeurs . . . Lith. Rigo Fes et Cie.   11.4 cm in rect. 16.6 × 11.8 cm.

> not in *Fr.*; repr. IG, 'A Fanny Elssler Portrait,' *Dancing Times* vol. LVI, no. 668; May, 1966, p. 411.

26. [Colour plate VI] (upper R:) No 29/(bottom:) Costume Espagnol/(on stone:) Deveria (facs. sign.)/A. Devéria del   Lith. de Lemercier à Paris./Paris, chez Aumont . . . et chez Rittner et Goupil . . . 27 cm in rect. 34.9 × 23.7 cm.

> *Fr.* 24 Var; Hall 93; never repr.

27. Fanny Elssler (facs. sign.)/(Ballet du Diable boiteux, 3e Acte)/ Lith. par Lafosse d'après Devéria et Barre   Im. de Lemercier, Benard & Cie/Paris, chez Rittner et Goupil . . . London, Ackermann & Co   28 cm in rect. 34.6 × 23.6 cm.

> *Fr.* 23; A/B 1450; EB 3rd, 58; repr. IG, *FE,* opp. p. 65, top; (close Var of B/S 22, pl. 18; Pirchan 31; Migel 27).

28. La Volière   Portrait of Mademoiselle F. Elssler/On Stone by Chas Parsons from a Drawing by J. D. Francis/Entered according to Act of Congress, in the year 1840, by G. Endicott . . ./ Litho. of Endicott . . . Fanny Elssler (facs. sign.)/Published by George Endicott . . . New York.   43.7 cm in double rect. 52.9 × 35.5 cm.

> not in *Amer.* I; repr. Delarue, p. 67 (the *Eng.* orig.: *Eng.* 55; B/S 27, pl. 19; IG, *Rambert,* 50, repr.; LM, *Images,* 62).

29A. Sylphide./Levasseur del./Imp. Zinco. Lith Kaeppelin et Cie . . ./(on stone:) Levasseur (facs. sign.) 16.6 cm in triple rect. 20.7 × 15.8 cm.

> *Fr.* 33; Hall 85; never repr.

29B. Fanny Elsler./Gez. v. Fr. Krüger . . . Lith. von Wild/Paris, publié par Goupil & Vibert . . . Druck u Verlag v. L. Sachse & Co Berlin . . . London published by Ackermann & Co   35.5 cm in rect. 49.9 × 34 cm.

> *Germ.* 79, repr. p. 20; Hall 86; A/B 1451; Pirchan 42.

30. Fanny Elssler (facs. sign.)/In the Cracovienne Dance, in the Ballet of/The Gipsey/E. Brown Jr del. Endicott's Lith./ New York, Published by Atwill.   25.3 cm in octagon 33.1 × 23.8 cm.

> *Amer.* I, 26; never repr. (the *Eng.* orig.: *Eng.* 56; B/S 24, pl. 16; *CBB,* opp. p. 147; Sitwell pl. 2; IG, *Rambert,* 60, repr.; *Fr.* Var: *Fr.* 579; repr. Migel, plate C).

31. Madlle Fanny Elssler in la Tarentule/Lith. & Pub. by N. Currier . . . New York   26.8 cm in octagon 31.8 × 23.2 cm.

> not in *Amer.* I; LM, *C/I,* 22, repr.

32. [Colour plate VII] Fanny Elssler/in the favourite dance/La Cachucha/Lith. & Pub. by N. Currier . . . New York/J. M. Mc Gee del.   25.8 cm in octagon 30.4 × 24 cm.

> *Amer.* I, 18b; Hall 28; LM, *C/I,* 13; never repr.

33. Fanny Elssler/Gemalt v. H. Inman in N. York   Gedr. v. J. B. Kuhn   Lith. v. B. Kohler in München, 1845   28.2 cm in printed rect. 44.3 × 35 cm.

> *Germ.* 71; repr. Khudyekov p. 170; Pirchan 82; Haskell, pl. 23, opp. p. 46; EB 3rd 60.

34. La Castilliana Bolero/Danced by/Madlle Fanny Elssler & Monsr Perrot/in the ballet divertissement/Le Delire d'un Peintre/J. Bouvier del.   Published by T. McLean . . ., Octr 5th, 1843   Printed at 70 St Martin's Lane   (she:) 23.9 cm in hexagon 37.3 × 27.8 cm.

> *Eng.* 58; B/S 21, pl. 17—with incorrect reproduction; Sitwell, pl. 3; IG, *FE,* opp. p. 161, top; IG, *Rambert,* 62 repr.

35. [Colour plate VIII] Fanny Elsler/Druck u Verlag v. J. E. Schreiber, Hamburg   24.7 cm.

> not cat.; never repr.

24. Fanny Elssler. Portrait with her sister Thérèse by Firmin Salabert (Paris, 1838)

OPÉRA
l'Ile des Pirates

A. Collin et C.ᵉ Editeurs r. Chapon. 3.

Lith. Rigo F.ᵉˢ et C.ᵉ r. Recher. 7

25. Fanny Elssler in *l'Ile des Pirates* (Paris, 1835)

27. Fanny Elssler as Florinde in *le Diable boiteux* from the statuette by Barre *fils* (Paris, 1837)

28. Fanny Elssler in *la Volière* (Paris, 1838)

29A. Fanny Elssler in *la Sylphide* (Paris, probably 1838)

29B. Fanny Elssler in *la Sylphide* (Berlin, probably 1842)

30. Fanny Elssler in *la Cracovienne* from *la Gypsy* (Paris, 1839)

31. Fanny Elssler in *la Tarentule* (New York, *c.* 1840)

33. Fanny Elssler at her dressing table (Park Theatre, New York, 1840)

34. Fanny Elssler with Jules Perrot in *la Castilliana Bolero* (London, 1843)

FANNY CERRITO
1817–1909

FANNY CERRITO WAS THE LAST OF THE GREAT dancers of the *Ballet romantique* to appear at the Opéra in Paris for ultimate consecration. She was already the darling of her birthplace, Naples, of la Scala, beginning with the spring season 1838, and of Her Majesty's Theatre where she appeared regularly each year beginning in 1840. Three years later, during the Carnaval-Lent season in Milan, the Scala audiences were sharply divided between 'Cerritisti' and 'Taglionisti', when the older ballerina was sharing the roster with her.

From the first London season every new work in which she appeared occasioned a popular print. 1840 saw a mainstay of her repertoire, Antonio Guerra's *le Lac des Fées* in which she is portrayed with the choreographer (no. 37 [Colour plate IX]) and floating through the air under a ballooning cloak (no. 38).

Two years later her major ballet was *Alma* for which she choreographed some of the dances with Deshayes and Perrot. Both Robert Jacob Hamerton (b. 1809) and Bouvier portrayed her in this role, their lithographs published by the rival houses of Spooner and McLean only one day apart (*Eng.* 23 and 24). From Bouvier's rendition (B/S 46, pl. 33; IG, *Rambert*, 49, repr.), a French version was pirated—without the houses of the town square behind her as she dances with a tambourine. It must date from 1847 when Cerrito appeared at the Opéra in the ballet, now called *la Fille de Marbre* (Oct. 20). This French variant lists the name of Frédéric Sorrieu (b. 1807) (no. 39). A music title from it, with Burgmüller's music and Sorrieu's name, presents *l'Aldeana Valse*, after a Spanish dance she performed in the Alhambra in Act II of the Paris ballet. At the earlier London premiere a Spanish dance had been featured in Scene IV. This dance was omitted when the ballet was abridged shortly after the London premiere. Perhaps the German town square of the English *Alma* did not accord with the palace in Granada of the Paris *Fille de Marbre* and was simply left out by Sorrieu.

On July 21, 1842, for her benefit at the end of the *Alma* season, Cerrito appeared with C. Camille in a *Varsovienne*.

A large print by 'E. K.' commemorated it (*Eng.* 25). It was also popularized in several music titles by J. Brandard (*Eng.* 26). We present one for 'Two Circassian Polkas' which regardless of its title, shows the two *danseuses* and the *pas de deux* at the benefit performance (no. 40). Still another *Varsovienne*, with Cerrito alone, was published two years later as number 4 of the series *The Favorites of the Ballet* (no. 41B). Although Chaffée catalogued four prints from this series, he did not know this example showing Cerrito.

Between these two *Varsoviennes*, 1843 provided her greatest role—in Perrot's *Ondine* (June 22), the choreographer dancing the role of the hero Matteo. Again, as with *Alma*, there were two different prints appearing within a few weeks of one another. Numa Blanc's, showing her appearance before a sea-shell (*Eng.* 29; B/S 54, pl. 38) was published by John Mitchell on July 15. Shortly thereafter, William Spooner issued the *Pas de l'Ombre* (*Eng.* 30), as drawn by James Henry Lynch (no. 41A). It must certainly be as much a favourite of Ivor Guest—who used it as frontispiece for his biography of the Neapolitan ballerina—as it is of mine!

Numa Blanc later did two other prints of Cerrito with her husband Arthur Saint-Léon. He portrayed them in *la Vivandière* (*Eng.* 32; repr. IG, *FC*, IXa, opp. p. 64, left), a success of 1844 which they danced during the next several years in London, and in Paris later. A 'mystery print', also by Blanc, shows them together in *la Manola*, a character dance. Beaumont and Sitwell reproduced it in 1938, but gave the title of the Elssler-Perrot *Castilliana Bolero* (our no. 34) on the explanatory note. Chaffée failed to include the print in his English catalogue. Even stranger, the print, unlike almost all major English lithographs, is undated! We present it in our 'Iconographer's Choice' as origin of a Portuguese music title adapted from it (no. 98 INSERT).

While Cerrito's name (as 'Miss Ceritto') was substituted for Carlotta Grisi's on *les Trois Grâces* in Paris (no. 61 [Colour plate XII]), while she was appearing in the *Pas de Quatre* (nos. 62–64) and the *Pas des Déesses* (no. 65 [Colour plate

XIII]) in London, she was also dancing elsewhere and in other works. A very successful Carnaval season was spent at the Teatro di Apollo in Rome with Arthur Saint-Léon, soon to be her husband. The prolific Battistelli lithographed and published a delightful print after a portrait by the Calabrian Natale Carta, showing, beside her, a *putto* holding the crown which was given to her by her Roman admirers (no. 36). Italian print-makers never viewed their subjects in the same way as Bouvier and Chalon, or Blanc and Brandard.

Six weeks before the *Pas des Déesses*, she starred, with Saint-Léon, in Perrot's *Lalla Rookh* (June 11, 1846). A well-known Brandard music title immortalized the event (not in *Eng.*; B/S 112, pl. 74). It shows the couple. We present an uncatalogued version which presents her alone (no. 42).

From their first Paris season, in 1847, comes another print from *la Fille de Marbre*, dated Nov. 15, 1847 (the premiere had been on Oct. 20). Saint-Léon, arms in 'high fifth', looks as though he is holding up drumsticks. They are actually straight feathers in his cap. He supports Cerrito's arabesque by his hips, as she holds the tambourine of no. 39 in front of her. The title of their dance is listed as the *Pas de la Fascination* (no. 43). It also appears, in pencil, on the earlier-described print.

Our next Cerrito lithograph is Venetian and probably dates from the Carnaval season there in 1848 (no. 44). It portrays the dancer *affrontée* and ably suggests her slightly overblown charm.

Back in Paris, in successive seasons came *la Vivandière* (1848), *le Violon du Diable* (1849) and *Stella ou les Contrebandiers* (1850)—each one was popular, *le Violon* having 50 performances and *Stella* 32, while they remained together at the Opéra. In March of 1851, they left Paris for the opening of the new *Teatro Real* in Madrid. In their repertoire were the recent Paris successes. Their Spanish premiere was in *le Violon du Diable* on April 4, followed by *Stella* on May 12. A unique lithograph, unknown in any public collection in Spain, one of the very few Spanish prints of a ballet dancer, as opposed to a native dancer, shows Cerrito in *la Sicilienne* from *Stella* (no. 45). With it, we close our iconography of Fanny Cerrito.

Returning from Madrid together, the now-estranged couple separated, she continuing to London, he remaining in Paris. Subsequently, she had success with *Orfa* (late 1852) in Paris, but very little after that. Through two seasons in Russia, and three more in London with the Royal Italian Opera at both Covent Garden (1855) and the Lyceum Theatre (1856–57), the career continued. She danced for the last time, in London, on June 18, 1857. She was forty. She lived for almost fifty-two years more, dying in 1909, the oldest of the great *danseuses* of the Romantic Ballet.

BIBLIOGRAPHY

Khudyekov, vol. III, pp. 265–278.

Guest, Ivor, *Fanny Cerrito, The Life of a Romantic Ballerina* (London, Phoenix House Ltd, 1956).

Guest, Ivor, *The Ballet of the Second Empire, 1847–1858*.

Migel, *The Ballerinas*, chapter 16, pp. 208–222.

36. Fanny Cerrito/Nel gran Teatro di Apollo in Roma Carnevale del 1845./V. Battistelli dis. N. Cav.ʳ Carta dip. Lit. Battistelli. 25.3 cm in rect. 29.3 × 23.6 cm.

  Ital. 57; Hall 33; A/B 890; repr. Khudyekov, p. 335; Haskell, pl. 19, opp. p. 38, R.

37. [Colour plate IX] Mad.ˡᵉ Cerito (facs. sign. Fanny Cerito) & Sig.ʳ Guerra (facs. sign. A. Guerra)/In the favorite Ballet of/"Le lac des Fées" By Guerra/From a drawing by Mʳˢ Philip Barnard On stone by Erxleben London, Published by R. Ackermann, . . . July 6th 1840 . . . Day & Haghe Lithʳˢ to the Queen. (he:) 29.3 cm in rect. 41.7 × 33.8 cm.

  Eng. 19; Hall 13; repr. B/S 50, pl. 35; IG, *Rambert*, 47.

38. Mademoiselle Cerrito./London, Published July 15th 1840 by J. Mitchell . . . à Paris, chez Rittner & Goupil . . ./J. Graf, Printer to Her Majesty/A. de Valentini, . . . J. S. Templeton Lith. 25.8 cm in hexagon 45.5 × 34.3 cm.

  Eng. 20; Hall 29; B/S 55, pl. 39; IG, *Rambert*, 45, not repr.

39. (untitled proof) (on stone:) F. Sorrieu (facs. sign.) Imp. Bertauts 26 cm.

  not cat.; repr. Levinson, *Meister*, no. 94, opp. p. 176 (the Eng. orig: *Eng.* 24; B/S 46, pl. 33; Sitwell, pl. 10; *CBB*, opp. p. 235; IG, *Rambert*, 49, repr.; the Fr. Var.: *Fr.* 580; repr. Migel 50).

40. (Cerrito and C. Camille) (top:) Two Circassian Polkas/ (bottom:) for the/Piano Forte/Composed by/Khue Lindoff/(on stone:) J. Brandard (facs. sign.)/Printed in Colors by M. & N. Hanhart/London, Leoni Lee & Coxhead . . . (dancer on left:) 18 cm in double rect. 27.7 × 23.4 cm.

  Eng. 26; never repr.

41A. Mad.ˡᵉ Fanny Cerito/In the Grand Ballet of/Ondine, ou, la Naiade/Scene Pas de l'Ombre/Drawn by J. H. Lynch/ London. Published by William Spooner, . . ., Augˢᵗ 5th 1843. 21.3 cm in octagon 34.2 × 27.6 cm.

  Eng. 30; Hall 14; B/S 53, pl. 37; IG, *FC*, frontispiece.

FANNY CERRITO

41B. The Favorites of the Ballet./4/Mad^{lle} Fanny Cerito The Varsovienne/William C. Steer, del. & lith.   19.3 cm in double octagon 24.3 × 17.8 cm.

Eng. series G, not cat.; never repr.

42. (untitled and clipped) (probable title:) Fanny Cerito in Lalla Rookh or the Rose of Lahore/(on stone:) J. Brandard (facs. sign.) 20.4 cm in tinted rect. 26.6 × 18.4 cm.

not cat.; repr. Cohen (ed.), *Dance as a Theatre Art* (1974), p. 89. (the orig. music title, with Saint-Léon: B/S 112, pl. 74; repr. IG, *FC*, XIIIa, opp. p. 96 left.)

43. (top:) La Mode, Revue Politique et Littéraire   15 Novembre 1847/(bottom:) Mme F. Cerito et M: S! Léon,/Pas de la Fascination./Dans le ballet de la Fille de marbre représenté à l'Opéra/Jules Rigo   Imp. Decan et Lebref   (he:) 16.5 cm.

not in *Fr.*; repr. Khudyekov, p. 270; IG, *FC*, XVIa, opp. p. 113 left.

44. Mad^{ela} Fanny Cerrito./(on stone:) Masutti (facs. sign.)/lit. Kier in Venezia. 25.2 cm.

Ital. 60; A/B 895; never repr.

45. Stella/La Siciliana/S: Fany Cerrito./Martinez lit?   Lit. Donon . . .   18.5 cm in tinted rect. 23 × 17.3 cm.

not cat.; never repr.

36. Fanny Cerrito. Portrait with a *putto* (Rome, 1845)

38. Fanny Cerrito in *le Lac des Fées* (London, 1840)

39. Fanny Cerrito in Alma (London, 1842)

40. Fanny Cerrito with Camille in *Two Circassian Polkas* (London, *c.* 1842)

41A. Fanny Cerrito in *Ondine* by J. H. Lynch (London, 1843)

41B. Fanny Cerrito in *The Varsovienne* (London, 1844)

42. Fanny Cerrito in *Lalla Rookh* (London, 1846)

43. Fanny Cerrito with Arthur Saint-Léon in the *Pas de Fascination* from *la Fille de Marbre* (Paris, 1847)

44. Fanny Cerrito (Venice, probably 1848)

45. Fanny Cerrito in *la Sicilienne* from *Stella* (Madrid, 1851)

CARLOTTA GRISI
1819–1899

THE SINGLE MOST IMPORTANT FACTOR THAT FORMS our memory of Carlotta Grisi is the fact that she created the title role in *Giselle*, on June 28, 1841, at the Paris Opéra. Our choice of prints mirrors this preponderance. Almost half of them present her in *Giselle*. But she had already been dancing for twelve years at that time, appearing first as *première danseuse* of the children's *corps de ballet* at la Scala from 1829. The earliest known print of her shows her five years later with Francesco Rosati, in Salvatore Taglioni's *L'Eredità* at the San Carlo in Naples (Sept. 2, 1834). It appears in one of the innumerable theatre almanacs of the period, but is entirely unknown and unpublished. Only its size militates against its inclusion here : it is not 'Glorious'. It will wait for a later publication.

Carlotta was fortunate, at Naples, in meeting Jules Perrot who became responsible for her artistic development and technical training. They lived together as husband and wife, but 'Our two turtle doves did not waste the time in making love which they could spend more profitably in suspended elevation.' (Charles de Boigne, *Petits Mémoires de l'Opéra*, p. 250). Perrot took her with him to London (1836), Vienna (1837–8) and la Scala (1838) and finally to Paris where they appeared together in *Le Zingaro*, a sort of ballet-opera at the Théâtre de la Renaissance, in which she both sang and danced (Feb. 29, 1840). It was the first step of a campaign to gain her admission to the Opéra.

The ballet critic of *la Presse*, Théophile Gautier, who had hailed Perrot's dancing and choreography at the Renaissance and commented on Carlotta's 'Very pretty dancer's voice,' . . . 'She knows how to dance, which is rare . . . she is good, but not better than good.' (*Histoire de l'Art dramatique en France*, II, 35), now constituted himself her champion. After she was finally hired for a single year by the Opéra, at a very modest salary, he reviewed many of her appearances in *pas de deux* inserted into several operas. And it was he who found the legend of the Wilis in the writings of his friend Heinrich Heine. It was the basic premise of his first performed ballet *Giselle* (see my *Ballets de Théophile Gautier*, chapters II and III).

Our first print of Carlotta in her greatest role shows her floating above her tomb in the second act of *Giselle*, by Bouvier (no. 46). It dates from 1842 in London, where Perrot revived the ballet, dancing opposite her in place of Lucien Petipa who had created the role of hero at the Opéra. While Bouvier was presenting an elegant, serene, slightly placid Grisi, Robert J. Hamerton was presenting her in one of the ugliest lithographs of the whole English gallery (no. 47). Her too-short skirt, uncontrolled arms and legs, and general air of *malaise* contrast unfavourably with the Bouvier picture. Only four weeks separate their publication : April 11th for the 'pretty print'; May 9th for the ghastly !

A French lithograph presents the same act of the ballet : No. 1 from the *Album du Théâtre* (no. 48). Here, as in several other Paris prints, the *danseuse* is shown with bare feet (see also nos. 11, 16, 61, 84 and 93, among others). This was entirely an artistic convention. The dancers always wore ballet-slippers, handstitched at the toes to protect the satin when they rose onto *pointes*. Not for these divinities were the metal-shank boxings of present-day toe shoes !

The four prints of our little gallery of music titles for *Giselle* probably represents less than a quarter of the total examples. It features three by Célestin Nanteuil (1813–73), a close friend of Théophile Gautier who was certainly the most fecund of the Paris *vignettistes*. Nanteuil's biography by Aristide Marie (Paris, H. Floury, 1924) lists more than 240 separate lithographs published for music titles. Only one of our three Nanteuil examples figures there (no. 50A). It shows Giselle disappearing into a grassy bank while the hero shudders in his grief. Earlier in the same act, Giselle reclines on a tree limb over the lake where the wilis are ready to drown the pensive hero who sits on a rock to the left (no. 49A). Again, Nanteuil has caught the poetic imagery of the *Apotheosis of the Romantic Ballet* (subtitle of Lifar's 1942 study of *Giselle*). Less successful is a view of Carlotta floating like a rag-doll in front of a staring hero (no. 49B).

Nanteuil's London *alter ego* was the equally prolific

Brandard. His version of *Giselle*, Act II, suggests a large mausoleum rather than a simple cross as her resting place. Recognizable is a new hero, Arthur Saint-Léon, who partnered both Carlotta and Fanny Elssler in London when the ballet was revived there in 1844. His mustache and goatee allow us to date this music title even though the *danseuse* is less readily identifiable! (no. 50B). *Giselle* had entered the 'public domain'. The role would henceforth belong to any ballerina capable of presenting its technical and dramatic demands.

Among Grisi's other great successes were the title roles in Gautier's *la Péri* (Paris, 1843) and Perrot's *la Esmeralda* (London, 1844), adapted from Victor Hugo's *Notre-Dame-de-Paris*. The English prints of each are among the loveliest of our gallery. The brothers Lynch, C. G. and James Henry (d. 1868) (who had drawn Cerrito in *Ondine* the previous year, see no. 41A), prepared a pose showing Carlotta kneeling under a *grand jeté* by Lucien Petipa (no. 51 [Colour plate X]). They had both appeared for Alfred Bunn at Drury Lane, beginning on Sept. 30, 1843. The print is dated Feb. 5, 1844. At that time both dancers were back in Paris, appearing not only in *la Péri*, but also in *Giselle*.

When Carlotta reappeared in London, it was at Her Majesty's Theatre. Perrot choreographed one of his masterpieces for her and appeared in it in the role of the poet Gringoire. Together, they are immortalized by Bouvier in *la Truandaise* from *Esmeralda* (no. 52 [Colour plate XI]). The print was published by Thomas McLean on Apr. 6, 1844, less than a month after the premiere of the ballet (Mar. 9).

Another success of this London season were the appearances of Carlotta and Perrot in *la Polka*, the ULTIMATE character dance. Polkamania had swept Western Europe, and Perrot was quick to capitalize on the vogue. Bouvier drew the sketch for a lithograph published by McLean in May, 1844. It is too well known! We prefer a German example, from Berlin, in which Bouvier's parentage is recognized by the garbled 'Gez. v. Bovier [*sic*]' (no. 53). The lithographer Blau at least took pains to have the figures in his variant face the same direction as the original.

The year of *Esmeralda* and *la Polka*, Carlotta was to have been immortalized as the dancer of the future in *les Trois Grâces* (no. 61 [Colour plate XII]) in the *Pas de Diane* from *la Jolie Fille de Gand*, her success of 1842 at the Opéra. But it was 'Miss Ceritto' whose name appeared under the depiction of Carlotta. Pregnancy and its problematical future for starring *danseuses* was the reason. 'A bird in the hand . . .!' But Carlotta did perform in the *Pas de Quatre* (1845– nos. 62–64), although not in the *Pas des Déesees* (1846). She was at Drury Lane that summer, appearing with James Sylvain, Elssler's partner in America, in her most recent Paris ballet, *Paquita*.

Like the other great *ballerine* of the Romantic Ballet, Carlotta eventually reached Russia where she appeared during three seasons between 1850 and 1853. Her St. Petersburg début was in her old war-horse *Giselle* (Oct. 8, 1850). The Russians were cold to her first act. They had already witnessed 'the mad scene' of Fanny Elssler. But her poetic interpretation of Act II restored Grisi to her rightful place. The major work mounted for her in St. Petersburg this first season was *The Naiade and the Fisherman* (premiere Jan. 30, 1851). Perrot, who partnered her there, simply adapted his *Ondine* which had been originally choreographed for Fanny Cerrito in London (see no. 41A). For an imperial performance in the gardens of Peterhof, on a stage specially constructed in the lake, Наяда И Рыбак (*Nayada i Ribak*) was presented and memorialized by the artist Adolf Jossifovitch Charlemagne (1822–1901) (no. 54). The print is dated July 4th. By that time both the leading dancers were far away—in London.

Carlotta returned again to Russia, with Mazilier as ballet master for her second season, and Perrot again for her third. When she danced for the last time early in March, 1853, she was not yet 34—youngest, at the end of her career, of the great dancers of the *Ballet romantique*.

BIBLIOGRAPHY

Khudyekov, vol. III, pp. 241–253.

Lifar, Serge, *Carlotta Grisi* (Paris, Editions Albin Michel, 1941).

Lifar, Serge, *Giselle Apothéose du Ballet Romantique* (Paris, Editions Albin Michel, 1942).

Beaumont, Cyril W., *The Ballet Called Giselle* (London, C. W. Beaumont, 1948).

Guest, Ivor, *Paris*, chapters 8–10, pp. 186–263.

Guest, Ivor, *The Ballet of the Second Empire 1847–1858*, chapter II, pp. 26–50.

Migel, *The Ballerinas*, chapter 15, pp. 195–207.

46. Carlotta Grisi (facs. sign)/In the Popular Ballet of/Giselle/ou les Wilis./London, Published by T. Mᶜ Lean . . . April 11ᵗʰ 1842./J. Bouvier del   Printed at the Genˡ Lithᶜ Estabˡ 17.5 cm in rect. with rounded top 37 × 27.8 cm.

   Eng. 73 ; EB 3rd 70 ; repr. Khudyekov, p. 241 ; B/S 31, pl. 23.

47. (a clipped copy with no titling, and showing only the figure) Madˡˡᵉ Carlotta Grisi/in the Popular Ballet of/Giselle or les Wilis/ London, Published by Wᵐ Spooner   May 9, 1842/R. J. Hamerton del./C. Graf lith.   25.8 cm.

   not cat. ; never repr.

48. (top:) Album du théâtre. No 1/(bottom:) Carlotta Grisi/(Rôle de Giselle dans le ballet de ce nom)/Paris, Garnot edit. en vente chez Masson . . . Imp. Lemercier. 13.8 cm in rect. 19.4 × 13.2 cm.

> *Fr.* 42; repr. Lifar, *Grisi*, pl. VIII.

49A. Deux Quadrilles/sur le Ballet/Giselle/Musique d'Ad: Adam/ Composés/Pour le Piano/par Musard/Londres, chez Cocks et C.ie Mayence et Anvers, chez Schott/Célestin Nanteuil (facs. sign.) Imp. Bertauts . . . Taille Douce de Boieldieu. (vignette:) 19 × 24.6 cm.

> *Fr.* 49; never repr.

49B. Giselle ou les Wilis/Mélodie/Tirée du Ballet de Giselle/ Musique d'Ad. Adam./Paroles de M.r L. Escudier./Dédiées/A Mademoiselle Dobrée/Paris chez J. Meissonnier . . ./Taille Douce de Boieldieu Bauve/Célestin Nanteuil (facs. sign.) Lith. Petit & Bertauts. (vignette:) 16.5 × 13.7 cm.

> *Fr.* 46; never repr.

50A. La Wili./Ballade Fantastique/Paroles de M.r A. Richomme. Musique d'Ad. Adam/A M.me Carlotta Grisi./(a sonnet)/ Celestin Nanteuil (facs. sign.) Imp. Petit & Bertauts/ Paris Publication de la France Musicale (vignette:) 18.3 × 14.6 cm.

> *Fr.* 47; repr. Beaumont, *Giselle*, opp. p. 52.

50B. (completely untitled, as clipped). (on stone:) J. Brandard (facs. sign.) (she:) 14.5 cm.

> not cat.; never repr.

51. [Colour plate x] Mad.lle Carlotta Grisi and Mons.r Petipa./In the Grand Ballet of/The Peri./London, Published by William Spooner . . . Feb.y 5.th 1844./Printed by M. & N. Hanhart/C. G. & J. H. Lynch, del.t (she:) 15.4 cm in octagon 35.5 × 27.4 cm.

> *Eng.* 78; Hall 12; EB 3rd 71; repr. Moore, 'The Petipa Family in America', *Dance Index* (vol. I, no. 5), May, 1942, p. 70; EB 3rd, *Ballets de Théophile Gautier*, pl. VII.

52. [Colour plate XI] Mad.lle Carlotta Grisi and Mon.r Perrot/In the very attractive Ballet/La Esmeralda/Published by T. McLean . . . April 6.th 1844/J. Bouvier del. Litho. 70 S.t Martins Lane. (she:) 23 cm in hexagon 37.5 × 28.4 cm.

> *Eng.* 81; Hall 26; IG, *Rambert*, 82; repr. B/S no. 28, pl. 21; Sitwell, pl. 5; *CBB*, opp. p. 242; Lifar, *Grisi*, pl. XI; Slonimsky, 'Jules Perrot', *Dance Index*, vol. IV, no. 12 (Dec. 1945), p. 206.

53. La Polka/Mad.lle Grisi & Mons.r Perrot/Verlag u. Eigenthum. v. Gebrüder Rocca/Gez. v. Bovier Lith. v. Blau. (she:) 19.5 cm in tinted rect. 27.5 × 22 cm.

> *Germ.* 115; Hall 27; never repr. (the Eng. orig: *Eng.* 80; B/S no. 37, pl. 28; Sitwell, pl. 7; IG, *Rambert,* 80, repr.) (the Fr. Var.: *Fr.* 585; repr. Slonimsky, 'Jules Perrot', p. 221; Migel, pl. H).

54. Balet na Ozerkach/1851 goda 4.go Iulaya/(Nayada i ribak)/Dess. Charlemagne Imp. par Munster Lith. Borell (she:) 3.4 cm in tinted rect. 20 × 29.1 cm.

> not cat.; repr. Slonimsky, 'Jules Perrot', p. 242 ('Epilegomena' by Chaffée).

46. Carlotta Grisi in *Giselle*, Act II. Floating over her tomb (Paris, 1841)

47. Carlotta Grisi in *Giselle*, Act II (London, 1842)

48. Carlotta Grisi in *Giselle*, Act II *Album du Théâtre*, no. 1

49A and B. Carlotta Grisi in *Giselle*, Act II:
[A] with Lucien Petipa
and [B] floating above her tomb.
MUSIC TITLES

50A.   Giselle returning to her tomb. MUSIC TITLE
50B.   Carlotta Grisi (or Fanny Elssler)
with Arthur Saint-Léon in *Giselle*, Act II.
MUSIC TITLE by J. Brandard

53. Carlotta Grisi with Jules Perrot in *la Polka*. German Variant after a London print, 1844

54. Carlotta Grisi with Jules Perrot in *The Naiade and the Fisherman* (Saint Petersburg, 1851)

LUCILE GRAHN

1819–1907

LUCILE GRAHN, 'BABY' OF THE FIVE GREATEST dancers of the Romantic Ballet, was only two days younger than Carlotta Grisi! We have become used to Italian names ending with 'i' or 'o'. Now, we find a second non-Italian. Elssler was Viennese. Grahn was Danish, the first product of the training of August Bournonville—a training which is still of major importance in Copenhagen today. Bournonville (1805–79) had gone to Paris in 1834, on leave of absence, with his young student Grahn. He performed twice at the Opéra and attended many performances of the balletic repertoire. Most important, they both saw Taglioni in *la Sylphide*. The major result for the Danish Ballet was a new *Sylphide*, the episodes of the original story kept *in toto* but with a new score by the Norwegian Baron Herman Løvenskjold (1815–70). Its Copenhagen premiere was on Nov. 28, 1836. James was danced by the choreographer Bournonville; Lucile Grahn, aged 17, was the new embodiment of Marie Taglioni.

She had already appeared as the heroine in Bournonville's *Valdemar* (1835), but now she found the role that was to personify her in future. She was henceforth 'the pale Sylphide of the North'. Copenhagen produced a lithograph to commemorate its new dancer (no. 56A). It showed her just over half length, appearing from a base of clouds. It was a print that was destined to have a long, eventful history—perhaps the most complicated in the evolution of ballet history.

Meanwhile, Grahn went to Paris again in 1837, this time falling under the spell of Fanny Elssler's *Cachucha*. Back in Copenhagen, she danced that character number in performances of Auber's *Fiorella* in Feb. 1838. The print which shows her in it was designed and lithographed by Emilius Bærentzen (1799–1868), the most prolific of the Danish artists for the ballet (no. 57). But recognition in Copenhagen was not sufficient; Paris still beckoned. She was dismissed when she disobeyed a summons home from Hamburg where she had appeared as guest artist in March, 1839. Her way to the Opéra was now open, and she signed a three-year contract to begin on June 1. With her came the two lithographs that showed her Copenhagen successes.

Paris, at this moment, had no need for Cachucha prints. It had Fanny Elssler's. But Taglioni, the Sylphide personified, was in St. Petersburg. So it was Grahn's Danish Sylphide that was immediately pirated. Before 1839 was over, the first volume of *les Belles Femmes de Paris* was published with an article on the new Opéra debutante and a French version of the Danish print (no. 56B). It was, obviously, reversed. The same print was reversed again when *La Sylphide, Modes, Littérature et Beaux Arts*, a publication having nothing to do with the ballet of its title, presented Grahn as no. 18 of a series of theatrical celebrities (no. 56C). The manuscript permission for printing, on another copy, lists Mar. 18, 1840 as date of publication. The new version faces in the original, Danish, direction.

The lithographer Charles Vogt who prepared this print, and the firm of Coulon et Cⁱᵉ who printed it, were, however, not yet finished! They were responsible for still another variant which Grahn took with her to St Petersburg for her performances there beginning in Jan., 1843. It is entitled 'Repertoire du théâtre russe 1843' and features yellow-brown tinted paper with complicated scalloped corners. It also faces the 'Danish direction'.

The piracies of the *Sylphide* print, however, were not yet finished! Grahn appeared at la Scala for the Carnaval-Lent season in 1844. She did not perform in that ballet, but two years later, the *Strenna teatrale*, a series of annual Milanese almanacs, presented an article, in French (signed 'H. L.'—probably Hippolyte Lucas), with a print showing her in her early Copenhagen and Paris role. Gaetano Cornienti, the Italian artist whose name figures on the new piracy, also reversed the version from *les Belles Femmes de Paris*. So the Italian 'Lucilla Grahn' still faces the earliest, Copenhagen, direction (no. 56D). New treatment of the chaplet of flowers in her hair, and the clouds, are also apparent. Such is the metier of the ballet iconographer!

During the short time she performed regularly at the Opéra

before she twisted her knee in rehearsal and had to convalesce for almost two years, Grahn sat for Henri Grevedon (1776–1860), already well-known for his portraits of Taglioni (1831) and Elssler (1835). His lovely portrait of the young Dane (no. 55) conveys an underlying determination to have her own way.

After a single, short season in Russia (spring, 1843) and the Carnaval-Lent at la Scala, which she shared with Fanny Elssler who appeared mainly in *Giselle*, Grahn began her conquest of London. She appeared immediately after Milan at Drury Lane, partnered by James Sylvain, former partner of Elssler in America. The ballet was *Lady Henrietta or the Statute Fair*, a work that had recently been premiered at the Opéra with Adèle Dumilâtre (see nos. 77A and B) and Maria (see no. 74), opposite Lucien Petipa (see nos. 51 and 71). Her major dance was the *Pas de Vénus* (no. 58). Brandard presented her *cabriole* and the foreshortened arms which connote some of the 'not-completely-stretched' limbs that we associate with the Romantic Ballet.

The following year, Grahn was ready for glory! She first appeared at Her Majesty's Theatre in Perrot's *Eoline ou la Dryade* (premiere Mar. 8, 1845) which opened the season. S. M. Joy, who pictured her dreamy flight above a pool (no. 59A), is not so well known as the lithographer Edward Morton who translated it onto the stone, and who lithographed no. 3 of Chalon's *Album d'Adieux* for Taglioni later the same season (no. 22C). It was Brandard who just earlier designed two lithographs showing the major *pas de deux* of the new ballet: the *Mazurka d'Extase* which she performed with Perrot who, as the gnome Rubezahl, danced opposite her. Brandard's designs were issued both as easel prints (dated Apr. 10, 1845) and as music titles. The former are entitled No. 1 *l'Invitation*

(no. 59B) and No. 4 *l'Extase* (*Eng.* 192). Where and what are numbers 2 and 3?

Even more important Grahn appearances this season were in the *Pas de Quatre* (July 12) with Taglioni, Carlotta and Fanny Cerrito (nos. 62–64). Even though, as the youngest, her variation was the first, Grahn 'had arrived'.

The next year was a repetition of 1845. At the beginning of the season she appeared with Perrot in his *Catarina ou la Fille du Bandit* (Mar. 3). Brandard's new lithograph, dated Apr. 21, 1846, featured the *Pas Stratégique* where she drilled an army of female bandits (no. 60). It became her most popular memento, appearing in at least four different German and Austrian versions (*Germ.* 117–119; 443, 466), as well as a Roman one (*Ital.* 115; repr., Migel, no. 59). Later that year, she appeared in the *Pas des Déesses* (no. 64 [Colour plate XIII]), again dancing the first of the variations. Her position as a ballerina of international stature was forever assured.

Grahn's career continued much longer than those of her older colleagues. In 1856 she married the tenor Friedrich Young (hence her frequent depiction as Lucile Grahn-Young in Germany), and for the next several years, she only accepted engagements that coincided with his. She was at Dessau and Leipzig between 1857 and 1861. Her career was technically not at an end until, in 1875, she ceased to be 'Ballet-Directrice' in Munich. She lived there for 32 more years, bequeathing her fortune to the city who named Lucile Grahn Strasse after her. She died on Apr. 4, 1907—aged almost 88. Her career of forty years was much longer than her colleagues. Only Cerrito survived her, and she was a nonagenarian at her death! The *Ballet Romantique* was dead, not only in its mystique but in its practitioners also.

BIBLIOGRAPHY

Khudyekov, vol. III, pp. 229–232.

Reumert, Elith, *Den Danske Ballets Historie* (København, Hjem-meets Forlag, 1922).

Neiiendam, Robert, *Lucile Grahn; en Skaebne i Dansen* (København, 1963).

Guest, Ivor, *Paris*, pp. 179–184.

Migel, Parmenia, *The Ballerinas*, chapter 13, pp. 168–178.

55. Melle Lucile Grahn./de l'Académie Royale de Musique/(on stone:) H. Grevedon (facs. sign.)/Imp. par Lemercier/Paris, publié par Goupil et Vibert . . . Berlin Verlag von L. Sachse & Cie London, pub. by the Anaglyphic Company . . . 29.5 cm in rect. 38.7 × 30.2 cm.

> Hall 1; repr. Khudyekov, p. 229; Levinson, no. 88, p. 167.

56A. Lucile Grahn/i Sylphiden./(on stone:) Em. Btz. ft. (facs. sign.)/Em. Bærentzen & Co lith. Inst.   14.5 cm.

> not cat.; repr. Reumert, p. 58 bottom (among many other Danish publications); Cornell, 'Hans Christian Andersen', *Dance Index*, vol. IV, no. 9 (Sept., 1945), p. 146, bottom L.

56B. (top:) Les belles femmes de Paris/(bottom:) Lucile Grahn/Artiste de l'Académie Royale/Imp. Lemercier, Benard et C.   14.4 cm.

> *Fr.* 40, repr. Pl. X, p. 147; Khudyekov, p. 230.

56C. Melle Lucile Grahn/La Sylphide/Modes, Littérature, Beaux Arts/Direction Rue d'Hanovre, 17/Lith. Coulon et Cie/N° 18   Ch. Vogt Lith.   14.2 cm.

> not in *Fr.*; repr. IG, *Paris*, no. 55; Haskell, pl. 34, opp. p. 49 left.

56D. Lucilla Grahn/Cornienti inc.   10.7 cm.

> *Ital.* 432; never repr.

57. Lucile Grahn/i Cachucha/Frit efter Natur af Em. Bærentzen Em. Bærentzen & Cⁱᵉ lith. Inst.   31.4 cm.

> not cat.; repr. Reumert, p. 59; Cornell, 'Andersen', p. 147, bottom.

58. Lucile Grahn/The Pas de Venus in the Ballet of/The Statute Fair/J. Brandard del. and lith/M. and N. Hanhart, lith printers/ Published May 10, 1844 by Messrs Fores   13.8 cm.

> not cat.; never repr.

59A. Mᵉˡˡᵉ Lucile Grahn/of Her Majesty's Theatre, in the character of/"Eoline ou la Dryade"/On Stone by Edward Morton from a Picture by S. M. Joy/M. & N. Hanhart, Lith. Printers./ London, Pub. July 14ᵗʰ, 1845 by J. Mitchell.   31.6 cm in rect. with rounded corners 41.8 × 33 cm.

> *Eng.* 70; Hall 9; repr. B/S 64, pl. 46; Sitwell, pl. 12; IG, *Rambert 76.*

59B. (top:) Ballet par Perrot   Eoline, ou la Driade.   Music par C. Pugni/(bottom:) Nº 1, L'Invitation/The Celebrated "Mazurka d'Extâse" danced by/Monsʳ Perrot & Madˡˡᵉ Lucile Grahn,/at/Her Majesty's Theatre./London, Published April 10ᵗʰ 1845 by Jullien/(on stone:) J. Brandard (facs. sign.)/J. Brandard del & Lith.   M. & N. Hanhart, Chromo Lith.   and at Milan, by Lucca   (she:) 15.9 cm in triple rect. 26.5 × 20.5 cm.

> *Eng.* 191; repr. B/S. 115, pl. 77.

60. Lucile Grahn (facs. sign.)/In Monsʳ Perrot's Ballet of/Catarina, ou la Fille du Bandit/J. Brandard delʳ & lith.   London, Pub⸝ lished April 21ˢᵗ 1846, by Messʳˢ Fores . . . Printed by M. & N. Hanhart 28.9 cm in rect. 40.7 × 27.9 cm.

> *Eng.* 51; EB 3rd 74; repr. Levinson, no. 91, p. 172; B/S 63, pl. 45; *CBB,* opp. p. 254.

55. Lucile Grahn. Portrait by Henri Grevedon

56A. Lucile Grahn in *I Sylphiden* (Copenhagen, 1836)

56C. The Second French pirating from *la Sylphide* (Paris, 1840)

56B. The French pirating from *les Belles Femmes de Paris* (Paris, 1839)

56D. The Italian pirating from the original French pirating (Milan, 1846)

57. Lucile Grahn in *la Cachucha* (Copenhagen, 1838)

58. Lucile Grahn in *Lady Henrietta or the Statute Fair* (London, 1844)

59A. Lucile Grahn in *Eoline ou la Dryade* (London, 1845)

59B. Lucile Grahn with Jules Perrot
in the *Mazurka d'Extase* from *Eoline ou la Dryade* (London, 1845)

60. Lucile Grahn in *Catarina ou la Fille du Bandit* (London, 1846)

[IX] 37. Fanny Cerrito with Antonio Guerra in *le Lac des Fées* (London, 1840)

[X] 51. Carlotta Grisi with Lucien Petipa in *la Péri* (Paris, 1843)

[XI] 52. Carlotta Grisi with Jules Perrot in *Esmeralda* (London, 1844)

[XII] 61. *Les Trois Grâces* Marie Taglioni, Fanny Elssler and Carlotta Grisi (with the name of 'Miss Ceritto') (Paris, 1844)

[XIII] 65. Fanny Cerrito, Arthur Saint-Léon, Marie Taglioni, and Lucile Grahn in the *Pas des Déesses* (London, 1846)

[XIV] 84. Carolina Rosati in *Coralia* (London, 1847)

[xv] 92. Katti Lanne in *Esmeralda* (Hamburg, late 1850s)

[XVI] 94. Marie Taglioni II as *la Fée aux Fleurs* in *Théa* (London, 1847)

THE APOTHEOSES

WE ARE USED TO *PAS DE TROIS*! IN TWO OF MARIUS Petipa's full-length ballets of the late 19th century: *Swan Lake*, Act I and *Sleeping Beauty*, Act IV ('Florestan and his two Sisters') occur two of the great classic dances for a man with two *danseuses*. Earlier, during the years of the Romantic Ballet, such a *pas de trois* was very uncommon, and was almost never immortalized by a print. A single American engraving, dated May 1, 1827, presents Mr. and Mrs. Conway and her sister Miss Deblin (*Amer.* I, 17). It seems unique! (There was a *Pas de Trois* in the first act of *la Sylphide* with the hero James between his bride-to-be Effie [the mortal] and the sylphide herself [the unattainable beloved], but we know of no prints showing it.)

Yet the authoritative icon of the *Ballet romantique* presents three (or perhaps, four) of the five great dancers whose careers we have just examined. But *les Trois Grâces* was not a *Pas de Trois*, was not even a dance at all! It was a study by Lejeune (probably Eugène) who manipulated the Barre statuettes of Taglioni (see no. 16A) and Elssler (see no. 27) to suggest 'the past' and 'the present' and added a similar figure of Carlotta Grisi in her *Pas de Diane* from *la Jolie Fille de Gand* (1842) for 'the future'. *Giselle* was certainly a more important role for her, but it was too close to Taglioni's *Sylphide* to provide sufficient contrast. A neo-classic dance was a better foil to the two statuettes. Just before the final publication, the name of Grisi which should have appeared on the wreath below the unslippered feet of the *danseuse* on the right, was changed to a barbarous 'Miss Ceritto'. Hence the supreme depiction of the Romantic Ballet presents 'Three or Four Graces'. Chaffée's exhaustive search for and study of this lithograph constitutes the covering essay for his catalogue of French dance prints. It is a must!

Les Trois Grâces was published June 1, 1844. It is one of the rarest of our gallery. We know of only five or six copies of it (two in Paris; one or two in London; two in America). There must be others, but they have not surfaced yet. Variants, however, obviously appeared very soon. The finest, with the name of Friedrich Dewehrt (b. 1808), is reproduced in Pirchan's *Fanny Elssler* (his no. 61), from the collection of the

Staatliche Porträtsammlung in Vienna (*Germ.* 101). Three American variants exist (*Amer.* I, 61a and b; 62), Nathaniel Currier's is not reversed, most probably because he revised again the direction when Sarony drew his own, reversed, onto the stone to conform more closely to the original. (Currier version repr. Moore, *Artists of the Dance*, frontispiece; LM, *C/I*, frontispiece; Migel 56.) They are good, and rare, prints, but cannot even suggest the elegant monumentality of the original. Chaffée mentioned an additional Italian variant: 'That we have seen but did not note in detail' (*Fr.* cat. p. 201) (*Ital.* 242). I have never found that version, but do possess two different titles for English music that feature reductions of the pose with the three *danseuses*. France was responsible for the icon, but it was London that presented dance *divertissements* in which these great female dancers appeared together.

Even before the *Pas de Quatre* in 1845, there had been a growing London interest in the simultaneous appearance of great *danseuses*. They had always 'graciously' performed in one another's benefit performances, but *amour propre* precluded dancing together until the artistic climate changed, particularly with the genius of Perrot as choreographer. In 1841, a *Jugement de Pâris* was announced, but not performed. Fanny Elssler partnered Adèle Dumilâtre in *Un Bal sous Louis XIV* (Apr. 6, 1843). Three and one-half months later, BY ROYAL COMMAND, the two Fannys, Elssler and Cerrito, appeared together in a *Pas de Deux* (July 20, and at least ten more performances; the premiere was the occasion of a State Visit by the Queen and Prince Albert). A pattern had been set.

The first of several realizations, and the most important, occurred on July 12, 1845 — the *Pas de Quatre*, 'The Romantic Ballet at its most Sublime' as Ivor Guest subtitles it (*London*, chapter XVI, p. 109). The problems of obliging the *danseuses* to allow the choreographer Perrot a free hand with the order of their variations has been told many times. Female reticence about public knowledge of specific ages was used by Benjamin Lumley, the Director of Her Majesty's Theatre, to resolve that delicate situation. So it was in London that the first of several 'super-number-one-special groups' drew raves from spectators and critics alike.

THE APOTHEOSES

The *Illustrated London News* immediately presented its woodcut of one of the poses in the glorious *Grand Pas* (July 19). From it, a completely unknown print entitled *The Dance of the Fairies* was published in New York, dated 1846 (no. 63). Brandard's easel-print and music title probably appeared next (no. 64). Chalon's depiction, lithographed by T. H. Maguire, was published on Sept. 8, many weeks after the last 1845 performance on July 19. It properly remains the authoritative depiction, used by Anton Dolin as the opening and closing pose for his re-creation of the event (first in 1941). The subsequent iconography of the *Pas de Quatre* is even more complicated than that of *les Trois Grâces*. Our favourite is a Viennese music title, published by Diabelli in 1848: Le Quatuor dansé à Londres/par . . . and then the names of the *danseuses*, with the substitution of Fanny Elssler's in place of Grahn's. (Repr. Cornell, 'Le Quatuor dansé à Londres par', *Dance Index*, vol. III, nos. 7–8, Jul.–Aug., 1944, cover and p. 124.) Vienna was always loyal to its own!

The tremendous success of the *Pas de Quatre* occasioned a series of other *grands divertissements* . . . 'steeple-chases which Lumley is pleased to have these ladies dance under the title of ballet', wrote Saint-Léon whose wife Cerrito appeared in most of them, and who personally danced in the next one (IG, '*Lettres d'un Maître de ballet*', p. 235). In 1846, Perrot's *Jugement de Pâris* featured *le Pas des Déesses* (no. 65 [Colour plate XIII]). Paris (Saint-Léon) in deciding which of the goddesses, Juno, Minerva or Venus (Taglioni, Grahn, Cerrito), was to be the recipient of the golden apple, did not avert the Trojan War, but he figures as the lone male in a female preserve.

The *Pas des Déesses* did not end the series of gala *divertissements*. 1847 witnessed revivals of both the *Pas de Quatre* (with Carolina Rosati replacing Grahn) and the *Pas des Déesses*. Taglioni appeared for the last time in the second of these revivals (Aug. 21, 1847). She arrived too late in the season to have appeared in the newest of Perrot's *Grands Pas*—*les Éléments* which featured Cerrito as Air, Rosati as Water, and Grisi as Fire (June 26, 1847). The next year was the choreographer's 'swan-song'. *Les Quatre Saisons* presented Cerrito, Grisi, Rosati and Marie Taglioni II (June 13, 1848). *Les Éléments* was also revived the same year. With Perrot gone, the 'grand assemblage' was attempted again two years later by Paul Taglioni. His *les Grâces* which presented Carlotta, his own daughter Marie Taglioni II, and Amalia Ferraris (May 2, 1850) is remembered by an elegant Chalon watercolour (repr. IG, *London*, XXIII, opp. p. 128).

It is not, however, for superb lithographs that we remember these later 'steeple-chases'. Each was simply depicted by a woodcut in the *Illustrated London News* (*les Éléments*—July 11, 1847; *les Quatre Saisons*—June 24, 1848; *les Grâces*—May 18, 1850; the first two repr. IG, *FC*, XIVa and b, opp. p. 97). The *Pas de Trois* for these *danseuses* had now become a successful balletic form.

London's interest in ballet had waned. Beside newspaper woodcuts, there is only one single dated English print later than these: Oct. 10, 1854 appears on the lithograph from a portrait of Adeline Plunkett in *la Manola* (*Eng.* 100). London had now absented herself from the Romantic Ballet. No subsequent English print will appear in our gallery.

BIBLIOGRAPHY
Chaffée, 'Three or Four Graces' (the French catalogue).
Guest, Ivor, *London*, chap. XVI, pp. 109–112.

61. [Colour plate XII] Les trois Grâces/Dessiné par Lejeune Imprimé par Lemercier Lith. par (Elssler in the centre:) 34.5 cm in triple rect. 44.8 × 37.6 cm.
    Fr. 110; repr. pl. IV, p. 134; repr. Khudyekov, p. 335; Levinson, no. 60, opp. p. 126; B/S 19, pl. 1 (as by Chalon); *CBB*, opp. p. 115 (see the text for reprs. of Vars).

62. The Celebrated/Pas de Quatre/composed by Jules Perrot/as danced at Her Majesty's Theatre, July 12th 1845, by the four eminent danseuses/Carlotta Grisi, Marie Taglioni, Lucile Grahn & Fanny Cerrito./Drawn from the life by Alfred E[d] Chalon Esq[re] R.A./A. E. Chalon R.A. T. H. Maguire/Proof/M. & N. Hanhart, Lithographic Printers . . . London. Published September 8 1845 by J. Mitchell, Publisher to Her Majesty . . . A Paris chez Goupil et Vibert . . . (Taglioni, in the centre:) 31.4 cm in double hexagon 46 × 40.6 cm.
    Eng. 94; EB 3rd 63; repr. B/S 8, pl. 7; *CBB*, opp. p. 251; IG, *FC*, XIIa, opp. p. 81 left; Migel 55.

THE APOTHEOSES

63. (top:) L. Grahn   C. Grisi   Taglioni   Cerito/(bottom:)
The Dance of the Fairies./Lith. & Pub. by J. Baillie/Entered
according to act of Congress, in the year 1846, by J. Baillie (the
group of four:) 10.7 cm in double rect. 20.8 × 28.9 cm.

 not cat.; never repr. (the orig. *Illustrated London News* woodcut: repr. IG,
 London, XVIIIa; IG, 'Dandies and Dancers', pp. 42–3).

64. Grand Pas de Quatre/Danced by   (their names)/(on stone:)
J. Brandard (facs. sign.)/J. Brandard del. & lith.   M. & N. Hanhart lith Printers. (the group of four:) 17.3 cm in rect. with
rounded top: 29.2 × 23.2 cm

 not in *Eng.*; repr. B/S 100, pl. 69; Haskell, pl. 17, opp. p. 36 in colour.

65. [Colour plate XIII] The Celebrated/Pas des Déesses/In the
Ballet,/Le Jugement de Paris/As danced at Her Majesty's Theatre
July, 1846./by the four eminent danseuses [*sic*]/Fanny Cerrito,
Marie Taglioni, Lucile Grahn & Mon! S! Leon./Drawn from
the Life by Jules Bouvier, Esqre/J. Bouvier Litho.   70 St. Martins
Lane/London, Published Sept. 8, 1846, by T. McLean.
(Saint-Léon:) 24.3 cm in double hexagon 46 × 36.5 cm (this
copy is slightly clipped along each side.).

 Eng. 93; B/S 9, not repr.; repr. *CBB*, opp. p. 259 (with the name of Rosati
 who replaced Grahn in the revival of 1847); Gregor 175; IG, *FC*, XIIb,
 opp. p. 81 right; EB 3rd, 64 cover.

62. Carlotta Grisi, Marie Taglioni, Lucile Grahn, and Fanny Cerrito in the *Pas de Quatre* (London, 1845)

63. The *Illustrated London News* pose of the *Pas de Quatre* used for 'The Dance of the Fairies' (New York, 1846)

64. Lucile Grahn, Fanny Cerrito, Marie Taglioni, and Carlotta Grisi in the *Pas de Quatre* by and after J. Brandard

THE CONTEMPORARIES

PREVIOUSLY, WE HAVE EXAMINED THE CAREERS OF the great dancers whose performances shaped the Romantic Ballet. Now, there remain other *danseuses* who appeared with them, many of them fine artists, but who never gained the supreme rank and thus are not remembered through the largest number of printed mementos.

Oldest among them was Lise Noblet (1801–52), two and one-half years older than Taglioni, but who had already been a leading dancer at the Opéra for nine years before the début of her younger rival there. She was a *premier sujet*. Her major role, before the arrival of Taglioni, was that of the Goddess of Love in J.-B. Blache's *Mars et Vénus, ou les Filets de Vulcain* (1826). This was followed by *Astolphe et Joconde* by Aumer (1827). Little over a year later she created the mimed role that was most often to be linked to her name . . . Fenella, the mute heroine of the Scribe-Auber *la Muette de Portici* (Feb. 29, 1828), one of the cornerstones of the operatic repertoire. Her depiction as Fenella by Achille Devéria (no. 66), who included it with the two later ones of Elssler (nos. 26 [Colour plate VI] and 27) and Taglioni's *la Sylphide* (no. 16A) in his *Costumes historiques*, complete the four dance prints of that monumental series. All are presented here.

Taglioni's arrival and eventual finding of her perfect repertoire relegated Noblet to second status despite her specific title. In *le Dieu et la Bayadère* (1830) she was 'the other woman' Néala, opposed to Taglioni's Zoloé. In *la Sylphide*, she was James Reuben's fiancée Effie, a role in which she was portrayed at least twice, first in no. 728 of the Martinet *Petite galérie dramatique* (French series A), and in plate 2 of the Laederich *Album de l'Opéra* (not in *Fr.*; repr. IG, *Paris*, no. 41). Until the coming of Fanny Elssler, she was *the* leading dancer at the Opéra after Taglioni. Our second print of her, not previously catalogued or reproduced, shows her in the *divertissement* of Auber's opera *le Lac des Fées* (1839) (no. 67).

The two Paulines—Leroux (1809–91) and Duvernay (1813–94)—were equally *filles de l'Opéra* with Noblet. Their consecration in prints, however, is as much from London. Leroux's Paris career extended from 1826 to 1844, with a hiatus between 1837 and 1840 for convalescence. The English print we present (no. 68) shows her in *The Devil in Love* (1843), Drury Lane adaptation of *le Diable amoureux* (Opéra, 1840) in which she created the role of the demon Urielle. It was catalogued by Chaffée from a composite sheet, in the Harvard Theatre Collection, showing reproductions of 18 lithographs (*Eng. 85*). He did not know that it was no. 1 of a series by Brandard, of which he catalogued no. 5 showing Clara Webster (*Eng. 128; B/S 96, pl. 68*). One of our prints of Grahn (no. 58) is no. 3 of the same series.

Duvernay, the protégée of Dr. Véron, appeared in London at Drury Lane in Elssler's *le Diable boiteux*, translated as *The Devil on Two Sticks* (Dec. 1, 1836). Her distinctive pink satin and black lace costume was the subject of many prints including one by John Frederick Lewis (1805–76) (*Eng. 45*) and another by Chalon (*Eng. 46*). Still others, not so often reproduced include our no. 70. She died, in 1894, after enjoying widowhood for more than thirty-four years with the fortune of her husband Stephens Lyne-Stephens. Old master paintings from her art collection still hang in the National Galleries, both of London and Washington, D.C.

Other slightly younger Opéra-trained *danseuses* include Maria (b. *c.* 1818), whose family name was Jacob although she never used it professionally, and Adèle Dumilâtre (1821–1901), remembered as the first Queen of the Wilis in *Giselle*. During eight years Adèle, who with her elder sister Sophie had the almost-unique distinction of having 'a ballet father', appeared in a series of ballets as second lead with Carlotta Grisi, or starring in others with less-popular dancers. *Eucharis* (1844) was not a great success—only six performances—but it occasioned a lithograph which, although catalogued (*Fr.* 592), has never been reproduced before (no. 77B). Her thin-faced elegance is ably caught by Léon Nöel (1807–84) who lithographed a portrait after Joseph Negelen (1792–1870) (no. 77A). Hippolyte Masson's Maria is an equally distinctive folio (no. 74). Her flashing eyes suggest the soubrette who seconded Carlotta in *le Diable à Quatre* (1845). It was she who, with Eugène Coralli, introduced the *Polka* onto the Opéra stage, as Grisi and Perrot were also showing it in London (see no. 53).

THE CONTEMPORARIES

The sisters Fijan, who later appeared professionally under the noble family name of Fitzjames, were two other products of the Opéra schooling. The elder, Louise (b. 1809), had the distinction of performing the role of the Abbess Helena in Meyerbeer's *Robert le Diable* (a role created by Taglioni in 1831) more than 200 times! She is presented in the *Pas Vénitien*, a fanciful dance which appeared as no. 11 of the series *les Annales de l'Opéra* (no. 69). It was soon pirated as design on an American music title—*The Boudoir Waltzes*—published in 1847 in Louisville, Kentucky and Cincinnati, Ohio (*Amer.* II, 48). Nathalie (b. 1819), the younger sister, appeared as leading dancer in Antonio Guerra's lone ballet at the Opéra, *les Mohicans* (1847). It was a disaster. Normally a failure was allowed three performances. It had only two! But Nathalie subsequently became a useful member of the dancing personnel in Paris. With Auguste Mabille (b. 1815), she appeared in the *Pas de Deux* of *Giselle*, Act I (now called the 'Peasant *Pas de Deux*'). She is pictured here, again with Mabille, in a lithograph showing a statue of them in the divertissement of *le Diable à Quatre* (1845). It is reproduced here for the first time (no. 76).

While the Opéra trained most of its *danseuses*, its leading male dancers usually came from elsewhere. We have already noted Antonio Guerra dancing with Taglioni (see no. 17) and Cerrito (see no. 37 [Colour plate IX]) in London. He had been schooled at the San Carlo in Naples. Lucien Petipa (1815–98), who partnered all of the great ballerinas of the *Ballet romantique*, was a product of his father's instruction, while the family was living and performing in Brussels. Before he became the regular partner of Carlotta in *Giselle* (see no. 49A) and *la Péri* (see no. 51 [Colour plate X]), he had made his Paris début with Fanny Elssler in one of her *Sylphide* performances (June 10, 1839). We see him, during these early Opéra years in the *divertissement* of Auber's *Gustave III ou le Bal masqué* (premiere 1833) (no. 71).

Jules Perrot (1810–92), whose début at the Opéra (1830) presented him opposite Taglioni, left in 1835. A fine classical dancer whose original theatrical vocation had been in Lyon as a youthful imitator of Mazurier (see no. 4), he achieved his apogee in London with the long series of brilliant ballets and *Grand Pas* which we have already noted (see nos. 34, 39, 41A, 42, 52–54 and Colour plate XI, 59A and B, 60, 62–65 and Colour plate XIII).

The last of the great *premiers danseurs* was Arthur Saint-Léon (1821–70) whose early training, like Petipa's, was with his father, in Stuttgart. He had already appeared there in a successful, professional début before entering the classes of Albert (see no. 1) in Paris. We have noted him in London where he was the preferred partner of Cerrito from 1842. She became his wife three years later. He has already appeared with her in our gallery in the *Pas des Déesses* (1846) (see no. 65 [Colour

plate XIII]) and in Paris (see no. 43). Now we see him, after the break-up of their marriage, at the *Théâtre-lyrique* in Paris in his own *Lutin de la Vallée* (Jan. 22, 1853). In this hybrid *opéra-ballet*, he appeared in several different disguises, including one as an old violinist (no. 79). This work was part of the repertoire he took to Portugal where he appeared for two seasons—1854–56, at the São Carlos in Lisbon. His most popular ballet there was *Saltarello*, adapted from another work at the *Théâtre-lyrique*—*le Danseur du Roi*, Oct. 22, 1854. The ultimate Lisbon consecration was an 1856 portrait by Santa Barbara (no. 78). The ballet master had now published his *Sténochorégraphie* (Paris, 1852). The year before the date on the portrait, he had received the cross of the Order of Christ from the Regent Ferdinand, husband of the Queen Regnant Maria II. Its ribbon is shown in his button-hole.

There were other *danseuses* who, like the male dancers, received initial training elsewhere than at the Opéra. Obvious is Elena I. Andreyanova (1816–57), the first Russian *Giselle* and *Péri*. She appears in an extremely rare seated portrait by Alexandrov (no. 73). Only slightly older than her, Elisa Albert-Bellon (c. 1815 or earlier–1892) was the daughter and pupil of Albert (see no. 1). A début at the Opéra in 1829 did not lead to a contract, but she danced there for parts of two years between 1842 and 1843. She had the distinction of being the only *danseuse* to appear in the title role of *Giselle* while Carlotta continued at the Opéra, dancing it twice in Sept., 1842. She figures here in the Viennese production of *le Diable amoureux*—*der Verliebte Teufel*, in a three-quarter length portrait by Adolf Dauthage (1825–83) (no. 72).

A more unusual case was Marie Guy-Stéphan (1818–73). In 1839, she is listed *première danseuse* in Bordeaux and an almost unknown print attests to that fact. She made an unsuccessful Opéra *début*, appearing with Lucien Petipa, in 1840, was not hired, but had success in London beginning the next year. She, like Pauline Leroux, danced at Drury Lane as Urielle in *The Devil in Love* (Paris: *le Diable amoureux*). She must have continued in Bordeaux, as a second print of her was published there in 1843. Meanwhile, two English lithographs present her: in 1842, dancing the *Cracovienne* from *Une Soirée de Carnaval* (*Eng.* 106, by Bouvier), one of Cerrito's successes, and in the *Boleras de Cadiz* (*Eng.* 107) (1844). She now did the completely unexpected and performed for several itinerant years throughout Spain, partnered at the beginning by Marius Petipa (1822–1910), Lucien's younger brother and subsequent ballet master at St. Petersburg. She appeared opposite Saint-Léon in *le Lutin de la Vallée* at the *Théâtre-lyrique* (1853) (see no. 79—there is a pendant print showing her). In it she appeared in a dance from Cadiz, the *Pas Gaditan*. That same year, she was the second named role in *Aelia et Mysis* at the Opéra, appearing again in a Spanish dance. We present her in an unidentified ballet by the fecund Victor Dollet (b. 1815). He was lithographing it from a portrait by Charles Sardou (b. 1806). It is uncatalogued, and not previously reproduced (no. 75).

Other non-French dancers of the same period include Augusta Nielsen (1822–1902), one of Grahn's replacements in Copenhagen who appeared in the character dance *la Lithuanienne* (1844). Three separate Danish prints attest its popularity. Since Migel has presented one of them by Bærentzen (her no. 60), we present another by Th. W. Pederson (probably Wilhelm Th. Pederson, 1820–59) (no. 80). It is more static than the Bærentzen example.

From Naples came Louise (1823–93), the daughter of Marie Taglioni's uncle Salvatore. She appeared in many ballets and opera *divertissements* during her almost nine years in Paris, including Carlotta's *Filleule des Fées* (1849), Cerrito's *Stella* (1850), a revival of *la Sylphide* (1852) in which she danced Noblet's role of Effie, and *Aelia et Mysis* (1853). Most of the depictions of her present the leader of the bees in *les Abeilles*, the *divertissement* created by Saint-Léon for inclusion in Halévy's opera *le Juif errant* (1852). We present one of those which has been completely unknown until now (no. 81). It is number 1 of a recognized series of three lithographs from designs by Joséphine Ducollet (see nos. 99A and B), who does not appear among Bénézit's biographies of artists.

Adeline Plunkett (1824–1910) came from Belgium. After a short London career at Her Majesty's Theatre where she was summarily dismissed by Benjamin Lumley, the director, she appeared at the Opéra in Carlotta's role in *la Péri*, beginning in 1845. A London print showing her in this ballet which she had danced at Drury Lane the previous year is, unfortunately, not in our collection (*Eng.* 99; B/S 84, pl. 59). The almost identical, French, music title from it is, however (no. 82). Victor Coindre who signed the new stone obviously

gave no credit to the British originator T. H. Maguire, lithographer of the fifth plate of Taglioni's *Album d'Adieux* (see no. 23B) and the Chalon *Pas de Quatre* (no. 62) two years before. Only a festoon of falling flowers in her hands, and the reversal of her position, suggest the variant.

Our last 'contemporary' of the greatest *danseuses* came from Philadelphia! Augusta Maywood (1825–76/7) made her début at the Opéra the same year as Grahn, but was six years younger. She left Paris to elope with her partner Charles Mabille (1817–58), younger brother of Auguste, the partner of Nathalie Fitzjames (see no. 76). After seasons in Marseille (1841–2) and Lyon (1842–3), the newly-weds danced in Lisbon (1843–5). She was the heroine of *Giselle* in the premiere of that ballet in the second and third of those cities. (Elisa Albert Bellon first created the role in Bordeaux; see no. 72.) Their marriage foundered, but they still performed together in Vienna until 1846 by which time she had reassumed her maiden name (it was actually the name of her step-father!).

The largest part of the remainder of Augusta's career took place in Italy where she had the original idea of travelling with the small, essential nucleus of a company performing its own repertoire in the various cities of the ballet circuit. From these years, we present an Ancona print signed by Augusto Bedetti, showing her as Esmeralda (the ballet was most often named *la Zingara* in Italy), with a laudatory sestet below (no. 83A). Parmenia Migel has already reproduced it (her no. 34) in *The Ballerinas*. Such is not the case with a Hamburg music title showing a vacuous dancer in the Auguste Maywood Polka. Until now, it has been unknown for many years (no. 83B). With her, we end the contemporaries of the great ballerinas.

66. (top right:) Nᵒ 2/(bottom:) Jeune Fille Napolitaine/(on stone:) Deveria (facs. sign.)/A. Devéria del.   Lith. de Lemercier/Paris, chez Aumont . . . London, published by Ch. Tilt   28.2 cm in rect. 34.8 × 23.7 cm.
   Fr. 78b; repr. (Var. a) IG, *Paris*, 31.

67. (top:) Costume de Mᶜˡˡᵉ Noblet/dans le Lac des Fées/(bottom:) Mosaïque gracieuse par L. Lassalle./Nᵒ 15/(on stone:) Louis Lassalle (facs. sign.)/Fourmage Editeur . . . Imp. d'Aubert & Cⁱᵉ   17.2 cm in double rect. 21.4 × 15.5 cm.
   not cat; never repr.

68. Nᵒ 1/Pauline Leroux/The Devil in Love/J. Brandard del. & lith./M. and N. Hanhart, lith. printers/Published Feb. 1ˢᵗ 1844 by Mᵉˢˢʳˢ Fores   18.9 cm.
   Eng. 85; never repr.

69. (top:) l'Opéra/(below:) 11/Mᵉˡˡᵉ Fitzjames/Pas Vénitien/Imp. par Lemercier/Guérard del . . . Desmaison lith./Paris (Mᵒⁿ Aumont) François Delarue . . . London, pub. 20 August 1844 by the Anaglyphic Company . . .   19.8 cm in triple rect. 26.1 × 21.4 cm.
   Fr. 561; never repr.

70. Madˡˡᵉ Duvernay as Florinda/in the/"Devil on Two Sticks"/ London. Lithographed, Printed & Publᵈ by G. E. Madeley . . ./ Proof/(Nᵒ 5. Fair Favorites)/Madeley, Litho: 21.7 cm.
   Eng. 157; Hall 7; never repr.

71. (top:) Gustave III ou le bal masqué/(below:) Costume de Mʳ Lucien Petipa./Edmond Sewrin del. Litho. de Pallard. 20.1 cm in triple rect. 24.8 × 14.6 cm.
   not in *Fr.*; repr. Khudyekov, p. 321.

THE CONTEMPORARIES

72. Elisa Albert Bellon (facs. sign.)/in dem Ballete der verliebte Teufel/Verlags-Eigenthum v A. Paterno's W: & Sohn in Wien/ (on stone:) Nach d. Natur v Dauthage (facs. sign.)/850/Gedr. b. J. Höfelich 32.4 cm.

Germ. 9; never repr.

73. (the whole in Cyrillic) E. I. Andreyanova/Pervaya Russkaya Tanzovitzaya/Fotographiya Alexandrovskogo Lit. Tuleva 12.3 cm in rect. 16.1 × 12.8 cm.

not cat.; repr. Lifar, *Giselle*, pl. XIX.

74. Maria (facs. sign.)/de l'Académie Royale de Musique/(on stone:) Hyppolite Masson (facs. sign.)/1843/Imprimé par Lemercier à Paris 27.2 cm.

not cat.; never repr.

75. Marie Guy Stephan. (facs. sign.)/(on stone:) Victor Dollet (facs. sign.)/V: Dollet, d'après C: Sardou Imprimé par Auguste Bry 37.6 cm.

not cat.; never repr.

76. (Base of statuette:) mabile et/Nathalie Fidejam/Dans/Diable a/ (on stone:) C. V./Le Monde Dramatique/Imp. Lemercier, Benard et C: (whole statuette:) 24.2 cm.

Fr. 35; never repr.

77A. M: Adèle Dumilâtre/de l'Académie Royale de Musique/ Peint par Negelen Imprimé par Lemercier à Paris Lith. par Léon Noël./Paris, publié par Jeannin ... London published April 1: 1843, by S. et J. Fuller ... 28.5 cm in five rects. 42.8 × 33.2 cm.

Fr. 15; never repr.

77B. (top:) Souvenirs de l'Opéra, N: 6/(in wreath:) A Dumilâtre (facs. sign.)/Adèle Dumilâtre/(dans Eucharis)/(on stone:) L. Loire (facs. sign.)/Paris, Garnot édit. Imp. Lemercier 18.4 cm in tinted rect. 24.3 × 17.3 cm.

Fr. 592; never repr.

78. A. M. Saint-Léon./(on stone:) S:ᵃ Barbara (facs. sign.)/1856/ Lith. de Lopes & Bastos ... 28.5 cm.

Cat. Campos Ferreira Lima, *Retratos ... litografados ...* (Guimarães, 1942), vol. I, no. 36; repr. *CBB*, opp. p. 314.

79. Arthur S: Léon/dans le/Le Lutin de la Vallée./Faivre del. et lith./Imp. Bertauts ... Paris (central figure:) 18 cm in tinted rect. 31.6 × 23.6 cm.

not cat.; never repr.

80. Augusta Nielsen/(la Lithuanienne)/Th. W. Pederson del Fortling lith ... Brødrene Berlings Stentrykteri 23.6 cm.

not cat.; never repr.

81. (top:) Célébrités Théâtrales N: 1/Grand Opéra/(below:) L. Taglioni (Fuchs)/Rôle de la Reine des Abeilles dans le divertisse-ment du Juif-errant/(facs. sign.)/(on stone:) Joséphine Ducollet (facs. sign.)/Paris, Masson ... Imp. Lemercier ... 21.8 cm in tinted rect. 27.4 × 20.8 cm.

not cat.; never repr.

82. (top:) Adeline Plunkett/Artiste de l'Académie Royale de Musique/(below:) Miranda/Polka des Salons pour le Piano/par/ A. Goria/Pr. 3 Fr./Paris, chez Chabal, Editeur de Musique .../ Imp. Bertauts, Paris/(on stone:) Victor Coindre (facs. sign.).

Fr. 87; never repr. (the Eng. orig: *Eng.* 99; Hall 6; B/S 84, pl. 59; IG, *Rambert*, 96).

83A. Ad/Augusta Maywood/Gli Anconitani nella Primavera del 1853./(sestet)/(on stone:) A. Bedetti (facs. sign.)/Ancona, Lit. Pieroni 17 cm in tinted rect. with rounded corners: 23.1 × 19 cm.

Ital. 147; A/B 2793; Winter, 'Augusta Maywood', *Dance Index*, II, nos. 1–2 (Jan.–Feb., 1943), no. 11; repr. Migel, *The Ballerinas*, no. 34.

83B. (top:) Auguste Maywood-Polka/(below:) pour Piano/par/ Aug. M. Canthal./Price 1/6 xxx/Schuberth & C:/Hamburg, Leipzig & New York. 13.2 cm.

not cat.; never repr.

66. Lise Noblet as Fenella in *la Muette de Portici* (Paris, 1828)

67. Lise Noblet in *le Lac des Fées* (Paris, 1839)

68. Pauline Leroux in *The Devil in Love* (London, 1844)

69. Louise FitzJames in the *Pas Vénitien les Annales de l'Opéra*, no. 11 (Paris, 1844)

70. Pauline Duvernay as Florinda in *The Devil on Two Sticks* (London, 1837)

71. Lucien Petipa in *Gustave III ou le Bal masqué* (Paris, 1833)

72. Elisa Albert-Bellon in *der Verliebte Teufel* (Vienna, 1850)

73. Elena Ivanovna Andreyanova (Saint Petersburg, *c.* 1840)

74. Maria [Jacob] Portrait by Hyppolite Masson (Paris, 1843)

75. Marie Guy-Stéphan in ballet costume by Victor Dollet after Charles Sardou

76. Nathalie FitzJames and Auguste Mabille in *le Diable à Quatre* (Paris, 1845)

77A. Adèle Dumilâtre
portrait by Léon Noël after Joseph Negelen (Paris, 1843)

77B. Adèle Dumilâtre in *Eucharis*.
Souvenirs de l'Opéra, no. 6 (Paris, 1844)

78. Arthur Saint-Léon. Portrait by Santa Barbara (Lisbon, 1856)

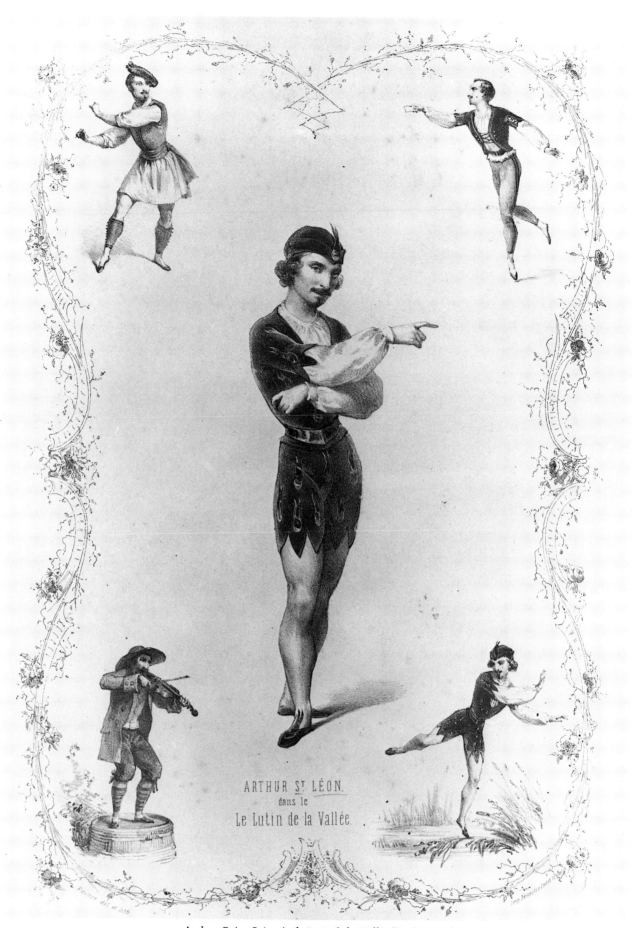

ARTHUR St. LÉON.
dans le
Le Lutin de la Vallée.

79. Arthur Saint-Léon in *le Lutin de la Vallée* (Paris, 1853)

80. Augusta Nielsen in *la Lithuanienne* (Copenhagen, 1844)

81. Louise Taglioni-Fuchs in the *Divertissement* of *le Juif errant* (Paris, 1852)

82. Adeline Plunkett in *la Péri* (Paris, 1845)

83B. Augusta Maywood in a Polka.
MUSIC TITLE from Hamburg

THE NEW GENERATION

BETWEEN 1825 AND 1840, WHILE THE GREATEST *danseuses* of the Romantic Ballet were making their débuts and finding their stellar vehicles, a series of births was producing what was to become the second generation of ballerinas. Unlike the period between 1804 (birth of Taglioni) and 1825 (Maywood), when most of the dancers were French-born and/or French-trained, the forthcoming generation was predominantly Italian. When Grisi (last at the Opéra in 1849) and Cerrito (1855) ended their Paris careers, their replacements were Carolina Rosati (1825–1905) and Amalia Ferraris (1830–1904; the *Enc. dello Spettacolo* says born in 1828) whose Opéra débuts occurred in 1853 and 1856 respectively. Their names alone are indicative. Neither was trained nor went through the ranks in Paris. They arrived as Stars, and stayed: Rosati for six years until 1859, Ferraris performing for the last time at the Opéra in March, 1863 just over six and a half years after her first Paris appearances.

Despite their ages at the time of the Opéra débuts (Rosati was almost 27, Ferraris 26), each had already had a long career. Rosati made her original début in Verona at age 10! The first dance print showing her is from Turin, dated 1838 (*Ital.* 108). She was then not yet 12. Ferraris appeared first in Taglioni's *Sylphide* at la Scala. She was 11 or 12. On the shoulders of formidable women such as these was the future of ballet to rest.

Both Ferraris and Rosati were already well known in London before they appeared in Paris. We show a print of Rosati in a London ballet, even though it was published in Paris (no. 84 [colour plate XIV]). In the title role of Paul Taglioni's *Coralia or the Inconstant Knight* (1847), she floats in a moon-lit landscape with a wide river and distant mountains. Our choice for a lithograph of Ferraris before her Paris triumph is in a perfect *attitude croisée derrière* (no. 90). It dates from Vicenza in 1853, and underlines her technical virtuosity. For Amalia Ferraris was one of that spectacular breed of the favourite pupils of the Milanese ballet master Carlo Blasis (1799–1878) who labelled them his 'Pleiades'. We shall soon meet others of them.

Among the most important ballets of the Rosati-and-

Ferraris years in Paris was *le Corsaire* (1856). It was loosely adapted from Byron's poem of the same name and featured, along with the last score of Adolphe Adam, the composer of *Giselle*, a bacchanalian orgy on a ship which foundered and sank in the waves . . . in the middle of the Opéra stage. Rosati, the greatest contemporary mime, portrayed Medora, the heroine. She is pictured on a music title by the fecund Henry Emy in that role (no. 85).

One of Ferraris's major Paris roles was the dancer Gazella in *l'Etoile de Messine* (1861). Its success is indicative of the increasing Italian take-over at the Opéra. The choreographer was Pasquale Borri (1820–84), lone *danseur* in the Blasis *Pléiade*. The composer was Niccolo Count Gabrielli; and what could be more Italian than the rousing tarentella that was a high point of the work. We present this *ballabile*, showing Ferraris with her French partner Louis Mérante (no. 91). It is an extremely rare example of a print showing a large group of dancers on stage. Audiences of the *Ballet romantique* preferred seeing only the leading stars!

Paris had already seen others of the Blasis-trained Pleiades. The first was Flora Fabbri. A Paris début in 1844 began seven seasons there, and she appeared also in London at both Drury Lane (1845 and 1846) and Covent Garden (1848). A Roman print from the Teatro Alibert in the fall of 1843, with her husband Luigi Bretin, shows them together in her father's ballet *la Zingarella* (no. 87). Her 'steely-pointes' are much in evidence.

Somewhat younger than Fabbri was Sofia Fuoco (1830–1916), another of the Blasis-trained prodigies. Her Paris début, aged 16, in *Betty*, partnered by Lucien Petipa (see nos. 51 [colour plate X] and 71), is remembered from a music title by the prolific brothers Schott whose main address was in Mainz, with others in Antwerp and Brussels and Paris itself (no. 89). A last Italian of these *danseuses* was Carolina Pochini (1836–1901), wife of Pasquale Borri. She never appeared at the Opéra although there had been some negotiations in 1853. Besides touring throughout Italy, she appeared also in Vienna as a full-length portrait in costume by Adolf Dauthage (1825–83), dated 1856, attests (no. 95).

Other non-French dancers also enjoyed enviable reputations which resulted in prints for our gallery. Katti Lanner (1831–1908), daughter of a Viennese orchestra leader and composer, had a long career throughout Europe and America. Her years as ballet mistress and choreographer at the Empire Theatre in London ended only the year before her death. From Hamburg comes a lithograph showing her in *Esmeralda* with the titles of four others of the ballets in her extensive repertoire (no. 92 [Colour plate XV]).

Perhaps 'the Germanies's' greatest contribution to the Romantic Ballet was the daughter of Paul Taglioni (see nos. 11, 14A and 14B) and Amalie Galster (see no. 9). Named after her aunt 'the great' Marie Taglioni, she is usually designated, as with royal families, as Marie Taglioni II (1833–91). Two English prints, however, list her name as Marie Paul Taglioni (*Eng.* 122–123). 1847 was the year of her London début, even before her first Berlin appearances. Only a month after the premiere of his *Coralia* with Carolina Rosati, Paul Taglioni choreographed a second ballet for her, *Théa ou la Fée aux Fleurs*. In it he cast his fourteen-year-old daughter as the Fairy of the Flowers. Her depiction in this role, pendant to the *Coralia* with Rosati (see no. 84 [Colour plate XIV]) completes the pair of the loveliest, most ornate prints of the Romantic Ballet (no. 94 [Colour plate XVI]).

From Denmark comes yet another of our examples showing non-French *danseuses*. During the early summer of 1849, August Bournonville presented a *Pas de Trois* for three of his promising pupils: the sisters Juliette (1831–1906) and Sophie Price (1832–1908) and their cousin Amalie (1831–1902). He had again lost the services of his leading *danseuse* when Augusta Nielsen (see no. 80) fled the stage in terror earlier in the year. Now, for the Casino Theatre, not the Royal Theatre, he arranged the *Pas de Trois Cousines* (no. 93). It is the charmer of the Danish gallery!

The native French dancers, *les filles de l'Opéra*, pale before the reputations of these international stars. Louise Fleury (b. 1826), was a pupil of Albert (see no. 1) who made a Paris début as Myrtha, the Queen of the Wilis in *Giselle*, early in 1843. She remained at the Opéra for another five years, but is better known for her performances in London, where she appeared first the year before her Paris début. Her major work was at Drury Lane where she created the title role in the London premiere of *The Beauty of Ghent* (Feb. 17, 1844). This was Carlotta Grisi's *Jolie Fille de Gand* (Opéra 1842) 'made English'. For this role in which she danced the *Pas de Diane* just as Carlotta had in Paris (see no. 61 [Colour plate XII]), several different artists created prints. Chalon did one (*Eng.*

66); Bouvier, two (*Eng.* 64, 65). We present the first of the Bouvier examples (no. 86A), since, unlike the other, it was not reproduced by Beaumont and Sitwell. Still another, unknown, depiction of Fleury in the *Pas de Diane* from this same ballet, appears as a catalogued plate 8 from the series *The Favorites of the Ballet* (*Eng.* 161). Interestingly, my example of the print shows the number '9' (no. 86B) which appears on a different plate of Fleury as Myrtha in *Giselle* (repr. Migel, cover). Fleury's later career coincided with that of Arthur Saint-Léon (see nos. 65 [Colour plate XIII], 78 and 79). She was his *première danseuse* during his two Lisbon seasons. She toured with him during the late 1850s throughout Central Europe; and she was his constant companion during the years of commuting between St. Petersburg and Paris before *Coppélia* and his premature death (1870).

A much more important native dancer was Emma Livry (1842–63). Illegitimate daughter of a minor soloist at the Opéra, she might have become the French stellar counterweight to the major Italian *ballerine* in Paris. But death by fire snuffed out the possibility. At 16, she starred in a revival of *la Sylphide*, so effectively that Taglioni came out of retirement to witness the triumph of her new avatar. The continuation of the relationship resulted in *le Papillon*, sole work choreographed by Taglioni (Nov. 26, 1860). In it Emma triumphed again as Farfalla, the butterfly, whose wings are burned when she approached too close to a lighted torch. Earlier in the ballet, she danced the *Valse des Rayons* in which she was photographed by Disdéri. This photograph served as basis for a lithograph by Jacolin. Despite previous reproduction, it is included again here (no. 96). It is the finest depiction of the ill-fated *danseuse* who might have revivified French ballet, but, instead, died before her 21st birthday.

A final part-French dancer must also be noted. Franceska Auriol (1829–62) was the daughter of Jean-Baptiste (1806–81), one of the finest acrobats and clowns of the first half of the nineteenth century. She is recognizable as Esmeralda in a fine English print with her husband the *danseur*-clown Richard Flexmore (*Eng.* 2, pl. XXII; B/S 80, pl. 57). It is dated 1848. The year before, she had appeared at the Paris Opéra dancing a *Rondeja* (cat. in Wild, *le Cirque iconographie*, 1869; no. 441) (the print at the *Bibliothèque et Musée de l'Opéra* and in the author's collection). Another Paris print, probably from the same year, shows her in *la Sylphide* (no. 88). Although far removed from Taglioni's ethereal creation, this lithograph has not been previously catalogued not reproduced. With it, we end the second generation of the *danseuses* of the Romantic Ballet.

84. [Colour plate XIV] (top:) Mad^elle^/Carolina Rosati/(bottom:) Coralia/Painted by De Valentini   Paris, impr. by Lemercier   Lith. by E. Desmaisons 18.3 cm in oval 39 × 30 cm on tinted paper: 50.4 × 37.5 cm.

> *Fr.* 91; repr. B/S 65, pl. 48, in colour.

85. (top:) à Madame Rosati/Rosati-Polka/Répertoire des bals de l'opéra/(bottom:) Composée sur des motifs du Ballet Le Corsaire,/par/Strauss./à Paris, maison Boieldieu, Édit:/(on stone:) Henry Emy (facs. sign.) Lith. Bertauts   22.3 cm.

> *Fr.* 92; repr. Khudyekov, p. 287.

86A. Louise Fleury (facs. sign.)/as/The Beauty of Ghent/J. Bouvier Del./Lithog. 70 St. Martins Lane/Pub. T. McLean . . . March 28th 1844   31 cm in hexagon 39.8 × 28.5.

> *Eng.* 64; Hall 1; B/S 75, not repr.

86B. The Favorites of the Ballet./9/Mad^lle^ Fleury   Beauty of Ghent   Pas de Diane/C. G. del. J. H. Lynch, Lith.   18.4 cm in octagon 24.6 × 17.8 cm.

> *Eng.* 161 (where number '8'); never repr.

87. Luigi Bretin   Flora Fabbri-Bretin/Primi Ballerini assoluti nel nobile Teatro Alibert/nel Ballo la Zingarella composto dal Coreografo/Giovanni Fabbri/Roma l'Autunno del 1843/V. Battistelli dis. Lit. Battistelli   (she:) 21.8 cm in double rect. 30.8 × 40.2 cm.

> *Ital.* 33, repr. title page; A/B 686; repr. Khudyekov, p. 343; *Enciclopedia dello Spettacolo*, IV, 1747.

88. (in wreath to lower right:) Auriol/Imp. par Thierry frères, Paris/Franceska Auriol/(on stone:) Plattel (facs. sign.)   17.7 cm on tinted paper 28.7 × 22.6 cm.

> not in *Fr.*; never repr.

89. (top:) Betty/Ballet en Deux Actes/Polka-Valse (left top:) Académie Royale de Musique/Melle Fuoco et M: Petipa/(right top:) Musique de/Amb. Thomas/(bottom:) Pour le Piano/par/Fréd. Burgmüller./Mayence, Anvers et Bruxelles/chez les fils de B. Schott   (she:) 16.1 cm.

> *Fr.* 39; Hall 4 (Petipa); repr. *CBB*, opp. p. 175.

90. Amalia Ferraris/Vicenza 1853./B. Marcovich fec: Vicenza, Lit. Longo   33.2 cm.

> *Ital.* 91; repr. LM, *Images*, 72.

91. (top:) Musée de Moeurs en Actions/(bottom:) 8./Scène de l'Opéra la Tarentelle. (Étoile de Messine)/Peint par Morlon   Imp. Lemercier . . . Paris   Lith. par Régnier, Bettannier, Morlon/Paris, Eugène Jouy. New York. Emile Seitz . . . (she: with upright tambourine) 18 cm in tinted rect. 39.6 × 52.7 cm.

> *Fr.* 122, repr. pl. XXVII, p. 182.

92. [Colour plate XV] Katti Lanner (facs. sign. in Gothic script)/Lith. Inst. v Ch: Fuchs, Hambrg   Lith. v. J. Puschkin/(in four inner corners clockwise from upper left:) Eleonore.   Faust. Sitala.   Uriella. 12.8 cm in ornamental frame: 19.7 × 16 cm.

> *Germ.* 135; never repr.

93. Sophie, Juliette, Amalie Price./(Pas des trois cousines)/Ed. Lehmann del. & lith.   Em. Bærentzen & C: lith Inst.   (central figure:) 24.8 cm in tinted rect. 37.5 × 30.5 cm.

> not cat.; Reumert, p. 87; Veale, 'The Dancing Prices of Denmark', *Dance Perspectives*, no. 11 (summer, 1961), inside cover.

94. [Colour plate XVI] (top:) Mad^elle^/Marie Taglioni/(bottom:) La Fée/aux/Fleurs/(no artists listed on this copy, but they should be the same as those in the companion print, no. 84)   25.4 cm in oval 39.2 × 30 cm on tinted paper: 51.2 × 37 cm.

> *Fr.* 107; Hall 15 (as Marie Taglioni I); repr. B/S 93, pl. 66.

95. Carolina Pochini/Verlag u Eigenthum v. Paterno in Wien. (on stone:) Dauthage (fac: sign.)/856   32.1 cm.

> *Germ.* 187; Hall 1; repr. Khudyekov, p. 347.

96. (top:) Le Papillon/(bottom:) Melle Emma Livry./au Ménestrel . . ./Jacolin (facs. sign.)/d'après la Phot. Disdéri.   Imp. Bertauts . . .   18.2 cm in tinted rect. 21.8 × 18.4 cm.

> *Fr.* 66, repr. pl. XXX, p. 189; Khudyekov, p. 296.

HENRY EMY

85. Carolina Rosati in *le Corsaire* (Paris, 1856)

86B. Louise Fleury in the *Pas de Diane* from *The Beauty of Ghent*,
Favorites of the Ballet, no. 9 (London, 1844)

87. Flora Fabbri with her husband Luigi Bretin in *la Zingarella* (Rome, 1843)

88. Franceska Auriol in *la Sylphide* (Paris, 1847)

89. Sofia Fuoco with Lucien Petipa in *Betty* (Paris, 1846)

90. Amalia Ferraris in attitude (Vicenza, 1853)

91. Amalia Ferraris with Louis Mérante and the corps de ballet in the Tarentella from *l'Etoile de Messine* (Paris, 1861)

93. Sophie, Juliette, and Amalie Price in the *Pas des trois cousines* (Copenhagen, 1849)

95. Carolina Pochini by Dauthage (Vienna, 1856)

96. Emma Livry in *le Papillon* (Paris, 1860)

ICONOGRAPHER'S CHOICE

IVOR GUEST, IN HIS LAUDATORY FOREWORD TO THIS collection, has ably shown the intimate and necessary relationship of the ballet historian to the dance iconographer. He has unhesitatingly acknowledged his debt to the cataloguers of prints who have helped him concretize the locales of the scenes surrounding the dancers whom he has treated—both onstage and off. I must now similarly acknowledge my debt to him and his rare colleagues who properly understand what research into dance and its history entail. The historical value of my text up until now has been based entirely upon works such as his. But my text has been little else than a string onto which the jewels of the prints themselves have been threaded to form self-contained necklaces. Ivor starts with the history and illustrates it with iconographic examples. I do the opposite: starting with the icons and grouping them into a semblance of historical continuity. I must now diverge even further from him. We leave behind the conventions of individual performer or specific generation to concentrate on the rare and the esoteric. The dance print as a historical document still remains as heretofore, but it is now presented as 'Iconographer's (rather than dance historian's) choice'.

Our first example is typical. Emelie Högqvist (1812–46) was a young Swedish *danseuse* whose potential was mentioned by Marie Taglioni during her single short visit to her birthplace Stockholm in September, 1841. Shortly thereafter, Emelie shifted her allegiance from dancing to acting, performed for several years in various plays and died at age 34. Why is she included here? All the reasons are non-historical. The lithograph showing her in the role of Aventurine in *I Polkan* (Dec. 7, 1845) is the largest and most imposing of all Swedish dance prints (the figure is more than 17″ high!) (no. 97A). It has only been reproduced once—in a Stockholm periodical of 1898. And what better way exists to 'lay claim' to a Swedish Gallery of dance prints which already contains fifteen examples and ten variants, all catalogued and ready to be published upon request.

A flying trip diagonally across Europe from Stockholm to Lisbon presents our second 'unknown ballerina'. Genoveva Monticelli (no dates found as yet) danced during the 1850

Carnaval season in Turin before appearing as leading dancer at the Theatro São Carlos in the Portuguese capital. There she remained for at least two seasons. The three-quarter length portrait of this very ugly divinity by Macphail, dated 1852, was duly catalogued by Henrique Campos Ferreira Lima in the first volume of his tiny *Retratos litografados* (no. 97B). So was the portrait of Saint-Léon by Santa Barbara (see no. 78). They constitute one-third of the dance lithographs in that catalogue. To those six, I have added at least 13 more! One of these is a music title for *A Sivigliana Passo Hespanhol* (no. 98). Here Monticelli appeared with her partner Valentino Cappon. Was it the artist Marchi, or the lithographic company Canongia & Cᵃ, or the ballerina herself who owned a copy of Numa Blanc's print of Cerrito and Saint-Léon in *la Manola*? (no. 98 INSERT). Certainly piracy was not dead.

Slightly more conventional travel takes us again to Paris. In his French catalogue, Chaffée listed prints of two minor *danseuses*, Louise Lucy-Barré in *l'Etoile du Rhin* (Fr. 12) and Octavie de Mélisse in *la Sylphide* (Fr. 77). Both include the name of Joséphine Ducollet as artist. And the second lithograph is titled 'Célébrités Théâtrales No. 2'. So a series was found! Our previous inclusion of the uncatalogued print showing the much-better-known Louise Taglioni as Queen of the Bees (see no. 81), also by Ducollet and with 'No. 1' of the same series across its top, further rounds out the group. An iconographer's task is to provide otherwise unobtainable information. No better reason exists for inclusion of these two ladies (nos. 99A and 99B). DeMélisse certainly did not dance the title role of *la Sylphide* in Paris despite 'Grand Opera' in the print's title. *L'Etoile du Rhin*, which supposedly featured Lucy-Barré, was not a Paris work—it appears neither in Ivor Guest's appendices to *The Ballet of the Second Empire* nor in Beaumont Wicks' exhaustive lists of dramatic offerings in the French capital. But she did appear elsewhere. Late in 1850 she arrived in New York where she hired George Washington Smith to partner her. But *l'Etoile du Rhin* was not in her American repertoire either. A ballet of that name, titled in English, was premiered at Drury Lane on Feb. 24, 1852. It starred Adeline Plunkett (see no. 82) and was given 40 times in three months. Ducy-Barré was not in its cast! In June, 1852, de Mélisse followed Ducy-Barré to New York, appearing at Niblo's, as well as in Boston where in February of the next year the company, which included Léontine Pougaud and the *danseur* Mège, disbanded. She did not appear in *la Sylphide* at that time. The 'Célébrités Théâtrales' were finished.

Two Italian *danseuses* are also to be noted. Possessed of the same pairs of first names, and the same initials, Bettoni and Bussola have little else in common. The career of Luigia Maria Bussola is well documented, largely through the information listed on the five Italian prints known of her (*Ital.* 39-43). After early seasons at la Scala in 1841 and 1842, she is noted in Verona in 1845, Reggio Emilia in 1846, and Brescia the next year. She then appeared in Lisbon, for three or four seasons, as predecessor of Monticelli (see nos. 97B and 98). A Portuguese print dated 1849 which was catalogued by Campos Ferreira Lima (vol. I, no. 12) is presently unfindable, either at the *Biblioteca naçionão* which never owned it, or at the São Carlos, which supposedly did when the little catalogue appeared. Returning from Portugal, Bussola appeared in Rome in 1851, Parma in 1853, Asti in 1855, and Turin at an unknown season when she danced the role of the *Figlia del Danubio*. This latter print was partially reproduced in the Italian catalogue (*Ital.* 42; p. 35). Now, I present a full-length one from the Roman autumn season of 1851 (no. 99C).

Maria Luigia Bettoni was older than Bussola. It was probably she who danced the role of Cupid in Salvatore Taglioni's *Pellia e Mileto* in 1827 at la Scala. Similarly she may have been the 'Luigia' at Cremona in Carnaval season of 1828. In 1834 she appeared in *Guillaume Tell* at the *Théâtre nautique* in Paris. For five years we have no word until the 'Primavera' season of 1839 when she danced with Teodoro Martin at the Carlo Felice of Genoa. From those performances we have the concrete evidence of a previously unknown lithograph (no. 99D). I did not obtain this print until after the publication of the Italian catalogue. Bettoni continued with a London season at Covent Garden in 1840, and, two years later, as 'prima ballerina francesa' (the 'dancing-dancer' rather than the 'acting-dancer') at la Scala for the Carnaval-Lent season. Like Emelie Högqvist shortly thereafter, she now changed from dancer to actress, using the name of Araldi, very possibly her married name. Again, without iconographic identification, another dancer of the Romantic Ballet would not be 'fleshed out' so well.

Mystery again shrouds the career of Carlotta DeVecchi. A 'Carolina' of the same name is listed as 'graduated student' performer at la Scala in 1839. (A reverse shift from 'Carlotta' to 'Carolina' also took place early in the career of Pochini—see no. 95; see *Ital.* 186-187, and p. 26.) The two deVecchis are probably the same. But what of another, or the same, deVecchi mentioned by Carlo Blasis in his *Notes on Dancing* (1847) who

was wanted in Paris but went to Lisbon instead (pp. 62-3). A Micheline and Jose (Guiseppe) deVecchi are listed there during the early and middle 1840s. Another (or the same) Micheline, with a Paolo, were at the São Carlos in 1853-54. What have they to do with Carlotta/Carolina? Carlotta reappears in the ballet *divertissements* at the Porte-Saint-Martin in Paris during the 1850s, and at Drury Lane, London, in 1852, appearing with Plunkett and Eugenio Durand in *Vert-Vert* (at the Opéra the previous year). Her ultimate consecration is iconographic. A grand folio print presents her in the 'Rôle de Paquita 1856' (no. 100). The date appears both on the stone and in the titling. The artist Antonio Greppi is listed minimally in Bénézit as a lithographer of portraits 'spéciale-ment de comédiens italiens'. That much is logical. But Carlotta Grisi's *Paquita* had left the repertoire of the Opéra in 1851, five years after its premiere. In London, it was only given one season while Grisi was at Drury Lane. Where was it presented with Carlotta deVecchi in 1856? Not at the Porte-Saint-Martin. But the identifiable icon remains as proof of a performance somewhere.

A similar case is presented by a lithograph of Pavulina Santi (certainly 'Paolina') (no. 101). It is a free adaptation, reversed, of an earlier print of Carlotta Grisi in the second act of *Giselle* (no. 101, INSERT) drawn by Alexandre Lacauchie for the *Galérie des Artistes dramatiques* (*Fr.* series L). The signature of the artist Tagliabue (probably Andrea, a pupil of the Brera in Milan) is not as significant as the presence of 'Im. Lemercier, Benard et C.'. This is a French print despite the Italian nationality of both artist and sitter. Paolina made a début in Vienna on Feb. 26, 1847 dancing a *pas de deux* with Pasquale Borri. She was then listed as 'pupil of [Augusta] Maywood'. She remained there several years, appearing later as the *seconde danseuse* 'Sainti' at the Monnaie in Brussels for the season 1849-50. The first ballet there that autumn, six days after the opening of the season, was with Lucile Grahn in *Giselle*. Was Sainti/Santi the Queen of the Wilis, or is the print later? She did perform in London at the Royal Italian Opera, Covent Garden, in 1853-54. But *Giselle* was not then in repertoire.

Even farther afield is an American adaptation of a London print. One of Chalon's finest depictions of Marie Taglioni was as Flore in the revival of Charles Didelot's *Flore et Zéphire* (1830; the print dated 1831) (no. 102 INSERT). It was certainly known in America. William R. Browne reversed it for his *The Highland Fling* and his partner Charles Risso lithographed it (no. 102). The dates of this partnership are from 1832-38, so, even before the arrival of Fanny Elssler in New York, American variants of European lithographs were being printed. Taglioni's long, bouquet-decorated tutu and floral headdress have been changed to a short (almost mid-thigh) kilt, with rolled plaid stockings and a large plumed hat. The sizes of the figures are identical. Is the *danseuse* supposed to be Effie, the mortal beloved of James Reuben, in Taglioni's *Sylphide*? We may never know, but the lithograph is CHOICE.

Another oddity of the Romantic Ballet was Jean (Giovanni) Rousset who had the unusual idea of naming his daughters for his former dancing partners. So there were Caroline (Pitrot), Thérésine (Teresa Coralli), Adeline (Adélaïde Mersy), and Clémentine (I have forgotten her namesake!) Rousset, who might constitute the starring personnel of a potential ballet troupe. Two of the sisters are noted first as *secondes danseuses* in Bordeaux in 1845. A print published there the next year of Thérézine [*sic*] and Adélaïde serves as memento. Caroline, most important *danseuse* of the family, had appeared earlier with her father in Parma in 1841. Now, the same year that her two sisters were dancing in Bordeaux, Caroline made her début as *première* at the Monnaie in Brussels (Sept., 1845). Less than four years later, for the benefit she shared with the ballet master Adrien on Mar. 29, 1849, was performed the Belgian premiere of *Catarina ou la Fille du Bandit*. Lucile Grahn who had created the ballet originally in London in 1846 did not dance the role in Brussels until the autumn after Caroline Rousset. A print adapted from Brandard's London one showing Grahn (see no. 60) was issued for Caroline. It lists her role as Catarina, *la Reine des Bandits* (no. 103). Despite printing in Paris, it is a Brussels souvenir— one of only four Belgian prints that I know. The whole family came to New York in the early 1850s with a repertoire which featured *Giselle* as well as *Catarina*. A music title showing all four sisters in a *Pas de Quatre*, looking charming, as well as medallion portraits of each, looking frightening, is 'Entered according to Act of Congress in the year 1852 . . .' (no. 104A). (Thank God for the American laws which forced identifying

dates on many of our prints!) Their repertoire now included a Teresina Polka, a Clementine Waltz, and an Adelaide Waltz from 'la Giselle'. The Rousset family deserves the recognition it receives here.

One last, unique, print deserves mention. It is a Hungarian music title (no. 104B). Its dating of late 1870s or 1880s makes it our most modern entry, but the treatment of its subject is not far removed from other music covers of the Romantic Ballet. What is special is the use of the Magyar language. Other Budapest works figure in the Austro-German catalogue, but they are titled in German! First indication, beside the unfamiliar language, is the name of the *danseuse*, her family name preceding her given one. This is standard practice in China and Japan, but the Hungarians are the only European people who have remained that close to their Asiatic heritage. Thus, Rotter Irma, who as Irma Rotter had performed at the Vienna Opera between 1865 and 1867, is shown as the Delibes-Mérante *Sylvia ou la Nymphe de Diane* (premiere: Opéra 1877). The lithography may have been done in Vienna, but the publisher Rózsavölgyi ès társa (and Company) lists Budapest. So there exists at least one Hungarian dance print. I hardly think it will serve as basis for a large national gallery!

Our 'Iconographer's Choice' could be extended many more times. A Romanian music title or one from Havana; rarities and odd variants of many kinds. And additional but equal representation of the greatest *premières danseuses*, their precursors, contemporaries and younger emulators. But our present voyage among the *Glories of the Romantic Ballet* is now finished. May it provide as much 'meat' for the ballet historian and collector of these mementos as it has offered 'fun' to the iconographer.

97A. Emelie Högqvist/i "Polkan."/(on stone:) Wm. Wohlfahrt pins (facs. sign.) 45 cm.

 not cat.; repr. 'Huru Jag kom till Balletten'. *Jolrosor* (Stockholm), 1898.

97B. Mme Genoveva Monticelli/Dedicado ao meriti d'esta insigne Artista, por alguns de seus admiradores/(on stone:) Macphail (facs. sign.)/Lith. de Lopes & Bastos . . . 1852. 26.2 cm in tinted rect. 35.5 × 28.2 cm.

 cat. Campos Ferreira Lima, *Retratos*, I, no. 26; never repr.

98. (top:) A Sivigliana/Passo Hespagnol/para Piano/(bottom:) Executado no Real Theatro de S. Carlos/por/Mme Monticelli e Mr. Cappon/na dança/Fenella./(on stone:) Marchi (facs. sign.)/Lith de Canongia & C^{a.}/Lisboa/Armazem de Muzica, Pianos . . . de J. I. Canongia & C^{a.} (she:) 17.7 cm.

 not cat.; never repr.

98. (INSERT). La Manolla./Mad^{lle.} Cerito and Monsr. St. Leon/of Her Majesty's Theatre/London Published by J. Mitchell . . ./Drawn from the Life by Monsr. Numa Blanc C. Graf, Lith. to Her Majesty (she:) 27 cm in octagon 33.3 × 27.7 cm.

 not cat.; repr. B/S, pl. 17 with incorrect titling; IG, *FC*, pl. VIb, opp. p. 33; EB 3rd, 67.

99A. (top:) Celebrites Theatrales, N°. 2/(bottom:) Melle. Octavie de Mélisse. (facs. sign.)/Rôle de la Sylphide/Paris, Masson Imp. Lemercier . . ./(on stone:) Joséphine Ducollet (facs. sign.) 23 cm in tinted rect. 30.8 × 24.1 cm.

 Fr. 77; Hall 1; never repr.

99B. (trimmed copy, so less printing than on no. 99A) (bottom):
L. Ducy Barré (facs. sign.: L. Ducy)/Rôle de l'Etoile du Rhin/
Paris Masson   Imp. Lemercier .../(on stone:) Joséphine
Ducollet (facs. sign.)   24 cm in tinted rect. (what remains
27 × 20.6 cm.

> *Fr.* 12; Hall 1; repr. Moore, 'George Washington Smith', *Dance Index*, IV,
> no. 6–8 (June–Aug., 1945), p. 108.

99C. Luigia Maria Bussola/Roma l'Autunno 1851.   23 cm.

> *Ital.* 43; A/B 735; repr. Khudyekov, p. 349.

99D. Maria Luigia Bettoni./Lit. Ponthenier/(on stone:) Deschiera
(??) (facs. sign.)   21.3 cm.

> not cat.; never repr.

100. Melle. Carlotta de-Vecchi/(Rôle de Paquita)./1856/Imp.
Lemercier, Paris/(on stone: left:) 1856. (right:) A. Greppi/
Paris.   30.3 cm in rect. 36 × 25.2 cm.

> not cat.; never repr.

101. Pavulina Santi/(on stone:) Tagliabue (facs sign.)   Im.
Lemercier, Benard et C.   19.8 cm in rect. 28.6 × 21.6 cm.

> not cat.; never repr.

101 (INSERT). (untitled, but Carlotta Grisi in *Giselle*, Act II) Lith.
de Rigo frères et Cie   Alex^dre Lacauchie/Paris. Publié par
Marchant. (Plate 63 of *Galérie des Artistes dramatiques*) 17.4 cm
in rect. 25.9 × 15.6 cm.

> *Fr.* 543; Hall 6; repr. Haskell, fig. 31, opp. p. 49.

102. The Highland Fling/(on stone:) Browne (facs. sign.)/Risso
lith. 27.8 cm.

> not cat.; never repr.; mentioned *Amer.* I, p. 29.

102 (INSERT). Mademoiselle Taglioni./From a drawing by A. E.
Chalon R.A. Drawn on Stone by R. J. Lane A.R.A./London
Published June 1831 by Dickinson .../Printed by C.
Hulmandel/Paris par Chas Motte ...   27.4 cm in octagon
32.3 × 23.4 cm.

> *Eng.* 109; Soloviev 7; Hall 26; A/B 4316; repr. B/S 2, pl. 2; IG, *Rambert*,
> 117; Migel 8.

103. Catarina, Reine des Bandits/rôle joué au grand Théâtre de
Bruxelles/par Mlle Caroline Rousset/Jules Petit del. et lith. Lith.
Prodhomme ...   Paris   24 cm in rect. with rounded top:
41.2 × 28.4 cm.

> not cat.; never repr. (compare no. 60).

104A. (top:) Favorite Dances of the/Rousset Family./(bottom:)
Entered according to Act of Congress in the Year 1852 .../
Arranged for the Piano by/John C. Scherpf./New York
Published by W^m. Vanderbeek .../Lith. of Endicott & Co.,
N.Y.   (*pas de quatre:*) 17.5 cm in ornamented horiz. frame:
21.3 × 30.5 cm.

> *Amer.* II, 71; repr. Odell, *Annals of the New York Stage*, vol. VI, opp. p. 158,
> bottom.

104B. Rotter Irma/urhïgynek./mély tisztelettel. [dedicated with deep
regard to]/Sylvia Négyes. [Quadrille]/zongorára szerzé [piano
composed by]/Pischinger A./Zenetanár. [Music teacher]/A
Kiadók sajátja [copyright]/Budapest/Rózsavölgyi ès társa. [R.
and Co.]/Lith. art. Anst. v. Jos. Eberle & Co. ... Wien   9.9 cm
in vert. oval: 12.5 × 9 cm.

> not cat.; never repr.

97A. Emelie Högqvist as Aventurine in *I Polkan*
(Stockholm, 1845)

97B. Genoveva Monticelli by Macphail (Lisbon, 1852)

98. Genoveva Monticelli with Valentino Cappon in the Sivigliana from *Fenella*
(Lisbon, 1852–53)

98 (INSERT).   Fanny Cerrito with her husband Arthur Saint-Léon in *la Manola*
(London, 1844)

99A. Octavie de Mélisse in *la Sylphide*

99B. Louise Ducy-Barré in *l'Etoile du Rhin*
from the series *Célébrités Théâtrales*, nos. 2 and 3

99C. Luigia Maria Bussola (Rome, 1851)

99D. Maria Luigia Bettoni (Genoa, 1839)

100. Carlotta de Vecchi in *Paquita* (Paris, 1856)

101. Paolina Santi in *Giselle* (Paris, 1850s)

101 (INSERT). Carlotta Grisi in *Giselle* (Paris, 1841)

102. The Highland Fling (New York, 1830s)

102 (INSERT).
Marie Taglioni as Flore in *Flore et Zéphire* (London, 1831)

103. Caroline Rousset as *Catarina, Reine des Bandits* (Brussels, 1846)

104A. The Four Rousset sisters in a *Pas de Quatre*
(New York, 1852)

104B. Irma Rotter in *Sylvia* (Budapest, *c*. 1880)

INDICES

(In the numbers that follow each name, page numbers precede plate numbers—which are given in italics. Colour plates are numbered with roman numerals.)

INDEX A
DANCERS, CHOREOGRAPHERS, BALLET MASTERS

INDEX B
ARTISTS (Designers, Engravers, Lithographers, Printers, Publishers)

Kuhn, J. B., 38; *33*

Lacauchie, Alexandre, 38, 121, 123; *25, 101 Insert*
Laederich, 85
Lake, W., 23; *14A, 14B*
Lane, Richard James, 21, 24, 123; *22A, 23C, 102 Insert*
Lassalle, Louis, 87; *67*
Lauter, 21
Lee, Leoni & Coxhead, 49; *40*
Lehmann, Edvard, 109; *93*
Lejeune, 22, 79, 80; *61; XII*
Lemercier, 38, 62, 71, 80, 87, 88, 109, 122, 123; *26, 48, 55, 61, 66, 74, 77A, 77B, 81, 84, 91, 99A, 99B, 100; VI, XII, XIV*
Lemercier, Benard & Cⁱᵉ, 38, 71, 88, 121, 123; *27, 56B, 76, 101*
Lépaulle, Gabriel, 21, 23; *11; III*
Levasseur, 12, 38; *1A, 3B, 29A*
Lewis, John Frederick, 85
Loire, L., 88; *77B*
Longo, 109; *90*
Lopes & Bastos, 88, 122; *78, 97B*
Lucca, 72; *59B*
Lynch, C. G. and J. H., 61, 62, 109; *51, 86B; X*
Lynch, James Henry, 22, 24, 48, 49; *23A, 41A*

Macphail, 120, 122; *97B*
Madeley, G. E., 87; *70*
Maguire, Thomas Herbert, 21, 22, 24, 80, 87; *23B, 62*
Marchant, 123; *101 Insert*
Marchi, 120, 122; *98*
Marcovich, B., 109; *90*
Martinet, Maison, 85
Martinez, 50; *45*
Masson (and Masson, Hippolyte), 62, 85, 88, 122, 123; *48, 74, 81, 99A, 99B*
Masutti, 50; *44*
McGee, John L., 37, 38; *32; VII*

McLean, Thomas, 23, 37, 38, 48, 61, 62, 81, 109; *17, 34, 46, 52, 65, 86A; XI, XIII*
Meissonnier, J., 62; *49B*
Mitchell, John, 23, 49, 72, 80, 122; *13, 38, 59A, 62, 98 Insert*
Morlon, 109; *91*
Morton, Edward, 22, 24, 71, 72; *22C, 59A*
Motte, C., 23, 123; *16B, 102 Insert*
Müller, G. Edouard, 13; *9*
Mulrenin, Bernard, 21, 23; *12*
Munster, 62; *54*

Nanteuil, Célestin, 60, 62; *49A, 49B, 50A*
Negelen, Joseph, 85, 88; *77A*
Noël, Léon, 85, 88; *77A*

Pallard, 87; *71*
Parsons, Charles, 38; *28*
Paterno, 109; *95*
Paterno's Witwe & Sohn, 88; *72*
Pederson, Wilhelm Th., 87, 88; *80*
Petit, Jules, 123; *103*
Petit & Bertauts, 62; *49B, 50A*
Pieroni, 88; *83A*
Plattel, 109; *88*
Ponthenier 123; *99D*
Prodhomme, 123; *103*
Puschkin, J. 109; *92; XV*

Rait (Wright?), 23; *21B*
Regnier, Bettannier, Morlon, 109; *91*
Ricordi, 12; *1A*
(also: Presso Gio. Ricordi and Presso Ricordi, Pozzi e C.)
Rigo, Frères, 38, 123; *25, 101 Insert*
Rigo, Jules, 50; *43*
Risso, Charles, 121, 123; *102*
Rittner & Goupil, 23, 38, 49; *12, 13, 16B, 26, 27, 38; VI*
Rocca Gebrüder, 62; *53*
Rózsavölgyi, 122, 123; *104B*

Sachse, L. & & Cᶜ, 12, 38, 71; *2, 29B, 55*

Salabert, Firmin, 22, 23, 36; *10, 24*
Santa-Barbara, 86, 88, 120; *78*
Sardou, Charles, 87; *75*
Sarony, Napoleon, 37, 79
"J.S." (Schindler, Johann Josef), 11, 12; *3A*
Schoppe, J. 12; *2*
Schreiber, J. E., 38; *35; VIII*
Schuberth & Cᵒ, 88; *83B*
Schott, 62, 107, 109; *49A, 89*
Seitz, Emile, 109; *91*
Sewrin, Edmond, 87; *71*
Smith, Edwin Dalton, 22, 23; *18, 19; IV, V*
Sorrieu, Frédéric, 48, 49; *39*
Soyer, Emma, 22
Spooner, William, 48, 49, 61, 62; *41A, 47, 51; X*
Steer, William C., 50; *41B*
Sudre, 23; *10*
Sully, Thomas, 37

Tagliabue (prob. Andrea), 121, 123; *101*
Taylor, Weld, 22, 23; *18, 19; IV, V*
Templeton, J. S., 22, 24, 49; *22B*, 38
(Thackeray, William Makepeace), 21, 23; *13*
Thierry, frères, 23, 109; *10, 88*
Tilt, Charles, 87; *66*
Tuleva, 88; *73*

'C.V.', 88; *76*
de Valentini, Alexandre, 49, 109; *38, 84; XIV*
Vanderbeek, 123; *104A*
Vigneron, 21
Vogt, Charles, 70, 71; *56C*

Wagstaff, Théophile, 21, 23; *13*
Watson, J., 23; *19; V*
Wild, 38; *29B*
Wohlfahrt, Wᵐ, 122; *97A*

Zinco, 38; *29A*

Introduction to Diesel Engines

Chapter Review

The following activities have been designed to help you refresh your knowledge of this chapter. Your instructor may require you to complete some or all of these activities as a regular part of your training program. You are encouraged to complete any activity that your instructor does not assign as a way to enhance your learning.

Matching

Match the following terms with the correct description or example.

A. Common rail

B. Compression ratio

C. Power density

D. Thermal efficiency

E. Torque

_____ **1.** A comparison between total cylinder volume and clearance volume.

_____ **2.** A measurement of rotational, or twisting, force transmitted from the crankshaft to the flywheel.

_____ **3.** A high-pressure injection system that electronically varies injection pressure, timing, and rate.

_____ **4.** The power an engine produces for its displacement.

_____ **5.** A comparison between the amount of energy released during combustion and energy available at the engine flywheel.

Multiple Choice

Read each item carefully, and then select the best response.

_____ **1.** Nikolaus Otto substantially improved engine efficiency by developing the _____.

    A. two-stroke cycle internal-combustion engine

    B. external combustion engine

    C. four-stroke internal-combustion engine

    D. steam engine

_____ **2.** An ancient device called a fire piston was Rudolf Diesel's inspiration for the first _____ combustion system.

    A. spark-ignition

    B. compression-ignition

    C. four-stroke

    D. fuel-injection

_____ **3.** Diesel engines inject liquid fuel under high pressure into the combustion chamber near the end of the ____ stroke.

    A. intake

    B. compression

    C. power

    D. exhaust

_____ **4.** At the 1897 Paris Exhibition the first biodiesel engine was introduced; it ran on a fuel derived from _____.
   A. soybean oil
   B. mineral oil
   C. peanut oil
   D. crude oil

_____ **5.** In the 1920s, _____ developed practical, compact injection pumps and governors that allowed the use of smaller diesel engines to power trucks, buses, and automobiles.
   A. Robert Bosch
   B. Rudolf Diesel
   C. Clessie Cummins
   D. David Packard

_____ **6.** The process of burning fuel using excess air is known as _____.
   A. stoichiometric combustion
   B. rich burn combustion
   C. indirect combustion
   D. lean burn combustion

_____ **7.** The use of higher compression ratios in diesel engines contributes to _____.
   A. higher engine efficiency
   B. lighter vehicle weights
   C. lower fuel consumption
   D. Both A and C

_____ **8.** The ability of an engine to accelerate at middle- and high-speed ranges is called _____.
   A. torque elasticity
   B. thermal efficiency
   C. compression efficiency
   D. stoichiometric combustion

_____ **9.** The measuring unit used for new fuel efficiency standards in the United States is _____.
   A. grams per mile
   B. miles per gallon
   C. ton miles per gallon
   D. Both A and C

_____ **10.** Starting in 2007, the EPA's diesel fuel regulations required fuel refineries to supply fuel containing fewer than _____ parts per million of sulfur.
   A. 1.5
   B. 15
   C. 150
   D. 1500

True/False

If you believe the statement to be more true than false, write the letter "T" in the space provided. If you believe the statement to be more false than true, write the letter "F".

_____ **1.** Virtually all emergency vehicles, such as ambulances, fire trucks, and tow trucks, use diesel engines.

_____ **2.** Compared to similarly sized gasoline-powered engines, diesel engines are 75–90% more fuel efficient.

_____ **3.** There are only two mechanisms used to ignite fuel in any engine: electric spark or heat generated through the compression of air.

_____ **4.** A compression-ignition combustion system utilizes a spark as its primary ignition source.

_____ **5.** The first working model of a diesel engine was fueled using coal dust, which was blasted into the combustion chamber using pressurized air.

_____ **6.** Today's diesel engines produce near-zero emissions, even when using petroleum fuel.

_____ **7.** The Ford Motor Company was the first manufacturer to mass-produce turbocharged diesel-powered engines like the kind used in today's vehicles.

_____ **8.** Diesel engines use substantially more fuel than similarly displaced gasoline-fueled engines to produce the same horsepower.

_____ **9.** Historically, diesel fuel has been less expensive because it is a by-product of gasoline production and requires less refining.

_____ **10.** A diesel engine requires significantly more scheduled maintenance than a gasoline-powered engine.

_____ **11.** Although diesels make up only 5% of all the registered vehicles on the road, they burn close to 22% of all transportation fuels.

_____ **12.** Some noxious emissions, such as carbon monoxide (CO) and hydrocarbon (HC) emissions, are much lower from diesel engines than from gasoline-powered engines.

_____ **13.** B-20 is a blend of 20% conventional diesel fuel combined with 80% biologically derived fuel.

_____ **14.** Developmental engines are now achieving injection pressures as high as 60,000 psi (4137 bar).

_____ **15.** New exhaust aftertreatment technology has enabled today's diesel engines to achieve close to zero emissions.

Fill in the Blank

Read each item carefully, and then complete the statement by filling in the missing word(s).

1. A _____ uses exhaust energy to compress air and pressurize the air intake system of an engine.

2. The primary benefit of turbocharging a diesel engine is an increase in power _____.

3. Both the steam engine and the Otto cycle engine had a low-thermal _____ compared to a diesel engine.

4. Compressing a gas will cause its _____ to increase.

5. The combustion chamber of a typical _____-ignition engine will reach temperatures in excess of 1000°F (538°C).

6. With smaller _____ volumes, diesel engines compress air twice as much as spark-ignition engines.

7. A diesel engine has significantly higher _____ output than a similarly displaced gasoline-fueled engine.

8. The "gear fast, run slow" strategy of heavy-duty, on-highway engines is also referred to as _____ _____.

9. The production of carbon dioxide (CO_2), a _____ gas, is 20–40% lower in diesel engines than in gasoline-fueled engines.

10. A reduction of _____ levels in diesel fuel began in mid-2006 to help manufacturers meet emissions standards.

11. To further reduce emissions, the _____ _____ _____, which is part of the Energy Independence and Security Act of 2007 (EISA) in the United States, indirectly mandates the use of B-20 fuel for 2011.

12. The latest _____ _____ injection systems electronically vary injection pressures and the duration of the injection event and produce multiple injection events during a combustion cycle.

13. A diesel _____ filter uses technology that filters and traps soot particles from the exhaust stream in a ceramic filter.

14. The exhaust aftertreatment technology unique to diesel engines that specifically targets NO_x emissions is called _____ _____ _____.

15. A new aftertreatment technology called a _____ catalytic converter breaks down exhaust emissions using a combination of specialized catalysts and high frequency AC electrical energy.

Skill Drills

Test your knowledge of skill drills by filling in the correct words in the photo captions.

1. Identifying and Interpreting a Vehicle Identification Number

Vehicle Production Year VIN Key

10th Digit in VIN	Production Year	10th Digit in VIN	Production Year
1	2001	C	2012
2	2002	D	2013
3	2003	E	2014
4	2004	F	2015
5	2005	G	2016
6	2006	H	2017
7	2007	J	2018
8	2008	K	2019
9	2009	L	2020
A	2010	M	2021
B	2011		

Step 1: Inspect the vehicle for a VIN identification plate or stamping in the following locations: the driver-side _____ _____, the top or side of right _____ _____ near the front of the vehicle, the left _____ post pillar, beneath the _____ on either the driver or passenger side of the vehicle, under a panel on the _____ on the passenger side of the vehicle (in the area where a _____ _____ would be found). Most vehicles have a VIN in _____ _____.

Step 2: Record the VIN and enter it into a _____ that identifies the VIN information, such as the type of _____ _____, gross vehicle _____, the type of _____, or the manufacturing _____ where the vehicle was produced. Or, identify the vehicle's _____ _____ using the chart.

Step 3: Connect an electronic _____ _____ to the vehicle's _____ _____ connector located next to the _____ _____ below the dash panel. Switch the _____ _____ on, but do not _____ the engine (key on, engine off [KOEO]).

Step 4: Navigate to a screen or window in the _____ _____ where the VIN is located and record the information. Compare the _____ VIN to the VIN stored in the engine's _____ _____ _____ to check whether they correspond.

2. Identifying and Interpreting an Engine Emission Decal

Step 1:   All medium- and heavy-duty emission decals are located on a vehicle's _____, not on the _____ as light-duty vehicle decals are. Inspect the _____ _____ and other engine surfaces for an _____ or _____ standard emission _____.

Step 2:   Record the engine _____ _____, horsepower, rated rpm, _____ rate, _____ adjustment specifications, and the _____ for emission control systems.

Step 3:   Use the acronyms along with OEM _____ _____, aftermarket _____, or _____ research to interpret what the acronyms mean.

Step 4:   Inspect the vehicle and _____ whether the vehicle is _____ with the systems listed on the _____.

Step 5:   List the _____ and report your _____.

3. Recording Engine and Trip Information

Step 1:   Turn the ignition switch of the vehicle to the _____-_____-_____ position.

Step 2:   Using a driver's information _____, navigate to find any _____ _____, fuel consumption, and _____ _____ data.

Step 3:   Using _____ software, connect to the vehicle's _____ _____ connector.

Step 4:   Download and store a _____ _____ report.

Step 5:   Record the engine's _____ _____ and _____ _____ from the appropriate screens.

Common Emission System Acronyms

Fill in the name of the emission system based on its acronym.

ECM = _____ _____ _____

TC   = _____

CAC = _____ _____ _____

DPF = _____ _____ _____

EGR = _____ _____ _____

SCR = _____ _____ _____

CCV = _____ _____ _____

LNT = _____ _____ _____

DOC = _____ _____ _____

LNC = _____ _____ _____

Crossword Puzzle

Use the clues in the column to complete the puzzle.

Across

3. The highest point the piston travels in a cylinder.

4. A fuel derived from a planet or animal source.

5. The ability of an engine to produce the torque needed to accelerate from medium to high engine speed while under load.

Down

1. Gases that are believed to contribute to global warming.

2. A strategy that takes advantage of a diesel engine's high torque output at low engine speeds by lowering drive axle gear ratios. The engine operates at lower rpm while operating at highway speeds.

ASE-Type Questions

Read each item carefully, and then select the best response.

_____ **1.** Technician A says that a diesel engine's higher compression ratio helps it to produce more power and use less fuel. Technician B says that higher compression ratios only help the diesel engine produce more torque. Who is correct?
A. Technician A
B. Technician B
C. Both Technician A and Technician B
D. Neither Technician A nor Technician B

_____ **2.** Technician A says that diesel engines inject fuel into the cylinder during the intake stroke. Technician B says that diesel engines inject fuel into the cylinder near the end of the compression stroke. Who is correct?
A. Technician A
B. Technician B
C. Both Technician A and Technician B
D. Neither Technician A nor Technician B

_____ **3.** Technician A says that diesel engines supply only enough air to completely burn all the fuel in the combustion chamber. Technician B says that diesel engines supply excess air to the combustion chamber to completely burn all the fuel in the combustion chamber. Who is correct?
A. Technician A
B. Technician B
C. Both Technician A and Technician B
D. Neither Technician A nor Technician B

_____ **4.** Technician A says that biodiesel fuel is too expensive to purchase and will soon become unavailable because there is no interest in using it. Technician B says more biodiesel will be used in the near future because there are laws requiring increased production and blending of biodiesel with regular diesel. Who is correct?
A. Technician A
B. Technician B
C. Both Technician A and Technician B
D. Neither Technician A nor Technician B

_____ **5.** Technician A says diesel engines only make up 5% of the vehicles on the road, which is the reason they produce less pollution. Technician B says diesels burn less fuel, which explains why they produce less air pollution. Who is correct?
A. Technician A
B. Technician B
C. Both Technician A and Technician B
D. Neither Technician A nor Technician B

_____ **6.** Technician A says a power stroke in a modern common rail engine only uses a single injection of fuel. Technician B says a late-model common rail diesel has multiple injection events during a combustion cycle. Who is correct?
A. Technician A
B. Technician B
C. Both Technician A and Technician B
D. Neither Technician A nor Technician B

_____ **7.** Technician A says the evaporation of diesel fuel from the tank of a diesel bus on a warm day produces more emissions than a car. Technician B says that diesel fuel does not produce a significant amount of emissions due to fuel evaporation. Who is correct?
A. Technician A
B. Technician B
C. Both Technician A and Technician B
D. Neither Technician A nor Technician B

_____ **8.** Technician A says that high horsepower (kilowatts) is the most important attribute an engine needs to pull heavy loads and accelerate quickly. Technician B says that high torque output is the most important attribute an engine needs to quickly climb hills. Who is correct?
   A. Technician A
   B. Technician B
   C. Both Technician A and Technician B
   D. Neither Technician A nor Technician B

_____ **9.** Technician A says increasing an engine's compression ratio will produce better fuel economy but less power output. Technician B says increasing an engine's compression ratio produces more power but increases fuel consumption. Who is correct?
   A. Technician A
   B. Technician B
   C. Both Technician A and Technician B
   D. Neither Technician A nor Technician B

_____ **10.** Technician A says that diesel engines can produce more power because air and fuel are not mixed during the intake stroke. Technician B says that diesel engines produce more power because they use excess air to burn fuel. Who is correct?
   A. Technician A
   B. Technician B
   C. Both Technician A and Technician B
   D. Neither Technician A nor Technician B

Careers, Employability Skills, and Workplace Practices

Chapter Review

The following activities have been designed to help you refresh your knowledge of this chapter. Your instructor may require you to complete some or all of these activities as a regular part of your training program. You are encouraged to complete any activity that your instructor does not assign as a way to enhance your learning.

Matching

Match the following terms with the correct description or example.

A. Operator's manual
B. Parts specialist
C. Primary sources
D. Secondary sources
E. Service campaign and recall

F. Shop or service manual
G. Supporting statement
H. Technical service bulletin (TSB)
I. Vehicle emission control information (VECI) label
J. Vehicle safety certification (VSC) label

_____ 1. A statement that urges the speaker to elaborate on a particular topic.

_____ 2. A label certifying that the vehicle meets the Federal Motor Vehicle Safety, Bumper, and Theft Prevention Standards in effect at the time of manufacture.

_____ 3. Secondhand information compiled from a variety of sources.

_____ 4. A label used by technicians to identify engine and emission control information for the vehicle.

_____ 5. The person who serves customers at the parts counters.

_____ 6. Information issued by manufacturers to alert technicians of unexpected problems or changes to repair procedures.

_____ 7. A document that contains information about a vehicle, which is a valuable source of information for both the owner and the technician.

_____ 8. A corrective measure conducted by manufacturers when a safety issue is discovered with a particular vehicle.

_____ 9. People who have direct experience with the same or a similar problem.

_____ 10. Manufacturer's or after-market information on the repair and service of vehicles.

Multiple Choice

Read each item carefully, and then select the best response.

_____ 1. To gain the Automotive Service Excellence (ASE) qualifications, candidates need a minimum of _____ year's working experience before taking an exam for each area of specialization.
   A. one
   B. two
   C. three
   D. four

_____ 2. The _____ administers technician certification procedures throughout the United States.
   A. Competitive Automotive Regulatory System
   B. National Highway Traffic Safety Administration
   C. National Institute for Automotive Service Excellence
   D. National Automotive Technical Association

_____ **3.** H-series Automotive Service Excellence (ASE) certification is designed specifically for _____.
  A. medium/heavy-duty truck technicians
  B. transit bus certification
  C. truck equipment
  D. school bus certification

_____ **4.** Making an attempt to see a situation from someone else's point of view is called _____.
  A. empathy
  B. active listening
  C. nonverbal feedback
  D. validation

_____ **5.** Body position, eye contact, and facial expression are all examples of _____.
  A. verbal feedback
  B. empathy
  C. nonverbal feedback
  D. defensive listening

_____ **6.** Which of the following phrases is an example of a supporting statement?
  A. "I understand."
  B. "I see."
  C. "Give me an example."
  D. "That must be frustrating for you."

_____ **7.** Speaking is a three-step process that includes all of the following, _except:_ _____.
  A. thinking about the message
  B. providing feedback
  C. checking whether the message is correctly understood
  D. accurately presenting the message

_____ **8.** When asking a customer an open question, you would begin with the word _____.
  A. why
  B. when
  C. where
  D. who

_____ **9.** When you read through the table of contents, introduction, conclusion, headings, and index until you find what we are looking for you are using a(n) _____ reading method.
  A. open
  B. selective
  C. comprehending
  D. absorbing

_____ **10.** Information from _____ sources tends to be more reliable since it is more generic and objective.
  A. primary
  B. direct
  C. secondary
  D. human

_____ **11.** A complete repair order should contain all of the elements of the three Cs; this includes all of the following, _except:_ _____.
  A. concern
  B. correction
  C. cause
  D. complication

_____ **12.** Which of the following determines the use of our personal space?
  A. Familiarity
  B. Gender
  C. Culture
  D. All of the above

_____ **13.** Manufacturers supply every new vehicle with a(n) _____, which is usually kept in the glove compartment.
- **A.** service bulletin
- **B.** operator's manual
- **C.** service manual
- **D.** service information program

_____ **14.** A(n) _____ lists how much time will be involved in performing a standard or warranty-related service or repair.
- **A.** labor guide
- **B.** technical service bulletin
- **C.** parts program
- **D.** inspection report

_____ **15.** In order to determine the total cost of the service, you need to know all of the following, *except*: _____.
- **A.** the labor cost
- **B.** the tax amount
- **C.** the cost of gas and consumables you used to service the vehicle
- **D.** the service history

True/False

If you believe the statement to be more true than false, write the letter "T" in the space provided. If you believe the statement to be more false than true, write the letter "F".

_____ **1.** In the United States, ASE certification is a mandatory requirement to work in the trade.

_____ **2.** All ASE's heavy-duty certifications are designed in a way that the number represents the subject matter and the letter represents the classification of the vehicle type.

_____ **3.** Nonverbal feedback includes thoughts and feelings that interfere with our listening, such as our own assumptions, emotions, and prejudices.

_____ **4.** In order to empathize with someone you must first agree with him or her.

_____ **5.** A closed question only allows an individual to answer with a simple yes or no.

_____ **6.** Instructions should contain information about who, what, when, where, why, and directions for how a task should be completed.

_____ **7.** The first step of the researching process is to look for information or clues that can help solve the problem.

_____ **8.** Technical assistance hotlines put you in contact with professionals who can assist you in diagnosing a particularly difficult problem over the phone.

_____ **9.** If a problem is noticed with a piece of workshop equipment such as a defective automotive lift, a lockout/tagout procedure should be followed.

_____ **10.** A service information program is specific to one year and make/model of a particular vehicle.

Fill in the Blank

Read each item carefully, and then complete the statement by filling in the missing word(s).

1. Skilled _____ are vital to ensure commercial vehicles stay on the road, operating efficiently, safely, and reliably.

2. Health and safety legislation demand strict adherence by employers to _____ in the use of certified personal and shop safety equipment for all workers.

3. The active _____ focuses all of his or her attention on the speaker, including verbal and nonverbal messages.

4. A _____ statement such as "I see" or "Tell me more" indicates to the customer that you are paying attention.

5. A _____ question requires a specific answer, and there is usually only one answer.

6. When taking a _____ message, make sure you get the person's name and organization, contact details, the date and time, and a summary of the message.

7. Being part of a _____ allows us to share ideas, knowledge, and resources and complement each other's strengths and weaknesses.

8. A repair order can become a _____ document in a lawsuit and can be used by the court to determine if the shop has any liability in the situation.

9. Most shops should have a _____ inspection form that needs to be completed on a regular basis, typically weekly or monthly, although some tasks may need to be performed daily.

10. By following the checklist on a vehicle _____ form a technician can check all of the components in a systematic way and ensure that they are operational or serviceable.

11. All aspects of our physical appearance, including our clothes, jewelry, hairstyle, posture, and outward demeanor, culminate to create the _____ _____ made in any encounter.

12. Being _____, clocking in on time, for example, demonstrates a good work attitude and professionalism.

13. The quality of _____ _____ influences people to choose us over our competitors and makes people feel good about continuing to buy our products or services.

14. A typical _____ _____ _____ is issued by manufacturers and contains step-by-step procedures and diagrams on how to identify if there is a fault and perform an effective repair.

15. A fault within the locking mechanism of a seatbelt that results in the seatbelt not operating as a restraint when it should would cause a manufacturer to issue a mandatory _____.

Labeling

Label the following diagrams with the correct terms.

   1. Identifying vehicle information labels:

A. _____

B. _____

C. _____

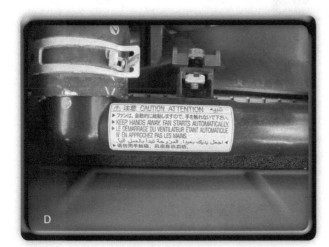

D. _____

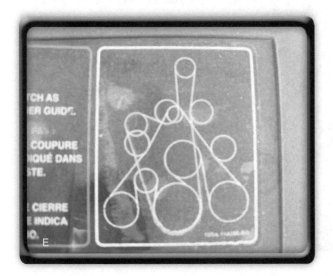

E. _____

Skill Drills

Test your knowledge of skill drills by filling in the correct words in the photo captions.

1. Locating Parts Information on the Computer:

Step 1: Log in to the application using the appropriate _____ and _____.

Step 2: Enter the _____, make, _____, and engine and _____ number information into the system in the appropriate places.

Step 3: Search for the _____ you require to conduct the _____ or _____.

Step 4: The _____ _____ will provide a list of possible matches for you to select from. If the initial search does not produce what you are looking for, try changing the _____ _____. Keep searching until you find the information.

Step 5: Gather information on the identified parts, including _____ _____, _____, _____, and _____.

Step 6: Print, _____ down, or directly _____ an _____ for the desired parts.

2. Identifying Information Needed and Service Requested:

Step 1: Locate a _____ _____ used in your shop.

Step 2: Familiarize yourself with the repair order, and _____ the following _____ on the repair order:

    a. _____

    b. Customer details: _____ and _____, daytime _____ number

    c. Vehicle details: _____, make, model, _____, _____ reading, VIN

    d. Customer _____ _____: Note any additional information that is required on your shop's _____ _____.

Step 3: Following the shop _____, determine the _____ for the tasks that are listed.

Step 4: Use the repair order to carry out the requested _____ or _____. Fill in the repair order with _____ of the cause of the customer concern(s) and the _____(s) conducted.

3. Reviewing a Vehicle Service History:

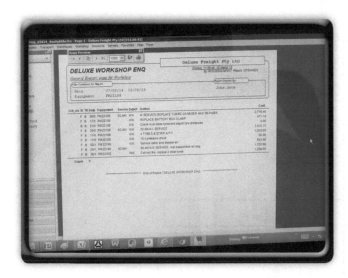

Step 1: Locate the service _____ for the vehicle. This may be in shop _____ or in the service history _____ within the vehicle glove compartment. Some shops may keep the vehicle's service history on a _____.

Step 2: Familiarize yourself with the _____ _____ of the vehicle.

  a. On what _____ was the vehicle first serviced?

  b. On what date was the vehicle _____ serviced?

  c. What was the most _____ _____ performed?

  d. Was the vehicle ever serviced for the _____ _____ more than _____?

Step 3: Compare the vehicle service history to the manufacturer's _____ maintenance requirements and list any _____.

  a. Have all the services been _____?

  b. Have all the _____ been checked?

  c. Are there any _____ items?

Crossword Puzzle

Use the clues in the column to complete the puzzle.

Across

4. A complete list of all the servicing and repairs that have been performed on a vehicle.
5. A statement that shows common interest in the topic being discussed.

Down

1. A form used by shops to collect information regarding a vehicle coming in for repair, also referred to as a work order.
2. A computer software program for identifying and ordering replacement vehicle parts.
3. A label that lists the type of coolant installed in the cooling system.
6. A guide that provides information to make estimates for repairs.

ASE-Type Questions

Read each item carefully, and then select the best response.

_____ 1. Technician A says that maintaining an appearance of neatness is important as it conveys to the customer the idea of careful, professional technicians. Technician B says that a dirty and cluttered shop indicates that the shop gets a lot of quality work done. Who is correct?
  A. Technician A
  B. Technician B
  C. Both Technician A and Technician B
  D. Neither Technician A nor Technician B

_____ 2. Technician A says researching the service information is a waste of time. Technician B says that researching the service information saves time. Who is correct?
  A. Technician A
  B. Technician B
  C. Both Technician A and Technician B
  D. Neither Technician A nor Technician B

_____ 3. Technician A says that an example of an open question is: "What are the conditions like when your A/C is not working?" Technician B says that an example of an open question is: "Does your A/C work at all?" Who is correct?
  A. Technician A
  B. Technician B
  C. Both Technician A and Technician B
  D. Neither Technician A nor Technician B

_____ 4. Technician A says that labor guides are necessary for the service writer to quote prices for a customer on the repair bill. Technician B says that labor guides are what the customer pays and that warranty pays more for labor using a different labor guide. Who is correct?
  A. Technician A
  B. Technician B
  C. Both Technician A and Technician B
  D. Neither Technician A nor Technician B

_____ 5. Technician A says joining the commercial vehicle service industry in its repair and service sector as a service technician is the most popular trade pathway. Technician B says the position of a service technician allows for maximum exposure to the most recent technological developments and advancements in the industry. Who is correct?
  A. Technician A
  B. Technician B
  C. Both Technician A and Technician B
  D. Neither Technician A nor Technician B

_____ 6. Technician A says that hybrid vehicle is a specialized area in commercial vehicle service and repair in which a technician can specialize. Technician B says that the manufacturing of parts is a specialized area in commercial vehicle service and repair in which a technician can specialize. Who is correct?
  A. Technician A
  B. Technician B
  C. Both Technician A and Technician B
  D. Neither Technician A nor Technician B

_____ 7. Technician A states that it is a lifelong learning process to perfect your communication skills. Technician B states that learning and applying good communication skills will not save you time but it will help you avoid or get through tricky situations.
  A. Technician A
  B. Technician B
  C. Both Technician A and Technician B
  D. Neither Technician A nor Technician B

_____ **8.** While discussing effective writing, Technician A says a repair order can never be considered a legal document. Technician B says writing is one of the most important tasks a technician does on a daily basis. Who is correct?
   A. Technician A
   B. Technician B
   C. Both Technician A and Technician B
   D. Neither Technician A nor Technician B

_____ **9.** Technician A says you should always escort customers in the shop to keep them safe and continue any conversation in the customer write-up area as soon as possible. Technician B says customers should be given safety glasses to enter a shop, and the shortest amount of time possible should be spent with the customer in the shop. Who is correct?
   A. Technician A
   B. Technician B
   C. Both Technician A and Technician B
   D. Neither Technician A nor Technician B

_____ **10.** Technician A says being focused on customer service means you are fully engaged in providing the highest level of service that you can. Technician B says one of the most important parts of customer service is repairing the vehicle correctly the first time. Who is correct?
   A. Technician A
   B. Technician B
   C. Both Technician A and Technician B
   D. Neither Technician A nor Technician B

Safety, Personal Protection Equipment, and First Aid

Chapter Review

The following activities have been designed to help you refresh your knowledge of this chapter. Your instructor may require you to complete some or all of these activities as a regular part of your training program. You are encouraged to complete any activity that your instructor does not assign as a way to enhance your learning.

Matching

Match the following terms with the correct description or example.

A. Double-insulated
B. Ear protection
C. First aid
D. Hazardous material
E. Heat buildup

F. Internal bleeding
G. Occupational Safety and Health Administration (OSHA)
H. Shock
I. Strain
J. Threshold limit value (TLV)

_____ 1. The maximum allowable concentration of a given material in the surrounding air.

_____ 2. The loss of blood into the body cavity from a wound; there is no obvious sign of blood.

_____ 3. An injury caused by the overstretching of muscles and tendons.

_____ 4. Protective gear worn when the sound levels exceed 85 decibels, when working around operating machinery for any period of time, or when the equipment you are using produces loud noise.

_____ 5. Any material that poses an unreasonable risk of damage or injury to persons, property, or the environment if it is not properly controlled during handling, storage, manufacture, processing, packaging, use and disposal, or transportation.

_____ 6. Government agency created to provide national leadership in occupational safety and health.

_____ 7. The immediate care given to an injured or suddenly ill person.

_____ 8. A dangerous condition that occurs when the glove can no longer absorb or reflect heat and heat is transferred to the inside of the glove.

_____ 9. Tools or appliances that are designed in such a way that no single failure can result in a dangerous voltage coming into contact with the outer casing of the device.

_____ 10. Inadequate tissue oxygenation resulting from serious injury or illness.

Multiple Choice

Read each item carefully, and then select the best response.

_____ 1. The federal agency that provides regulations and procedures designed to help prevent worker fatalities and workplace injuries and illnesses is called the _____.
   A. Occupational Safety and Health Administration
   B. Environmental Protection Agency
   C. National Transportation Safety Board
   D. Automotive Safety Council

_____ 2. The federal government agency that deals with issues related to environmental safety is called the _____.
   A. National Association for Environmental Management
   B. National Environmental Health Association
   C. Environmental Protection Agency
   D. Occupational Safety and Health Administration

_____ 3. The signal word _____ indicates a potentially hazardous situation, which, if not avoided, may result in minor or moderate injury.
   A. alert
   B. danger
   C. warning
   D. caution

_____ 4. A _____ background is used for emergency-type signs, such as for first aid, fire protection, and emergency equipment.
   A. red
   B. blue
   C. green
   D. yellow

_____ 5. Running engines produce dangerous exhaust gases, including _____.
   A. carbon dioxide
   B. hydrogen dioxide
   C. carbon monoxide
   D. Both A and C

_____ 6. A _____ fire involves flammable liquids or gaseous fuels.
   A. class A
   B. class B
   C. class C
   D. class K

_____ 7. A fire extinguisher marked with a green triangle is approved to fight a _____ fire.
   A. class A
   B. class B
   C. class C
   D. class D

_____ 8. If you are cleaning up dust after a repair, you should use a(n) _____.
   A. low-pressure wet cleaning method
   B. dry sweeping method
   C. HEPA vacuum cleaner
   D. Either A or C

_____ 9. What type of gloves should be used to protect your hands from exposure to greases and oils?
   A. Chemical gloves
   B. Light-duty gloves
   C. Cloth gloves
   D. Leather gloves

_____ 10. Safety glasses must be marked with "_____" on both the lens and frame.
   A. polarized
   B. UV protection
   C. Z87
   D. heavy duty

_____ 11. When you approach the scene of an accident or emergency, you should _____.
   A. make sure there are no other dangers, and assist only if it is safe to do so
   B. check to see if the victim is responsive and breathing
   C. have a bystander call 9-1-1
   D. All of the above

_____ 12. If a chemical splashes into the eye, hold the eye wide open and flush with warm water for at least _____, continuously and gently.
   A. 5 minutes
   B. 10 minutes
   C. 15 minutes
   D. 20 minutes

_____ 13. A _____ fracture involves bleeding or the protrusion of bone through the skin.
   A. simple
   B. open
   C. complicated
   D. All of the above

_____ 14. A _____ occurs when a joint is forced beyond its natural movement limit causing stretching or tearing in the ligaments that hold the bones together.
   A. dislocation
   B. strain
   C. sprain
   D. simple fracture

_____ 15. A _____ burn involves blistering and damage to the outer layer of skin.
   A. first-degree
   B. second-degree
   C. third-degree
   D. All of the above

True/False

If you believe the statement to be more true than false, write the letter "T" in the space provided. If you believe the statement to be more false than true, write the letter "F".

_____ **1.** Almost all accidents are avoidable or preventable by taking a few precautions.

_____ **2.** Danger is usually indicated by black text with a yellow background.

_____ **3.** A pictorial message allows a safety message to be conveyed to people who are illiterate or who do not speak the local language.

_____ **4.** Gasoline engines fitted with a catalytic converter can be run safely indoors.

_____ **5.** All electric tools must be equipped with a ground prong or double-insulated. If they are not, do not use them.

_____ **6.** Three elements must be present at the same time for a fire to occur: fuel, oxygen, and heat.

_____ **7.** The shop should have a material safety data sheet for each hazardous substance or dangerous product.

_____ **8.** You should always use compressed air to blow dust from components or parts before attempting to work on them.

_____ **9.** Coming into frequent or prolonged contact with used engine oil can cause dermatitis and other skin disorders, including some forms of cancer.

_____ **10.** Over-the-ear style hearing protection has a higher noise-reduction rating than in-the-ear style protection.

_____ **11.** Safety glasses should only be worn when there is a chance of direct impact or debris damage to the eyes.

_____ **12.** Gas welding goggles can be worn instead of a welding mask when assisting a person using an electric welder.

_____ **13.** It is necessary to use a full face shield when using solvents and cleaners, epoxies, and resins or when working on a battery.

_____ **14.** You should always remove watches, rings, and jewelry before starting work.

_____ **15.** If an object punctures the victim's skin and becomes embedded in the victim's body you should remove the object and apply a sterile dressing.

Fill in the Blank

Read each item carefully, and then complete the statement by filling in the missing word(s).

1. Personal _____ equipment refers to items of safety equipment like safety footwear, gloves, clothing, protective eyewear, and hearing protection.

2. _____ routes are a safe way of escaping danger and gathering in a safe place where everyone can be accounted for in the event of an emergency.

3. A _____ is anything that could hurt you or someone else, and most workplaces have them.

4. To prevent accidents, a machinery guard or a _____ painted line on the floor usually borders large, fixed machinery such as lathes and milling machines.

5. Poor _____ safety practices can cause shocks and burns, as well as fires and explosions.

6. The _____ used in electric droplights are very vulnerable to impact and must not be used without insulating cage protection.

7. All flammable items should be kept in an approved _____ storage container or cabinet, with firefighting equipment close at hand.

8. The acronym _____ should be followed when operating a fire extinguisher.

9. A fire _____ is designed to smother a small fire and is very useful in putting out a fire on a person.

10. Most shops use _____ materials daily, such as cleaning solvents, gasket cement, brake fluid, and coolant.

11. A(n) _____ _____ _____ is used to flush the eye with clean water or sterile liquid in the event that you get foreign liquids or particles in your eye.

12. Used oil and fluids will often contain dangerous chemicals and impurities and need to be safely _____ or disposed of in an environmentally friendly way.

13. A shop safety _____ is a valuable way to identify unsafe equipment, materials, or activities so they can be corrected to prevent accidents or injuries.

14. Before you undertake any activity, think about all potential hazards and select the correct _____ _____ _____ based on the risk associated with the activity.

15. The proper _____ provides protection against items falling on your feet, chemicals, cuts, abrasions, and slips.

16. _____ cream looks and feels like a moisturizing cream, but it has a specific formula to provide extra protection from chemicals and oils.

17. A disposable _____ _____ is made from paper with a wire-reinforced edge that is held to your face with an elastic strip.

18. Safety _____ must be worn when servicing air-conditioning systems or any other system that contains pressurized gas.

19. Good _____ is about always making sure the shop and your work surroundings are neat and kept in good order.

20. _____ bleeding is the loss of blood from a wound where the blood can be seen escaping.

Labeling

Label the following diagrams with the correct terms.

1. Identify the following fire extinguisher types:

A. _____

B. _____

C. _____

D. _____

2. Identify the following forms of hand protection:

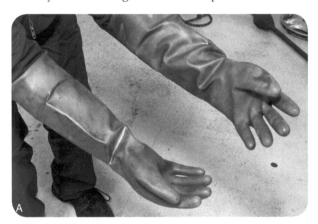

A. _____

B. _____

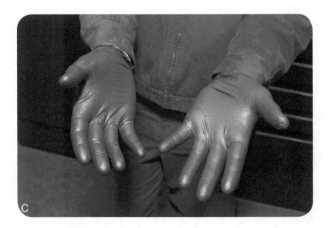

C. _____

D. _____

3. Identify the following forms of eye protection:

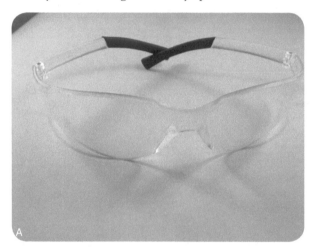

A. _____

B. _____

C. _____

D. _____

E. _____

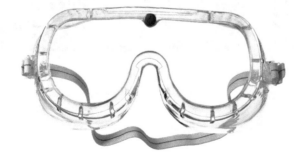

Skill Drills

Test your knowledge of skill drills by filling in the correct words in the photo captions.

1. Identifying Hazardous Environments:

Step 1: Familiarize yourself with the shop _____. Study and understand the various _____ _____ around your shop. Identify _____ and plan your _____ route. Know the designated _____ point and go there in an emergency.

Step 2: Check for air _____. Locate the extractor _____ or _____ outlets and make sure they are not obstructed in any way. Locate and observe the operation of the exhaust _____ hose, pump, and outlet used on the vehicle's _____ pipes.

Step 3: Check the _____, _____, and _____ of fire extinguishers in your shop. Be sure you know when and how to use each type of _____ _____.

Step 4: Find out where _____ materials are kept, and make sure they are _____ properly.

Step 5:   Check the _____ and _____ on the air compressor and air guns for any _____ or excessive wear. Be particularly careful when troubleshooting _____ _____. Never pull the _____ while inspecting one. Severe _____ damage can result.

Step 6:   Identify _____ _____ and _____ associated with activities in your shop. Ask your supervisor for information on any special _____ in your particular shop and any special avoidance _____, which may apply to you and your working environment.

2. Identify Information on a Safety Data Sheet:

Step 1:   Once you have studied the information on the _____ _____, find the _____ for that particular material. Always check the _____ _____ to ensure that you are reading the most recent update.

Step 2:   Note the _____ and _____ names for the material, its manufacturer, and the emergency _____ _____ to call.

Step 3:   Find out why this material is potentially _____. It may be _____, it may _____, or it may be _____ if inhaled or touched with your bare skin. Check the threshold _____ _____ (TLVs). The concentration of this material in the air you _____ in your shop must not exceed these figures. There could be physical symptoms associated with breathing harmful _____. Find out what will happen to you if you suffer _____ to the material, either through breathing it or by coming into physical _____ with it. This will help you take safety precautions, such as eye, face, or skin _____, wearing a mask or _____ while using the material, or _____ your skin afterwards.

Step 4:   Note the _____ _____ for this material so that you know at what temperature it may catch fire. Also note what kind of _____ _____ you would use to fight a fire involving this material. The _____ fire extinguisher could make the emergency even worse.

Step 5:   Study the _____ for this material to identify the _____ conditions or other materials that you should _____ when using this material. It could be _____, moisture, or some other chemical.

Step 6:   Find out what special _____ you should take when working with this material. This will include personal protection for your _____, _____, or _____ and storage and use of the material.

Step 7:   Be sure to _____ your _____ of your SDS from time to time. Be confident that you know how to _____ and _____ the material and what action to take in an _____, should one occur.

Crossword Puzzle

Use the clues in the column to complete the puzzle.

Across

4. A list of the steps required to get the same result each time a task or activity is performed.

6. A fracture that involves no open wound or internal or external bleeding.

7. The displacement of a joint from its normal position; it is caused by an external force stretching the ligaments beyond their elastic limit.

8. An injury in which a joint is forced beyond its natural movement limit.

Down

1. A place where hazards exist.

2. Protective gear that includes items like hairnets, caps, or hard hats.

3. Protective gear used to protect the wearer from inhaling harmful dusts or gases.

5. A guiding principle that sets the shop direction.

ASE-Type Questions

Read each item carefully, and then select the best response.

_____ 1. Technician A says that exposure to solvents may have long-term effects. Technician B says that accidents are almost always avoidable. Who is correct?
   A. Technician A
   B. Technician B
   C. Both Technician A and Technician B
   D. Neither Technician A nor Technician B

_____ 2. Technician A says that both OSHA and the EPA can inspect facilities for violations. Technician B says that a shop safety rule does not have to be reviewed once put in place. Who is correct?
   A. Technician A
   B. Technician B
   C. Both Technician A and Technician B
   D. Neither Technician A nor Technician B

_____ 3. Technician A says that both caution and danger indicate a potentially hazardous situation. Technician B says that an exhaust extraction hose is not needed if the vehicle is only going to run for a few minutes. Who is correct?
   A. Technician A
   B. Technician B
   C. Both Technician A and Technician B
   D. Neither Technician A nor Technician B

_____ 4. Technician A says that firefighting equipment includes safety glasses. Technician B says that a class A fire extinguisher can be used to fight an electrical fire only. Who is correct?
   A. Technician A
   B. Technician B
   C. Both Technician A and Technician B
   D. Neither Technician A nor Technician B

_____ 5. Technician A says that a good way to clean dust off brakes is with compressed air. Technician B says that asbestos may be in current auto parts. Who is correct?
   A. Technician A
   B. Technician B
   C. Both Technician A and Technician B
   D. Neither Technician A nor Technician B

_____ 6. Technician A says that personal protective equipment (PPE) does not include clothing. Technician B says that the PPE used should be based on the task you are performing. Who is correct?
   A. Technician A
   B. Technician B
   C. Both Technician A and Technician B
   D. Neither Technician A nor Technician B

_____ 7. Technician A says that appropriate work clothes include loose-fitting clothing. Technician B says that you should always wear cuffed pants when working in a shop. Who is correct?
   A. Technician A
   B. Technician B
   C. Both Technician A and Technician B
   D. Neither Technician A nor Technician B

_____ 8. Technician A says that a hat can help keep your hair clean when working on a vehicle. Technician B says that chemical gloves may be used when working with solvent. Who is correct?
   A. Technician A
   B. Technician B
   C. Both Technician A and Technician B
   D. Neither Technician A nor Technician B

_____ **9.** Technician A says that barrier creams are used to make cleaning your hands easier. Technician B says that hearing protection only needs to be worn by people operating loud equipment. Who is correct?
   A. Technician A
   B. Technician B
   C. Both Technician A and Technician B
   D. Neither Technician A nor Technician B

_____ **10.** Technician A says that tinted safety glasses can be worn when working outside. Technician B says that welding can cause a sunburn. Who is correct?
   A. Technician A
   B. Technician B
   C. Both Technician A and Technician B
   D. Neither Technician A nor Technician B

Basic Tools and Lubricants

Chapter Review

The following activities have been designed to help you refresh your knowledge of this chapter. Your instructor may require you to complete some or all of these activities as a regular part of your training program. You are encouraged to complete any activity that your instructor does not assign as a way to enhance your learning.

Matching

Match the following terms with the correct description or example.

A. Air-impact wrench
B. Alkalis
C. Bench vice
D. Chassis dynamometer
E. Coolant
F. Copper
G. Double flare
H. Flashback arrestor
I. Hygroscopic
J. Impact driver

K. Lockout/tagout
L. Morse taper
M. Non-ferrous metals
N. Peening
O. Ratchet
P. Rattle gun
Q. Socket
R. Telescoping gauge
S. Tin snips
T. Vernier caliper

_____ 1. A term used to describe the action of flattening a rivet through a hammering action.

_____ 2. A non-ferrous, pure metal that can be alloyed (combined) with other metals but is not combined with iron.

_____ 3. An enclosed metal tube commonly with 6 or 12 points to remove and install bolts and nuts.

_____ 4. A seal that is made at the end of metal tubing or pipe.

_____ 5. A safety system designed to ensure that faulty equipment or equipment in the middle of repair is not used.

_____ 6. A generic term to describe a handle for sockets that allows the user to select direction of rotation.

_____ 7. Chemical compounds that have a pH value greater than 7. They are commonly used in toy batteries and bleaches.

_____ 8. When brake fluid absorbs water from the atmosphere.

_____ 9. Cutting device for sheet metal, works in a similar fashion to scissors.

_____ 10. A device that securely holds material in jaws while it is being worked on.

_____ 11. Tool used for measuring distances in awkward spots such as the bottom of a deep cylinder.

_____ 12. A fluid that contains special anti-freezing and anti-corrosion chemicals mixed with water.

_____ 13. A tool powered by compressed air designed to undo tight fasteners.

_____ 14. Pure metals such as copper; can also be used in alloys.

_____ 15. A tool that is struck with a blow to provide an impact turning force to remove tight fasteners.

_____ 16. An accurate measuring device for internal, external, and depth measurements that incorporates fixed and adjustable jaws.

_____ 17. A machine with rollers that allows a vehicle to attain road speed and load while sitting still in the workshop.

_____ 18. The most common air tool in an automotive workshop; also called the air-impact wrench.

_____ **19.** A spring-loaded valve installed on oxyacetylene torches as a safety device to prevent flame from entering the torch hoses.

_____ **20.** A tapered mounting shaft for drill bits and chucks in larger drills and lathes.

Multiple Choice

Read each item carefully, and then select the best response.

_____ **1.** Stainless steel rulers are commonly _____ in length.
- **A.** 12"
- **B.** 24"
- **C.** 36"
- **D.** All of the above

_____ **2.** To measure the precise diameter of a part or item such as a valve stem, you would use a(n) _____.
- **A.** outside micrometer
- **B.** inside micrometer
- **C.** feeler gauge
- **D.** depth micrometer

_____ **3.** To measure the trueness of a rotating disc brake rotor or camshaft, you would use a(n) _____.
- **A.** outside micrometer
- **B.** vernier caliper
- **C.** dial indicator
- **D.** feeler gauge

_____ **4.** A _____ is used to check the flatness of a surface, often used to measure the amount of warpage the surface of a cylinder head has.
- **A.** feeler gauge
- **B.** straight edge
- **C.** dial indicator
- **D.** depth micrometer

_____ **5.** The most common type of drill bit is the _____. It has a point with cutting flutes that form a common angle of 118 degrees.
- **A.** morse taper
- **B.** SDS bit
- **C.** brad point bit
- **D.** twist drill

_____ **6.** A _____ is designed not to bounce back when it hits something.
- **A.** ball-peen hammer
- **B.** dead-blow hammer
- **C.** club hammer
- **D.** rubber mallet

_____ **7.** Technicians sometimes use a _____ to remove bolts whose heads have rounded off.
- **A.** cold chisel
- **B.** pry bar
- **C.** cross-cut chisel
- **D.** gasket scraper

_____ **8.** A _____ has the coarsest teeth, with approximately 20 teeth per 1 inch (25 mm). It is used when a lot of material must be removed quickly.
- **A.** coarse bastard file
- **B.** rough file
- **C.** second-cut file
- **D.** warding file

_____ 9. The name for the _____ comes from its shape; it is used to hold parts together while they are being assembled, drilled, or welded.
   A. D-clamp
   B. F-clamp
   C. G-clamp
   D. P-clamp

_____ 10. To cut a brand-new thread on a blank rod or shaft, you would use a(n) _____.
   A. tap
   B. die
   C. puller
   D. extractor

_____ 11. When marks need to be drawn on an object such as a steel plate to help locate a hole to be drilled, a _____ is used to mark the points so they will not rub off.
   A. starter punch
   B. pin punch
   C. wad punch
   D. prick punch

_____ 12. A(n) _____ is a device able to communicate electronically with and extract data from the vehicle's one or more on-board computers.
   A. scan tool
   B. dynamometer
   C. multimeter
   D. oscilloscope

_____ 13. A waste recovery system is incorporated into _____ where contaminated washer fluids can be captured for environmentally friendly disposal.
   A. spray-wash cabinets
   B. brake washers
   C. solvent tanks
   D. pressure washers

_____ 14. A _____ uses high pressure to blast small abrasive particles to clean the surface of parts.
   A. pressure washer
   B. spray-wash cabinet
   C. sand or bead blaster
   D. cleaning gun

_____ 15. A(n) _____ is a break in the electrical circuit where either the power supply or earth circuit has been interrupted.
   A. open circuit
   B. short circuit
   C. grounded circuit
   D. All of the above

_____ 16. Batteries are filled with a dangerous and corrosive liquid called _____.
   A. sulphuric acid
   B. hydrochloric acid
   C. muriatic acid
   D. nitric acid

_____ 17. The purpose of engine oil is to_____
   A. reduce unwanted friction
   B. cool the engine
   C. absorb shock loads
   D. All of the above

_____ 18. Also known as mineral oil, _____ is used mainly as a cleaning agent in the automotive industry.
   A. petrol oil
   B. paraffin
   C. PAO oil
   D. ethylene

_____ **19.** An alloy of zinc and copper, _____ is used to make some metal nuts, bolts, and bushes.
   A. chrome
   B. brass
   C. tin
   D. cast iron
_____ **20.** When carbon and other materials are alloyed with iron they form _____.
   A. aluminum
   B. chrome
   C. graphite
   D. steel

True/False

If you believe the statement to be more true than false, write the letter "T" in the space provided. If you believe the statement to be more false than true, write the letter "F".

_____ **1.** Tools are identified as metric or imperial by markings identifying their sizes, or by the increments on measuring instruments.
_____ **2.** A micrometer should always be stored with its measuring surfaces touching in order to maintain its calibration.
_____ **3.** Morse taper is a system for securing drill bits to drills.
_____ **4.** Grinding wheels and discs usually have a maximum safe operating speed printed on them.
_____ **5.** An air hammer is not as efficient as a hand chisel and hammer for driving and cutting.
_____ **6.** Combination wrenches usually have either different-sized heads on each end of the wrench, or heads the same size but with different angles.
_____ **7.** Six- and 12-point sockets fit the heads of hexagonal-shaped fasteners. Four- and 8-point sockets fit the heads of square-shaped fasteners.
_____ **8.** Waterpump pliers are often called Channellocks, after the company that first made them.
_____ **9.** The most common screwdriver is the Phillips or Pozidriv screwdriver.
_____ **10.** A pry bar is designed to remove a gasket without damaging the sealing face of the component.
_____ **11.** A warding file is thinner than other files and comes to a point; it is used for working in narrow slots.
_____ **12.** A taper tap, known as a plug tap, is used to tap a thread into a hole that does not come out the other side of the material.
_____ **13.** A tube-flaring tool is used to flare the end of a tube so it can be connected to another tube or component.
_____ **14.** Blind rivets are so named because there is no need to see or reach the other side of the hole in which the rivet goes to do the work.
_____ **15.** The engine dynamometer measures engine performance through a vehicle's driven wheels.
_____ **16.** Pneumatic foot controls are usually used on a tire changer to allow both hands of the technician to be free to work on the tire.
_____ **17.** Oxyacetylene torches are used by technicians to heat, braze, weld, and cut metal.
_____ **18.** Slow battery chargers incorporate microprocessors to monitor and control the charge rate so that the battery receives the correct amount of charge according to its state of charge.
_____ **19.** Propylene glycol is a chemical that resists freezing but is very toxic to people and animals.
_____ **20.** Gear oil is the lubricant used in transmissions, transfer cases, and differentials.

Fill in the Blank

Read each item carefully, and then complete the statement by filling in the missing word(s).

1. A measuring _____ is a flexible type of ruler that is useful for measuring longer distances and is accurate to a millimeter or fraction of an inch.
2. A _____ ball gauge is good for measuring small holes where telescoping gauges cannot fit.
3. A _____ tool may be stationary, such as a bench grinder, or portable, such as a portable electric drill.

4. A drill _____ is a device for gripping drill bits securely in a drill.

5. A(n) _____ grinder uses discs rather than wheels.

6. The _____ wrench has an open-end head on one end and a closed-end head on the other. Both ends are usually the same size.

7. A speed _____ is the fastest way to spin a fastener on or off a thread by hand, but it cannot apply much torque to the fastener.

8. The traditional _____ wrench is a hexagonal bar with a right-angle bend at one end.

9. The _____ screwdriver fits into spaces where a straight screwdriver cannot and is useful where there is not much room to turn it.

10. Magnetic pickup tools and mechanical _____ are very useful for grabbing items in tight spaces.

11. The _____ is used for the general cutting of metals. The frames and blades are adjustable and rated according the number of teeth and hardness of the saw.

12. When materials are too awkward to grip vertically in a plain vice, it may be easier to use an offset _____ .

13. Screw _____ are devices designed to remove screws, studs, or bolts that have broken off in threaded holes.

14. Gear _____ consist of three main parts: jaws, a cross-arm, and a forcing screw.

15. A typical _____ or blind rivet has a body, which forms the finished rivet, and a mandrel, which is discarded when the riveting is completed.

16. Pressure _____ gauges are a particular type of pressure gauge that measures "negative" pressure below atmospheric pressure.

17. Wheel _____ systems are often incorporated into a special-purpose vehicle hoist and use light beams with calibration equipment.

18. Automatic transmission fluid must lubricate the internal gears, bearings, and bushes of the transmission, yet have a large enough _____ of friction to allow the clutches to grab and not slip.

19. Diesel fuel oil is a derivative of _____ oil that is used to power diesel engines, also known as compression ignition or CI engines.

20. Like stainless steel, _____ is a bright, shiny corrosion-resistant metal and is used mostly for decorative purposes, such as on hubcaps.

Labeling

Label the following diagrams with the correct terms.

1. Identify the types of air tools:

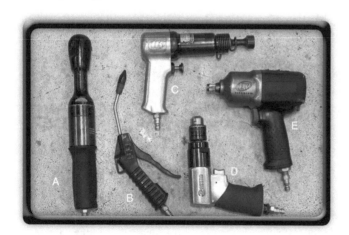

A. _____

B. _____

C. _____

D. _____

E. _____

2. Identify the components of a socket:

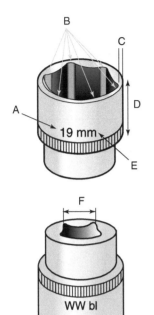

A. _____

B. _____

C. _____

D. _____

E. _____

F. _____

3. Identify the types of pliers:

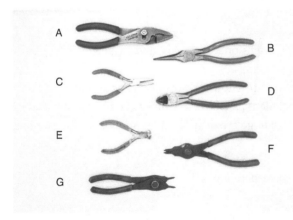

A. _____

B. _____

C. _____

D. _____

E. _____

F. _____

G. _____

4. Identify the types of hammers:

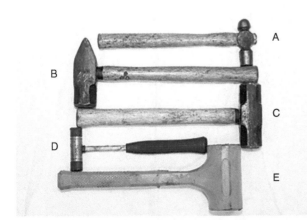

A. _____

B. _____

C. _____

D. _____

E. _____

5. Identify the components of a flare tool:

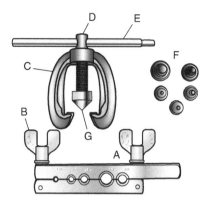

A. _____

B. _____

C. _____

D. _____

E. _____

F. _____

G. _____

Materials Used in the Vehicle Industry

Match the following materials used in the automotive industry with the correct description.

A. Bakelite	**F.** Melamine
B. Cork	**G.** Nylon
C. Fiberglass	**H.** Perspex
D. Glass	**I.** Rubber
E. Graphite	**J.** Silicone rubber

_____ **1.** A metal glass that is used in some timing belts.

_____ **2.** A synthetic rubber that is used for spark plug high-tension leads, seals, and gaskets.

_____ **3.** Used for windscreens, windows, and headlight coverings.

_____ **4.** A synthetic resin that was used primarily in the construction of distributor caps and rotors.

_____ **5.** A tough, clear plastic used as partitions on instrument panels. It resembles glass by its transparency.

_____ **6.** A black substance that is often used as an additive to grease or sprayed on, used as a lubricant in automotive applications.

_____ **7.** Used in the manufacture of tires.

_____ **8.** A synthetic plastic material that is used in the construction of some bushings.

_____ **9.** Often used in combination with rubber to form gaskets for engine blocks.

_____ **10.** A compound used to make synthetic resins and used for moulding some lightweight vehicle body parts.

Skill Drills

Test your knowledge of skill drills by filling in the correct words in the photo captions.

1. Measuring Using an Outside Micrometer:

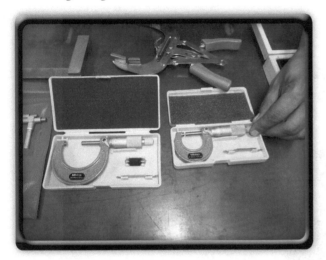

Step 1:   Select the correct of micrometer. Verify that the _____ and _____ are _____ and that it is _____ properly.

Step 2:   _____ the _____ of the part you are measuring.

Step 3:   In your _____ hand, hold the _____ of the micrometer between your little finger, _____ finger, and palm of your hand, with the _____ between your thumb and forefinger.

Step 4:   With your _____ hand, hold the part you are measuring and place the _____ over it.

Step 5:   Using your _____ and forefinger, lightly _____ the ratchet. It is important that the correct amount of force is applied to the _____ when taking a measurement. The spindle and _____ should just _____ the component, with a slight amount of _____ when the micrometer is removed from the measured piece. Be careful that the part is _____ in the micrometer so the reading is correct. Try _____ the micrometer in all directions to make sure it is square.

Step 6:   Once the micrometer is properly _____, tighten the _____ mechanism so the _____ will not turn.

Step 7:   Read the micrometer and _____ your reading.

Step 8:   When all readings are finished, _____ the micrometer, position the spindle so it is _____ _____ from the anvil and return it to its protective case.

2. Measuring Using a Dial Bore Gauge:

Step 1:   Select the correct _____ of the dial bore gauge you will use and fit any _____ to it.

Step 2:   Check the _____ and adjust it as necessary.

Step 3: Insert the dial bore gauge into the _____. The accurate measurement will be at exactly _____ degrees to the bore. To find the accurate measurement, _____ the dial bore gauge _____ slightly back and forth until you find the centered position.

Step 4: Read the _____ to determine the bore _____.

Step 5: Always _____ the dial bore gauge and return it to its _____ _____ when you have finished using it.

3. Measuring Using Vernier Callipers:

Step 1: Verify that the vernier calliper is _____ (zeroed) before using it. If it is not zeroed, _____ your mentor, who will get you a _____ vernier calliper.

Step 2: Position the _____ correctly for the measurement you are making. Internal and external readings are normally made with the vernier calliper positioned at _____ degrees to the _____ of the component to be measured. Length and _____ measurements are usually made _____ to or in line with the object being measured. Use your thumb to press or withdraw the _____ _____ to measure the outside or inside of the part.

Step 3: Read the _____ of the vernier calliper, being careful not to change the position of the _____ _____. Always read the dial or face _____ on. A view from the _____ can give a considerable parallax error. Parallax error is a visual error caused by viewing measurement markers at an incorrect _____.

4. Measuring Using a Dial Indicator:

Step 1: Select the gauge type, size, attachment, and _____ that fit the part you are measuring. Mount the dial indicator _____ to keep it _____.

Step 2: Adjust the _____ so that the _____ is at 90 degrees to the part you are measuring and _____ it in place.

Step 3:   _____ the part one complete turn and locate the _____ spot. _____ the indicator.

Step 4:   Find the point of maximum _____ and note the reading. This will indicate the _____-_____ value.

Step 5:   Continue the _____ and make sure the _____ does not go below zero. If it does, _____ the indicator and remeasure the point of _____ variation.

Step 6:   Check your readings against the manufacturer's _____. If the _____ is _____ than the specifications allow, consult your supervisor.

Crossword Puzzle

Use the clues in the column to complete the puzzle.

Across

3. The shaft of a pop rivet.

5. Precise measuring tools designed to measure small distances and are available in both millimeter (mm) and inch calibrations.

6. A term used to generically describe an internal thread-cutting tool.

8. Tools powered by electricity or compressed air.

9. A generic term to describe tools that tighten and loosen fasteners with hexagonal heads.

10. A device that converts and stores electrical energy through chemical reactions.

Down

1. A renewable fuel made by chemically combining natural oils from soybeans (or cottonseeds, canola, etc.; animal fats; or even recycled cooking oil) with an alcohol such as methanol (or ethanol).

2. Also called feeler blades; flat metal strips used to measure the width of gaps, such as the clearance between valves and rocker arms.

4. Pliers designed to cut protruding items level with the surface.

7. A highly flammable liquid that can dissolve other substances.

ASE-Type Questions

Read each item carefully, and then select the best response.

_____ 1. Technician A says that you would use an outside micrometer to measure the bottom of a cylinder. Technician B says that you would use a telescoping gauge to measure the bottom of a cylinder. Who is correct?
   A. Technician A
   B. Technician B
   C. Both Technician A and Technician B
   D. Neither Technician A nor Technician B

_____ 2. Technician A says to use nippers to cut through soft metal. Technician B says to use an Allen key. Who is correct?
   A. Technician A
   B. Technician B
   C. Both Technician A and Technician B
   D. Neither Technician A nor Technician B

_____ 3. Technician A says pressure compression gauges are used to measure the compression pressures inside an engine cylinder. Technician B says pressure compression gauges can identify overall condition and pressure leakage situations that could be caused by a range of engine faults. Who is correct?
   A. Technician A
   B. Technician B
   C. Both Technician A and Technician B
   D. Neither Technician A nor Technician B

_____ 4. Technician A says the most commonly used pair of pliers in the shop is the needle-nosed plier. Technician B says the most common is the snap-ring plier. Who is correct?
   A. Technician A
   B. Technician B
   C. Both Technician A and Technician B
   D. Neither Technician A nor Technician B

_____ 5. Technician A says bolt cutters cut hardened rods. Technician B says tin snips can cut thin sheet metal. Who is correct?
   A. Technician A
   B. Technician B
   C. Both Technician A and Technician B
   D. Neither Technician A nor Technician B

_____ 6. Technician A says that a drift punch is also named a starter punch because you should always use it first to get a pin moving. Technician B says a center punch centers a drill bit at the point where a hole is required to be drilled. Who is correct?
   A. Technician A
   B. Technician B
   C. Both Technician A and Technician B
   D. Neither Technician A nor Technician B

_____ 7. Technician A states that a tap handle has a right angled jaw that matches the squared end that all taps have. Technician B states that to cut a thread in an awkward space, a T-shaped tap handle is very convenient. Who is correct?
   A. Technician A
   B. Technician B
   C. Both Technician A and Technician B
   D. Neither Technician A nor Technician B

_____ 8. Technician A states that there are many applications for blind rivets, and various rivet types and tools may be used to do the riveting. Technician B states that a typical pop or blind rivet has a body, which will form the finished rivet, and a mandrel, which is discarded when the riveting is complete. Who is correct?
   A. Technician A
   B. Technician B
   C. Both Technician A and Technician B
   D. Neither Technician A nor Technician B

_____ **9.** Technician A says a battery could discharge if the vehicle is not started for as little as one month due to normal vehicle drains. Technician B says slow charging a battery is less stressful on a battery than fast charging. Who is correct?

   A. Technician A
   B. Technician B
   C. Both Technician A and Technician B
   D. Neither Technician A nor Technician B

_____ **10.** Technician A says engine oil reduces wear on moving parts. Technician B says engine oil absorbs shock loads. Who is correct?

   A. Technician A
   B. Technician B
   C. Both Technician A and Technician B
   D. Neither Technician A nor Technician B

Fasteners, Locking Devices, and Lifting Equipment

Chapter Review

The following activities have been designed to help you refresh your knowledge of this chapter. Your instructor may require you to complete some or all of these activities as a regular part of your training program. You are encouraged to complete any activity that your instructor does not assign as a way to enhance your learning.

Matching

Match the following terms with the correct description or example.

A. Allen head screw

B. Bolt

C. Fasteners

D. Flat washers

E. Screws

F. Taper key

G. Tensile strength

H. Torque

I. Torx bolt

J. Vehicle hoist

_____ **1.** Devices that securely hold items together, such as screws, cotter pins, rivets, and bolts.

_____ **2.** In reference to fasteners, the amount of force it takes before a fastener breaks.

_____ **3.** A type of vehicle lifting tool designed to lift the entire vehicle.

_____ **4.** Spread the load of a bolt head or a nut as it is tightened and distribute it over a greater area.

_____ **5.** A type of threaded fastener with a thread on one end and a hexagonal head on the other.

_____ **6.** Often found in vehicle engines in places such as cylinder heads to blocks, where particular tightening sequences are required.

_____ **7.** Usually smaller than bolts and are sometimes referred to as metal threads. They can have a variety of heads and are used on smaller components.

_____ **8.** Sometimes called a cap screw, it has a hexagonal recess in the head, which fits a hex wrench.

_____ **9.** Used to prevent the free rotation of gears or pulleys on a shaft; used to anchor a pulley to a shaft or a disc to a driving shaft.

_____ **10.** The twisting force applied to a shaft that may or may not result in motion.

Multiple Choice

Read each item carefully, and then select the best response.

_____ **1.** A self-locking or _____ nut is highly resistant to being loosened by the kind of vibration that engines and vehicles experience.

    A. torx

    B. castellated

    C. nylock

    D. spring

_____ **2.** When a _____ nut is screwed onto a bolt that has been drilled in the right spot, a split pin can be passed through them both and then spread open to lock the nut in place.

    A. castellated

    B. spring

    C. nylock

    D. shake proof

_____ 3. The external version of a _____ has teeth on the outside and the internal version has teeth on the inside; one type has both.
    A. tab washer
    B. serrated edge shake-proof washers
    C. castellated washer
    D. torx washer

_____ 4. Bolts, nuts, and studs are designated by their _____.
    A. thread diameter
    B. grade
    C. pitch
    D. All of the above

_____ 5. The coarseness of any thread is called its _____.
    A. depth
    B. pitch
    C. grade
    D. tensile strength

_____ 6. Torque value is specified in _____.
    A. foot pounds
    B. megapascals
    C. newton meters
    D. Either A or C

_____ 7. As long as a bolt is not tightened too much, it will return to its original length when loosened. This is called _____.
    A. yield
    B. torque
    C. elasticity
    D. stretch

_____ 8. A torqueing procedure called _____ is considered a more precise method to tighten torque-to-yield bolts using a multistep process.
    A. torque angle
    B. sequencing
    C. torque gauging
    D. pitch gauging

_____ 9. Used to keep components in place where shearing forces are high _____ are used in high-pressure pumps to keep valve plates anchored in position.
    A. taper pins
    B. rawl pins
    C. dowel pins
    D. split pins

_____ 10. A _____ is usually attached to levers that have to slide along a shaft to allow engagement of a part.
    A. feather key
    B. parallel key
    C. taper key
    D. gibb-head key

_____ 11. A _____ is designed to be pulled out easily and is used when a gear or a pulley has to be attached to a shaft.
    A. taper key
    B. feather key
    C. gibb-head key
    D. parallel key

_____ 12. A(n) _____ is designed to conduct heat laterally to transfer heat from the combustion chamber to the coolant faster.
    A. sealing bead
    B. anisotropic gasket
    C. O-ring
    D. fire ring

_____ **13.** Mechanical seals called _____ are used to seal holes in the engine block that were left during original manufacture to remove the sand core during the casting process.
- **A.** welch plugs
- **B.** stopper plugs
- **C.** core plugs
- **D.** Either A or C

_____ **14.** Slings are normally made out of _____.
- **A.** webbing material
- **B.** wire rope
- **C.** chain
- **D.** All of the above

_____ **15.** A(n) _____ is a common type of hydraulic jack that is mounted on four wheels, two of which swivel to provide a steering mechanism.
- **A.** sliding-bridge jack
- **B.** floor jack
- **C.** bottle jack
- **D.** air jack

True/False

If you believe the statement to be more true than false, write the letter "T" in the space provided. If you believe the statement to be more false than true, write the letter "F".

_____ **1.** Bolts are always threaded into a nut or hole that has an identical thread cut inside.

_____ **2.** Studs can have different threads on each end.

_____ **3.** On both metric and imperial bolts the size indicates the diameter of the bolt head.

_____ **4.** The higher a bolt's grade number, the lower the tensile strength.

_____ **5.** Torque-to-yield bolts cannot be reused because they have been stretched into their yield zone and would very likely fail if re-torqued.

_____ **6.** A helical insert is used to repair damaged bolt holes.

_____ **7.** Parallel keys are used to anchor a pulley to a shaft or a disc to a driving shaft.

_____ **8.** The most widely used seal for rotating parts is the lip-type dynamic oil seal.

_____ **9.** O-rings are generally effective at sealing high pressures where the differential speed between the opposing surfaces is minimal.

_____ **10.** In engines that use a timing chain or timing gears the front main seal is located in a housing bolted to the front of the engine block.

_____ **11.** For cork, felt, or neoprene gaskets, a light coat of adhesive spray is used on each surface of the block and the gasket.

_____ **12.** Sliding-bridge jacks are specialized jacks for lifting and lowering transmissions during removal and installation.

_____ **13.** Every vehicle hoist in the workshop must have a built-in mechanical locking device so the vehicle hoist can be secured at the chosen height after the vehicle is raised.

_____ **14.** Once you drive a vehicle over an inspection pit you can inspect and service the vehicle underside without fear of the vehicle toppling over.

_____ **15.** A crane is only as good as the slings connecting it to the equipment to be moved.

Fill in the Blank

Read each item carefully, and then complete the statement by filling in the missing word(s).

1. A(n) _____-_____ screw is made of a hard material that cuts a mirror image of itself into the hole as you turn it.

2. A(n) _____ nut does not need to be held when started but it is not as strong as a conventional nut.

3. A flat _____ is used to protect the surface underneath from being marked by the nut or head as it turns and tightens down.

4. The metric system uses _____ stamped on the heads of metric bolts and on the face of metric nuts.

5. A(n) _____-_____ compound neutralizes the chemical reaction that causes some metals to react with each other and bind together.

6. If a bolt continues to be tightened and stretched beyond its _____ point, it will not return to its original length when loosened.

7. _____ pins are often used to hold components on rotating shafts.

8. The _____ gasket seals and contains the pressures of combustion within the engine, between the cylinder head and the engine block.

9. To seal the rotating parts of an engine, a(n) _____ seal is needed.

10. Room temperature _____ oxygen-safe silicone is used to help seal fiber gaskets and gasket joints.

11. The maximum operating capacity of lifting equipment is usually expressed as the safe _____ _____.

12. Chain blocks and mobile _____ are often used together to lift larger components inside heavy vehicle workshops.

13. Jack _____ are adjustable supports used with vehicle jacks designed to support a vehicle's weight once a vehicle has been raised by a vehicle jack.

14. A(n) _____ lifting hoist provides workshop flexibility as they can be easily moved to any area of a standard workshop floor.

15. An engine _____, or mobile floor crane, is capable of lifting very heavy objects, such as engines while they are being removed from a vehicle.

Labeling

Label the following diagrams with the correct terms.

1. Identify the bolt dimensions:

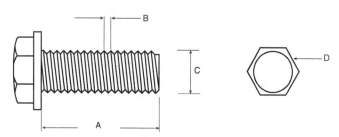

A. _____

B. _____

C. _____

D. _____

2. Identify the washer types:

A. _____

B. _____

C. _____

D. _____

3. Identify the types of locking keys:

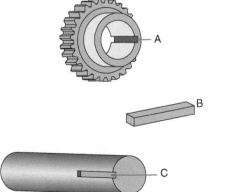

A. _____

B. _____

C. _____

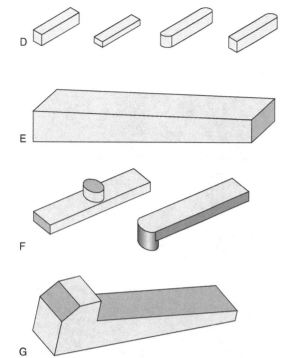

D. _____

E. _____

F. _____

G. _____

4. Identify the chain fittings:

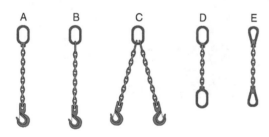

A. _____

B. _____

C. _____

D. _____

E. _____

Skill Drills

Test your knowledge of skill drills by filling in the correct words in the photo captions.

1. Using a Torque Wrench and Torque Angle Gauge:

Step 1: Identify the _____ _____ either through the manufacturer's specifications or, in some cases, stretch bolts themselves have a specific _____ on the head of the bolt. In addition, the diameter of the _____ of the bolt is _____ than the threaded diameter.

Step 2: Check the specifications. Determine the correct _____ value and _____ for the bolts or fastener you are using. This will be in _____ -pounds (ft-lb). Also check the torque _____ specifications for the bolt or fastener, and whether the procedure is one step or more than one step.

Step 3: Tighten the _____ to the specified torque. If the component requires _____ bolts or fasteners, make sure to _____ them all to the same _____ _____ in the sequence and follow the _____ that are specified by the manufacturer. Some torqueing procedures could call for _____ or more steps to complete the torqueing process.

2. Fitting a Formed Head Gasket:

Step 1: Obtain an assembly that will need a gasket _____, in this case the _____ gasket.

Step 2: Remove the _____ _____ and keep track of the head _____.

Step 3: Remove the old _____.

Step 4: Clean the mating _____ with the proper cleaning _____.

Step 5: Select a _____ according to the manufacturer's _____.

Step 6: Inspect the gasket for _____ or other _____.

Step 7: Select a _____ that is manufacturer recommended.

Step 8: Spread the _____ on the _____ surfaces according to the manufacturer's specifications.

Step 9: Align the _____ with the mating surface.

Step 10: Assemble the components and tighten the _____ to their _____ specification and tightening _____.

3. Removing and Replacing Lip-Type Seals:

Step 1:   Use a component that requires a _____ _____ seal, usually a _____.

Step 2:   Inspect the assembly for _____, sharp _____, or _____.

Step 3:   _____ the assembly and assess seal _____.

Step 4:   Seal failure can include a broken _____ _____ or a _____ component at the sealing surface.

Step 5:   Remove the seal with an oil seal _____.

Step 6:   Measure and record the housing _____ diameter, the _____ diameter, and _____ of the seal landing.

Step 7:   Select the recommended _____ seal.

Step 8:   Compare the _____ seal with the _____ to make sure they are the same _____.

Step 9:   Lubricate the _____ and the seal with clean _____ before fitting the new _____ over the shaft, making sure that the seal _____ faces into the housing.

Step 10:   Locate the seal in the _____ according to the manufacturer's specifications.

Step 11:   Press the seal into the housing with the sealing lip _____ the fluid being sealed.

Step 12:   Use a _____ to make sure the seal is snugly fit.

Step 13:   Check the installation and make sure the _____ _____ is correct.

4. Lifting a Vehicle Using a Hydraulic Hoist:

Step 1:   Read and follow the safety instructions that are provided with the four-post hoist. They should be displayed near the lift operating _____. Also verify the vehicle's _____ and compare it against the hoist's safe load _____. Check the hydraulic system for any and _____ the steel cables for any sign of _____. Make sure there are no oil _____ around or under the hoist. The four-post hoist should be completely _____ before you attempt to drive the vehicle onto it.

Step 2:   The platform may have built-in wheel _____ or attachments for wheel _____ equipment. A set of bars is normally mounted at the _____ of each ramp to prevent the vehicle from being _____ off the front of the four-post hoist. At the back will be _____ that allow the vehicle to be driven onto the four-post hoist. The back of the ramps will _____ upwards when the hoist is _____ and prevent the vehicle from _____ off the back.

Step 3:   Prepare to use the vehicle hoist _____. With the aid of an assistant _____ the driver, or a large _____ in front of the hoist, drive the vehicle _____ and _____ onto the four-post hoist and position it centrally. If the vehicle has front wheel _____, drive the vehicle forward until the _____ lock into the _____.

Step 4:   Get out of the vehicle and check that it is correctly _____ on the platform. If it is, apply the _____ _____.

Step 5:   Make sure the hydraulic hoist area is _____. Move to the controls and _____ the vehicle until it reaches the appropriate _____ height. If the four-post hoist has a manual _____ mechanism, lock it in place to _____ whatever _____ device is used.

Step 6:   Before the four-post hoist is _____, remove all _____ and _____ from the area and _____ up any spilled _____. Remove the safety device or _____ the lift before lowering it. Make sure no one is near the area. Once the four-post hoist is fully lowered, carefully _____ the vehicle off the hoist with the help of a _____.

5. Using Engine Hoists and Stands:

Step 1:   Prepare to use the engine _____. Lower the _____ _____ and position the lifting end and chain over the _____ of the engine.

Step 2:   Wear appropriate PPE, such as _____ _____, during the entire operation, beginning with _____ the chain, steel cable, or sling, and bolts to make sure they are in good condition. Before you use the crane, make sure the chain/sling is rated _____ than the weight of the item to be lifted. Also _____ that the lifting arm is only extended to the length of its lifting _____ applicable to the weight of the item to be lifted. Only use _____ lifting equipment, nothing homemade. Look carefully around the component that is about to be lifted to determine if it has _____ _____ or other anchor points.

Step 3:   If the engine or component has _____ _____, attach the _____ with D-_____ or chain _____. If you need to screw in _____ and spacer _____ to lift the engine, make sure you use the correct bolt and spacer _____ for the chain or cable. Screw the bolts until the _____ is held _____ against the component.

Step 4:   Attach the hoist's _____ under the _____ of the sling and raise the engine hoist just enough to lift the engine to take _____ the up on the cable, chain, or sling. Double-check the sling and attachment points for _____. The engine's or component's _____ _____ _____ should be directly under the engine hoist's hook, and there should be no _____ or _____ in the chain or sling.

Step 5:   _____ the engine hoist until the engine is clear of the _____ and any obstacles. Slowly and _____ move the engine hoist and lifted component to the new location with _____ ground clearance to prevent _____ and potential _____ of the whole crane.

Step 6:   Make sure the engine is _____ correctly. You may need to place _____ under the engine to stabilize it. Once you are sure the engine is _____, lower the engine hoist and _____ the _____ and any securing fasteners. Finally, return the equipment to its _____ area.

Crossword Puzzle

Use the clues in the column to complete the puzzle.

Across

1. A tool used to measure the rotational or twisting force applied to fasteners.
2. Usually smaller than bolts and are sometimes referred to as metal threads. They can have a variety of heads and are used on smaller components. The thread often extends from the tip to the head so they can hold together components of variable thickness.
5. A washer that compresses as the nut tightens; the nut is spring loaded against this surface, which makes it unlikely to work loose.
6. A type of vehicle jack that uses oil under pressure to lift vehicles.
7. Helps prevent fasteners from loosening; it is applied to one thread, then the other fastener is screwed onto it. This creates a strong bond between them, but one that stays plastic, so they can be separated by a wrench.

Down

1. A certificate issued when lifting equipment has been checked and deemed safe.
3. A metal spring wrapped circularly around the inside of a lip seal to keep it in constant contact with the moving shaft.
4. Used to prevent the free rotation of gears or pulleys on a shaft and can be used to secure a gear wheel on its shaft.
5. A type of threaded fastener with a thread cut on each end, as opposed to having a bolt head on one end.

ASE-Type Questions

Read each item carefully, and then select the best response.

_____ **1.** Technician A says seals are usually used on stationary components and gaskets are used on rotating parts. Technician B says seals are usually used on rotating parts whereas gaskets are used for stationary components. Who is correct?
  A. Technician A
  B. Technician B
  C. Both Technician A and Technician B
  D. Neither Technician A nor Technician B

_____ **2.** Technician A says the purpose of gaskets and seals is to keep critical fluids from leaking and to keep contaminants out. Technician B disagrees. Who is correct?
  A. Technician A
  B. Technician B
  C. Both Technician A and Technician B
  D. Neither Technician A nor Technician B

_____ **3.** Technician A says a garter spring is used in lip-type seals. Technician B says it is used to maintain high pressure without fluid leaking. Who is correct?
  A. Technician A
  B. Technician B
  C. Both Technician A and Technician B
  D. Neither Technician A nor Technician B

_____ **4.** Technician A says that hoists should be inspected and certified periodically. Technician B says that safety locks do not need to be applied before working under a vehicle, unless you will be working for more than 10 minutes. Who is correct?
  A. Technician A
  B. Technician B
  C. Both Technician A and Technician B
  D. Neither Technician A nor Technician B

_____ **5.** Technician A says that an engine sling should have an angle greater than 90 degrees. Technician B says that all slings and lifting chains should be inspected for damage prior to use. Who is correct?
  A. Technician A
  B. Technician B
  C. Both Technician A and Technician B
  D. Neither Technician A nor Technician B

_____ **6.** Technician A says that you should have a co-worker help guide you onto an inspection pit. Technician B says that all lights should be on in the pit before driving over it. Who is correct?
  A. Technician A
  B. Technician B
  C. Both Technician A and Technician B
  D. Neither Technician A nor Technician B

_____ **7.** Technician A says if a fastener is overtightened, it could become damaged or could break. Technician B says if a fastener is undertightened, it is likely to be satisfactory. Who is correct?
  A. Technician A
  B. Technician B
  C. Both Technician A and Technician B
  D. Neither Technician A nor Technician B

_____ **8.** Technician A says torque specifications for bolts and nuts in vehicles will usually be contained within workshop manuals. Technician B says that in practice, most torque specifications call for the nuts and bolts to have oiled threads prior to tightening. Who is correct?
  A. Technician A
  B. Technician B
  C. Both Technician A and Technician B
  D. Neither Technician A nor Technician B

_____ **9.** Technician A says one of the tools used to repair damaged bolt holes is the helical insert, more commonly known by its trademark, Heli-coil. Technician B says Heli-coils are made of coiled wire and are inserted into a tapped hole that is larger than the desired hole. Who is correct?
   A. Technician A
   B. Technician B
   C. Both Technician A and Technician B
   D. Neither Technician A nor Technician B

_____ **10.** Technician A says a MLS head gasket has multiple layers that provide superior combustion sealing. Technician B says one of the most critical gaskets in automotive applications is the head gasket. Who is correct?
   A. Technician A
   B. Technician B
   C. Both Technician A and Technician B
   D. Neither Technician A nor Technician B

Basic Engine Terminology and Operating Principles

Chapter Review

The following activities have been designed to help you refresh your knowledge of this chapter. Your instructor may require you to complete some or all of these activities as a regular part of your training program. You are encouraged to complete any activity that your instructor does not assign as a way to enhance your learning.

Matching

Match the following terms with the correct description or example.

A. Bore
B. Combustion
C. Crankshaft throw
D. Dynamometer
E. Idle

F. Over-square engine
G. Square engine
H. Total cylinder volume
I. Under-square engine
J. Volumetric efficiency

_____ 1. An engine with an equal stroke and bore dimensions.

_____ 2. A device that measures engine or vehicle road speed and torque to calculate engine power.

_____ 3. The number of degrees of crankshaft rotation when both the intake and exhaust valves are open.

_____ 4. A chemical reaction between fuel and oxygen that releases heat.

_____ 5. An engine's minimum operational speed.

_____ 6. An engine with a stroke that is longer than the cylinder bore.

_____ 7. The diameter of a cylinder.

_____ 8. The sum of the cylinder displacement plus clearance volume.

_____ 9. The distance between the centerline of the main bearing journal and crankpin journal.

_____10. An engine with a stroke that is shorter than the cylinder bore dimension.

Multiple Choice

Read each item carefully, and then select the best response.

_____ 1. Which of these terms can be used interchangeably with the term "engine"?
   A. Power unit
   B. Motor
   C. Prime mover
   D. Both A and C

_____ 2. A(n) _____ engine is best suited for high-speed operation.
   A. square
   B. under-square
   C. over-square
   D. rectangular

_____ 3. The space remaining in a cylinder when the piston is at TDC is called the _____.
   A. clearance volume
   B. cylinder displacement
   C. compression zone
   D. cylinder volume

_____ **4.** The _____ is the largest structure of an engine.
- **A.** transmission
- **B.** cylinder block
- **C.** crankshaft
- **D.** crankcase

_____ **5.** The _____ converts the reciprocating action of the pistons into rotational movement.
- **A.** crankpin
- **B.** crankshaft
- **C.** main bearing journals
- **D.** camshaft

_____ **6.** The piston is attached to one end of a connecting rod by a pin called a _____.
- **A.** wrist pin
- **B.** crankpin
- **C.** piston pin
- **D.** Either A or C

_____ **7.** In imperial measurements, torque is expressed in units called _____.
- **A.** newton meters
- **B.** decibars
- **C.** foot-pounds
- **D.** None of the above

_____ **8.** Measurement of an engine's power output as a function of both torque and engine speed is known as _____.
- **A.** torque rise
- **B.** horsepower
- **C.** compression ratio
- **D.** displacement

_____ **9.** The amount of energy an engine converts into mechanical energy compared to what could theoretically be extracted from a pound of fuel is called _____.
- **A.** rated horsepower
- **B.** specific fuel consumption
- **C.** volumetric efficiency
- **D.** thermal efficiency

_____ **10.** Engines are classified by _____.
- **A.** type of fuel
- **B.** location of the camshaft
- **C.** cylinder bore diameter and displacement
- **D.** All of the above

True/False

If you believe the statement to be more true than false, write the letter "T" in the space provided. If you believe the statement to be more false than true, write the letter "F".

_____ **1.** An engine harnesses the heat from combustion.

_____ **2.** The term "motor" is sometimes used to describe engines used in off-road equipment and locomotives.

_____ **3.** The bore/stroke relationship predicts the best application for an engine.

_____ **4.** Square engines have a stroke ratio more useful for operating at low speed and developing peak torque.

_____ **5.** Compression ratio is a comparison between the cylinder volume when the piston is at BDC and when it reaches TDC.

_____ **6.** The crankshaft is used to operate the valves in the correct sequence.

_____ **7.** Idle is the maximum speed an engine can turn without a load.

_____ **8.** When low power or poor engine performance is reported, an engine stall test can be used to determine whether the problem is in the engine or transmission.

_____ **9.** Brake horsepower is measured with a dynamometer using a brake-like device called a prony brake to apply a load.

_____ **10.** Volumetric efficiency can be determined by weighing fuel consumed in an hour on a dynamometer and dividing the consumption by the output hp.

_____ **11.** Reciprocating engines are the most common type of external combustion engine.

_____ **12.** Changing the time when the intake valve opens and closes can improve engine performance and increase volumetric efficiency.

_____ **13.** The Miller cycle is sometimes referred to as a five-stroke cycle because the compression stroke is divided into two separate events.

_____ **14.** Navistar's EcoMotors EM100 design uses two cylinders and four pistons.

_____ **15.** Because diesel engines have less natural retarding force to slow a vehicle than a throttled SI engine, diesels often have an engine-based braking system to supplement service brake operation.

Fill in the Blank

Read each item carefully, and then complete the statement by filling in the missing word(s).

1. Stroke ratio is also referred to as _____.

2. Cylinder _____ = π × Radius² × Stroke

3. The _____ is usually defined as the area of the cylinder block below the cylinders, and it includes the oil pan/sump.

4. The part of the crankshaft that connects with the connecting rod is called the _____.

5. Engines have replaceable piston _____ to minimize gas leakage past the piston.

6. Poppet-type _____ are used to control the movement of gases into and out of the cylinder.

7. A _____ _____ or valve timing mechanism is used to coordinate the movement of the crankshaft with the camshaft and the valves.

8. The _____ is a heavy, round casting bolted to the end of the crankshaft.

9. Torque _____ is the difference between engine torque at its peak compared to torque at the maximum or rated rpm of the engine.

10. The power output of an engine measured at the maximum engine speed under SAE-defined standardized atmospheric pressure, humidity, and temperature is called _____ horsepower.

11. A _____ is the repetition of a set of events in a periodic pattern.

12. When both intake and exhaust valves are open together at the beginning of the intake stroke and end of the exhaust stroke, the condition is known as valve _____.

13. The _____ diesel engine designed in the 1930s still has, by far, the best hp-to-weight ratio of any diesel.

14. Diesel engines use high- and low-pressure _____ systems.

15. The air _____ system is responsible for providing fresh, clean, cool, dry, filtered air to the engine.

Labeling

Label the following diagrams with the correct terms.

1. Identify the components that convert combustion force into rotational power:

A. _____

B. _____

C. _____

D. _____

E. _____

2. Identify the major structures of a diesel engine block:

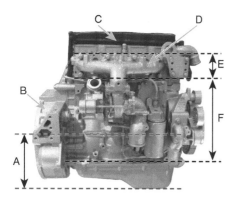

A. _____

B. _____

C. _____

D. _____

E. _____

F. _____

3. Identify the typical parts of a simple valve train mechanism:

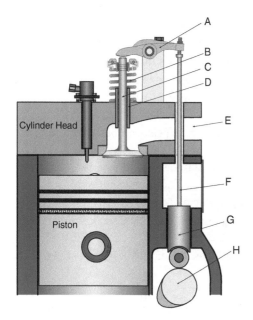

A. _____

B. _____

C. _____

D. _____

E. _____

F. _____

G. _____

H. _____

Skill Drills

Test your knowledge of skill drills by filling in the correct words in the photo captions.

1. Measuring Torque Rise

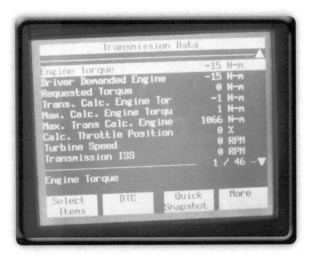

Step 1: Using a chassis _____ or a vehicle connected to a _____ with OEM software, run the vehicle through its entire engine operating range under _____. Use a _____ _____ or take snapshots of the engine data list during the trip using the feature in the OEM software.

Step 2: During a _____ _____, a vehicle that is _____ by using a gear that is one or two steps above where it should operate will move through peak _____ with a full _____ application. Record the trip using a _____ _____ feature within the OEM software.

Step 3: Operate the vehicle at _____ speed one or two _____ down from where it should be while the vehicle is under load, such as traveling up a hill. Again, _____ the data.

Step 4: Find the highest _____ _____ value recorded.

Step 5: Find the highest _____ value reached while the engine was at _____ speed.

Step 6: Calculate the _____ _____ using the following formula: _____ Torque – _____ Torque ÷ Rated Torque × 100 = Torque _____

Step 7: Determine whether the torque rise is more suited to _____ or _____-_____ use and _____ your findings with the vehicle's _____ _____.

2. Performing a Stall Test

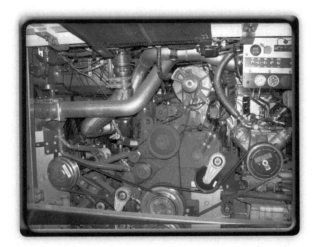

Step 1: Warm the engine to _____ temperature.

Step 2: Chock the _____ with purpose made _____ and apply the _____ _____.

Step 3: Using an appropriate electronic _____ _____ or OEM software, navigate to an engine _____ _____ screen and prepare a custom data list including engine _____ and _____ pressure. If fuel rates and exhaust _____ _____ are available, measure those, too.

Step 4: With the park brakes applied, depress the _____ until the engine reaches its _____ speed. Observe and _____ the engine rpm and compare it to the OEM specifications. Engine rpm that is _____ than the OEM specified rpm indicates that the engine is not producing enough _____.

Step 5: Make _____ recommendations to investigate other causes of low _____ power if the engine _____ _____ is more than _____ rpm below the OEM specifications.

Crossword Puzzle

Use the clues in the column to complete the puzzle.

Across

3. An engine that uses only atmospheric pressure, not pressurized air, to charge the cylinders with air.

5. An engine that pressurizes the air intake system to charge the cylinders with air.

Down

1. A measure of engine power, which is a function of both torque and engine speed.

2. The distance traveled by the piston from the top to the bottom of the cylinder.

4. A marketing term used by Caterpillar to describe a variety of technologies used to lower emissions and increase engine efficiency.

ASE-Type Questions

Read each item carefully, and then select the best response.

_____ 1. Technician A says that a diesel engine's high torque output is due to turbocharging. Technician B says a diesel engine's high torque output is due to its higher compression ratio. Who is correct?
   A. Technician A
   B. Technician B
   C. Both Technician A and Technician B
   D. Neither Technician A nor Technician B

_____ 2. Consider an engine with a high torque rise. Technician A says that it is best used in line haul highway tractors and can use a transmission with fewer gear steps. Technician B says that it is best used for vocational applications such as dump trucks, city buses, and delivery vehicles and needs to use a transmission with more gear steps. Who is correct?
   A. Technician A
   B. Technician B
   C. Both Technician A and Technician B
   D. Neither Technician A nor Technician B

_____ 3. Technician A says that diesel engines with high compression ratios produce more power, mix fuel and air better, and burn less fuel. Technician B says engines with high compression ratios need heavier, high-torque starting systems, more cylinder head bolts, and better sealing head gaskets. Who is correct?
   A. Technician A
   B. Technician B
   C. Both Technician A and Technician B
   D. Neither Technician A nor Technician B

_____ 4. Technician A says that engine torque output is varied by changing engine speed. Technician B says that more torque is produced by injecting and burning more fuel. Who is correct?
   A. Technician A
   B. Technician B
   C. Both Technician A and Technician B
   D. Neither Technician A nor Technician B

_____ 5. Technician A and B are discussing how to determine the correct direction of rotation when adjusting the valves and injectors of an inline six cylinder engine. Both valves are closed on Cylinder 1 as the engine turns past TDC. The next valve to open is the intake valve. Technician A says the engine is being turned correctly. Technician B says you cannot tell whether the engine is being turned correctly by looking at valve opening. Who is correct?
   A. Technician A
   B. Technician B
   C. Both Technician A and Technician B
   D. Neither Technician A nor Technician B

_____ 6. Technician A says that long valve overlap periods help keep the exhaust valves and piston crowns cool. Technician B says that longer valve overlap helps fill the cylinder with more air, especially when the engine is turbocharged. Who is correct?
   A. Technician A
   B. Technician B
   C. Both Technician A and Technician B
   D. Neither Technician A nor Technician B

_____ 7. Technician A says that diesel engines use longer stokes than SI engines. Technician B says that SI engines use longer strokes than diesel engines. Who is correct?
   A. Technician A
   B. Technician B
   C. Both Technician A and Technician B
   D. Neither Technician A nor Technician B

_____ **8.** Technician A says that diesel engines are reciprocating engines. Technician B says that the use of a flywheel classifies any engine a rotary engine. Who is correct?
   A. Technician A
   B. Technician B
   C. Both Technician A and Technician B
   D. Neither Technician A nor Technician B

_____ **9.** Technician A says that a diesel's high torque output is due to its slow speed characteristics and short crankshaft throws. Technician B says that a diesel's high torque output is created when more air and fuel are added to the cylinder. Who is correct?
   A. Technician A
   B. Technician B
   C. Both Technician A and Technician B
   D. Neither Technician A nor Technician B

_____ **10.** Technician A says that an engine's rated horsepower is determined by measuring power output on a dynamometer. Technician B says that rated horsepower information is on the engine emission decal. Who is correct?
   A. Technician A
   B. Technician B
   C. Both Technician A and Technician B
   D. Neither Technician A nor Technician B

Diesel Engine Emissions

Chapter Review

The following activities have been designed to help you refresh your knowledge of this chapter. Your instructor may require you to complete some or all of these activities as a regular part of your training program. You are encouraged to complete any activity that your instructor does not assign as a way to enhance your learning.

Matching

Match the following terms with the correct description or example.

A. Carbon dioxide (CO_2)

B. Carbon monoxide (CO)

C. Greenhouse gas (GHG)

D. Ozone

E. Photochemical smog

_____ **1.** A gas classified as contributing to global warming because it traps heat in the atmosphere.

_____ **2.** A type of air pollution that gives the atmosphere a hazy, reddish-brown color.

_____ **3.** A harmless, colorless, odorless gas which is a by-product of combustion.

_____ **4.** A noxious gas molecule composed of three oxygen molecules.

_____ **5.** A regulated poisonous gas emission which is odorless, colorless, and tasteless.

Multiple Choice

Read each item carefully, and then select the best response.

_____ **1.** Which of the following is an example of a greenhouse gas?

    A. Hydrocarbon

    B. Carbon dioxide

    C. Ozone

    D. Oxides of nitrogen

_____ **2.** What type of emission is formed from unburned fuel?

    A. Hydrocarbon

    B. Greenhouse gas

    C. Nitrous oxide

    D. Carbon dioxide

_____ **3.** Which of the following is created as a result of the incomplete combustion of carbon-based fuels?

    A. Nitrogen dioxide

    B. Carbon dioxide

    C. Carbon monoxide

    D. All of the above

_____ **4.** Volatile organic compounds cause NO_x to break down and form _____.

    A. ozone

    B. soot

    C. smog

    D. All of the above

_____ **5.** Which of the following is the only type of regulated particulate matter that is visible to the naked eye?
  A. PM-2.5
  B. PM-10
  C. PM-50
  D. PM-75

_____ **6.** Crankcase emissions are composed of _____.
  A. cylinder blow-by gas
  B. sulfur
  C. oil droplets
  D. Both A and C

_____ **7.** Incomplete combustion is caused by _____.
  A. inadequate combustion time
  B. improperly mixed air and fuel
  C. insufficient combustion heat and pressure
  D. All of the above

_____ **8.** The United States and Canada follow emission standards established by the _____.
  A. Environmental Protection Agency
  B. European Union
  C. Japanese Ministry of Land, Infrastructure and Transportation
  D. All of the above

_____ **9.** European manufacturers introduced _____ systems that allow optimization of engine power output while reducing particulate emissions close to North American standards without a fuel penalty.
  A. diesel particulate filters
  B. selective catalytic reduction
  C. engine manufacturer diagnostics
  D. emission monitoring

_____ **10.** The "useful life" of a heavy-duty engine is defined as _____.
  A. 110,000 miles (177,000 km) or 10 years
  B. 185,000 miles (297,728 km) or 15 years
  C. 435,000 miles (700,065 km) or 10 years
  D. 500,000 miles (804,672 km) or 15 years

True/False

If you believe the statement to be more true than false, write the letter "T" in the space provided. If you believe the statement to be more false than true, write the letter "F".

_____ **1.** Technological advances made to meet emissions standards have produced cleaner engines that are more efficient and powerful.

_____ **2.** The first emissions standards for heavy-duty diesel engines were established in the 1950s.

_____ **3.** More particulate is left on the road by a truck's tires than is emitted from late-model diesel engine emissions.

_____ **4.** Modern gasoline-powered vehicles no longer produce carbon monoxide.

_____ **5.** Ozone can damage lung tissue, sting eyes, irritate the nose, and aggravate respiratory problems such as asthma and bronchitis.

_____ **6.** Fuel injector spray characteristics influence the type and quantity of exhaust emissions produced.

_____ **7.** Diesel engines produce higher hydrocarbon emissions than gasoline-fueled engines.

_____ **8.** Difficult-to-burn fuel molecules called aromatic molecules cause a characteristic smell from diesel exhaust at idle and low speed.

_____ **9.** Oxides of nitrogen are formed in the diesel combustion chamber from the tiny drops of fuel sprayed into the chamber near the end of the compression stroke.

_____ **10.** Diesel engines have a lower maximum engine speed than gasoline engines because they will not completely burn fuel at high speed.

———— **11.** Vehicles and equipment sold for on- or off-highway use in North America must have an emission decal affixed to the vehicle or engine.

———— **12.** Engine manufacturer diagnostics apply to all 1997 and newer heavy-duty engines used in vehicles over 24,000-lb (10,886-kg) gross vehicle weight rating.

———— **13.** Tier 1 emission standards are the final, cleanest standard of the four phases.

———— **14.** Opacity testing is the common measurement for evaluating smoke density from diesel engines.

———— **15.** EMD systems check the functioning of the fuel delivery system, exhaust gas recirculation system, particulate filter, and emissions-related circuit continuity and rationality for the engine control module inputs and outputs.

Fill in the Blank

Read each item carefully, and then complete the statement by filling in the missing word(s).

1. Emissions that are hazardous to human or plant life are identified as _____.

2. Hydrocarbons in the atmosphere react with NO_2 in the presence of sunlight to form photochemical _____.

3. Particulate matter between 5 and 50 nanometers in diameter is classified as nano, or _____.

4. The biggest hazard of burning fuel containing _____ is that it reacts with other combustion by-products to increase the formation of particulate matter.

5. Close to 50% of hydrocarbon emissions from diesel engines originate from above the top compression ring between the piston crown and the cylinder wall in an area called the _____ _____.

6. The first emissions standards limited peak smoke _____ for heavy-duty diesels.

7. When _____ _____ _____ were introduced for all on-highway heavy-duty diesels, exhaust-based reduction became a major strategy for reducing diesel emissions.

8. Heavy-duty _____-_____ _____ are part of the newest emission legislation and use a more sophisticated set of emission standards that were introduced in 2010.

9. Emission standards for off-road equipment are referred to as _____ 1, 2, 3, and 4 emission standards.

10. The _____ _____ lamp joined other lamps on the instrument panels of heavy-duty vehicles to meet HD-OBD requirements.

Crossword Puzzle

Use the clues in the column to complete the puzzle.

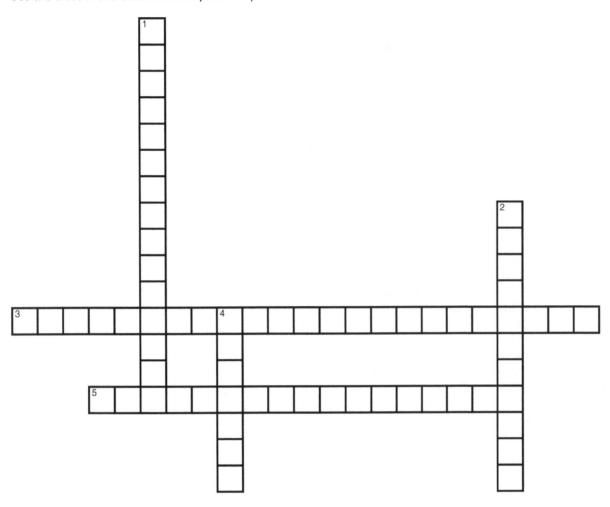

Across

3. Any carbon-containing molecule that is highly reactive.
5. A category of noxious emissions composed of a combination of very small solid or liquid particles.

Down

1. A diagnostic strategy used by the engine control module to evaluate whether emission-related systems are functioning correctly.
2. A molecule, often a fuel, composed of hydrogen and carbon atoms.
4. A measure of the percentage of light blocked by exhaust smoke which is used to evaluate exhaust gas density.

ASE-Type Questions

Read each item carefully, and then select the best response.

_____ 1. Technician A says that creating clean diesel engines has resulted in diesels using more fuel and less power output compared to older engines. Technician B says that even the latest engine technology has not allowed diesels to operate as cleanly as spark ignited gasoline engines. Who is correct?
   A. Technician A
   B. Technician B
   C. Both Technician A and Technician B
   D. Neither Technician A nor Technician B

_____ 2. While discussing the reasons for banning of diesel engines, Technician A says that diesel engines make up only 5% of the vehicles on the road but produce 24% of the transportation emissions, which is disproportionately higher emissions compared to spark ignition gasoline-fueled vehicles. Technician B says that diesels will produce fewer emissions for every ton of weight hauled compared to spark-ignited gasoline-fueled engines. Who is correct?
   A. Technician A
   B. Technician B
   C. Both Technician A and Technician B
   D. Neither Technician A nor Technician B

_____ 3. While discussing greenhouse gas emissions and diesels, Technician A says that carbon dioxide emissions are regulated through fuel economy standards. Technician B says that there are no direct carbon dioxide standards for diesel powered trucks or buses in North America or Europe. Who is correct?
   A. Technician A
   B. Technician B
   C. Both Technician A and Technician B
   D. Neither Technician A nor Technician B

_____ 4. Technician A says that carbon monoxide emissions are higher from diesels than gasoline engines. Technician B says that diesel engines produce little or no carbon monoxide gas compared to gasoline engines. Who is correct?
   A. Technician A
   B. Technician B
   C. Both Technician A and Technician B
   D. Neither Technician A nor Technician B

_____ 5. Technician A says that black smoke from the exhaust of a diesel engine is evidence of particulate emission. Technician B says that black smoke is just soot which will harmlessly fall to the ground. Who is correct?
   A. Technician A
   B. Technician B
   C. Both Technician A and Technician B
   D. Neither Technician A nor Technician B

_____ 6. Technician A says that crankcase vapors have oil droplets that categorize the emission as a hydrocarbon. Technician B says that only gases are considered hydrocarbon emissions and oil droplets qualify crankcase emissions as a type of particulate emission. Who is correct?
   A. Technician A
   B. Technician B
   C. Both Technician A and Technician B
   D. Neither Technician A nor Technician B

_____ 7. Technician A says that diesel exhaust has a noxious component that is 5 to 10 times greater than the noxious component of spark-ignited gasoline-fueled engines. Technician B says that the noxious part of diesel exhaust is many times less than the noxious component of spark-ignited gasoline-fueled engines. Who is correct?
   A. Technician A
   B. Technician B
   C. Both Technician A and Technician B
   D. Neither Technician A nor Technician B

_____ **8.** Technician A says that diesel engine crankcase vapors are made up of primarily air leaking past the piston rings and can be vented directly to the atmosphere since it has no hydrocarbon or fuel in the air. Technician B says that crankcase vapors are classified as particulate emissions and are not vented to the atmosphere on late model engines. Who is correct?

   A. Technician A
   B. Technician B
   C. Both Technician A and Technician B
   D. Neither Technician A nor Technician B

_____ **9.** Technician A says that high crevice volume in a diesel engine is responsible for producing excessive amounts of particulate emissions. Technician B says that high crevice volume produces excessive amounts of NO_x emissions. Who is correct?

   A. Technician A
   B. Technician B
   C. Both Technician A and Technician B
   D. Neither Technician A nor Technician B

_____ **10.** Technician A says the Malfunction Indicator Lamp (MIL) replaces other warning lamps to indicate an engine related fault. Technician B says the MIL is used only to indicate emission related faults. Who is correct?

   A. Technician A
   B. Technician B
   C. Both Technician A and Technician B
   D. Neither Technician A nor Technician B

Diesel Engine Combustion Systems

Chapter Review

The following activities have been designed to help you refresh your knowledge of this chapter. Your instructor may require you to complete some or all of these activities as a regular part of your training program. You are encouraged to complete any activity that your instructor does not assign as a way to enhance your learning.

Matching

Match the following terms with the correct description or example.

A. Compression ignition (CI)

B. Direct injection (DI)

C. Indirect injection (IDI)

D. Rate-shaped injection

E. Stoichiometric ratio

_____ **1.** A diesel combustion chamber design that has a piston-formed combustion bowl and a multi-orifice nozzle.

_____ **2.** An ignition system that initiates combustion using heat derived from only the compression of air.

_____ **3.** The minimum mass of air required to completely burn all fuel in the combustion chamber so that no fuel or air remains after combustion.

_____ **4.** A diesel combustion chamber that uses a precombustion chamber formed in the cylinder head and a pintle nozzle.

_____ **5.** An injection strategy that carefully regulates the amount of fuel injected into a cylinder per degree of crank angle rotation.

Multiple Choice

Read each item carefully, and then select the best response.

_____ **1.** A(n) _____ engine is a compression ignition engine that injects fuel during the intake stroke.

A. direct injection compression ignition

B. homogeneous charge compression ignition

C. indirect injection compression ignition

D. natural gas compression ignition

_____ **2.** When diesel fuel is injected and the engine will not start, _____ smoke, which consists of vaporized fuel, will emerge from the exhaust pipe during cranking.

A. white

B. black

C. blue

D. gray

_____ **3.** The temperature at which diesel fuel will ignite when heated (approximately 380–500°F) is known as its _____.

A. flash point

B. preignition temperature

C. auto-ignition temperature

D. stoichiometric ratio

_____ **4.** Diesel engines use _____ combustion, which uses more air than necessary to burn fuel and has the advantage of reducing fuel consumption.
   A. lean burn
   B. rich burn
   C. stoichiometric
   D. stratified

_____ **5.** The quantity of fuel injected in a diesel engine is controlled by a governor, which first measures _____ to determine how much fuel should be injected.
   A. engine load
   B. engine speed
   C. throttle pedal position
   D. All of the above

_____ **6.** When a combustion chamber burns fuel in layers that vary in air–fuel ratios, it is known as _____ combustion.
   A. stoichiometric
   B. stratified
   C. lean burn
   D. overlap

_____ **7.** Engines are designed to produce peak combustion pressure at approximately _____ of crankshaft rotation after top dead center.
   A. 3° to 5°
   B. 10° to 15°
   C. 15° to 20°
   D. 25° to 30°

_____ **8.** The geometric configuration of the piston bowl is determined by _____.
   A. fuel spray penetration
   B. turbulence
   C. spray angle
   D. All of the above

_____ **9.** The appearance of combustion slobber on an exhaust stack as a result of prolonged engine idle is known as _____.
   A. wet stacking
   B. spittle streaking
   C. slurry trailing
   D. All of the above

_____ **10.** An injection strategy that carefully regulates the amount of fuel injected into a cylinder per degree of crank angle rotation is called _____.
   A. pilot injection
   B. indirect injection
   C. rate-shaped injection
   D. stratified injection

True/False

If you believe the statement to be more true than false, write the letter "T" in the space provided. If you believe the statement to be more false than true, write the letter "F".

_____ **1.** When preignition detonation occurs in an SI system, cylinder temperatures, rather than the spark plug, ignite the air–fuel mixture.

_____ **2.** A diesel engine's efficiency is limited to lower compression ratios.

_____ **3.** Pressure and temperature increase proportionally when compression ratio rises.

_____ **4.** Normal cranking speeds for medium- and large-bore diesels are between 150 and 250 rpm.

_____ **5.** Engines that use high compression ratios also have increased mechanical efficiency.

_____ **6.** In diesel engines, intake air is throttled for the purpose of controlling power.

_____ **7.** During full-load conditions, when maximum quantities of fuel are injected, excess air dilutes the heat of combustion, which prevents damage to cylinder components and valves.

_____ **8.** When injection takes place later than normal, the injection event is referred to as having retarded timing.

_____ **9.** Indirect injection chambers use injectors with multi-orifice nozzles, which spray fuel in at high pressure.

_____ **10.** Offset combustion chambers create uneven piston crown temperatures.

_____ **11.** During ignition delay, the afterburn phase is characterized by uncontrolled combustion in a cylinder until all accumulated fuel is burned.

_____ **12.** Direct injection chambers do not allow the engine to warm up from idle; in fact, an engine will cool down below operating temperature when idled.

_____ **13.** Most engine manufacturers recommend that late-model diesel engines should idle for no more than 3 minutes.

_____ **14.** The Comet and the Ricardo Comet are types of direct injection combustion chambers.

_____ **15.** An integrated pressure-sensing glow plug includes a pressure sensor that measures cylinder pressure for closed-loop feedback of combustion pressure.

Fill in the Blank

Read each item carefully, and then complete the statement by filling in the missing word(s).

1. Antiknock additives, also known as _____ boosters, increase the temperature-pressure thresholds where preignition takes place and enables a spark ignition engine to use higher compression ratios.

2. Of all engines, the _____ engine is the most efficient combustion system due to its ability to extract the greatest amount of mechanical energy from burning fuel.

3. An engine with a high compression ratio extracts more _____ using the same amount of fuel compared to an engine with a lower compression ratio.

4. The time period between the beginning of fuel injection and the actual ignition of fuel in a combustion chamber is known as _____ _____.

5. Engines with very high compression ratios have the disadvantage of producing more _____ vibration than engines with lower compression ratios.

6. A _____ ratio occurs when the minimum quantity of air is present in the combustion chamber to completely burn all fuel with neither air nor fuel remaining after the combustion event.

7. The absence of a throttle plate increases the efficiency of diesel engines because it eliminates _____ _____, which is energy expended by an engine to move air in and exhaust out of the cylinders.

8. To maintain peak combustion pressure, the _____ of the injection event needs to vary with engine speed and load change.

9. Cylinder _____ is created by the shape of the combustion bowl.

10. A(n) _____ direct injection chamber uses two valves per cylinder.

11. The characteristic "knock" or combustion noise from diesel engines is caused by _____ _____.

12. When soot produced by partially burned fuel mixes with liquids, such as lube oil, it produces combustion _____, a black gooey liquid that leaks from exhaust manifold joints and exhaust pipes when engines are excessively idled.

13. A _____ injection of fuel 8–10° before the main injection event shortens, and can almost eliminate, ignition delay.

14. A _____-_____ nozzle uses multiple spray holes to distribute and atomize fuel.

15. To reduce wait-to-start times, an instant start _____ _____ system uses two heating elements connected together in series.

Labeling

Label the following diagrams with the correct terms.

1. Identify the components of an indirect diesel combustion chamber:

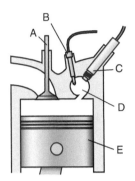

A. _____

B. _____

C. _____

D. _____

E. _____

2. Identify the components of a glow plug:

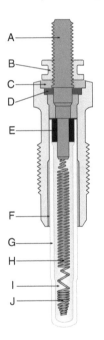

A. _____

B. _____

C. _____

D. _____

E. _____

F. _____

G. _____

H. _____

I. _____

J. _____

Skill Drills

Test your knowledge of skill drills by filling in the correct words in the photo captions.

1. Measuring Idle Time:

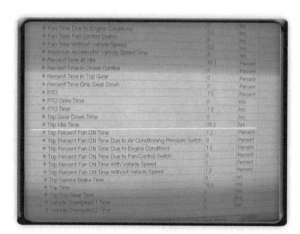

Step 1: Connect an _____ _____ _____ (OEM) service tool or other appropriate software or electronic service tool to the vehicle's _____ _____ _____ (DLC).

Step 2: Navigate to the _____ menu items that report trip _____ or trip _____.

Step 3: Locate and record _____ _____ as percentage of total engine _____ _____.

Step 4: If available, also report the _____ of time spent in _____ _____.

Step 5: Report your results and make _____ recommendations to reduce _____ _____.

2. Adjusting Idle Speed and Shut-Down Timer:

Step 1: Identify the correct _____ _____ for the _____.

Step 2: Using OEM _____ or other electronic _____ _____, navigate to the programmable engine _____ screen.

Step 3: Review the idle speed. Enter a new _____ _____ if the current setting is unacceptable. If a truck's mirrors _____ and other cab _____ are a problem, idle speed can be _____. If the vehicle easily _____ when engaging the _____ or runs rough due to too _____ an idle speed, increase the engine _____ speed at idle. Customer _____ may be required to make changes to customer programmable parameters.

Step 4:   Navigate to the programmable engine _____ screen for the idle _____ _____ _____. The time setting in _____ on this feature will shut down the _____, but the vehicle _____ system and _____ will remain active until the _____ _____ is turned off. When engine operation is required again, the driver must simply either push the _____ or turn the ignition to start the engine again. Touching the clutch or _____ _____ will reset the timer to _____ minutes.

Step 5:   A cold or hot _____ temperature _____ feature may accompany the shut-down timer adjustment. In very hot weather, the _____ _____ may be required by the driver; in very _____ weather, the engine may need to _____ to help keep the engine from _____ _____ too much.

3. Inspecting Air Intake Heaters and Glow Plugs:

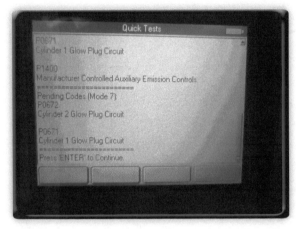

Step 1:   Obtain the _____ _____ to determine whether the fault is with the _____ _____ _____ or the _____ _____.

Step 2:   With the key off, disconnect the leads to the _____ _____ _____ and measure the _____ of the electrical heating elements. If any circuit has _____ resistance (generally no more than a few ohms) the circuit is _____.

Step 3:   If the air intake heater circuit resistance is satisfactory, switch the _____ _____ on while measuring the _____ to the air intake heater. To simulate a _____ _____ condition, the engine should be cold or the intake air and coolant _____ should be disconnected. A high amperage _____ will supply _____ _____ to the electric heating element.

Step 4:   If no _____ is supplied by the relay, check the relay _____, which is switched to _____ through the electronic _____ _____ (ECM). Use a _____ wire to _____ the terminal to determine if the relay will _____ and supply _____ to the heater.

Step 5:   Using a _____, check the battery _____ _____ to the _____ to determine whether current is supplied to the relay. Battery _____ should appear at the relay at all times.

Step 6:   For glow plugs, measure the electrical _____ of each plug. Connect the _____ _____ of a test _____ to the battery _____. When the _____ is touching the terminal tip of the plug, the test light will faintly glow if the glow plug has _____.

Step 7:   Report your findings and make _____ recommendations for _____.

Crossword Puzzle

Use the clues in the column to complete the puzzle.

Across

3. A small injection event taking place 8–10° before the main injection event.
5. A fuel nozzle that sprays fuel through a single hole.

Down

1. The temperature at which fuel will produce adequate vapor to ignite if exposed to an open source of ignition such as a spark or flame.
2. The time period between the beginning of fuel injection and actual ignition of fuel in a combustion chamber.
4. A chemical reaction between oxygen and fuel molecules in which heat is released.

ASE-Type Questions

Read each item carefully, and then select the best response.

_____ 1. Technician A says that a diesel engine's higher compression ratio helps mix air and fuel better. Technician B says that higher compression ratio engines generally require more cylinder head bolts. Who is correct?
   A. Technician A
   B. Technician B
   C. Both Technician A and Technician B
   D. Neither Technician A nor Technician B

_____ 2. Technician A says that diesel engines have greater torsional vibration because they have lean-burn combustion systems. Technician B says torsional vibration is not a problem when gear trains are moved to the rear of an engine. Who is correct?
   A. Technician A
   B. Technician B
   C. Both Technician A and Technician B
   D. Neither Technician A nor Technician B

_____ 3. Technician A says diesel engines supply only enough air to completely burn all the fuel in the combustion chamber. Technician B says diesel engines supply excess air, which lowers exhaust temperatures. Who is correct?
   A. Technician A
   B. Technician B
   C. Both Technician A and Technician B
   D. Neither Technician A nor Technician B

_____ 4. Technician A says that a diesel engine will maintain an operating temperature sufficient to heat a truck cab or bunk when idled at minimum idle speed. Technician B says that a diesel engine will cool down when idling and should be checked for overheating conditions only after loading the engine. Who is correct?
   A. Technician A
   B. Technician B
   C. Both Technician A and Technician B
   D. Neither Technician A nor Technician B

_____ 5. Technician A says the most efficient and powerful diesels have compression ratios between 23:1 and 25:1. Technician B says that compression ratios above 23:1 will reduce engine power output. Who is correct?
   A. Technician A
   B. Technician B
   C. Both Technician A and Technician B
   D. Neither Technician A nor Technician B

_____ 6. Technician A says that glow plugs are needed in some diesels to heat the air inside the cylinder to enable an engine to start. Technician B says that glow plugs are needed by some engines to vaporize fuel to get an engine to start. Who is correct?
   A. Technician A
   B. Technician B
   C. Both Technician A and Technician B
   D. Neither Technician A nor Technician B

_____ 7. Technician A says that DI combustion chambers have always been cleaner and quieter than IDI chambered engines. Technician B says IDI engines cannot turn as fast as DI engines and are harder to start. Who is correct?
   A. Technician A
   B. Technician B
   C. Both Technician A and Technician B
   D. Neither Technician A nor Technician B

_____ **8.** Technician A says that after an engine starts and warms up, white smoke indicates only an engine misfire condition. Technician B says that white smoke during cranking indicates coolant is leaking into a cylinder. Who is correct?
   A. Technician A
   B. Technician B
   C. Both Technician A and Technician B
   D. Neither Technician A nor Technician B

_____ **9.** Technician A says that IDI engines need to use multi-orifice nozzles to mix air and fuel well. Technician B says that only DI combustion chambers use multi-orifice nozzles. Who is correct?
   A. Technician A
   B. Technician B
   C. Both Technician A and Technician B
   D. Neither Technician A nor Technician B

_____ **10.** Technician A says pilot injection helps an engine to operate quietly by shortening the ignition delay period. Technician B says high-cetane fuel reduces combustion noise associated with ignition delay. Who is correct?
   A. Technician A
   B. Technician B
   C. Both Technician A and Technician B
   D. Neither Technician A nor Technician B

Cylinder Components

Chapter Review

The following activities have been designed to help you refresh your knowledge of this chapter. Your instructor may require you to complete some or all of these activities as a regular part of your training program. You are encouraged to complete any activity that your instructor does not assign as a way to enhance your learning.

Matching

Match the following terms with the correct description or example.

A. Articulating piston

B. Cam ground piston

C. Hypereutectic piston

D. Slipper skirt piston

E. Trunk piston

_____ **1.** A two-piece piston design that uses a separate aluminum skirt connected to an alloy steel crown through a piston pin.

_____ **2.** A piston design that is dimensionally longer than it is wide, with a full piston skirt.

_____ **3.** A piston design that has a portion of the skirt removed on both non-thrust sides of the piston to provide clearance for the crankshaft counterweights.

_____ **4.** An elliptically shaped piston that expands to a round, symmetrical shape after it is warmed up.

_____ **5.** A piston that has high silicon content (16–20% silicon).

Multiple Choice

Read each item carefully, and then select the best response.

_____ **1.** The US Environmental Protection Agency imposes new design features on cylinder components through legislated standards called _____.

A. thermal compliance guidelines

B. hardness standards

C. durability requirements

D. longevity standards

_____ **2.** The surface of the piston that slides directly against the cylinder wall to stabilize piston movement is called the _____.

A. crown

B. skirt

C. ring belt

D. shell

_____ **3.** The force of a piston against the side of a cylinder wall during the compression stroke produces _____.

A. major side thrust

B. cylinder glazing

C. minor side thrust

D. piston skirt scoring

_____ **4.** Single-piece alloyed steel pistons called _____ are the newest innovation in diesel piston design.
   A. trunk pistons
   B. cam ground pistons
   C. slipper skirt pistons
   D. MONOTHERM pistons

_____ **5.** Large operating clearances between a piston and cylinder wall can result in a noise that can be heard during warm-up and light-load operation called _____.
   A. piston slap
   B. bore squeal
   C. engine knock
   D. ring ping

_____ **6.** Which of the following piston ring alloys is the best material to use for compression rings?
   A. Aluminum
   B. Gray cast iron
   C. Ductile iron
   D. Steel

_____ **7.** Connecting rods are _____ to relieve stress risers and add additional fatigue strength.
   A. nitrogen hardened
   B. hypereutectic
   C. shot-peened
   D. anodized

_____ **8.** Prolonged idling of diesel engines causes _____.
   A. excessive soot loading
   B. slobber production
   C. cylinder glazing
   D. All of the above

_____ **9.** Oil baked into the cross-hatch finish of the cylinder walls that prevents the piston rings from effectively sealing is called _____.
   A. cylinder glazing
   B. patina
   C. mirroring
   D. soot loading

_____ **10.** When replacing piston rings, the end gaps of all piston rings should be placed _____ apart in a three-ring pack.
   A. 60°
   B. 90°
   C. 120°
   D. 180°

True/False

If you believe the statement to be more true than false, write the letter "T" in the space provided. If you believe the statement to be more false than true, write the letter "F".

_____ **1.** EPA standards require that heavy-duty diesels must have a useful life of 15 years or 185,000 miles (297,729 km).

_____ **2.** Slipper skirt pistons enable the use of shorter connecting rods, which permits the manufacture of vertically smaller, lighter, more compact engines.

_____ **3.** Cast pistons are able to withstand higher cylinder pressures and temperatures than forged pistons.

_____ **4.** Aluminum, when heated, will expand four to seven times more than ferrous metal.

_____ **5.** Piston rings transfer as much as two-thirds of the heat from the pistons to the cylinder walls.

_____ **6.** Refinements to ring design, cylinder bore finishing techniques, and engine oils have helped produce engines that can operate for more than a million miles of use before the piston rings need to be replaced.

_____ **7.** Chrome ring face material is primarily used to retain oil for lubrication.

_____ **8.** The rectangular ring is the ring shape of choice for most engine manufacturers today.

_____ **9.** The piston pin bore is usually offset toward the major side thrust portion of the cylinder.

_____ **10.** Proper alignment of the connecting rod and cap is made by matching up the markings on the cap and rod to identify the assembled position.

_____ **11.** Split fracture connecting rods allow the rod and cap to be separated along a predetermined fracture line.

_____ **12.** The best method for removing hard carbon deposits from aluminum pistons is to buff them using a grinder with a wire wheel attachment.

_____ **13.** The presence of vertical cracks in the piston bowl or piston pin bore usually indicates a bonding problem between the piston skirt and crown.

_____ **14.** A break-in period is needed to seat rings as well as other engine parts, including bearings, valve guides, piston pins, and cam bushings.

_____ **15.** A compression test is used to measure the percentage of gas leakage past the piston rings.

Fill in the Blank

Read each item carefully, and then complete the statement by filling in the missing word(s).

1. The _____, or top of the piston, is subjected to cylinder pressure and tremendous heat.

2. Additional piston material, called the pin _____, reinforces the area around the pin.

3. Eliminating the dead air of the _____ _____ area can lower hydrocarbon exhaust emissions by as much as 50%.

4. A _____ piston is made from aluminum alloy billets that are stamped into shape using dies.

5. A micro-finish _____, or machining of fine lines, is commonly used on forged piston skirts to retain oil.

6. An _____-_____ insert reinforces the top ring piston land, which can prevent the top of the weaker aluminum of the ring land from fracturing and breaking away.

7. A(n) _____ ring seals in compression gases that escape past the top rings and assists in oil control.

8. The _____ _____ ring is usually a low-tension type of ring and has no significant gas pressure acting upon it.

9. A trapezoidal _____ _____ is most commonly used with a full floating piston pin.

10. Select fit rod sets can be identified by the _____ marks that uniquely identify the weight variation of the rod.

11. High _____ _____ thickens the oil and reduces the required time or distance service intervals between oil changes.

12. When new rings are installed into a cylinder, a new _____-_____ finish needs to be made on the cylinder wall.

13. When liquids enter the combustion chamber and eliminate the little clearance volume remaining in a diesel engine, a condition called _____ _____ occurs.

14. Pressure in the crankcase is measured in inches (centimeters) of water column using a _____ gauge.

15. The precision measuring tool used to measure taper wear in a cylinder is called a _____ _____ gauge.

Labeling

Label the following diagrams with the correct terms.

1. Identify the components of a typical articulated piston and connecting rod:

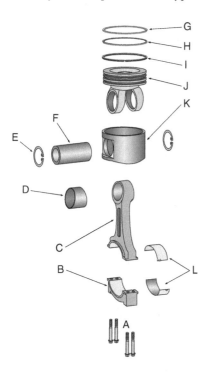

A. _____

B. _____

C. _____

D. _____

E. _____

F. _____

G. _____

H. _____

I. _____

J. _____

K. _____

L. _____

2. Identify the features of a connecting rod:

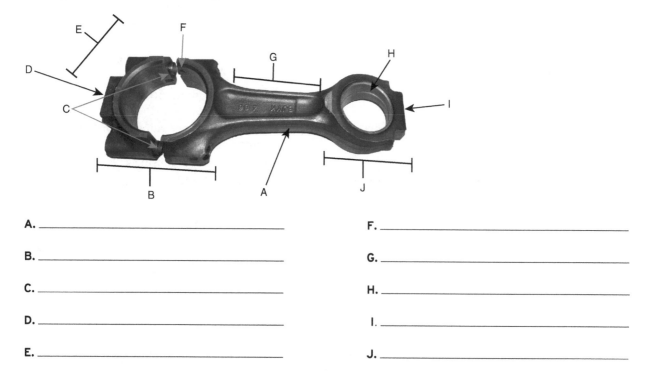

A. _____

B. _____

C. _____

D. _____

E. _____

F. _____

G. _____

H. _____

I. _____

J. _____

Crossword Puzzle

Use the clues in the column to complete the puzzle.

Across

3. The area between the piston crown and cylinder wall above the top compression ring.

4. A process used to harden aluminum by electrochemically reacting oxygen with aluminum.

5. A condition where dirt is drawn into an engine; this causes premature abrasive wear of the cylinder walls and rings.

Down

1. A property that allows two metals to slide against one another with minimal friction or wear.

2. The process of hardening a metal's surface by heating the metal and quenching it with cyanide salts.

ASE-Type Questions

Read each item carefully, and then select the best response.

_____ 1. Technician A says that excessive idling of a diesel engine will cause cylinder walls to glaze and piston rings to stick. Technician B says idling an engine regularly for long periods of time causes piston rings to break. Who is correct?
   A. Technician A
   B. Technician B
   C. Both Technician A and Technician B
   D. Neither Technician A nor Technician B

_____ 2. Technician A says that oil control rings are designed to scrape as much oil as possible from the cylinder walls. Technician B says oil control rings leave a metered amount of oil on the cylinder walls. Who is correct?
   A. Technician A
   B. Technician B
   C. Both Technician A and Technician B
   D. Neither Technician A nor Technician B

_____ 3. Technician A says compression rings in a diesel are rectangular to extend engine life. Technician B says that the top compression rings have a barrel face to provide effective sealing. Who is correct?
   A. Technician A
   B. Technician B
   C. Both Technician A and Technician B
   D. Neither Technician A nor Technician B

_____ 4. Technician A says that piston ring markings identify the type of ring and its location in a piston ring groove. Technician B says ring markings are used to ensure the rings are installed facing downward. Who is correct?
   A. Technician A
   B. Technician B
   C. Both Technician A and Technician B
   D. Neither Technician A nor Technician B

_____ 5. Technician A says that after rebuilding an engine, the engine should be operated at low load and low speed to prevent any catastrophic damage and help break in an engine. Technician B says that an engine should be operated under a heavy load as soon as possible after ring replacement. Who is correct?
   A. Technician A
   B. Technician B
   C. Both Technician A and Technician B
   D. Neither Technician A nor Technician B

_____ 6. After discovering broken rings in an engine, Technician A says that the rings were most likely broken due to improper installation. Technician B says the rings were broken due to excessive cylinder taper. Who is correct?
   A. Technician A
   B. Technician B
   C. Both Technician A and Technician B
   D. Neither Technician A nor Technician B

_____ 7. Technician A says that most high horsepower diesel engines use trunk type pistons. Technician B says that most high horsepower diesel engines today use pistons with steel crowns. Who is correct?
   A. Technician A
   B. Technician B
   C. Both Technician A and Technician B
   D. Neither Technician A nor Technician B

_____ 8. Technician A says a scuffed piston skirt and burnt piston crown in one cylinder of a recently overhauled engine is likely due to a damaged or improperly aligned oil cooler nozzle. Technician B says the engine was overheated. Who is correct?
   A. Technician A
   B. Technician B
   C. Both Technician A and Technician B
   D. Neither Technician A nor Technician B

_____ **9.** While discussing the cause of a cracked piston crown with a vertical crack through the inner edge of the combustion bowl, Technician A suggests that the piston has a manufacturing defect. Technician B suggests excessive use of starting fluid cracked the piston. Who is correct?

    A. Technician A

    B. Technician B

    C. Both Technician A and Technician B

    D. Neither Technician A nor Technician B

_____ **10.** Technician A says that a compression test of an engine's cylinders is the best method to use to diagnose a worn-out engine. Technician B says that measuring crankcase pressure is the best method to identify a worn-out engine. Who is correct?

    A. Technician A

    B. Technician B

    C. Both Technician A and Technician B

    D. Neither Technician A nor Technician B

Cylinder Blocks and Crankshafts

Chapter Review

The following activities have been designed to help you refresh your knowledge of this chapter. Your instructor may require you to complete some or all of these activities as a regular part of your training program. You are encouraged to complete any activity that your instructor does not assign as a way to enhance your learning.

Matching

Match the following terms with the correct description or example.

  A. Deep-skirt block   **D.** Tunnel-bore block

  B. Ladder-frame block   **E.** Warp anchor

  C. Parent bore block

_____ **1.** A block design that has holes cast and bored in the block for the cylinders with the pistons inserted directly into these holes; also known as a no-sleeve block.

_____ **2.** A block design that has the cylinder head and the cylinder block bolted together by tie bolts; sliding steel sleeves, which are locked in the block, accept the cylinder head bolt from one side and the tie bolt from the other.

_____ **3.** A block design with sides that extend exactly to the centerline of the crankshaft bearings and a separate, additional section that attaches to the crankcase and the oil pan and incorporates the main bearing caps into one unit.

_____ **4.** The speeding up and slowing down of the crankshaft caused by alternating compression and power strokes of the engine cylinder.

_____ **5.** A block configuration with a bottom edge that extends well below the crankshaft's centerline.

Multiple Choice

Read each item carefully, and then select the best response.

_____ **1.** Metal made from iron ore with a carbon content of 3–5% is known as _____.
    A. cast iron
    B. carbonated iron
    C. crystalized iron
    D. graphite iron

_____ **2.** Holes made in a block to flush sand out of small passageways during casting are called _____.
    A. core plugs
    B. casting plugs
    C. frost plugs
    D. Either A or C

_____ **3.** An engine block building technique that starts with squeezing powdered iron alloys into molds at high pressures and then heating them to bond the metal particles together is called _____.
    A. compacted graphite iron
    B. induction hardening
    C. sintered graphite
    D. Either A or C

_____ **4.** The distance of rod journal offset from the main bearing journals is known as the _____.
   A. stroke
   B. throw
   C. radius
   D. Either A or C

_____ **5.** A six-cylinder engine will have _____ of spacing between the rod journals.
   A. 45°
   B. 90°
   C. 120°
   D. 180°

_____ **6.** A circular-shaped machining applied to the rod and main journal surface between the journal and the crankshaft cheek is called a _____.
   A. fillet radius
   B. counterweight
   C. elastomer dampener
   D. vibration dampener

_____ **7.** The hardening process that involves heating the shaft and introducing cyanide salt or liquid into the heating chamber with the crankshaft is called _____.
   A. induction hardening
   B. nitriding
   C. sintering
   D. Either A or C

_____ **8.** Vibration dampeners that use rubber as the primary material to absorb harmonic vibrations and reduce torsional stress on the crankshaft are called _____ dampeners.
   A. viscous
   B. ductile
   C. malleable
   D. elastomer

_____ **9.** The primary purpose of the _____ is to provide inertia between power impulses to keep the engine rotating.
   A. flywheel
   B. main bearing
   C. crankshaft
   D. counterbalance shaft

_____ **10.** A variation of the deep-skirt block known as a _____ block uses additional horizontally placed bolts to connect the crankcase walls of the block to the main bearing caps.
   A. cross-bolted
   B. tie-bolted
   C. bolster-bolted
   D. All of the above

_____ **11.** Honing stones are used to produce a _____ finish on the cylinder walls.
   A. symmetrical
   B. polished
   C. cross-hatch
   D. matte

_____ **12.** The ability of a bearing to absorb particle contamination is known as _____.
   A. conformability
   B. embeddability
   C. compatibility
   D. fatigue strength

_____ **13.** The difference in height between the bearing and the cap or web is called bearing _____.
   A. crush
   B. thrust
   C. protrusion
   D. spread

_____ **14.** Top-stop flange breakage is caused by _____.
  A. improper torqueing of the cylinder head
  B. improper positioning of the head gasket fire ring
  C. uneven flange height above the deck
  D. All of the above
_____ **15.** Cylinder taper is measured using a _____.
  A. micrometer
  B. dial bore gauge
  C. inside telescoping gauge
  D. Both A and C

True/False

If you believe the statement to be more true than false, write the letter "T" in the space provided. If you believe the statement to be more false than true, write the letter "F".

_____ **1.** Moving the gear train to the rear of the engine can dramatically reduce gear train noise.
_____ **2.** Cast iron is as strong as steel.
_____ **3.** After rough casting, diesel blocks are often stored at high temperatures for a day or two to heat treat and "season" them.
_____ **4.** Primary balance is achieved when the movement of one piston counterbalances the movement of another.
_____ **5.** The two most common processes used to harden bearing surfaces of the crankshaft are induction hardening and nitriding.
_____ **6.** Balance rotates in opposition to one another at twice the engine speed to counter secondary imbalance forces.
_____ **7.** Once a dry cylinder sleeve has been inserted and pressed into place it can no longer be removed.
_____ **8.** Mid-stop liners occupy less overall space than top-stops allowing the block to be a few millimeters shorter.
_____ **9.** During normal operating conditions, a continuous supply of clean oil will keep the shaft and bearing surfaces separated due to the hydrodynamic wedge.
_____ **10.** The ability of a bearing to carry a load is known as conformability.
_____ **11.** Thrust bearings are used to control endplay in a crankshaft.
_____ **12.** Excessive skirt clearance will result in piston knock or slap.
_____ **13.** Diesel engine cylinder walls wear out faster than their gasoline engine counterparts.
_____ **14.** Most bearing failures are caused by problems with lubrication.
_____ **15.** Insufficient endplay can be the result of a misaligned main bearing cap.

Fill in the Blank

Read each item carefully, and then complete the statement by filling in the missing word(s).

1. The transmission, cylinder head(s), and all other major engine parts are bolted or connected to the _____ _____.

2. When used in small, six-cylinder diesel engines, _____ can eliminate more than 77 lb (35 kg) of weight compared to a similar engine block made from cast iron.

3. Coatings of tool-grade hardness iron carbon alloys can be achieved by a plasma-spraying technique developed by Mercedes-Benz called _____ technology.

4. When the crankshaft counterweights offset the weight of the piston and connecting rod assembly, _____ balance is achieved.

5. The main purpose of the _____ in a reciprocating engine is to convert the linear motion of the connecting rod assemblies into rotational movement.

6. The crankshaft is supported along its centerline by the main bearing _____.

7. The mass of the _____ can substantially suppress torsional vibration at its end of the crankshaft.

8. Silicone fluid is used in _____ dampeners to tune out harmonic and torsional vibrations.

9. A _____ vibration absorber provides torsional control by producing forces that directly cancel the forces that produce torsional vibration.

10. A number of medium-duty engines incorporate specialized torsional vibration dampening springs in the flywheel construction called _____ _____ flywheels.

11. The major advantage of _____ _____ liners is the direct contact of coolant with the sleeve that enables rapid heat transfer from the cylinder to the coolant.

12. Detroit Diesel's DD series engines use _____ bearings.

13. A measuring tool that consists of a strip of oil-soluble plastic material and packaging printed with a thickness gauge is called _____.

14. Measuring and adjusting _____ is one of the most critical operations when rebuilding a sleeved engine.

15. Long stoke engines will have more wear mid-stoke as well due to a higher amount of _____ thrust.

Labeling

Label the following diagrams with the correct terms.

1. Identify the components of a crankshaft:

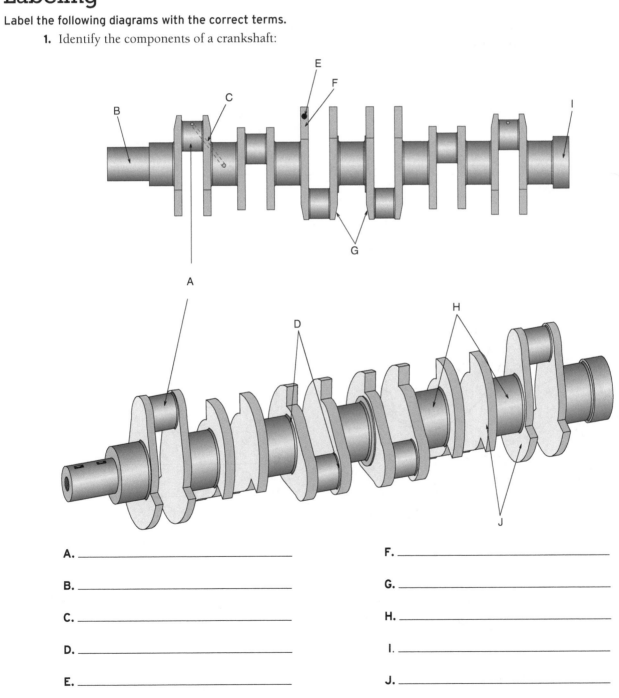

A. _____   F. _____

B. _____   G. _____

C. _____   H. _____

D. _____   I. _____

E. _____   J. _____

2. Identify the components of a dual mass flywheel:

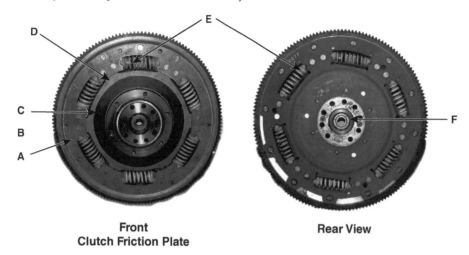

Front
Clutch Friction Plate

Rear View

A. _____   D. _____

B. _____   E. _____

C. _____   F. _____

3. Identify the parts of a set of main bearings:

Main Bearings

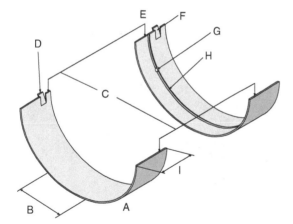

A. _____

B. _____

C. _____

D. _____

E. _____

F. _____

G. _____

H. _____

I. _____

Skill Drills

Test your knowledge of skill drills by filling in the correct words in the photo captions.

1. Measuring Liner Protrusion

Step 1:   Inspect the liner _____ for _____, cracks, and the correct machined depth. Generally, the machined depth is only measured if there has been a problem with _____ or the counterbore has been _____.

Step 2:   Thoroughly clean the _____ and _____. Any dirt or other material will prevent the liner from _____ properly.

Step 3:   Install and lubricate the _____ _____. Seals are lubricated only after they are installed to prevent _____ and _____ when the liner is installed. Slide a small _____ beneath the _____ and move around the liner circumference several times to make sure the _____ is not _____. Generally, seals are not lubricated with petroleum-based products; this prevents rapid _____ if the seals are not oil compatible. _____ is often used as an effective lubricant.

Step 4:   Insert the _____ into the _____ _____. Do not force the liners into the block. Instead, use the OEM prescribed tool to _____ the liner into the block. Hammering or hitting the flange can **dent** the flange surface, which causes a _____ _____. The OEM prescribed tools will protect the liner _____ and sealing surfaces from damage. They can be used to install the liner _____ into the _____ and, in some cases, _____ the liner into the block.

Step 5:   Clamp the _____ in the _____ with the OEM prescribed _____ or _____ _____, following the manufacturer's procedures.

Step 6:   Using a _____ _____ and _____, measure the liner protrusion in _____ or _____ places. Protrusion is measured as the distance between the _____ _____ and a very specific point on the _____; this point varies between _____.

Step 7:   Compare the measured _____ against the manufacturer's specifications values. Variation from side to side should not exceed _____" (0.025 mm). If it does, it is usually due to a piece of _____ beneath the flange or a _____ O-ring. Remove, check, and reinstall the liner if the liner variations are _____ from side to side. Install a selective _____ beneath any _____ _____ that sits too low.

2. Measuring Crankshaft Endplay

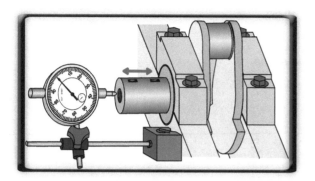

Step 1: Place a dial indicator _____ _____ on the engine block. Place the
_____ _____ on the vibration _____.

Step 2: If the vehicle is equipped with a _____ transmission, push on the _____.
With the clutch depressed, _____ the dial indicator. Alternatively, a _____
_____ between the _____ and flywheel _____ _____
inspection hole can be used to pull the flywheel _____.

Step 3: Push the _____ forward using a pry bar between the flywheel and the _____
_____ in the flywheel housing.

Step 4: Observe and record the measurement on the _____ _____. Specifications are
generally in the range of _____–_____" (0.102–0.483 mm). The specifications
may seem large, but bearing _____ must be wide enough to allow _____ to flow
on both sides of two _____ _____ or bearing _____.

Step 5: Make service recommendations to _____ and _____ the _____
_____ or remove the _____ _____ and perform further inspection
of the engine.

Crossword Puzzle

Use the clues in the column to complete the puzzle.

Across

3. A vibration that sends pressure waves moving back and forth along the crankshaft.
4. Two separate spring-loaded gears incorporated into a single unit to reduce gear rattle caused by torsional vibration.
5. The speeding up and slowing down of the crankshaft caused by alternating compression and power strokes of the engine cylinder.

Down

1. A heat treatment process that involves passing alternating electric current through coils of heavy-gauge wire surrounding the material to be hardened; through magnetic induction, heat is produced in the metal, which is then quenched with water to produce a hard, wear-resistant metal surface.
2. Pinholes produced in cylinder block walls, heads, and liner sleeves as a result of the collapse of tiny water vapor bubbles formed when coolant vaporizes on hot cylinder wall surfaces.

ASE-Type Questions

Read each item carefully, and then select the best response.

_____ 1. While examining a coolant leak from a weep hole on the side of a Detroit S60 engine, Technician A says the leak is caused by a leaking liner O-ring. Technician B says the coolant leak is due to cavitation of the cylinder block. Who is correct?
   A. Technician A
   B. Technician B
   C. Both Technician A and Technician B
   D. Neither Technician A nor Technician B

_____ 2. Technician A says that mid-stop liners help reduce engine block weight. Technician B says half-stop liners are used to minimize the likelihood of a coolant leak into the engine oil. Who is correct?
   A. Technician A
   B. Technician B
   C. Both Technician A and Technician B
   D. Neither Technician A nor Technician B

_____ 3. Technician A says that when using Plastigauge, Plastigauge that becomes wider indicates a smaller oil clearance between a crankshaft and main bearing. Technician B says the Plastigauge will become narrower when bearing oil clearances are smaller. Who is correct?
   A. Technician A
   B. Technician B
   C. Both Technician A and Technician B
   D. Neither Technician A nor Technician B

_____ 4. While installing new rod bearing inserts, the shells protruded very slightly above the margin of the bearing cap. Technician A says this is normal. Technician B says that wrong bearings are producing this result. Who is correct?
   A. Technician A
   B. Technician B
   C. Both Technician A and Technician B
   D. Neither Technician A nor Technician B

_____ 5. Technician A says that rear gear trains are used to shorten the length of the engine block. Technician B says that rear gear trains reduce engine vibration. Who is correct?
   A. Technician A
   B. Technician B
   C. Both Technician A and Technician B
   D. Neither Technician A nor Technician B

_____ 6. Technician A says that liner protrusion can be measured with a flat bar and feeler blades. Technician B says a dial indicator mounted on a sled should be used. Who is correct?
   A. Technician A
   B. Technician B
   C. Both Technician A and Technician B
   D. Neither Technician A nor Technician B

_____ 7. While examining a heavy, flat steel plate bolted to the oil pan rails and main bearing caps, Technician A suggests it is used to stiffen the crankcase to reduce torsional twisting. Technician B says the plate is used to prevent oil from splashing up onto the cylinder walls and causing high oil consumption. Who is correct?
   A. Technician A
   B. Technician B
   C. Both Technician A and Technician B
   D. Neither Technician A nor Technician B

_____ 8. Technician A says that crankshaft endplay is controlled by the fillet radius of the crankshaft journals. Technician B says that the main bearings limit crankshaft endplay. Who is correct?
   A. Technician A
   B. Technician B
   C. Both Technician A and Technician B
   D. Neither Technician A nor Technician B

_____ **9.** Technician A says that a defective vibration dampener will cause the accessory drive belts of an engine to jump off the drive pulleys. Technician B says a defective vibration dampener will cause the crankshaft or even the camshaft to break. Who is correct?

A. Technician A

B. Technician B

C. Both Technician A and Technician B

D. Neither Technician A nor Technician B

_____ **10.** Technician A says that the upper shell of a main bearing is identified by a marking on the back of the shell. Technician B says that the upper main bearing shell will always have a hole in it. Who is correct?

A. Technician A

B. Technician B

C. Both Technician A and Technician B

D. Neither Technician A nor Technician B

Cylinder Heads and Valve Train Mechanisms

Chapter Review

The following activities have been designed to help you refresh your knowledge of this chapter. Your instructor may require you to complete some or all of these activities as a regular part of your training program. You are encouraged to complete any activity that your instructor does not assign as a way to enhance your learning.

Matching

Match the following terms with the correct description or example.

A. Cross-flow cylinder head

B. In-block camshaft

C. Overhead camshaft engine

D. Parallel flow head

E. Reverse-flow cylinder head

_____ **1.** An engine that has only the valves, rocker levers, and bridges located in the cylinder heads above the piston; the camshaft is located in the engine block.

_____ **2.** A head design that features intake and exhaust manifolds on the same side of the engine and short, large ports that are joined together to provide a more compact engine design with adequate airflow to the cylinders.

_____ **3.** A head design with the intake and exhaust manifolds located on opposite sides of an inline engine to improve engine breathing characteristics.

_____ **4.** An engine that has the camshaft located in the cylinder head.

_____ **5.** A cylinder head with no exhaust manifolds on the outside of the cylinder head; instead, short exhaust runs are fed directly to the turbocharger located in the V between the cylinder banks.

Multiple Choice

Read each item carefully, and then select the best response.

_____ **1.** Cylinder heads are classified by _____.
- **A.** exhaust and intake port arrangement
- **B.** type of material
- **C.** valve train arrangement
- **D.** All of the above

_____ **2.** The _____ head is sometimes referred to as the uniflow design
- **A.** reverse-flow
- **B.** cross-flow
- **C.** parallel flow
- **D.** variable flow

_____ **3.** What are the most common type of intake and exhaust valves used in diesel engines?
- **A.** Check valves
- **B.** Poppet valves
- **C.** Butterfly valves
- **D.** Gate valves

_____ **4.** Valve seats have a minimum of _____ angle cuts to ensure good gas flow and proper transfer of heat from the valve face.
  A. two
  B. three
  C. four
  D. five

_____ **5.** A _____ converts the linear change of the cam profile to the reciprocating motion used to open and close the valves.
  A. rocker arm
  B. lifter
  C. pushrods
  D. valve bridge

_____ **6.** The lobes on a camshaft are used to control _____.
  A. valve timing
  B. valve lift
  C. valve duration
  D. All of the above

_____ **7.** Cylinder head bolts use specialized _____ threads like those used to retain main and rod bearing caps.
  A. tapered
  B. rolled
  C. split
  D. squared

_____ **8.** The _____ method requires initial bolt tightening with a torque wrench and then turning the bolt an additional number of degrees past this point.
  A. torque-turn
  B. torque to yield
  C. torque plus angle
  D. Either A or C

_____ **9.** An estimated 80% of new engines are designed with _____ gaskets as standard equipment.
  A. graphite
  B. fiber-based
  C. multilayer steel
  D. neoprene

_____ **10.** Which of the following methods is used to check cylinder heads for cracks?
  A. Dye penetrant
  B. Pressure testing
  C. Magnetic flux
  D. All of the above

True/False

If you believe the statement to be more true than false, write the letter "T" in the space provided. If you believe the statement to be more false than true, write the letter "F".

_____ **1.** Cylinder heads can't be produced using aluminum due to their tendency to warp, crack, or melt when overheated.

_____ **2.** The reverse-flow cylinder head is the most popular intake and exhaust port arrangement.

_____ **3.** Single-piece cylinder head castings are more likely to experience head gasket failure at the rear of the engine where coolant temperatures are hottest.

_____ **4.** Exhaust valves are usually larger than intake valves.

_____ **5.** All premium diesel engines use replaceable valve seat inserts.

_____ **6.** Rotating a valve slightly each time it opens can eliminate localized hot spots that can lead to valve burning.

_____ **7.** Rocker arms are sometimes called crossheads, yokes, or bridges.

_____ **8.** Overhead camshaft engines often use one camshaft for the intake valves and a second camshaft for the exhaust valves.

_____ **9.** Torque to yield bolts can be reused if they do not show signs of pitting, corrosion, or thread damage.

_____ **10.** Most valve bridges and crossheads are adjustable.

Fill in the Blank

Read each item carefully, and then complete the statement by filling in the missing word(s).

1. When made from _____ _____ _____, diesel cylinder heads have approximately the same weight as aluminum but also possess higher strength and rigidity than steel.

2. The shape of the _____ _____ of most diesels is designed to impart a twisting or spinning motion to the air as it enters the cylinder to increase turbulence.

3. Another term for an _____-_____ camshaft arrangement is a pushrod engine because the camshaft actuates the valves through a pushrod and rocker lever.

4. Valves are located in _____ that are either cast into the cylinder head or removable.

5. A valve _____ holds the valve closed on the seat and maintains tension on the valve train when the valve is open.

6. A large valve _____ helps create a power profile that delivers higher torque at high speed and heavy load.

7. A _____ transmits the cam actuation force from the followers to the rocker levers.

8. The _____ requires correct timing to the engine to ensure the valves open at precisely the correct time in relation to piston position.

9. The size, number, and grade of _____ are increased in four-stroke diesels in comparison to two-stroke diesels and spark-ignition engines.

10. A traditional technique for clamping cylinder heads to the block requires the use of a torque wrench and a _____ pattern sequence for torqueing the head bolts down in the correct sequence.

Labeling

Label the following diagrams with the correct terms.

1. Identify the major engine components:

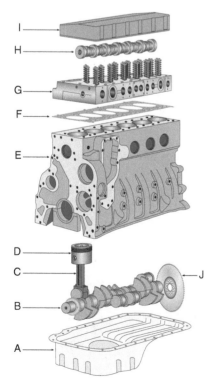

A. _____

B. _____

C. _____

D. _____

E. _____

F. _____

G. _____

H. _____

I. _____

J. _____

2. Identify the type of intake and port arrangement:

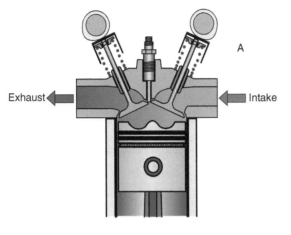

Exhaust   Intake

A

A. _____

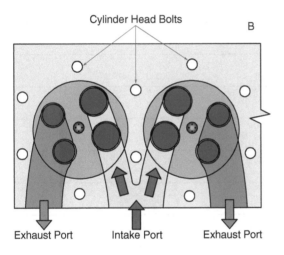

Cylinder Head Bolts   B

Exhaust Port   Intake Port   Exhaust Port

B. _____

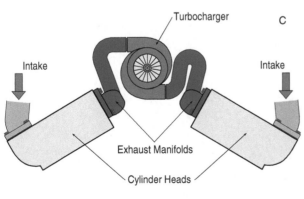

Turbocharger   C

Intake   Intake

Exhaust Manifolds

Cylinder Heads

C. _____

3. Identify the components of an overhead camshaft valve train:

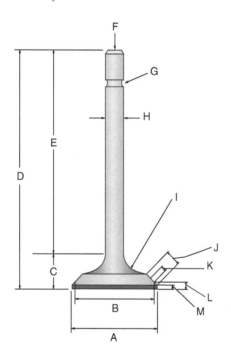

A. _____

B. _____

C. _____

D. _____

E. _____

F. _____

G. _____

4. Identify the nomenclature associated with poppet valves:

A. _____

B. _____

C. _____

D. _____

E. _____

F. _____

G. _____

H. _____

I. _____

J. _____

K. _____

L. _____

M. _____

5. Identify the nomenclature of a camshaft lobe:

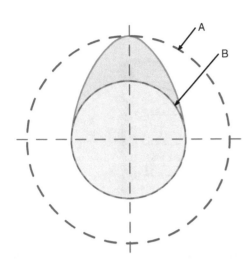 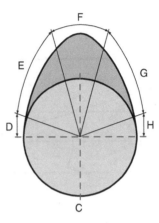

A. _____

B. _____

C. _____

D. _____

E. _____

F. _____

G. _____

H. _____

Skill Drills

Test your knowledge of skill drills by filling in the correct words in the photo captions.

1. Measuring Cylinder Head Warpage:

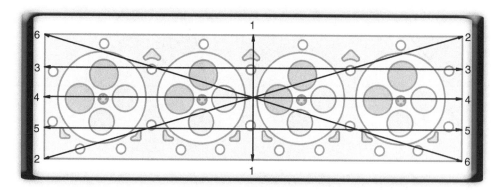

Step 1: Thoroughly clean the cylinder head and block deck surfaces with _____. Remove any foreign material, _____, or _____ with a cleaning pad. Choose a cleaning pad that removes soft material but not _____; this will protect the _____ surfaces from damage that more aggressive abrasives and tools can cause.

Step 2: Use a purpose-made straight edge. Lay the straight edge along the flat _____ _____ surface. Try to slide a _____ gauge or _____ gauge between the straight edge and the _____. Any gaps between the straight edge and the surface indicate _____ of the head _____. A general specification allows no more than 0.006" (0.152 mm) of warpage in _____" (30 cm) of casting surface when using MLS _____. This means a _____" (0.152 mm) thickness gauge should generally be used to check for warpage, but check the manufacturer's specifications to be sure. Much smaller _____ are permissible on smaller _____ used in automobile engines.

Step 3: Check for warpage in the _____ and _____ directions as well as across the _____ _____. Follow the figure when measuring.

Step 4: If the _____ blade slipped beneath the _____ _____ and there is little resistance when pulling on the blade, it indicates a _____ or _____ of the head surface. If the clearance is beyond _____, make a service recommendation for the cylinder head to be _____ by a machine shop. Note, though, that due to the small clearance space between _____ and _____ on diesel engines, very little, if any, material can be machined from the _____ _____ to correct warpage. Always check specifications for head _____ if a head has been machined.

Step 5: Check the cylinder block _____ using the same procedures as checking the cylinder _____.

Crossword Puzzle

Use the clues in the column to complete the puzzle.

Across

3. A material produced from powdered iron alloys squeezed into molds at high pressures and then heated to bond the metal particles together; also known as sintered graphite.

4. The speeding up and slowing down of the crankshaft caused by alternating compression and power strokes of the engine cylinder.

5. The component that maintains the seal around the combustion chamber at peak operating temperatures and pressures and keeps air, coolants, and engine oil in their respective passages over all temperatures and pressures.

Down

1. Two separate spring-loaded gears incorporated into a single unit to reduce gear rattle caused by torsional vibration.

2. The angle in crankshaft degrees that both the intake and exhaust valves are open; overlap occurs at the end of the exhaust stroke and the beginning of the intake stroke.

ASE-Type Questions

Read each item carefully, and then select the best response.

_____ **1.** Technician A says that the cam gear rotates two times faster than the crank gear. Technician B says the cam gear rotates at half the engine speed. Who is correct?
   A. Technician A
   B. Technician B
   C. Both Technician A and Technician B
   D. Neither Technician A nor Technician B

_____ **2.** While examining a valve spring from an engine that is being overhauled, Technician A says that valve springs should be checked for free length and cracks. Technician B says the spring should be checked for compressed spring pressure, nicks, and straightness. Who is correct?
   A. Technician A
   B. Technician B
   C. Both Technician A and Technician B
   D. Neither Technician A nor Technician B

_____ **3.** While installing a cylinder head, Technician A says the threads of cylinder head bolts must be lubricated before installation. Technician B says that only the underside of the bolt head requires lubrication and the threads only need to be clean. Who is correct?
   A. Technician A
   B. Technician B
   C. Both Technician A and Technician B
   D. Neither Technician A nor Technician B

_____ **4.** An engine has arrived at the shop with a popping noise through the intake manifold. Technician A says that it is likely a worn-out exhaust cam lobe causing the problem. Technician B says it is a worn camshaft intake lobe that is likely the problem. Who is correct?
   A. Technician A
   B. Technician B
   C. Both Technician A and Technician B
   D. Neither Technician A nor Technician B

_____ **5.** When adjusting the valve clearances on the engine, Technician A says the valves are closed when the valve lifter or follower is on the inner base circle of the camshaft lobe. Technician B says that valves are always adjusted when closed while the lifter or follower is on the camshaft lobe nose. Who is correct?
   A. Technician A
   B. Technician B
   C. Both Technician A and Technician B
   D. Neither Technician A nor Technician B

_____ **6.** Technician A says that before reusing any head bolt it should be inspected for nicks and pitting. Technician B says the service manual should be consulted before reusing because some bolts can only be used once. Who is correct?
   A. Technician A
   B. Technician B
   C. Both Technician A and Technician B
   D. Neither Technician A nor Technician B

_____ **7.** Technician A says that rear gear trains are used on engines because they operate with less noise. Technician B says that rear gear trains are used because they have less wear than a front gear train mechanism. Who is correct?
   A. Technician A
   B. Technician B
   C. Both Technician A and Technician B
   D. Neither Technician A nor Technician B

_____ **8.** Technician A says that overhead cam engines with unit injectors can provide the greatest actuation force for highest injection pressures. Technician B says that pushrod engines using a low-mounted camshaft can provide the same force as an overhead camshaft engine to its unit injectors. Who is correct?

    A. Technician A

    B. Technician B

    C. Both Technician A and Technician B

    D. Neither Technician A nor Technician B

_____ **9.** Technician A says that fiber gaskets are the best and most commonly used gaskets in modern diesel engines. Technician B says that MLS gaskets are the most commonly used head gaskets. Who is correct?

    A. Technician A

    B. Technician B

    C. Both Technician A and Technician B

    D. Neither Technician A nor Technician B

_____ **10.** Technician A says that a leaking head gasket can be detected by checking for overpressurization of coolant and excessive gas bubbles in the engine coolant. Technician B says that it is best to remove the oil pan and pressurize the cooling system to check for a head gasket leak. Who is correct?

    A. Technician A

    B. Technician B

    C. Both Technician A and Technician B

    D. Neither Technician A nor Technician B

Diesel Engine Lubrication Systems

Chapter Review

The following activities have been designed to help you refresh your knowledge of this chapter. Your instructor may require you to complete some or all of these activities as a regular part of your training program. You are encouraged to complete any activity that your instructor does not assign as a way to enhance your learning.

Matching

Match the following terms with the correct description or example.

A. Additives   **D.** Polyalphaolefin (PAO)

B. Base stock   **E.** Viscosity

C. Multigrade oil

_____ **1.** A blend of a several different oils with different viscosities.

_____ **2.** A measure of oil's resistance to flow.

_____ **3.** A manmade base stock used in place of mineral oil.

_____ **4.** Chemicals that improve the original properties of the base stock oil.

_____ **5.** The raw mineral processed from crude oil.

Multiple Choice

Read each item carefully, and then select the best response.

_____ **1.** Lubrication systems in a diesel engine are designed to _____.
A. remove dirt, abrasives, and contaminants
B. absorb shock loads between bearings and gears
C. cool internal engine parts
D. All of the above

_____ **2.** There are _____ distinct classifications of oils that are recognized by API performance specifications.
A. two
B. three
C. four
D. five

_____ **3.** The center section of the API service symbol identifies the oil's _____.
A. performance standard
B. viscosity rating
C. API certification
D. base stock type

_____ **4.** The _____ suffix indicates that the oil provides a higher level of protection against changes to viscosity related to soot loading and viscosity loss due to oil molecule shear in diesel engines.
A. SAE
B. PLUS
C. API
D. EGR

_____ **5.** Which type of oil additive prevents water from combining with engine oil?
  A. Dispersants
  B. Oxidation inhibitors
  C. Emulsifiers
  D. Antifoaming additives

_____ **6.** Approximately 70% of the base stock of synthetic oils is made from _____.
  A. polytetrafloeraethylene
  B. polyalkylene glycol
  C. dialkyldithiophosphate
  D. polyalphaolefin

_____ **7.** The primary disadvantage of synthetic oil is its _____.
  A. low-temperature viscosity
  B. high-temperature performance
  C. significantly higher cost
  D. low resistance to chemical breakdown

_____ **8.** A _____ separates the crankcase from the oil pan reservoir to prevent the crankshaft from whipping engine oil stored in the pan.
  A. slosh baffle
  B. windage tray
  C. crankcase cover
  D. filter housing

_____ **9.** Oil pans are made out of _____.
  A. fiberglass
  B. stamped steel
  C. aluminum
  D. All of the above

_____ **10.** Oil pumps used to pressurize the lubrication system of a diesel engine are _____ pumps, usually constructed with a closed gear or gerotor design.
  A. impulse
  B. positive displacement
  C. velocity
  D. valveless

_____ **11.** A _____ filter is capable of removing particles as small as 2–5 microns.
  A. cellulose
  B. paper
  C. micro-glass
  D. thread mesh

_____ **12.** When oil turns _____, it is usually a sign that coolant has leaked into it.
  A. gray
  B. milky white
  C. brown
  D. Any of the above

_____ **13.** Every _____ gallons of fuel consumed by a diesel engine produces enough contaminants to use up 1 quart of oil.
  A. 25
  B. 30
  C. 45
  D. 60

_____ **14.** Abnormally high oil pressure as defined by OEM specifications is usually caused by _____.
  A. defective oil pressure regulating valve
  B. tight engine bearings
  C. plugged filters
  D. thick oil

_____ **15.** The rear main oil seal can begin to leak as a result of _____.
   A. excessive bearing clearances
   B. metal filings in the crankcase
   C. abrasive dirt
   D. Any of the above

True/False

If you believe the statement to be more true than false, write the letter "T" in the space provided. If you believe the statement to be more false than true, write the letter "F"

_____ **1.** At a molecular level, the forces attracting oil molecules to metal surfaces are greater than the forces causing oil molecules to adhere to one another.

_____ **2.** DLD-1, DLD-2, and DLD-3 are the Society of Automotive Engineers standard designations.

_____ **3.** Oils having a viscosity with low numbers such as 0, 5, or 10 flow more easily than viscosities of 20, 30, or 50.

_____ **4.** Oil with a high viscosity index will change viscosity faster than oil with a low viscosity index.

_____ **5.** Motor oils are comprised typically of 90–95% base stock; the remaining 5–10% of the oil volume is made of chemical additives.

_____ **6.** Pour point depressants lower oil's freezing point in cold conditions.

_____ **7.** Oil additives go through no testing except by the U.S. Environmental Protection Agency to certify they are not environmentally noxious.

_____ **8.** Because synthetic oils have a lower coefficient of friction, they are highly recommended for use during break-in periods.

_____ **9.** Almost all diesel engines use oil coolers because the cooling of pistons and other internal engine parts is performed using lubrication oil.

_____ **10.** Engine oil should never exceed 212°F (100°C).

_____ **11.** The media used for air, coolant, and oil filtration can be used interchangeably.

_____ **12.** The purpose of the anti-drain back valve is to prevent the oil in the engine from returning to the crankcase when the engine is shut down.

_____ **13.** Spin-on filters are exempt from EPA regulations regarding hazardous waste.

_____ **14.** Software-based oil-life calculations use a formula or algorithm with input variables for engine operating conditions to determine oil life.

_____ **15.** The best method used to identify the location of an oil leak is tracing dye, which is easily detected with an ultraviolet light.

Fill in the Blank

Read each item carefully, and then complete the statement by filling in the missing word(s)

   1. Without _____ to minimize the effects of friction, the engine would be quickly destroyed and or seized.

   2. Engine oils are classified by the _____ _____ _____ and will carry a designation indicating their suitability for engine applications.

   3. Oil _____ is a performance criteria defined by the Society of Automotive Engineers.

   4. Multigrade oil's main advantage is improved _____-_____ characteristics with less engine drag.

   5. An additive ingredient called viscosity index _____ can be used to control the viscosity index properties of lubrication oil.

   6. Reserve alkalinity additives ensure the oil does not become _____ from products of combustion.

   7. For years _____ has been considered as a lubricity additive to keep moving parts operating smoothly inside fuel injection systems.

   8. The _____ is the deepest part of the oil pan where the oil pump pickup tube is located.

   9. Because the oil pump can produce more oil flow than the engine can use, an oil pressure _____ _____ is used to control oil pressure.

10. The oil filter _____ _____ is a feature that allows oil to pass from the dirty side to the clean side of the filter if resistance or restriction is excessive across the filter media.

11. The percentage of _____ refers to the total amount of particles that are suspended in the oil.

12. The recommended _____ _____ interval is calculated by multiplying the quantity of oil in the oil pan by the number of barrels of fuel burned.

13. An oil _____ sensor is an electrical device that measures the amount of soot loading in engine oil.

14. In the absence of any sensor capable of comprehensively measuring oil quality, _____ _____ _____ is recommended.

15. When checking the engine oil level, the acceptable oil level range is stamped on the oil _____.

Labeling

Label the following diagrams with the correct terms

1. Identify the components of a diesel oil circuit:

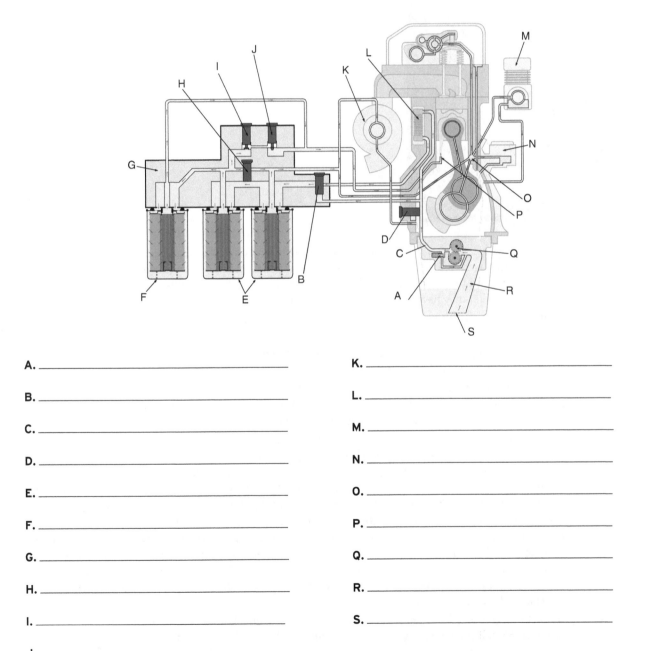

A. _____

B. _____

C. _____

D. _____

E. _____

F. _____

G. _____

H. _____

I. _____

J. _____

K. _____

L. _____

M. _____

N. _____

O. _____

P. _____

Q. _____

R. _____

S. _____

Skill Drills

Test your knowledge of skill drills by filling in the correct words in the photo captions

1. Replacing a Spin-On Oil Filter:

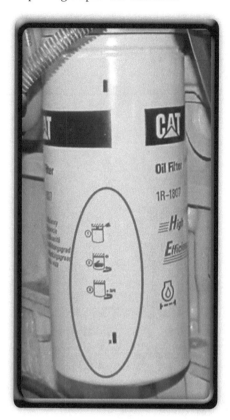

Step 1: With the engine _____, remove the filter with a filter wrench. A large _____-_____ filter wrench assisted with a _____ _____ can be used to remove a tight filter. Occasionally, _____-_____belt wrenches are used to remove _____ filters. To prevent hot oil from scalding your hand when the filter is removed, the filter may have an _____ punched into the _____ to allow oil to _____ before removal.

Step 2: Visually inspect the filter _____ for any _____ or _____. Ensure that the old filter _____ is _____.

Step 3: Fill the new filter with oil. Put _____ in the unfiltered _____ holes of the _____ (the _____ filter hole returns filtered oil to the _____).

Step 4: Lubricate the filter _____ with oil or a smear of _____. This will help prevent the gasket from _____ on the filter base and from _____ when the filter is _____. It is also necessary to _____ the gasket to enable easy _____ during the next service.

Step 5: Spin the new filter on _____ _____. Note the _____ or _____ at the top of the filter _____, which indicate how far the new filter should be tightened after _____ the filter to the _____ using hand force only. Most filters are tightened a _____ or _____ turn beyond hand tight. Tightening the filter further could potentially _____ the filter base, which is often _____. The filter can also be damaged and internal leaks will form if it is _____. If the filter is too _____, it will _____.

Step 6: If the engine is being started for the first time after an _____, it should be prelubricated with _____ oil through an _____ _____. As an additional precaution to prevent damage to _____ and other moving parts from oil _____, disable the _____ system by disconnecting an ignition _____ or _____ and _____ _____, or using a remote starter button. Crank, but do not start, the engine until oil _____ appears on the _____ gauge in the instrument cluster. Electronic gauges can be read if only the cam and crank sensors are _____.

Step 7: After the engine is _____ and oil pressure is _____, check for _____. Reset any maintenance monitors to indicate when the next _____ filter and oil _____ is required.

2. Locating an Oil Leak:

Step 1:   Obtain the correct type of _____ _____ _____. There are _____ that are only compatible with oil, fuel, coolant, or refrigerant. Choose the _____ _____.

Step 2:   Bring the engine to _____ temperature and add the _____ amount of dye to the _____ _____ as recommended by the dye _____.

Step 3:   Road-test the vehicle with the engine _____ _____. When checking for a leak, it is important to get the engine oil to _____ temperature. High oil _____ and _____ oil will reveal _____ quicker than _____, _____-_____ oil.

Step 4:   After running the engine for _____-_____ minutes, shut the engine off and examine the engine using a _____ _____. Some kits use _____ _____ to power compact 12-volt lights. The newest dyes reflect a bright _____-_____ at a leak path when using the UV light. The use of _____ with _____ lenses further enhances the appearance of the dye, making even _____ leaks easier to detect in tight spots.

Step 5:   If uncertain about the actual spot leaking, _____ the area with an _____ _____ and _____ the area with the engine running.

Step 6:   Record your _____ and make a _____ recommendation based on your _____.

Crossword Puzzle

Use the clues in the column to complete the puzzle.

Across

3. Oil made from base stock that is synthetically derived or manufactured.

5. An electrical device that measures the amount of soot loading in engine oil.

Down

1. A filter element consisting simply of filter media unenclosed by a metal container.

2. A measurement of the total amount of change in an oil's viscosity due to temperature.

4. The measurement of a lubricant's reserve alkalinity, which aids in the control of acids formed during the combustion process.

ASE-Type Questions

Read each item carefully, and then select the best response

_____ 1. Technician A says all heavy-duty diesels use 15W-40 engine oil in the summer. Technician B says newer engines use 10W-30 oil. Who is correct?

   A. Technician A
   B. Technician B
   C. Both Technician A and Technician B
   D. Neither Technician A nor Technician B

_____ 2. Technician A says that low-sulfur oil needs to be used today to prevent damage to exhaust aftertreatment systems. Technician B says that today's oils should have low ash content. Who is correct?

   A. Technician A
   B. Technician B
   C. Both Technician A and Technician B
   D. Neither Technician A nor Technician B

_____ 3. Technician A says that viscosity index improvers thicken oil when it becomes hot and thins it when it becomes cold. Technician B says that viscosity index improvers thin oil when it's hot and thicken it when it's cold. Who is correct?

   A. Technician A
   B. Technician B
   C. Both Technician A and Technician B
   D. Neither Technician A nor Technician B

_____ 4. Technician A says that synthetic oils can be used to extend oil change intervals because they do not become contaminated as quickly with soot and dirt as conventional oil. Technician B says that synthetic oils can be used longer because they do not oxidize as quickly as conventional oil. Who is correct?

   A. Technician A
   B. Technician B
   C. Both Technician A and Technician B
   D. Neither Technician A nor Technician B

_____ 5. Technician A says that diesel engine oil turns black faster than oil in a spark-ignition engine because the oil composition and quality are different between the two oils. Technician B says that there is no difference between diesel engine and spark-ignition engine oil. Who is correct?

   A. Technician A
   B. Technician B
   C. Both Technician A and Technician B
   D. Neither Technician A nor Technician B

_____ 6. Technician A says that diesel engine oil operates at higher temperatures than spark-ignition engine oil because it cools pistons. Technician B says that diesel engine oil operates at close to coolant temperature. Who is correct?

   A. Technician A
   B. Technician B
   C. Both Technician A and Technician B
   D. Neither Technician A nor Technician B

_____ 7. Technician A and Technician B are discussing reasons for an abnormal amount of ash plugging of a diesel particulate filter. Technician A says that the cause is likely the use of oil incompatible with a DPF. Technician B says it's likely because the engine is worn out and using too much oil. Who is correct?

   A. Technician A
   B. Technician B
   C. Both Technician A and Technician B
   D. Neither Technician A nor Technician B

_____ 8. Technician A says that engine oil can warm up faster than engine coolant. Technician B says that engine oil can never warm up faster than engine coolant. Who is correct?

   A. Technician A
   B. Technician B
   C. Both Technician A and Technician B
   D. Neither Technician A nor Technician B

_____ **9.** Technician A says tracking oil consumption for a few weeks for a truck with a complaint of high oil consumption is the best place to start diagnosing the problem. Technician B says pulling down the main bearing caps to inspect for worn bearings is the best place to start diagnosing the problem. Who is correct?
   A. Technician A
   B. Technician B
   C. Both Technician A and Technician B
   D. Neither Technician A nor Technician B

_____ **10.** Technician A recommends backward flushing an oil cooler with solvent after repairing an engine that had damaged bearings. Technician B says that servicing the oil cooler when bearings are damaged is unnecessary. Who is correct?
   A. Technician A
   B. Technician B
   C. Both Technician A and Technician B
   D. Neither Technician A nor Technician B

Diesel Engine Cooling Systems

Chapter Review

The following activities have been designed to help you refresh your knowledge of this chapter. Your instructor may require you to complete some or all of these activities as a regular part of your training program. You are encouraged to complete any activity that your instructor does not assign as a way to enhance your learning.

Matching

Match the following terms with the correct description or example.

A. Electrolyte

B. Ethylene glycol

C. Heat exchanger

D. Propylene glycol

E. Thermal efficiency

_____ **1.** The ability of an engine to convert the energy content of fuel into mechanical force.

_____ **2.** The base chemical from which the majority of anti-freezes are made.

_____ **3.** A substance that can conduct current.

_____ **4.** An anti-freeze base that is nontoxic and environmentally friendly.

_____ **5.** A system that transfers heat from coolant to the atmosphere.

Multiple Choice

Read each item carefully, and then select the best response.

_____ **1.** The best heavy-duty on-highway diesel engines operate at approximately 45% thermal efficiency; the remaining energy is _____.

    A. emitted by the exhaust system

    B. radiated to the atmosphere

    C. absorbed by the cooling system

    D. All of the above

_____ **2.** Compressed intake air is cooled using _____.

    A. air-to-air aftercooling

    B. charge air coolers

    C. liquid heat exchangers

    D. Any of the above

_____ **3.** Every 1-psi (7-kPa) increase in cooling system pressure increases the boiling point of the coolant by approximately _____.

    A. 1°F

    B. 2°F

    C. 3°F

    D. 4°F

_____ **4.** The primary ingredient of engine coolant is _____.

    A. water

    B. ethylene glycol

    C. phosphate

    D. propylene glycol

_____ **5.** Inorganic additive technology is commonly marketed using the term _____.
   A. "supplemental coolant additive"
   B. "nitrite additive technology"
   C. "diesel coolant additive"
   D. Both A and C

_____ **6.** When _____ is added to coolant, it forms a thin, protective film on the coolant side of the engine cylinder walls and other surfaces to reduce cavitation erosion.
   A. alkaline
   B. magnesium
   C. nitrite
   D. electrolyte

_____ **7.** A coolant with a pH of 7 is considered _____.
   A. acidic
   B. neutral
   C. alkaline
   D. corrosive

_____ **8.** The optimal mixture of water to coolant for removing heat and providing corrosion protection is _____.
   A. 50/50
   B. 60/40
   C. 40/60
   D. 70/30

_____ **9.** The suggested color of Type III anti-freeze is _____.
   A. green
   B. pink
   C. blue
   D. orange

_____ **10.** Anti-freeze that contains corrosion inhibitors made from organic acids is considered _____ coolant.
   A. low oxidation
   B. extended-life
   C. hybrid
   D. neutral pH

_____ **11.** What type of red-colored anti-freeze uses non-carboxylate acids, such as benzoate, from benzoic acid, to form the additive package?
   A. Nitrated organic acid technology
   B. Type IV OAT Anti-freeze
   C. Hybrid Organic Acid Technology
   D. Fully Formulated Anti-freeze

_____ **12.** A _____ thermostat stops the flow of coolant to the top radiator hose, causing coolant to be redirected through a passageway and back to the water pump inlet for recirculation into the engine.
   A. blocking
   B. pressure relief
   C. chocking
   D. Both A and C

_____ **13.** The volume of air moved by an engine fan is determined by the _____.
   A. number of blades
   B. fan pitch
   C. fan speed
   D. All of the above

_____ **14.** A _____ fan drive system is commonly found in off-road equipment and transit buses where cooling demands can exceed the ability of a conventional fan drive system.
   A. variable speed
   B. hydraulic
   C. hub type
   D. viscous

_____ **15.** The use of a _____ is necessary when testing the freeze protection of the coolant in the cooling system.
- **A.** hydrometer
- **B.** hygrometer
- **C.** refractometer
- **D.** Either A or C

True/False

If you believe the statement to be more true than false, write the letter "T" in the space provided. If you believe the statement to be more false than true, write the letter "F".

_____ **1.** Thermal efficiency is measured as a percentage of the potential energy content in fuel compared with the engine's ability to convert the potential energy into mechanical energy.

_____ **2.** Almost all diesel engines use oil coolers that circulate engine coolant to remove heat from the engine oil.

_____ **3.** Ethylene glycol is both nontoxic and environmentally friendly.

_____ **4.** Diesel engine cooling systems operate at pressures between 15 and 20 psi, which is much higher than gasoline engines.

_____ **5.** Core plugs are designed to relieve pressure from frozen coolant to prevent engine damage.

_____ **6.** Cavitation erosion is unique to diesel engines.

_____ **7.** Coolant for diesel-fueled engines and coolant for gasoline-fueled engines are identical.

_____ **8.** In the past, coolant has included mixtures of alcohol and water as well as water mixed with honey and soluble oils.

_____ **9.** Propylene glycol requires a higher concentration than ethylene glycol to provide the same freeze protection.

_____ **10.** Mixing IAT with OAT, HOAT, and NOAT anti-freezes will severely damage the engine's cooling system.

_____ **11.** Overflow tanks use a line connected to the radiator just below the pressure cap, allowing the movement of coolant back and forth during the cooling system's thermal cycles.

_____ **12.** Water filters on diesel engines contain pucks of DCA additive, which is dissolved within minutes of coolant circulating through the filter.

_____ **13.** A temperature-controlled modulating fan clutch is coupled to the drive mechanism through a highly viscous silicone fluid.

_____ **14.** Constant torque spring clamps are designed to prevent cold weather leaks, and they do not require any adjustment after installation.

_____ **15.** White exhaust smoke that smells sweet is an indication of an EGR cooler leak.

Fill in the Blank

Read each item carefully, and then complete the statement by filling in the missing word(s).

1. The cooling system removes excess heat from the engine and releases it to the atmosphere through the _____.

2. Surge tanks, overflow reservoirs, and large radiator tanks are used to help buffer coolant _____.

3. Increasing cooling system _____ will prevent engine damage and loss of coolant by increasing the temperature at which coolant will boil.

4. Cooling systems must provide for the _____ of coolant to prevent pumps and coolant passageways in the cylinder head from becoming air bound, or blocked by an accumulation of steam.

5. The principle of inducing current flow by using dissimilar metals and an electrolyte is called the _____ effect.

6. Some of the _____ that collects in the cooling system comes from calcium and magnesium in the water used for cooling and some is produced by additives in the anti-freeze.

7. Both OAT and IAT were developed primarily to treat or condition the cooling system to reduce the effects of _____ erosion.

8. In all liquid-cooled engines, the _____ controls the flow of coolant through the radiator.

9. If ingested, 4 ounces (113 grams) of _____ _____ will cause fatal kidney failure in humans after a couple of days.

10. The primary disadvantage of using _____ as a nontoxic base for anti-freeze is that its freeze protection temperature is high in comparison to ethylene glycol.

11. To maintain the correct level of additives, Type I coolant requires _____ to ensure the correct levels of nitrite and other inhibitors are present.

12. Type II and type III anti-freeze are differentiated by the type of _____ that they use.

13. In a _____-_____ radiator the coolant flows from a top-connected hose, through a side-mounted tank, into cooling tubes, and across the radiator to another side-mounted tank.

14. To ensure positive circulation of coolant, an engine-driven _____ _____ moves coolant through the cooling system.

15. A _____ valve in a choking thermostat enables trapped steam to vent through a closed thermostat.

Labeling

Label the following diagrams with the correct terms.

1. Identify the components of a cooling system:

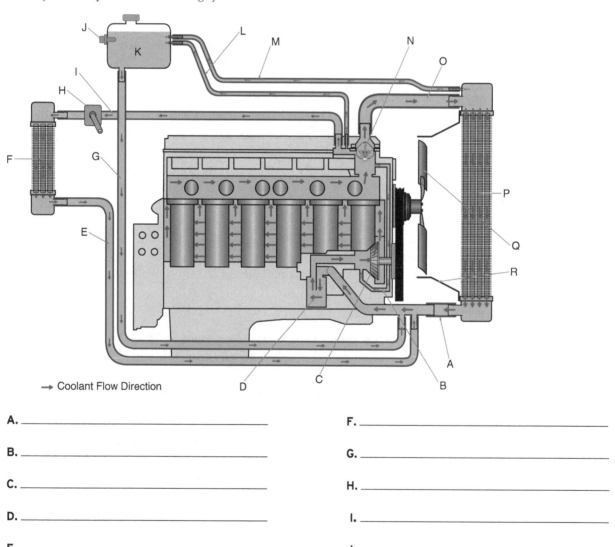

→ Coolant Flow Direction

A. _____   F. _____

B. _____   G. _____

C. _____   H. _____

D. _____   I. _____

E. _____   J. _____

K. _____

L. _____

M. _____

N. _____

O. _____

P. _____

Q. _____

R. _____

2. Identify the parts of a chocking thermostat:

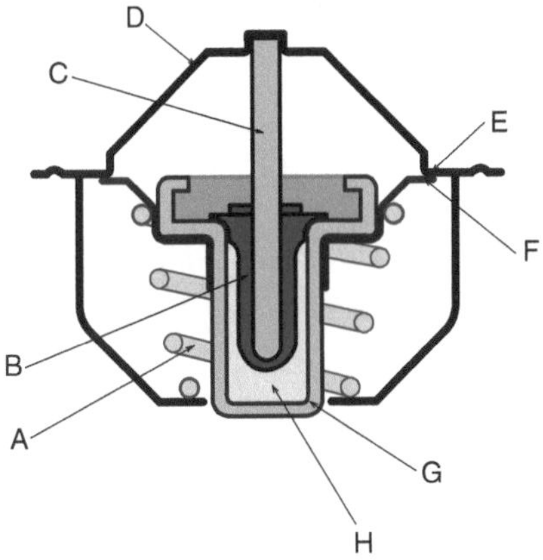

A. _____

B. _____

C. _____

D. _____

E. _____

F. _____

G. _____

H. _____

Skill Drills

Test your knowledge of skill drills by filling in the correct words in the photo captions.

1. Inspecting for a Leaking EGR Cooler:

Step 1:   Pressurize the _____ _____ and inspect for obvious external _____.

Step 2:   Remove the EGR valve and _____ it to see if it looks _____ and _____. If the EGR valve is located after the _____ _____, coolant leaks will wet the valve. EGR valves on the _____ side of the EGR system will not become wetted with coolant.

Step 3:   While the cooling system is _____, disconnect the _____ _____ of the _____ and check for visible leaks.

Step 4:   Disconnect the EGR cooler _____ and _____ exhaust _____. Using a _____-_____ kit with a _____ adapter, plug the exhaust inlet and outlets and _____ the block-off _____ _____ using the EGR clamps.

Step 5:   Pressurize the _____ side of the EGR _____ using the block-off kit with shop air supplied at _____ psi (207 kPa).

Step 6:   Shut off the compressed air to the cooler while it is pressurized and wait **30** minutes. There should be no _____ _____ in 30 minutes. Any drop indicates the cooler is _____.

Step 7:   Check for _____ _____ in the _____ _____ and from the _____ _____. If air bubbles are present, replace EGR _____.

2. Testing Coolant Nitrite or DCA/SCA Levels:

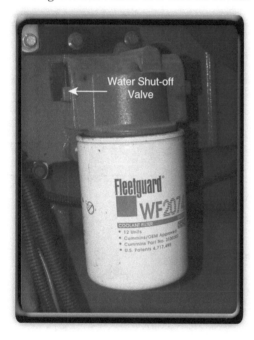

Step 1:   Identify the type of _____ _____ using coolant _____. The decal next to the _____ _____ may not be correct if the coolant has been _____ or _____ with other coolant formulations.

Step 2:   Using a manufacturer or aftermarket _____ _____, dip the _____ into the coolant and _____ any excess _____ off of the strip.

Step 3:   Using the _____ on the test strip _____, compare the color of the _____ _____ on the test strip against the chart _____.

Step 4:   Determine the level of _____ in the cooling system in parts per _____ or as a _____.

Step 5:   Using the _____ _____ or test strip manufacturer's recommendations, determine the amount of _____ that may be needed based on the coolant _____. The level may be _____, too high, or too low.

Step 6:   Drain the coolant to correct _____ nitrite levels, which can lead to _____ of cooling system _____, particularly _____. Add the correct amount of _____, _____, or _____ based on the cooling system _____ and coolant anti-freeze formulation.

3. Using a Hydrometer to Test the Freeze Point of the Coolant:

Step 1: Remove the _____ _____. Be sure the cooling system is _____ before removing the _____.

Step 2: Determine the type of _____-_____ and verify that the _____ is designed to be used with it.

Step 3: Place the hydrometer _____ into the coolant and _____ the _____ on top of the tool.

Step 4: Release the ball to draw in a _____ of _____. Make sure the _____ of _____ drawn in is above the _____ line.

Step 5: Read the _____ on the _____ to verify the _____ _____ of the coolant.

Step 6: Return the coolant sample to the _____ or _____ _____.

4. Using a Refractometer to Test the Freeze Point of the Coolant:

Step 1: Remove the _____ _____. Be sure the _____ system is _____ before removing it.

Step 2: Determine the _____ of anti-freeze and _____ that the _____ is designed to be used with it.

Step 3: Place a _____ _____ of coolant on the _____ _____ on the top of the tool.

Step 4: Hold the _____ roughly level under a _____, look through the _____, and read the _____ to verify the freeze protection of the coolant.

Step 5: Return the coolant sample to the _____ or _____ _____.

Crossword Puzzle

Use the clues in the column to complete the puzzle.

Across

3. A condition in which excessive amounts of air or steam bubbles are dissolved in coolant, diminishing the coolant's effectiveness.

4. An additive package that is only used with ELC, which is added at the midpoint of the coolant's life.

5. The transfer of heat into the cooling system from the combustion chamber.

Down

1. An additive used to treat cooling systems to reduce the effects of cavitation erosion.

2. Erosion in cylinder block walls, heads, and liner sleeves as a result of the collapse of tiny water vapor bubbles formed when coolant vaporizes on hot cylinder wall surfaces.

ASE-Type Questions

Read each item carefully, and then select the best response.

_____ 1. Technician A says that blue anti-freeze is long-life anti-freeze. Technician B says that blue anti-freeze is propylene glycol–based anti-freeze. Who is correct?
   A. Technician A
   B. Technician B
   C. Both Technician A and Technician B
   D. Neither Technician A nor Technician B

_____ 2. Technician A says that an engine in a late-model truck or bus that is slow to warm up will set a fault code for the cooling system. Technician B says that slow warm up is normal for diesels and as long as an engine reaches operating temperature there will be no fault code. Who is correct?
   A. Technician A
   B. Technician B
   C. Both Technician A and Technician B
   D. Neither Technician A nor Technician B

_____ 3. Technician A says that ethylene glycol–based anti-freeze is too toxic to be used and has been replaced by other formulations of anti-freeze. Technician B says that propylene glycol anti-freeze is toxic and is being replaced by glycerin-based anti-freeze. Who is correct?
   A. Technician A
   B. Technician B
   C. Both Technician A and Technician B
   D. Neither Technician A nor Technician B

_____ 4. Technician A says that a drop in the coolant level in the surge tank or coolant overflow reservoir when the engine cools indicates an internal engine leak. Technician B says that the drop in the level is normal. Who is correct?
   A. Technician A
   B. Technician B
   C. Both Technician A and Technician B
   D. Neither Technician A nor Technician B

_____ 5. Technician A says that pressurization of the cooling system takes place to enable coolant to remove more heat from the engine. Technician B says pressurization is needed to keep the coolant from boiling. Who is correct?
   A. Technician A
   B. Technician B
   C. Both Technician A and Technician B
   D. Neither Technician A nor Technician B

_____ 6. Technician A says that anti-freeze is added to coolant to protect the coolant from freezing and lowers the boiling point. Technician B says anti-freeze lowers the freeze point and raises the boiling point of coolant. Who is correct?
   A. Technician A
   B. Technician B
   C. Both Technician A and Technician B
   D. Neither Technician A nor Technician B

_____ 7. Technician A says the problem with new long-life anti-freeze is it can produce silicate dropout, which plugs cooling system passages. Technician B says that the problem with long life anti-freeze is that it is not compatible with all cooling system materials. Who is correct?
   A. Technician A
   B. Technician B
   C. Both Technician A and Technician B
   D. Neither Technician A nor Technician B

_____ **8.** Technician A says the advantage of hydraulic fan drive mechanisms is that they can turn faster than engine speed. Technician B says that on–off engine fans use less power than viscous type fan drives. Who is correct?
A. Technician A
B. Technician B
C. Both Technician A and Technician B
D. Neither Technician A nor Technician B

_____ **9.** Technician A says that when pressurizing a cooling system to check for leaks, a technician should never use a pressure higher than the pressure rating of the pressure cap. Technician B says that pressure testing the cooling system should be at 15–18 psi (103–124 kPa). Who is correct?
A. Technician A
B. Technician B
C. Both Technician A and Technician B
D. Neither Technician A nor Technician B

_____ **10.** Technician A says that diesel engine cooling systems are slow to warm up because diesel fuel does not burn as hot as gasoline and the systems are larger. Technician B says that diesel engine cooling systems have more heat loads but are only slow to warm up at idle. Who is correct?
A. Technician A
B. Technician B
C. Both Technician A and Technician B
D. Neither Technician A nor Technician B

Diesel Fuel Properties and Characteristics

Chapter Review

The following activities have been designed to help you refresh your knowledge of this chapter. Your instructor may require you to complete some or all of these activities as a regular part of your training program. You are encouraged to complete any activity that your instructor does not assign as a way to enhance your learning.

Matching

Match the following terms with the correct description or example.

A. Distillation

B. Ethanol

C. Fischer-Tropsch reaction

D. Methanol

E. Transesterification

_____ 1. A process that replaces glycerin in vegetable oil or animal fat with alcohol molecules.

_____ 2. A process used to create synthetic liquid diesel fuel from vaporized hydrocarbons.

_____ 3. Alcohol-based fuel made from starches and sugars.

_____ 4. A fuel made from wood or cellulose.

_____ 5. The process of boiling petroleum oil to separate oil molecules into fractions or cuts based on the boiling point temperature of each fraction.

Multiple Choice

Read each item carefully, and then select the best response.

_____ 1. The first biodiesel fuel was made out of _____.

A. soybeans

B. peanut oil

C. vegetable oil

D. corn

_____ 2. ATSM grade _____ fuel contains impurities and other characteristics that will damage on-highway engines and should never be used in them.

A. 1-D

B. 2-D

C. 3-D

D. 4-D

_____ 3. Diesel fuels intended for home heating oil and agricultural machinery are dyed _____ because they are taxed at a lower rate and not to be used in vehicles for on-highway use.

A. red

B. blue

C. orange

D. amber

_____ 4. Ultra-low-sulfur diesel fuel is designated with the identifier _____, which is appended to the fuel grade.

A. D10

B. LSD20

C. S15

D. ULS50

_____ **5.** The _____ of a fuel is defined as the temperature to which the fuel must be heated to produce a vapor that will ignite when exposed to a spark or open flame.
   A. boiling point
   B. flash point
   C. cloud point
   D. auto-ignition temperature

_____ **6.** The temperature at which wax begins to give fuel a hazy or milky appearance is called the _____ point.
   A. pour
   B. cloud
   C. brume
   D. frost

_____ **7.** Using B100 fuel will result in a _____.
   A. 67% reduction in unburned HCs
   B. 48% reduction in CO
   C. 47% reduction in PM emissions
   D. All of the above

_____ **8.** Biodiesel is manufactured from _____.
   A. algae
   B. beef tallow
   C. soybeans
   D. All of the above

_____ **9.** The _____ is responsible for diesel fuel specifications and test methods for petroleum-based diesel fuel and biodiesel fuel.
   A. NTSB
   B. EPA
   C. ASTM
   D. EISA

_____ **10.** Cetane boosters, detergents, lubricity additives, and smoke suppressants are considered _____.
   A. engine performance enhancers
   B. fuel stability enhancers
   C. contaminant control additives
   D. fuel handling additives

True/False

If you believe the statement to be more true than false, write the letter "T" in the space provided. If you believe the statement to be more false than true, write the letter "F".

_____ **1.** Coal dust was the original diesel fuel.

_____ **2.** ASTM-defined diesel fuel standards apply only to fuels that are refined in North America.

_____ **3.** Coal, carbon monoxide, and gases produced by decomposing wood and other plant material can all be used to manufacture synthetic diesel fuel.

_____ **4.** Biodiesel fuels must be treated to reduce their sulfur content.

_____ **5.** The lowest permissible auto-ignition temperature of diesel fuel sold in North America is 212°F (100°C).

_____ **6.** The lubricating properties of diesel fuel are provided by compounds such as fats and waxes that are already naturally present in diesel fuel.

_____ **7.** Gasoline or alcohol can be mixed with diesel fuel to minimize fuel gelling and improve combustion.

_____ **8.** Fatty acid methyl ester (FAME) fuels are another name given to biodiesel fuels produced through transesterification.

_____ **9.** Fuel with a low cetane number ignites sooner and burns faster than a fuel with a high cetane number.

_____ **10.** The American Petroleum Institute is a regulatory body that develops standards for measuring fuel density.

Fill in the Blank

Read each item carefully, and then complete the statement by filling in the missing word(s).

1. "Diesel fuel" is a generic term that refers to a range of fuels burned in _____ ignition engines.

2. A chemical process invented in Germany during the 1920s called the Fischer-Tropsch reaction is used to manufacture _____-_____-_____ diesel fuel.

3. The _____ content of diesel fuel affects particulate matter emissions.

4. The characteristic odor of diesel exhaust is attributed to the _____ content of diesel fuel.

5. When fuel reaches its _____ point, it can no longer pass through lines and filters.

6. The higher the _____ measure of a liquid, the thicker and more viscous it is.

7. The use of straight vegetable oil can lead a build-up of carbon in the injector nozzle called _____ that leads to reduced fuel flow and irregular injector spray patterns.

8. The _____ number is a measure of the ignition quality of fuel and refers to the fuel's ignitability under compression.

9. In the United States, all manufacturers of fuel additives must register their product with the _____ _____ _____, which, in turn, evaluates the products for adverse human health or negative environmental impact.

10. Fuel density is measured with a fuel _____ _____.

Fraction Matching

Match each type of fuel to its correct fraction in the distillation process.

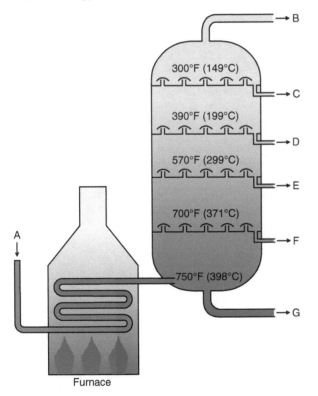

_____ 1. Lubricating oil

_____ 2. Kerosene

_____ 3. Paraffin wax

_____ 4. Gasoline

_____ 5. Fuel oil

_____ 6. Crude oil

_____ 7. Diesel

_____ 8. Asphalt

_____ 9. Gas

_____ 10. Jet fuel

Skill Drills

Test your knowledge of skill drills by filling in the correct words in the photo captions.

1. Determining a Fuel's ASTM Grade:

ASTM Grade	API Number	Density	Btu Heating Value
1-D	38–45	6.675–6.950 lb/gal. (800–833 g/L)	132,900–137,000 per gallon (35,108–36,192 per liter)
2-D	30–38	6.960–7.296 lb/gal. (834–874 g/L)	137,000–141,800 per gallon (36,192–37,460 per liter)
4-D	20–28	7.396–7.787 lb/gal. (886–933 g/L)	143,100–148,100 per gallon (37,803–39,124 per liter)

Step 1:   Obtain a _____ sample from the vehicle or equipment _____ _____ and place the sample in a _____ _____.

Step 2:   Using a purpose-made fuel _____, measure the fuel's _____ and _____ number.

Step 3:   Using a _____ provided by the hydrometer's manufacturer, look up the _____-_____ API number for the fuel. Because the _____ of a fuel is affected by _____, the corrected API value provides the API number that the fuel would have at _____ _____.

Step 4:   Using the _____ standard, _____ the _____ _____ with the ranges for 1-D, 2-D, and 4-D ASTM grades of fuel.

Step 5:   Report the information on a _____ or _____ _____.

2. Detecting Water in Diesel Fuel:

Step 1:   Take a fuel sample and examine it against a _____ background. Look for _____, which indicates high amounts of _____ _____ in fuel.

Step 2:   Using a good quality _____ paste, dip the _____ into a _____ sample to check for _____. For vehicle fuel tanks and underground reservoirs, the paste can be applied to the end of a long _____ _____ or _____. The _____ of the paste will change instantly when it contacts _____.

Step 3:   Place a _____ ounce (500 mL) sample of _____ in a clear glass beaker or jar. Slowly add _____–_____ ounces (50–100 mL) of methanol to the jar. Only _____ alcohol (methanol) should be used because it does not mix with _____ _____. (_____ can be mixed with diesel fuel and will _____ water in the fuel.) The methanol will _____ on the diesel fuel.

Step 4:   Allow the two liquids to _____ and _____.

Step 5:   Mark the container _____ with a _____ at the point of _____ _____.

Step 6:   Vigorously _____ and _____ the _____ and _____ together for 1 minute. Let the sample _____ and _____ for approximately _____ minutes.

Step 7:   Note the new _____ line between the _____ and _____ and mark it with another _____ on the container wall.

Step 8:   Because methanol will _____ water, its volume will _____ if it dissolves any water from the fuel. If _____ was present in the fuel sample, the line of liquid separation after mixing will be _____ the first marked line on the container wall. The difference between the two lines of separation is _____ to the fuel's _____ content. The water is now _____ _____ with the _____.

Step 9:   Report your findings. If necessary, make a _____ recommendation to drain _____ _____ from _____ _____.

3. Evaluating Fuel Quality:

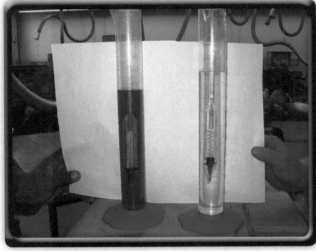

Step 1:   Obtain a fuel _____ and allow the fuel to _____ in a _____ for a few minutes.

Step 2:   Place a piece of _____ _____ behind the beaker to reflect through the fuel and _____ examine the _____.

Step 3:   Record the _____ and _____ of the fuel. Observe any _____ or _____ of fuel from other liquids or particles in the beaker. Fuel becomes _____ as it ages. Fuel contaminated with _____ _____ that has also gone stale turns _____. Microorganisms may even be _____ in fuel.

Step 4:   Use a rapid hand motion to draw a sample of the fuel _____ toward you. Smell the _____ and note the _____ of the fuel. Fuel, as it ages, will gradually lose its _____ smell and begin to change to having a smell similar to _____, _____, plasticine, or _____. The presence of microorganisms will give the fuel a foul _____ smell.

Step 5:   Record your observations and make a service recommendation. A fuel system with significant _____ should be _____ and _____ and the filters replaced. A _____ booster may be recommended for fuel that has become slightly _____ but not contaminated. Recommend a fuel _____ if fuel is to remain _____ for several months, but do not recommend long-term storage of _____.

Crossword Puzzle

Use the clues in the column to complete the puzzle.

Across

3. A fuel's lubricating quality.

5. A measure of a fluid's flow characteristics, or thickness.

Down

1. The quantity of fuel evaporating at a particular temperature.

2. The different petroleum products that make up a barrel of oil, which are separated by the distillation process.

4. A fuel treatment that kills microorganisms.

ASE-Type Questions

Read each item carefully, and then select the best response.

_____ **1.** Technician A says straight vegetable oil (SVO) can be burned in a diesel engine without causing any long-term problems for engine durability. Technician B says SVO will damage injectors. Who is correct?
  A. Technician A
  B. Technician B
  C. Both Technician A and Technician B
  D. Neither Technician A nor Technician B

_____ **2.** Technician A says that adding alcohol to diesel fuel is a good practice because it keeps fuel from waxing when it is cold and it improves engine starting. Technician B says wax in fuel should be removed at the refinery because it causes low power complaints in hot weather. Who is correct?
  A. Technician A
  B. Technician B
  C. Both Technician A and Technician B
  D. Neither Technician A nor Technician B

_____ **3.** Technician A says that adding a little gasoline to diesel fuel will help a diesel engine start faster in cold weather, reduce combustion noise, and improve power output. Technician B says that adding gasoline to diesel fuel will make starting worse, increase combustion noise, and accelerate fuel system wear. Who is correct?
  A. Technician A
  B. Technician B
  C. Both Technician A and Technician B
  D. Neither Technician A nor Technician B

_____ **4.** Technician A says that 2-D fuel provides the most power and best fuel economy for an on-highway diesel engine. Technician B says that 1-D is the best fuel for producing power and good fuel economy. Who is correct?
  A. Technician A
  B. Technician B
  C. Both Technician A and Technician B
  D. Neither Technician A nor Technician B

_____ **5.** Technician A says that 4-D fuel should not be used in on-highway diesel engines. Technician B says that 3-D cannot be recommended for diesel engines. Who is correct?
  A. Technician A
  B. Technician B
  C. Both Technician A and Technician B
  D. Neither Technician A nor Technician B

_____ **6.** Technician A says that diesel fuel's low volatility is why so many diesel fuel pump islands appear to have a lot of spilled fuel. Technician B says that fuel spills at diesel pump islands are more common than those at gasoline pumps because truck drivers are careless when refueling. Who is correct?
  A. Technician A
  B. Technician B
  C. Both Technician A and Technician B
  D. Neither Technician A nor Technician B

_____ **7.** Technician A says that winter grades of diesel fuel are more likely to produce a low-power complaint because winter fuel has a lower Btu content than fuel retailed during the summer months. Technician B says that winter fuel blends will plug fuel filters easier than fuel prepared for summer seasons which explains winter fuel low power complaints. Who is correct?
  A. Technician A
  B. Technician B
  C. Both Technician A and Technician B
  D. Neither Technician A nor Technician B

_____ **8.** Technician A says that microorganisms that grow in diesel fuel and plug filters feed on fuel molecules. Technician B says that the microorganisms grow in water contained in diesel fuel. Who is correct?

    A. Technician A

    B. Technician B

    C. Both Technician A and Technician B

    D. Neither Technician A nor Technician B

_____ **9.** Technician A says that the smell of diesel exhaust is produced by the complete combustion of diesel fuel. Technician B says that unburned hydrocarbons produce the characteristic smell of diesel exhaust. Who is correct?

    A. Technician A

    B. Technician B

    C. Both Technician A and Technician B

    D. Neither Technician A nor Technician B

_____ **10.** Technician A says that thinner, low viscosity diesel fuel will produce more power because more fuel can be injected. Technician B says that low viscosity fuel tends to leak around plungers and barrels in high-pressure injection equipment and less fuel is injected. Who is correct?

    A. Technician A

    B. Technician B

    C. Both Technician A and Technician B

    D. Neither Technician A nor Technician B

Low-Pressure Fuel Systems

Chapter Review

The following activities have been designed to help you refresh your knowledge of this chapter. Your instructor may require you to complete some or all of these activities as a regular part of your training program. You are encouraged to complete any activity that your instructor does not assign as a way to enhance your learning.

Matching

Match the following terms with the correct description or example.

A. Absolute micron rating

B. Bleeder screw

C. Hydroscopic

D. Priming

E. Sending units

_____ **1.** An electrical device, usually a variable-resistance rheostat, that supplies a voltage signal to an analog-type dash gauge proportional to the fuel level.

_____ **2.** A process that removes any air that may have entered the fuel system and prevents introduction of unfiltered fuel into the system.

_____ **3.** The largest sized particle that the fuel filter media will allow to pass.

_____ **4.** The ability to mix and absorb water.

_____ **5.** A component located in the fuel system that allows trapped air to escape from the filter when priming.

Multiple Choice

Read each item carefully, and then select the best response.

_____ **1.** All of the following are functions of the low-pressure fuel system **EXCEPT**?
A. remove water contamination
B. regulate fuel temperature
C. meter the correct quantity of fuel for injection
D. prevent wax gelling

_____ **2.** Which of the following is a poor material choice for fuel tanks?
A. Zinc
B. Aluminum
C. Steel alloy
D. Plastic

_____ **3.** Fuel tank pickups used in medium-duty applications are usually integrated with a _____.
A. fuel filter
B. fuel level sending unit
C. pressure relief valve
D. rollover valve

_____ **4.** Most fuel system wear takes place with particle contamination of _____ in diameter.
A. 3–5µ
B. 5–7µ
C. 8–10µ
D. 11–13µ

_____ **5.** Black tar-like organic particles that naturally occur in 2-D diesel fuels are called _____.
  A. fungi
  B. bacteria
  C. asphaltenes
  D. hydroscopic particles

_____ **6.** The most common and most destructive contaminant found in fuel systems is _____.
  A. sodium
  B. bacteria
  C. fungi
  D. water

_____ **7.** It is the job of the _____ filter to remove the bulk of free water and contaminants from the fuel.
  A. primary
  B. desiccant
  C. secondary
  D. microglass

_____ **8.** Fuel heaters use _____ to warm the fuel.
  A. electric current
  B. engine oil
  C. warm coolant
  D. Either A or C

_____ **9.** A _____ pump is used to supply fuel at low pressure, usually not more than 7 pounds per square inch.
  A. piston-type
  B. diaphragm pump
  C. gear pump
  D. Either A or C

_____ **10.** When the engine is not running and the fuel system requires purging of air or filling of a filter, a _____ provides the piston action to develop pressure differentials needed to move the fuel.
  A. hand primer
  B. bleeder screw
  C. priming button
  D. Either A or C

True/False

If you believe the statement to be more true than false, write the letter "T" in the space provided. If you believe the statement to be more false than true, write the letter "F".

_____ **1.** The fuel tank allows fuel returned from the engine to cool after absorbing heat from the engine and fuel injectors.

_____ **2.** Fiberglass is the best lightweight material choice for fuel tanks used in mobile applications.

_____ **3.** Contact with fuel will close the rollover valve to prevent fuel from leaking from the tank.

_____ **4.** Fuel lines are not allowed to be routed through a vehicle's passenger or driver compartment.

_____ **5.** When two fuel tanks are used, the return flow splitter valve equally divides return fuel flow from the engine to maintain identical fuel levels in each tank.

_____ **6.** Contamination usually occurs before the fuel is pumped into a vehicle's fuel tank.

_____ **7.** Sometimes referred to as "humbugs," bacteria and fungi can multiply throughout a fuel system and eventually clog fuel filters.

_____ **8.** Spin-on fuel and oil filters are exempt from hazardous waste regulations.

_____ **9.** Most in-tank electric pumps are the positive displacement, roller vane–type using permanent magnet–type electric motors.

_____ **10.** Detroit Diesel's DD series engines can perform an automated fuel system test that includes an evaluation of the low-pressure system called the Fuel System Integrity Check.

Fill in the Blank

Read each item carefully, and then complete the statement by filling in the missing word(s).

1. At low temperatures, the _____ content in diesel fuel can cause it to become too viscous to properly flow through filters and lines.

2. A tank _____ is necessary to allow air into the tank and some fuel vapors to escape.

3. The _____ _____ _____ collects fuel from the injectors, fuel pump, and relief valves and returns the fuel to the tank.

4. Every fuel tank is equipped with an electrical _____ _____ that transmits the fuel level to the instrument panel in the operator's cab.

5. The smallest particle visible to the human eye is 40 _____ in diameter.

6. Filter media can remove emulsified water by a process called _____, where smaller water droplets merge to form heavier droplets.

7. A _____–_____ separator is a filtration device that removes water from fuel, extends the life of a filter.

8. The _____ filter is located between the primary filter and the high-pressure fuel injection system.

9. The _____-_____-_____ module will alert the operator via the instrument display if there is too much water in the fuel filter housing or fuel–water separator filter.

10. High-pressure common rail systems often use a fuel _____ to prevent heat from causing the fuel to lose viscosity and density.

Labeling

Label the following diagrams with the correct terms.

1. Identify the components of a typical low-pressure fuel system using unit injectors:

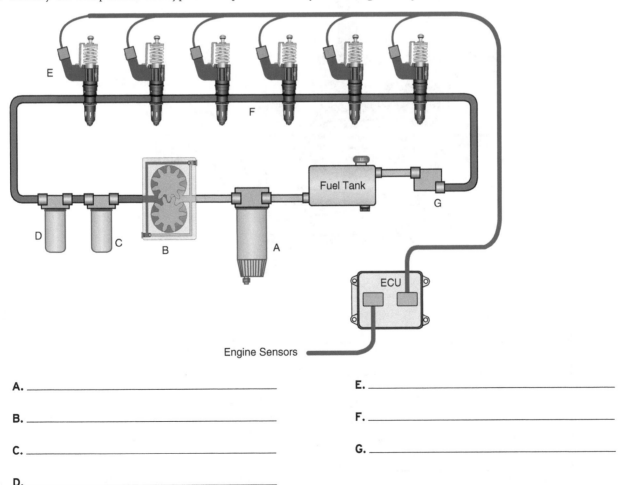

A. _____

B. _____

C. _____

D. _____

E. _____

F. _____

G. _____

2. Identify the components of a fuel heater:

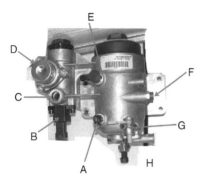

A. _____

B. _____

C. _____

D. _____

E. _____

F. _____

G. _____

H. _____

3. Identify the components of a diaphragm fuel pump:

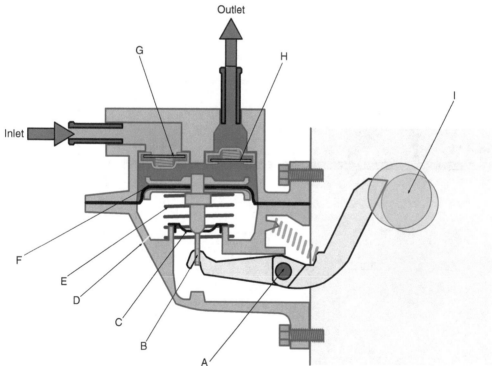

A. _____   F. _____

B. _____   G. _____

C. _____   H. _____

D. _____   I. _____

E. _____

Skill Drills

Test your knowledge of skill drills by filling in the correct words in the photo captions.

1. Performing a Primary Fuel Filter Suction-Side Pressure Test (page 458):

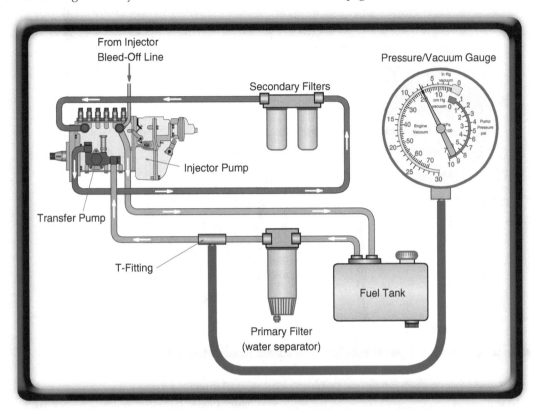

Step 1:   Obtain an accurate, high-quality _____-_____ gauge capable of measuring pressure in inches (millimeters) of _____ and _____ in tenths of inches, or a _____ gauge that measures in inches (millimeters) of water (H_2O). An electronic pressure _____ or a _____ vacuum-pressure gauge is best.

Step 2:   Connect the _____ to the _____ side of the _____ filter using a quick-connect fitting, which may need to be _____ in the system if one was not equipped by the OEM. A T-fitting may also be used in the _____ _____ between the _____ filter and _____ pump, but there is usually a _____ _____ and _____ in the filter system.

Step 3:   Start the engine and run it at _____-_____ (full throttle, no load). Observe and record the _____ reading. A slight _____ pressure is normal, but a _____ negative pressure means the _____ is _____ or there is a _____-_____ restriction before the _____. Generally, if the negative pressure is less than _____-_____" (203–254 mm) Hg or _____-_____ psi (28–34 kPa), the filter is operating satisfactorily and still has _____ _____ remaining. If the restriction is between _____-_____" (305–457 mm) Hg, recommend that the _____ be _____. Always refer to manufacturer's specifications.

2. Measuring Primary Filter Restriction (page 459):

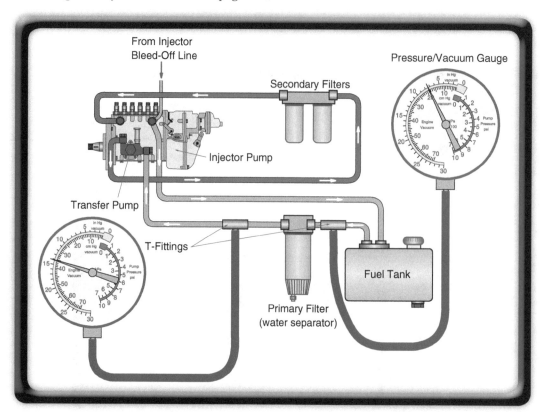

Step 1: Install _____-_____ fittings and attach pressure _____ gauges to both the _____ and _____ sides of the _____ filter. An electronic pressure _____ can be used. Alternately, use the same gauge and take _____ on both sides of the _____ during _____ separate _____.

Step 2: Start the _____ and operate it at _____ speed.

Step 3: Observe and record the _____ difference between the two _____. Most _____ filters will have less than _____ psi (0.7 kPa) difference between the two readings.

Step 4: If the filter restriction is approaching _____–_____" (127–203 mm) Hg or _____–_____ psi (17–28 kPa), recommend filter _____.

3. Performing a Primary Fuel Filter Suction-Side Restriction Test (page 460):

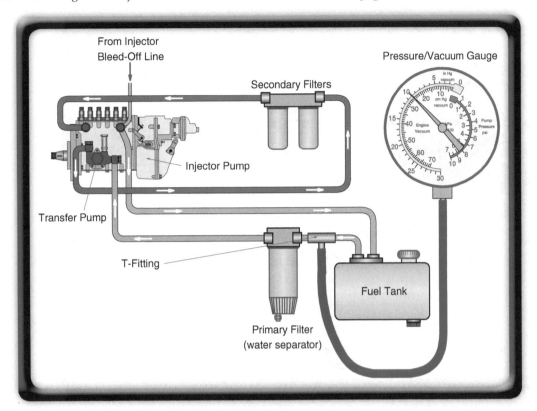

Step 1:   Install a _____-_____ fitting and attach a _____-
_____ gauge to the _____ side of the _____ filter. An electronic
_____ _____ can be used.

Step 2:   Start the engine and operate it at _____ _____.

Step 3:   Observe and record the _____ reading. A pressure lower than _____" (254 mm) Hg or
_____ psi (34 kPa) is too _____ and the _____ _____ to the
primary _____ should be _____ for problems. Recommend that the fuel tank
_____ _____ be inspected for _____.

4. Measuring Secondary Filter Output Pressure (page 461):

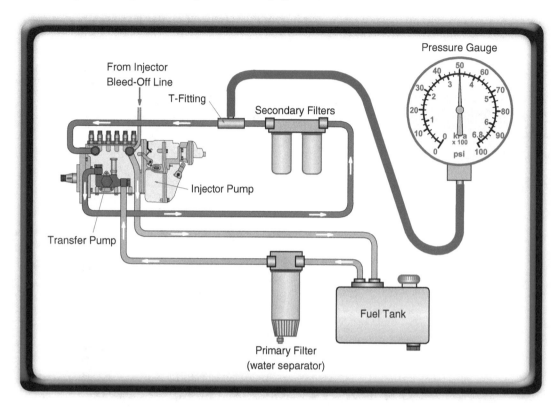

Step 1:   Obtain an accurate, high-quality _____ _____ capable of measuring pressure in psi (kPa). An _____ pressure _____ or a _____ pressure gauge is best.

Step 2:   Connect the gauge to the _____ side of the _____ filter using a quick-connect fitting, which may need to be _____ in the system if one was not equipped by the OEM. There is always a _____ _____ or _____ to access measurement of the _____ fuel _____.

Step 3:   Start the engine and run it at _____-_____ (full throttle, no load). Observe and _____ the _____ reading. Most _____ filters operate at pressures of _____–_____ psi (345–552 kPa). Compare the _____ pressures with the manufacturer's _____.

Step 4:   Make a _____ recommendation to _____ the _____ filter if the _____ pressures are approaching or _____ the manufacturer's specifications.

Crossword Puzzle

Use the clues in the column to complete the puzzle.

Across

2. A unit of measure equal to 0.001 mm.

4. A positive displacement fuel supply pump that sweeps fuel around the gear housing between pump gear teeth and can pressurize the output side to very high pressure.

5. A device that warms fuel to keep wax dissolved in the fuel.

Down

1. When the paraffin or wax content of the fuel causes fuel to become too viscous to properly flow through filters and lines due to low temperatures.

3. A type of wax dissolved in diesel fuel.

ASE-Type Questions

Read each item carefully, and then select the best response.

_____ 1. Technician A says that tanks storing diesel fuel should never be made from galvanized steel. Technician B says that diesel fuel should never be stored in tanks that contain copper or copper alloys. Who is correct?
  A. Technician A
  B. Technician B
  C. Both Technician A and Technician B
  D. Neither Technician A nor Technician B

_____ 2. Technician A says that the primary filter helps extend the life of the secondary filter. Technician B says that the primary filter is located between the engine's high-pressure injection system and the secondary filter. Who is correct?
  A. Technician A
  B. Technician B
  C. Both Technician A and Technician B
  D. Neither Technician A nor Technician B

_____ 3. Technician A says that a fuel heater located in a filter housing is the best way to prevent wax and ice crystals from restricting fuel flow. Technician B says that ethanol can be used to dissolve wax and prevent water from crystalizing in fuel filters. Who is correct?
  A. Technician A
  B. Technician B
  C. Both Technician A and Technician B
  D. Neither Technician A nor Technician B

_____ 4. Technician A says that a float sensor is used in a filter housing to measure the level of water to determine when the filter should be drained. Technician B says that a probe in the bottom of a fuel filter, which measures the difference between the conductivity of water and fuel, is used to switch on the water-in-fuel warning lamp. Who is correct?
  A. Technician A
  B. Technician B
  C. Both Technician A and Technician B
  D. Neither Technician A nor Technician B

_____ 5. Technician A says that primary filters typically use chemically treated paper filter media with a micron rating of more than 10 microns. Technician B says that synthetic filter media is used to separate bound, or coalesced, water from fuel inside a primary filter. Who is correct?
  A. Technician A
  B. Technician B
  C. Both Technician A and Technician B
  D. Neither Technician A nor Technician B

_____ 6. Technician A says that coolant is used to heat fuel in fuel–water separators. Technician B says that electrical heating elements keep water and wax from plugging the filter in a fuel–water separator. Who is correct?
  A. Technician A
  B. Technician B
  C. Both Technician A and Technician B
  D. Neither Technician A nor Technician B

_____ 7. Technician A says that a gear pump requires no check valve to prevent fuel from draining back to the tank. Technician B says a leaking hand primer pump check valve will allow fuel to drain back to the tank even if there is a gear pump. Who is correct?
  A. Technician A
  B. Technician B
  c. Both Technician A and Technician B
  D. Neither Technician A nor Technician B

_____ **8.** Technician A says that a restricted fuel filter will produce a low-power complaint under load but will not cause the engine to stall at idle. Technician B says hot fuel can cause a low-power complaint under load but will not cause the engine to stall at idle. Who is correct?
  A. Technician A
  B. Technician B
  C. Both Technician A and Technician B
  D. Neither Technician A nor Technician B

_____ **9.** Technician A says that electric priming pumps prevent suction-side air leaks in a fuel system. Technician B says that electric priming pumps are used to purge air from the suction-side fuel lines during filter changes and prior to engine start-up. Who is correct?
  A. Technician A
  B. Technician B
  C. Both Technician A and Technician B
  D. Neither Technician A nor Technician B

_____ **10.** Technician A says the best indication of when a fuel filter should be changed is based on how much distance a vehicle has traveled. Technician B says that the fuel filter should be changed whenever the oil is changed. Who is correct?
  A. Technician A
  B. Technician B
  C. Both Technician A and Technician B
  D. Neither Technician A nor Technician B

Functions of High-Pressure Fuel Systems

Chapter Review

The following activities have been designed to help you refresh your knowledge of this chapter. Your instructor may require you to complete some or all of these activities as a regular part of your training program. You are encouraged to complete any activity that your instructor does not assign as a way to enhance your learning.

Matching

Match the following terms with the correct description or example.

A. Atomization

B. Distribution

C. Hunting

D. Metering

E. Timing

_____ **1.** A rhythmic change in engine rpm at idle speed caused by uneven delivery of fuel.

_____ **2.** In the high-pressure injection system, the beginning of the injection event in the combustion cycle relative to crank rotation.

_____ **3.** The mixing of fuel and air in the cylinders during the injection event.

_____ **4.** The process of breaking up liquid fuel into a fine mist.

_____ **5.** Measurement of the correct quantity of fuel for each cylinder required for various speed and load conditions demanded of the engine.

Multiple Choice

Read each item carefully, and then select the best response.

_____ **1.** High-pressure injection systems perform all of the following tasks **EXCEPT**?

A. atomize the fuel

B. time the injection of fuel

C. regulate fuel temperature

D. control the rate of fuel delivery

_____ **2.** The _____ contains a microprocessor, various microcontrollers, memory, and software to execute instructions to operate the engine.

A. metering module

B. electronic control module

C. governor

D. calibration module

_____ **3.** Irregular or inconsistent fuel delivery causes the governor to readjust the quantity of fuel metered and correct the engine's speed; this correction is called _____.

A. loping

B. compensation

C. hunting

D. Either A or C

_____ **4.** A _____ detects misfiring or a cylinder with a low-power contribution.

A. cylinder balance test

B. injection timing test

C. cylinder cutout test

D. engine load test

_____ 5. Peak cylinder pressure should occur approximately _____ degrees of crankshaft rotation after top dead cylinder.
   A. 5–10
   B. 10–15
   C. 15–20
   D. 20–25

_____ 6. In modern fuel injection systems, _____ means the quantity of fuel injected per degree of crank angle rotation.
   A. injection rate
   B. fuel economy
   C. fuel rate
   D. pressurization rate

_____ 7. A rate-shaping strategy called _____ delivers a small quantity of fuel to the combustion chamber 8–10 degrees before the main injection.
   A. pilot injection
   B. preconditioning
   C. split-shot injection
   D. Either A or C

_____ 8. Poor mixing of air and fuel can cause _____.
   A. inadequate combustion turbulence
   B. nozzle dribble
   C. excessive ignition delay time
   D. Both A and C

_____ 9. Low compression pressure and excessive ignition delay are caused by _____.
   A. large fuel droplet size
   B. inadequate pre-ignition temperatures
   C. poor mixing of air and fuel
   D. inadequate combustion time

_____ 10. One major source of injection lag is a phenomenon, called _____ which causes a magnetic field to build up relatively slowly in the injector's electrical solenoid.
   A. reactive inductance
   B. inductive capacitance
   C. reactive resistance
   D. Either A or C

True/False

If you believe the statement to be more true than false, write the letter "T" in the space provided. If you believe the statement to be more false than true, write the letter "F".

_____ 1. Diesel engines use a throttle plate located in the air intake to regulate engine speed and power.

_____ 2. Compensation is observed when one or more cylinders are cut out and the engine maintains a set idle speed.

_____ 3. Calibration codes are given different names by manufacturers including injection quantity adjustment, the E-Trim, and the adaptation value.

_____ 4. A cylinder cutout test measures the crankshaft velocity changes for each cylinder compression and power stroke to identify cylinder misfiring, unbalanced power contributions, and mechanical problems.

_____ 5. The two most important factors influencing burn rate are cylinder pressure and temperature.

_____ 6. As the engine speeds up, injection and combustion events speed up proportionally.

_____ 7. Optimal timing for emissions negatively impacts fuel economy in North American diesel engines.

_____ 8. Fuel pressurized to thousands of pounds per square inch can easily penetrate skin, causing bodily harm, blood poisoning, and even death.

_____ 9. Modern diesel engines typically use 5–6 spray holes per injector.

_____ 10. Injection lag describes the time delay that occurs between the start of fuel pressurization and the moment when injection actually occurs.

Fill in the Blank

Read each item carefully, and then complete the statement by filling in the missing word(s).

1. Based on input data, the _____ uses linkage or software to calculate or move fuel control linkage to change the amount of fuel injected.

2. Optimal metering of injection quantities and fuel timing are calculated using a mathematical _____.

3. Idle _____ involves making adjustments to injection quantities based on changes to crankshaft speed produced during every power impulse.

4. The appropriate _____ code must be entered into the ECM each time a new injector is installed or an injector is moved.

5. The _____ _____ period is the time period between the injection of fuel and its actual point of ignition.

6. Burn time is expressed in _____ of crankshaft rotation.

7. A post-combustion injection after the main combustion event reduces the production of _____ inside the cylinder.

8. Finer _____ means fuel ignites sooner, burns faster, and burns more completely.

9. A _____ valve minimizes the backflow of fuel into an injection system in order to maintain line pressure between injections.

10. A plugged injector _____ can cause uneven distribution patterns resulting in performance and emission problems.

Labeling

Label the following diagrams with the correct terms.

1. Identify the type of diesel injection system:

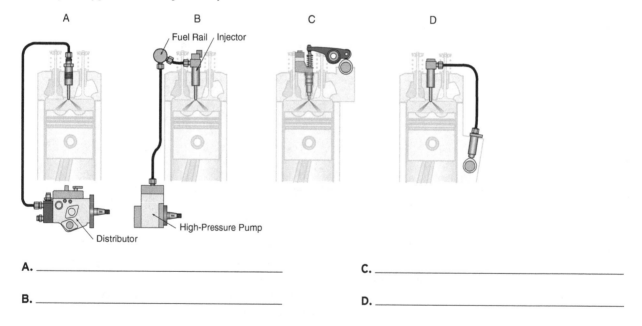

A. _____

B. _____

C. _____

D. _____

2. Identify the various calibration codes found on an injector:

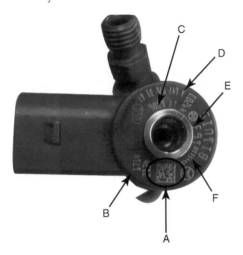

A. _____

B. _____

C. _____

D. _____

E. _____

F. _____

3. Identify the components of a pressure-sensing glow plug:

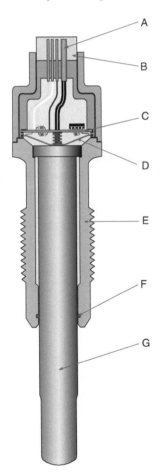

A. _____

B. _____

C. _____

D. _____

E. _____

F. _____

G. _____

Skill Drills

Test your knowledge of skill drills by filling in the correct words in the photo captions.

1. Changing an Injector Calibration Code:

Step 1:   Place the vehicle's _____ in _____ and apply the _____
_____.

Step 2:   Connect Detroit Diesel _____ _____ (DDDL) software to the vehicle
_____ _____ connector and switch on the _____ key.

Step 3:   Navigate to "Retrieve injector _____" in the _____ _____ and
bring up the Injector Calibration _____.

Step 4:   Remove the _____ _____ and record all _____ calibration
_____ if this has not already been done.

Step 5:   Compare the _____ injector calibration _____ against the _____
codes in the _____ Calibration _____.

Step 6:   If there are any _____ between the _____ injector calibration codes and
codes in the Injector Calibration window, _____ them. If any injectors have been
_____, update the calibration _____ in the Injector Calibration window.

Step 7:   Enter the engine _____ password in the _____ software (the Detroit Diesel
default password is usually _____).

Step 8:   Select the _____ Function button to _____ any calibration _____
changes to the _____.

Step 9:   Run the _____ until it reaches _____ temperature and _____ that
engine operation is _____.

2. Performing a Cylinder Balance Test:

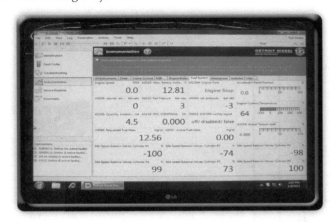

Step 1:   Start and run the _____ until it reaches _____ temperature. Place the transmission in _____ and apply the _____ _____.

Step 2:   Connect DDDL _____ to the vehicle _____ _____ connector.

Step 3:   Navigate to the _____ menu and then to the _____ _____ tab.

Step 4:   Observe and record the _____ _____ _____ _____ for each _____ while the engine is at _____.

Step 5:   Analyze the results. The _____ will apply a positive or negative _____ factor to the _____ of the injector _____ _____. A _____ value means _____ fuel is injected to compensate for low _____ pressure. A _____ value indicates a _____ pulse width signal is used to remove some fuel from the cylinder. A _____% change means the _____ cannot add or remove any fuel and the cylinder _____ will not be the same as other cylinders. Generally, any value over _____% indicates a problem with the _____. These problems range from the need for a valve _____ to _____ in the injector, high-pressure fuel system, or a base engine mechanical condition.

Crossword Puzzle

Use the clues in the column to complete the puzzle.

Across

4. Compressing fuel to the degree required for an injection event.

5. A mathematical formula used to solve a problem.

Down

1. A response by the fuel system governor to a loss of contribution from one or more cylinders. The governor increases the quantity of fuel injected into the other cylinders to maintain idle speed.

2. The energy required to pull air past a throttle plate or move gases in and out of the cylinder.

3. A device that regulates the quantity of fuel injected into the cylinders.

ASE-Type Questions

Read each item carefully, and then select the best response.

_____ 1. Technician A says a long injector response time from a magnetic solenoid is due mostly to the speed of the electric current through long wire windings. Technician B says a long injector response time is caused primarily by heavy, high-inertia control valves. Who is correct?
   A. Technician A
   B. Technician B
   C. Both Technician A and Technician B
   D. Neither Technician A nor Technician B

_____ 2. Technician A says a slow build-up of the injection rate, which provides a ramp-shaped injection discharge rate shape for the main injection event, reduces carbon monoxide emissions. Technician B says the ramp-shaped injection rate shape reduces NO_x emissions. Who is correct?
   A. Technician A
   B. Technician B
   C. Both Technician A and Technician B
   D. Neither Technician A nor Technician B

_____ 3. While discussing the steps to perform when changing an injector in a late-model engine, Technician A says that uploading a fuel injector calibration code helps the engine to run more smoothly. Technician B says that replacing the old code with the one on the new injector enables the ECM to compensate for small variations to injection quantity unique to each injector. Who is correct?
   A. Technician A
   B. Technician B
   C. Both Technician A and Technician B
   D. Neither Technician A nor Technician B

_____ 4. While checking contributions from each cylinder for a late-model electronically controlled engine, Technician A says that the purpose of adaptive cylinder balance is to reduce combustion noise so diesels run more quietly. Technician B says adaptive balance reduces emissions and helps an engine run more smoothly. Who is correct?
   A. Technician A
   B. Technician B
   C. Both Technician A and Technician B
   D. Neither Technician A nor Technician B

_____ 5. Technician A says that when a diesel engine has an increased load and its speed remains constant, injection timing must advance. Technician B says that under those conditions injection timing should retard. Who is correct?
   A. Technician A
   B. Technician B
   C. Both Technician A and Technician B
   D. Neither Technician A nor Technician B

_____ 6. While discussing possible causes of black smoke from the exhaust of an older heavy-duty diesel engine, Technician A says that black smoke from an engine under acceleration indicates the engine is producing plenty of power. Technician B says that smoke could indicate the injector nozzle spray holes are worn out. Who is correct?
   A. Technician A
   B. Technician B
   C. Both Technician A and Technician B
   D. Neither Technician A nor Technician B

_____ **7.** After assembling an engine and discovering one of the vibration-insulating high-pressure fuel line clamps was missing, two technicians discussed potential consequences if the clamp remained missing from the engine. Technician A says that the line will crack due to vibration caused by pressure pulses. Technician B says that a single missing clamp on thick-walled steel lines will have no effect on the line. Who is correct?
   A. Technician A
   B. Technician B
   C. Both Technician A and Technician B
   D. Neither Technician A nor Technician B

_____ **8.** Technician A says that multiple injection events from an injector to reduce emissions results in less torque produced from an engine. Technician B says that multiple injection events during a combustion cycle are used to reduce heat loads in a cylinder. Who is correct?
   A. Technician A
   B. Technician B
   C. Both Technician A and Technician B
   D. Neither Technician A nor Technician B

_____ **9.** While discussing potential ways to increase power output from an engine, Technician A says that advancing injection timing a few degrees will increase power output. Technician B says that advancing injection timing a few degrees will reduce fuel consumption. Who is correct?
   A. Technician A
   B. Technician B
   C. Both Technician A and Technician B
   D. Neither Technician A nor Technician B

_____ **10.** Technician A says that cutting out one cylinder at idle to check for a misfire condition will reduce idle speed by close to 100 rpm in a six-cylinder engine idling at 600 rpm if the cylinder is operating properly. Technician B says it is not possible to detect a misfiring cylinder at idle by noting a change in idle speed during cylinder cutout testing for any cylinder. Who is correct?
   A. Technician A
   B. Technician B
   C. Both Technician A and Technician B
   D. Neither Technician A nor Technician B

Hydraulic Nozzles

Chapter Review

The following activities have been designed to help you refresh your knowledge of this chapter. Your instructor may require you to complete some or all of these activities as a regular part of your training program. You are encouraged to complete any activity that your instructor does not assign as a way to enhance your learning.

Matching

Match the following terms with the correct description or example.

A. Electronic unit injectors (EUI)

B. Hydraulic nozzle holder

C. Multi-orifice nozzle

D. Pintle nozzle

E. Throttle pintle nozzle

_____ **1.** The nozzle body that encloses the nozzle assembly containing passageways connecting the high-pressure injection line to the nozzle valve.

_____ **2.** A fuel nozzle which sprays fuel through a single hole.

_____ **3.** A fuel nozzle that uses multiple spray holes to atomize and distribute fuel.

_____ **4.** A type of injector that changes the rate of injection from the nozzle through the shape of the nozzle valve; also called a delay nozzle.

_____ **5.** An electrically controlled injector incorporating timing, metering, atomization, and pressurization functions into a single unit or injector.

Multiple Choice

Read each item carefully, and then select the best response.

_____ **1.** The _____ is the valve in the nozzle that seals the end of the nozzle tip when it is not injecting fuel.
   A. nozzle valve
   B. pintle valve
   C. needle valve
   D. Either A or C

_____ **2.** Particulate matter, including soot, and oxides of nitrogen are produced from having _____ in the combustion chamber.
   A. too much fuel
   B. uneven fuel distribution
   C. not enough fuel
   D. too much air

_____ **3.** The amount of time necessary for combustion is dependent on _____.
   A. atomization
   B. fuel quality
   C. cylinder pre-ignition temperature
   D. All of the above

_____ **4.** A calibrated escape of fuel around the nozzle valve that lubricates and cools the valve is called _____.
   A. forward leakage
   B. atomization
   C. back leakage
   D. turbulence

_____ **5.** The most common technique for making holes in newer injector nozzles is _____.
   A. electric discharge machining
   B. twist drilling
   C. laser machining
   D. punching

_____ **6.** The point when fuel delivery begins is called the _____.
   A. nozzle injection pressure
   B. beginning of injection
   C. activation point
   D. Either A or C

_____ **7.** The time between the start of injection pressurization and the point when fuel is actually delivered is called _____.
   A. injection lag
   B. injection differential
   C. injection delay
   D. Either A or C

_____ **8.** Which of the following hydraulic nozzles would be used in a direct injection diesel engine?
   A. Pintle nozzle
   B. Throttle nozzle
   C. Multi-orifice nozzle
   D. Delay nozzle

_____ **9.** Carbon deposits, wear, or abrasion of the seat can cause _____ from the nozzle tip.
   A. forward leakage
   B. chatter
   C. back leakage
   D. Either A or C

_____ **10.** Excessive emissions of black or gray smoke, cylinder misfire at all load and speed conditions, and burned piston crowns usually indicate _____.
   A. nozzle tip leakage
   B. plugged orifices
   C. a nozzle is stuck open
   D. leakoff

True/False

If you believe the statement to be more true than false, write the letter "T" in the space provided. If you believe the statement to be more false than true, write the letter "F".

_____ **1.** Direct injection combustion chambers have very high turbulence in comparison to indirect injection chambers.

_____ **2.** Liquid fuel droplets vaporize and burn from the inside outward.

_____ **3.** The size or weight of the fuel droplet multiplied by its velocity determines the kinetic energy possessed by the droplet.

_____ **4.** Injection velocities of fuel can approach 1243 miles per second (2000 km per second) at full load.

_____ **5.** Newer unit injectors and common rail injectors use high-pressure fuel only to unseat the nozzle valve and begin injection.

_____ **6.** Only a single injector in an engine needs to be equipped with an integrated nozzle valve lift sensor to correct injection timing for all cylinders.

_____ **7.** Today's on-highway diesel engines primarily use indirect injection combustion chambers.

_____ **8.** Pintle nozzles are used only in direct injection combustion chambers.

_____ **9.** Newer multi-orifice nozzles may have as many as 13 spray holes in the tip.

_____ **10.** The two-spring two-stage injector nozzle mechanically controls injection rate by discharging fuel at two different rates.

Fill in the Blank

Read each item carefully, and then complete the statement by filling in the missing word(s).

1. The term _____ is often used to encompass the operation of a hydraulic nozzle.

2. Proper _____ of fuel is especially critical to reducing the formation of noxious emissions.

3. Combustible vapors originate from the fuel _____ surface as it encounters air friction and absorbs heat produced during the compression stroke.

4. Fine _____ helps fuel burn hot, fast, and more completely, leaving less residue.

5. A smoothing process, known as _____ _____ _____, enhances flow characteristics by removing resistance to fuel flow and permits increased delivery of fuel.

6. Nozzle opening pressure is determined by the pressure _____ between the spring force holding the valve on the nozzle body seat and the surface area of the nozzle valve in the annulus.

7. An identification number stamped on a nozzle's _____ identifies the nozzle and helps differentiate it from similarly shaped nozzles.

8. Nozzle opening pressure is higher in _____-_____ nozzles to produce the atomization, penetration, and distribution of fuel necessary for direct injection combustion chambers.

9. Because nozzle geometry is a compromise to promote good mixture preparation over all operating ranges, manufacturers are working on _____ orifice nozzles, or coaxial nozzles.

10. Nozzle _____ during bench testing of an injector is an indication of a clean nozzle valve with good seat contact.

Labeling

Label the following diagrams with the correct terms.

1. Identify the parts of a multi-orifice nozzle:

Multi-orifice Nozzle

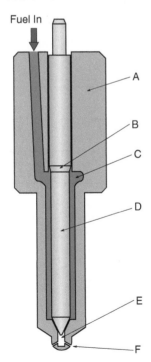

A. _____

B. _____

C. _____

D. _____

E. _____

F. _____

2. Identify the parts of a pintle nozzle:

Pintle Nozzle

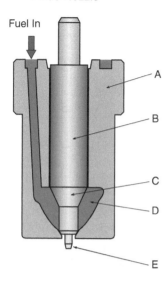

Fuel In

A. _____

B. _____

C. _____

D. _____

E. _____

3. Identify the typical components of a nozzle holder:

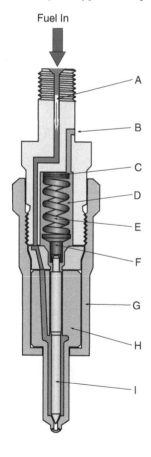

Fuel In

A. _____

B. _____

C. _____

D. _____

E. _____

F. _____

G. _____

H. _____

I. _____

Skill Drills

Test your knowledge of skill drills by filling in the correct words in the photo captions.

1. Testing Nozzle Spray Patterns:

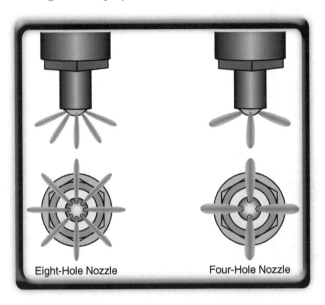

Eight-Hole Nozzle   Four-Hole Nozzle

Step 1: Disconnect the high-pressure _____ _____, then cap the nozzle fuel line _____ _____ with protective _____ caps.

Step 2: Remove the _____ from the engine. Inspect and _____ the _____ with _____. Check for missing _____ _____ or improperly installed nozzles, which will leak _____ combustion _____ around the nozzle _____.

Step 3: Set up the nozzle _____ _____ by filling it with the appropriate _____ fluid. The fluid should be _____ _____ fluid or an _____ test fluid, not _____ _____.

Step 4: Purge the nozzle tester of air by _____ the _____ several times until _____ fluid appears from the _____-_____ line.

Step 5: Ensure that the _____ area is clean and use clean _____ containers, clean _____, and clean _____ to produce satisfactory results.

Step 6: Install the proper nozzle–to–tester _____ that matches the _____-_____ fitting on the _____. Connect the _____ to the _____ _____.

Step 7: Bleed _____ from the nozzle. This is done by opening the _____ _____ and _____ the tester handle _____–_____ quick strokes to expel _____ from the injector nozzle. Test fluid should _____ from the _____ _____ in the nozzle _____. If the nozzle is _____ or the _____ is _____, the nozzle should be _____ or _____.

Step 8: Carefully _____ the spray _____ of the nozzle by _____ the tester _____ rapidly and noting the characteristics of the _____ _____ forming from the nozzle orifices.

Step 9: Spray should originate from each _____ and the spray _____ from each orifice should be the same _____ and _____ in shape. The spray should be well _____ and _____-_____ as it leaves the injector nozzle. Injectors showing _____ spray patterns should be _____ or _____.

Step 10: Listen for _____ _____ and, if observed, _____ it along with your other observations. If _____ nozzle in a _____ doesn't _____, and the rest do, recommend _____ or _____ of the nozzle.

2. Measuring NOP:

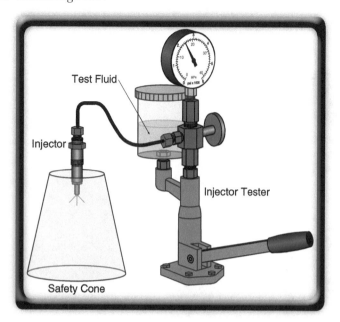

Step 1: Install the _____ in the _____ _____ following Steps 1–7 in Skill Drill 1: Testing Nozzle Spray Patterns.

Step 2: Observe and record the _____ by _____ the injector nozzle _____ and noting the _____ at which the _____ _____ lifts and fuel begins to _____ from the nozzle _____. Injector NOPs _____ according to the _____ of _____ and manufacturer's _____.

Step 3: Compare the injector's _____ with the manufacturer's specifications. Recommend _____ or _____ if the _____ does not _____ fall within an acceptable range.

3. Measuring Valve Seat Leakage (Forward Leakage):

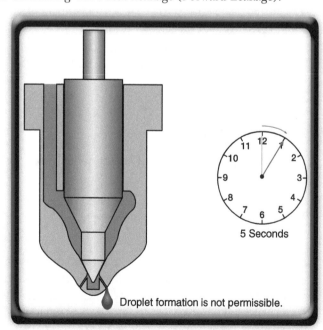

5 Seconds

Droplet formation is not permissible.

Step 1: Install the _____ in the _____ _____ following Steps 1–7 in Skill Drill 1: Testing Nozzle Spray Patterns.

Step 2: Slowly bring the _____ _____ applied to the nozzle to _____ psi (34 bar) less than the manufacturer's specified _____.

Step 3: Maintain this pressure for at least _____ seconds. Observe whether any _____ form on the _____ _____. Do this by _____ the _____ _____ to see whether it is _____. Some _____ is allowed on _____-_____ nozzles as long as there is no _____ formation within _____ seconds. It is acceptable for a _____ to form on the tip of a _____ nozzle, but if the droplet _____ _____ within _____ seconds, it is not acceptable.

4. Measuring Back Leakage:

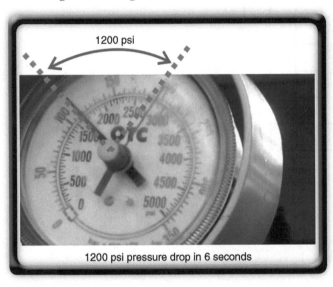

1200 psi

1200 psi pressure drop in 6 seconds

Step 1: Install the _____ in the _____ _____ following Steps 1–7 in Skill Drill 1: Testing Nozzle Spray Patterns.

Step 2: Slowly bring the _____ applied to the _____ to _____ psi (689 kPa) less than _____.

Step 3: Close the _____ in the line to the _____. This _____ the _____ in the nozzle under _____.

Step 4: Observe and record the _____ _____ on the tester gauge _____ seconds after _____ the tester _____.

Step 5: Typically, a _____ _____ of _____–_____ psi (21–60 bar) in _____ seconds indicates that the _____ surfaces inside the _____ are not leaking excessively and that the nozzle _____-_____-_____ clearances are _____. If the pressure drop is less than _____ psi (21 bar), the nozzle is not getting proper _____ and should be _____ or _____. If the pressure drop is more than _____ psi (60 bar), the nozzle is leaking _____ and should be _____ or _____.

Crossword Puzzle

Use the clues in the column to complete the puzzle.

Across

4. The process of breaking up liquid fuel into a fine mist.

5. Leakage of an injector nozzle from the spray holes, which indicates that the nozzle valve-to-seat seal is poor.

Down

1. The time delay that occurs between the start of fuel pressurization and the moment when injection actually takes place; also known as injection delay.

2. A tool used by technicians that supplies pressurized fuel to injector nozzles which is used to evaluate the condition of fuel nozzles.

3. A high-pitched noise or chirping sound produced by the high-speed cycling of the nozzle valve opening and closing with contact between the valve and seat.

ASE-Type Questions

Read each item carefully, and then select the best response.

_____ **1.** Technician A says a closed hydraulic nozzle allows combustion gases to mix with fuel inside the nozzle. Technician B says a closed nozzle has no fuel return line back to the fuel tank. Who is correct?
  A. Technician A
  B. Technician B
  C. Both Technician A and Technician B
  D. Neither Technician A nor Technician B

_____ **2.** Technician A says that direct injection combustion chambers use pintle spray nozzles. Technician B says that only multi-orifice nozzles are used in direct injection engines. Who is correct?
  A. Technician A
  B. Technician B
  C. Both Technician A and Technician B
  D. Neither Technician A nor Technician B

_____ **3.** Technician A says that the nozzles used by direct injection engines mix air and fuel faster and produce less combustion noise than nozzles used in indirect injection engines. Technician B says that before the introduction of electronically controlled direct injection systems, indirect injection engines produced less noise with fewer emissions and had higher maximum engine rpm in comparison with direct injection engines. Who is correct?
  A. Technician A
  B. Technician B
  C. Both Technician A and Technician B
  D. Neither Technician A nor Technician B

_____ **4.** Technician A says that fewer, smaller spray holes on an injector tip will atomize fuel better than an injector with larger, more numerous holes. Technician B says that fewer, larger spray holes in an injector tip will produce better fuel atomization. Who is correct?
  A. Technician A
  B. Technician B
  C. Both Technician A and Technician B
  D. Neither Technician A nor Technician B

_____ **5.** Technician A says that nozzle opening pressure (NOP) is adjusted with selective shims placed on top of the nozzle spring. Technician B says that NOP is electronically controlled in some of the latest injectors. Who is correct?
  A. Technician A
  B. Technician B
  C. Both Technician A and Technician B
  D. Neither Technician A nor Technician B

_____ **6.** Technician A says that hydraulic servo injectors use hydraulically balanced nozzle valves. Technician B says that servo hydraulic injectors require piezoelectric actuators. Who is correct?
  A. Technician A
  B. Technician B
  C. Both Technician A and Technician B
  D. Neither Technician A nor Technician B

_____ **7.** Technician A says that injection lag takes place when the time between the actual beginning of injection (BOI) lags behind the time when pressurization of the injector takes place. Technician B says that injection lag is caused by poor quality fuel with a low cetane number. Who is correct?
  A. Technician A
  B. Technician B
  C. Both Technician A and Technician B
  D. Neither Technician A nor Technician B

_____ **8.** While examining the purpose of a nozzle lift sensor, Technician A says that the sensor helps calibrate the amount of nozzle lift an engine's injectors should have. Technician B says the sensor helps produce more precise injection timing. Who is correct?

A. Technician A

B. Technician B

C. Both Technician A and Technician B

D. Neither Technician A nor Technician B

_____ **9.** When replacing an injector in an engine, Technician A says it is only important to make sure the replacement injector belongs to the same family or model of engines. Technician B says it is important that the replacement injector has a spray pattern that matches the shape of the combustion bowl in the piston. Who is correct?

A. Technician A

B. Technician B

C. Both Technician A and Technician B

D. Neither Technician A nor Technician B

_____ **10.** Technician A says that a driver may be correct in the complaint that an engine has less power after properly replacing and adjusting injectors. Technician B says that fuel consumption should decrease after replacing worn-out injectors. Who is correct?

A. Technician A

B. Technician B

C. Both Technician A and Technician B

D. Neither Technician A nor Technician B

Governors

CHAPTER 18

Governors

Chapter Review

The following activities have been designed to help you refresh your knowledge of this chapter. Your instructor may require you to complete some or all of these activities as a regular part of your training program. You are encouraged to complete any activity that your instructor does not assign as a way to enhance your learning.

Matching

Match the following terms with the correct description or example.

A. High idle
B. Peak torque
C. Rated speed
D. Torque control
E. Torque rise

_____ **1.** An engine's maximum speed with a load.

_____ **2.** The regulation of fuel entering the cylinders to produce an appropriate amount of torque for a given engine speed.

_____ **3.** The engine speed at which cylinder pressures are highest.

_____ **4.** The difference between peak torque and torque at rated speed.

_____ **5.** The maximum speed at which an engine turns without a load.

Multiple Choice

Read each item carefully, and then select the best response.

_____ **1.** Exceeding the rated rpm on a diesel can produce excessive _____ emissions.
   A. carbon monoxide
   B. particulate matter
   C. nitrogen oxide
   D. hydrogen

_____ **2.** Governors are designed to _____.
   A. measure engine speed
   B. sense operator demand
   C. regulate the quantity of fuel injected into the cylinders
   D. All of the above

_____ **3.** For on-highway diesel engines, peak torque is commonly found at _____ of the rated speed.
   A. one-third
   B. one-half
   C. two-thirds
   D. three-quarters

_____ **4.** The point where maximum fuel economy and horsepower coincide is called the _____.
   A. command point
   B. rated torque
   C. fulcrum point
   D. peak horsepower

_____ **5.** A mechanical governor typically uses _____ to sense engine speed.
   A. throttle linkage
   B. centrifugal force
   C. speed sensors
   D. a fuel gauge

_____ **6.** Mechanisms known as _____ improve ride quality and reduce emissions by slowing down control rack travel during acceleration and deceleration.
   A. load controllers
   B. torque controllers
   C. pulse dampeners
   D. Either A or C

_____ **7.** Programmable governor features such as horsepower, maximum torque output, and torque rise are examples of _____.
   A. chassis manufacturer-specific features
   B. customer-specified parameters
   C. engine OEM manufacturer-specific features
   D. technician-specified parameters

_____ **8.** Which of the following programmable governor features is **NOT** a customer-specified parameter?
   A. Progressive shift
   B. Tachometer calibration
   C. Idle shutdown timer
   D. Low gear torque reduction

_____ **9.** Mechanisms and adjustments within the _____ governor regulate only the engine idle speed and maximum engine speeds.
   A. combination
   B. variable speed
   C. automotive
   D. isochronous

_____ **10.** The _____ governor is able to maintain more precise engine speed control than other types of governors.
   A. isochronous
   B. variable speed
   C. combination
   D. automotive

True/False

If you believe the statement to be more true than false, write the letter "T" in the space provided. If you believe the statement to be more false than true, write the letter "F".

_____ **1.** Air–fuel ratio controls minimize the production of PM emissions or black smoke produced during engine acceleration.

_____ **2.** The Imperial measuring unit for torque is the newton meter.

_____ **3.** The droop curve can be managed both mechanically and electronically.

_____ **4.** Engines using highly sensitive governors are prone to hunting.

_____ **5.** Vocational vehicles, city buses, and off-road equipment engines use high torque rise governing.

_____ **6.** There is a direct mechanical connection between the throttle lever and the control rack.

_____ **7.** Electronic engine governors use principles of electronic signal processing to regulate fueling.

_____ **8.** All on-highway diesel engines manufactured today are partial-authority systems.

_____ **9.** Combination governors are mechanical governors that can combine the characteristics of the automotive governor and the variable speed governor.

_____ **10.** Gear-down protection limits engine rpm until a minimum road speed is reached.

Fill in the Blank

Read each item carefully, and then complete the statement by filling in the missing word(s).

1. Emission _____ on diesel engines indicate maximum engine speed or rated rpm.

2. Programmable _____ are measurable values about engine system operation that can be changed using service software.

3. Upper speed _____ occurs as engine fueling decreases when the engine approaches its rated speed.

4. The _____ _____ plots engine torque, fuel consumption, and horsepower against engine speed.

5. A feature called _____-_____ speed control will supply increased torque and more engine rpm when climbing hills with heavy loads and reduce torque when it senses the vehicle is unloaded or only lightly loaded.

6. Engine fueling takes place by moving an actuator such as the _____ _____ _____, which in turn changes the quantity of fuel injected into the cylinders.

7. A state of _____ exists when flyweight force equals spring force.

8. Mechanical governors use _____ that act through mechanical linkage and respond to centrifugal force.

9. Full-authority governing is more commonly referred to as _____ engine management.

10. Sometimes referred to as an all-speed governor, the _____ speed governor automatically changes the amount of fuel injected to regulate engine speed, which is based only on accelerator pedal position.

Labeling

Label the following diagram with the correct terms.

1. Identify the parts of a mechanical governor:

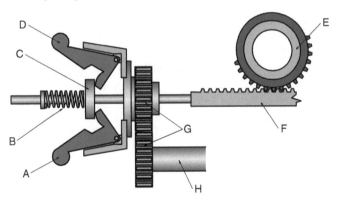

A. _____

B. _____

C. _____

D. _____

E. _____

F. _____

G. _____

H. _____

Skill Drills

Test your knowledge of skill drills by filling in the correct words in the photo captions.

1. Testing Maximum Engine Speed for a Mechanical Governor:

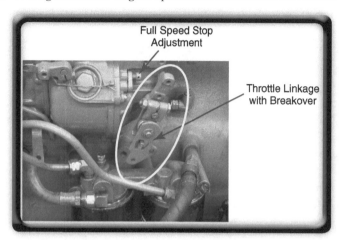

Step 1: After checking for full accelerator _____ _____, start the engine and allow it to run at _____ rpm.

Step 2: Check the _____ _____ on the engine or the engine's service literature to find its _____ _____ speed or _____ rpm.

Step 3: Slowly push on the _____ _____ to bring the _____ to full accelerator pedal _____.

Step 4: Observe and record the _____ engine rpm and _____ the accelerator pedal.

Step 5: Return the vehicle to _____, allow the _____ speed to slow, then turn off the _____.

Step 6: If the engine reached _____ _____ rpm, the governor _____ condition is acceptable. The engine should typically reach _____–_____% above rated rpm speed with no _____ acceleration. If the engine did not reach target _____, recommend governor and injection pump _____.

2. Adjusting Maximum Vehicle Speed:

Step 1:   Connect a data link _____ to the vehicle's data link _____.

Step 2:   Using _____ software, locate the group of vehicle _____ programmable _____. A separate _____ is provided for making _____ in OEM software.

Step 3:   Identify the _____ that is appropriate for the _____ and change the VSL _____ number. A customer _____ may be required to _____ and _____ the parameter.

Step 4:   Check that the chosen _____ is _____ than or _____ to peak torque rpm plus _____. If an acceptable vehicle _____ is not attainable, recommend another _____ _____ or _____ to increase engine rpm. If an _____ vehicle speed is not attained, engine _____ and _____ _____ will be adversely affected.

3. Adjusting Engine Protection Fault Response:

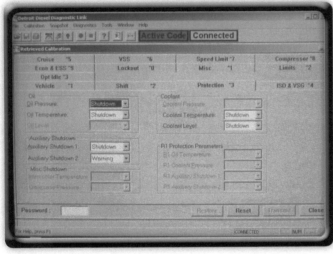

Step 1:   Connect OEM software to the vehicle's _____ _____ connector with the key _____, engine _____.

Step 2:   Navigate to the _____ parameters for engine _____ faults.

Step 3:   Determine which _____ will be _____ in the engine _____ system.

Step 4:   Determine what _____ _____ will be used to _____, _____, or _____ the engine.

Step 5:   Adjust the protection _____ system to one of _____ different settings:
- Off
- Warning: The _____ lamp on the _____ turns on.
- Derate: The warning lamp on the _____ turns on and engine power is _____.
- Shutdown: The warning lamp on the dash turns on, engine power is reduced, and then the _____ shuts down after _____ seconds. The red _____ _____ light will _____ before shutdown occurs.

Step 6:   Adjust the _____ menu items for whether the _____ button will be _____ to override the _____ feature and for the number of times the override _____ can override shutdown before _____ the key. This feature is not available in all _____.

Crossword Puzzle

Use the clues in the column to complete the puzzle.

Across

3. The inability of a governor to keep the engine speed below the high idle speed when it is rapidly accelerated.
4. An abuse condition where an engine is operated under heavy load below an acceptable operating speed range.

Down

1. The change or difference in engine speed caused by a change in load.
2. A rhythmic change in engine rpm at idle speed caused by uneven fueling of cylinders.
5. An engine's minimum operational speed.

ASE-Type Questions

Read each item carefully, and then select the best response.

_____ 1. Technician A says that any type of governor will always attempt to maintain engine idle speed even if two or three cylinders are misfiring. Technician B says that only a variable speed governor will compensate for a misfire loss from one or two cylinders and maintain idle speed. Who is correct?

   A. Technician A
   B. Technician B
   C. Both Technician A and Technician B
   D. Neither Technician A nor Technician B

_____ 2. Technician A says that any type of governor will work well when pulling heavy loads in off-road conditions without surging and causing driveline damage. Technician B says that an automotive governor is best suited to those operating conditions. Who is correct?

   A. Technician A
   B. Technician B
   C. Both Technician A and Technician B
   D. Neither Technician A nor Technician B

_____ 3. Technician A says that misadjusted governor parameters for gear-down protection could cause a low-power complaint. Technician B says that misadjusted progressive shifting parameters are more likely to cause a low-power complaint while accelerating to highway speed. Who is correct?

   A. Technician A
   B. Technician B
   C. Both Technician A and Technician B
   D. Neither Technician A nor Technician B

_____ 4. While discussing possible causes of a low-power complaint on an engine using a mechanical governor, Technician A says that weak governor springs can cause the problem. Technician B says that a leaking tube connecting the intake manifold and air–fuel ratio control device can cause the problem. Who is correct?

   A. Technician A
   B. Technician B
   C. Both Technician A and Technician B
   D. Neither Technician A nor Technician B

_____ 5. While advising a customer about the consequences of increasing maximum engine rpm with a power-up device, Technician A says that the engine will produce more smoke. Technician B says the problem with emissions can be corrected by adjusting the air–fuel ratio control. Who is correct?

   A. Technician A
   B. Technician B
   C. Both Technician A and Technician B
   D. Neither Technician A nor Technician B

_____ 6. Technician A says that an engine with multi-torque capabilities will supply more torque and engine rpm when operating in hilly terrain. Technician B says a multi-torque engine will supply more torque only when operating in cruise control. Who is correct?

   A. Technician A
   B. Technician B
   C. Both Technician A and Technician B
   D. Neither Technician A nor Technician B

_____ 7. Technicians A and B are discussing which engine is best used to pull tree stumps from some land on a farm. The decision is being made between two engines in two different medium-duty pickup trucks. Technician A says the engine with a peak torque of 850 ft-lb (1152 Nm) and 325 horsepower (242 kW) is ideal for pulling stumps. Technician B says the other truck with a peak torque of 650 ft-lb (881 Nm) and 400 horsepower (198 kW) is better. Who is correct?

   A. Technician A
   B. Technician B
   C. Both Technician A and Technician B
   D. Neither Technician A nor Technician B

_____ **8.** Technicians A and B are making programmable parameter adjustments for the governor used by an engine to drive a REPTO that is operating a hydraulic pump on a concrete mixer. Technician A says that the PTO throttle switch should be configured so the engine governor drives the PTO using variable speed governing. Technician B says that the engine should be set up to use variable speed governing when the PTO is operating. Who is correct?

    A. Technician A

    B. Technician B

    C. Both Technician A and Technician B

    D. Neither Technician A nor Technician B

_____ **9.** Technician A says that it is important to push the accelerator pedal to the floor once and then release it when starting a mechanically governed diesel engine. Technician B says the injection pump will automatically go to half throttle when cranking and nothing needs to be done. Who is correct?

    A. Technician A

    B. Technician B

    C. Both Technician A and Technician B

    D. Neither Technician A nor Technician B

_____ **10.** Technician A says that a diesel engine needs a governor to prevent a commercial vehicle from wasting fuel. Technician B says a diesel engine needs a governor to regulate fuel delivery because diesels are very sensitive to slight changes in the amount of fuel injected and can overspeed. Who is correct?

    A. Technician A

    B. Technician B

    C. Both Technician A and Technician B

    D. Neither Technician A nor Technician B

Multiple Plunger Injection Pumps

Chapter Review

The following activities have been designed to help you refresh your knowledge of this chapter. Your instructor may require you to complete some or all of these activities as a regular part of your training program. You are encouraged to complete any activity that your instructor does not assign as a way to enhance your learning.

Matching

Match the following terms with the correct description or example.

A. Charging gallery

B. Dynamic timing

C. Effective stroke

D. Spill timing

E. Static timing

_____ **1.** The distance the plunger moves between fill port closing and spill port opening.

_____ **2.** A passageway for fuel surrounding all the barrels of the injection pump.

_____ **3.** Changes in pump timing when an engine is running.

_____ **4.** Pump timing that is adjusted when an engine is stopped.

_____ **5.** A procedure that can be performed on an engine to verify or adjust pump to engine timing.

Multiple Choice

Read each item carefully, and then select the best response.

_____ **1.** To vary the quantity of fuel required for multiple plunger injection pumps, a(n) _____ metering system accurately meters the fuel used for each injection event.
  A. port-helix
  B. rack and pinion
  C. electronic
  D. pneumatic

_____ **2.** Inline multiple plunger injection pumps haven't been used on-highway light- or medium-duty diesel applications in North America since the late 1990s because they are not capable of _____.
  A. controlling the air–fuel ratio
  B. using an electronic governing system
  C. meeting strict emission requirements
  D. varying the beginning of injection

_____ **3.** The highest injection pressure available from a Bosch P7100 inline pump is approximately _____.
  A. 14,250 psi (983 bar)
  B. 16,500 psi (1138 bar)
  C. 19,500 psi (1344 bar)
  D. 25,500 psi (1758 bar)

_____ **4.** Caterpillar uses an exclusive, patented system call _____ metering.
  A. port-helix
  B. scroll
  C. wobble plate
  D. piston

_____ **5.** Bosch type _____ pumps have the highest pressure and volume output and are commonly used for medium- and heavy-duty on- and off-highway applications.
   A. A
   B. H
   C. P
   D. MW

_____ **6.** The governor is connected to the _____.
   A. pinion gear
   B. control sleeve
   C. control vane
   D. control rack

_____ **7.** A _____ eliminates the unpredictable variable of injection delay in timing the combustion event.
   A. timing mechanism
   B. nozzle valve sensor
   C. shut-off solenoid
   D. All of the above

_____ **8.** Injection pump plunger speed and duration of injection are primarily dependent on the shape of the _____.
   A. pump camshaft
   B. delivery valve
   C. nozzle lift
   D. helix

_____ **9.** High-pressure fuel injection lines are most often constructed using _____.
   A. reinforced copper
   B. seamless steel tubing
   C. zinc tubing
   D. Any of the above

_____ **10.** When setting initial static pump to engine timing the use of _____ can assist in the adjustment of the lift to port closure point to the appropriate engine position.
   A. pointers
   B. timing indicators
   C. timing pins
   D. All of the above

True/False

If you believe the statement to be more true than false, write the letter "T" in the space provided. If you believe the statement to be more false than true, write the letter "F".

_____ **1.** Because of the arrangement of high-pressure components, multiple plunger injection systems are referred to as pump-line-nozzle fuel systems.

_____ **2.** Some multiple plunger injection systems can match the capabilities of full-authority electronically controlled fuel systems.

_____ **3.** Fill and spill ports allow fuel to enter the barrel in the space above the plunger.

_____ **4.** Fuel enters the injection pump from a low-pressure supply pump at anywhere between 5 and 10 psi (34 and 69 kPa).

_____ **5.** Lift to port closure is considered the beginning of the injection event when adjusting the pump to engine timing, either on a calibration bench or in the field.

_____ **6.** The beginning of injection event occurs when the helix groove uncovers the spill port, venting fuel pressure from above the plunger to the spill port.

_____ **7.** To stop fuel delivery and engine operation, the vertical grooves in the sides of the pumping plunger are rotated to align with the fill and spill ports.

_____ **8.** The shape of the helix can be used to change injection timing.

_____ **9.** Partial-authority systems have a mechanical linkage that connects the accelerator pedal to the pump.

_____ **10.** Injection lines are fabricated to be the same length and diameter to ensure that the fuel pressure wave arrives at each cylinder at exactly the same time.

Fill in the Blank

Read each item carefully, and then complete the statement by filling in the missing word(s).

1. A multiple plunger injection pump is a fuel system configuration that uses piston-like barrel and plunger assemblies that are actuated by a _____ to pressurize fuel for injection.

2. A _____-_____ fuel system is a mechanical-electrical hybrid fuel system design in which the governor and timing controls are typically electronic and not solely mechanical.

3. Most multiple plunger pumps use a port-helix metering system, which uses a _____ and _____ assembly.

4. When the control rack moves from side to side in a linear direction, this motion is transferred through the _____ gear to the driving vane, which causes the plunger to simultaneously rotate.

5. An _____ valve is similar to a pressure regulator.

6. The _____ valve operates as a one-way check to allow fuel to remain at relatively high pressure in the fuel injection line.

7. To mechanically produce _____ injection timing, notches or slots are machined into the top of the pumping plungers.

8. To minimize the effect of pressure wave reflections, the delivery valve has a _____ function built into its shape.

9. Dynamic timing can be checked using an injection pulse transducer device, called a _____ _____ _____, attached to the fuel injection line.

10. Pumps are evaluated on test benches also known as _____ benches.

Labeling

Label the following diagrams with the correct terms.

1. Identify the major components of a multiple plunger injection pump:

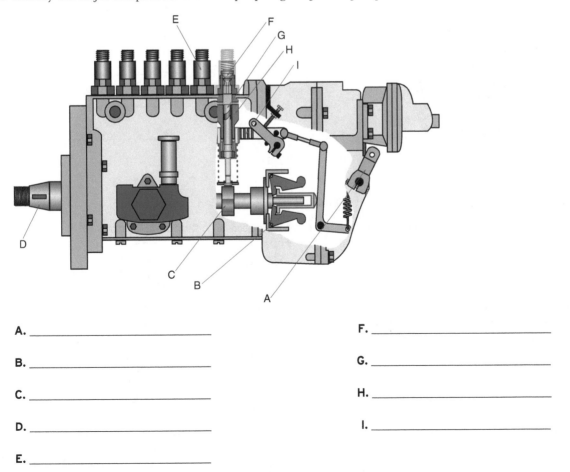

A. _____	F. _____
B. _____	G. _____
C. _____	H. _____
D. _____	I. _____
E. _____	

2. Identify the components of a plunger and barrel assembly:

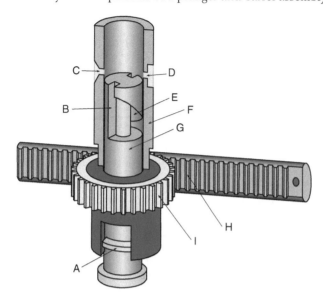

A. _____

B. _____

C. _____

D. _____

E. _____

F. _____

G. _____

H. _____

I. _____

3. Identify the components of a timing mechanism:

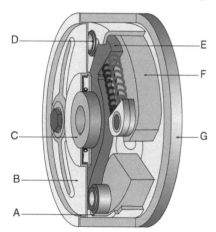

A. _____

B. _____

C. _____

D. _____

E. _____

F. _____

G. _____

4. Identify common camshaft profiles found in multiple plunger injection pumps:

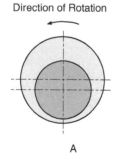
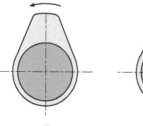
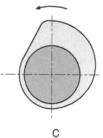
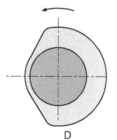

A. _____

B. _____

C. _____

D. _____

Skill Drills

Test your knowledge of skill drills by filling in the correct words in the photo captions.

1. Replacing a Delivery Valve:

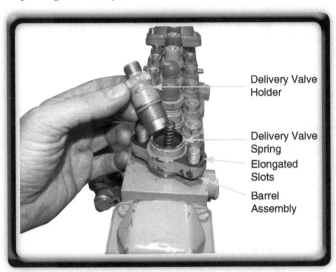

Delivery Valve
Holder

Delivery Valve
Spring

Elongated
Slots

Barrel
Assembly

Step 1:   Clean the engine and _____ _____ thoroughly before attempting to remove any
parts. Use compressed air to remove any _____ or small _____ particles that
remain on the _____ _____ after power washing. Remember that any dirt and
debris inside the _____ _____ will produce a _____.

Step 2:   Disconnect the _____ lines and _____ them while performing this procedure.

Step 3:   Remove the delivery valve _____ using a special _____-point _____. Some
well-made _____-point _____ can also be effectively used for this work. A sealing
_____ may give some resistance when removing the _____ from the pump
_____.

Step 4:   Remove the _____ _____ _____ from the holder if it is removed
with the holder. Otherwise, use a _____ to remove the valve seat, _____
_____, and _____.

Step 5:   Using a _____, remove and _____ the copper _____
_____ located _____ the delivery valve holder.

Step 6:   Install a new copper _____ _____.

Step 7:   If the _____ is being _____ after _____ particles are removed,
reinstall the delivery valve after _____ it.

Step 8:   Install a new delivery valve, _____, and _____ from a _____
_____.

Step 9:   Reinstall the delivery valve _____ with a new _____-_____ O-ring
and _____ to specifications.

Step 10: Repeat the above _____ with the other pump _____.

Step 11: Reinstall the _____ _____. Run the engine and _____ for
_____.

Crossword Puzzle

Use the clues in the column to complete the puzzle.

Across

2. An injection pump adjustment procedure that is made when the remaining pumping elements are adjusted to obtain lift to port closure (in 60-degree intervals for a six-cylinder pump) after the initial setting on cylinder 1.

4. A low-pressure fuel system pressure regulating valve for an injection pump that uses a ball and spring assembly. The overflow valve helps purge vapor from fuel and keeps fuel temperatures cool inside the pump.

5. A component used by multiple plunger injection pumps to produce low friction reciprocating motion of the plungers.

Down

1. A component used by multiple plunger injection pumps that actuates plungers that pressurize fuel for injection.

3. Adjustments of the control rack to pinion, rack travel, or rotation of barrels to ensure that that the delivery of fuel from each plunger is the same throughout the entire speed range of the pump.

ASE-Type Questions

Read each item carefully, and then select the best response.

_____ 1. Technician A says that injection lag caused by the use of a control rack causes injection timing to retard. Technician B says that injection lag caused by the swelling of injection lines potentially reduces the amount of fuel delivered. Who is correct?
   A. Technician A
   B. Technician B
   C. Both Technician A and Technician B
   D. Neither Technician A nor Technician B

_____ 2. Technician A says that an inline injection pump will turn at the same speed as the engine because it is driven by the camshaft. Technician B says that the injection pump will turn at half the engine speed because it is driven directly by the crankshaft dive gear. Who is correct?
   A. Technician A
   B. Technician B
   C. Both Technician A and Technician B
   D. Neither Technician A nor Technician B

_____ 3. When discussing the procedure used to install an inline injection pump, Technician A says that the crank should be positioned at top dead center for cylinder 1 using the timing mark on the front crank pulley. Technician B says that the valves on cylinder 1 should be checked after removing the valve cover to confirm that the engine is at top dead center for cylinder 1. Who is correct?
   A. Technician A
   B. Technician B
   C. Both Technician A and Technician B
   D. Neither Technician A nor Technician B

_____ 4. Technician A says that movement of the control rack travel in a multiple plunger injection pump is controlled by the governor. Technician B says that control rack travel goes to a full fuel position when the engine is cranking. Who is correct?
   A. Technician A
   B. Technician B
   C. Both Technician A and Technician B
   D. Neither Technician A nor Technician B

_____ 5. Technician A says that a nozzle lift sensor is used to provide feedback to an ECM regarding the quantity of fuel injected by a nozzle. Technician B says that the sensor is responsible for precisely identifying the beginning of the injection event. Who is correct?
   A. Technician A
   B. Technician B
   C. Both Technician A and Technician B
   D. Neither Technician A nor Technician B

_____ 6. Technician A says that a diesel engine cannot run backward or reverse its direction of rotation. Technician B says it can, depending on the style of injection pump camshaft. Who is correct?
   A. Technician A
   B. Technician B
   C. Both Technician A and Technician B
   D. Neither Technician A nor Technician B

_____ 7. Technicians A and B are discussing the potential cause of a fuel leak from a crack in a high-pressure fuel line. Technician A says the line broke because the pump's governor was tampered with. Technician B says it broke because the fuel line clamp insulators were worn out and did not clamp the line tightly enough to prevent vibration. Who is correct?
   A. Technician A
   B. Technician B
   C. Both Technician A and Technician B
   D. Neither Technician A nor Technician B

_____ **8.** Technicians A and B are discussing the replacement of a cracked high-pressure fuel line. Technician A says that the replacement line must be ordered for the correct cylinder because the lines are different lengths from the injection pump to each cylinder. Technician B says that it is best to order the replacement lines for all the cylinders to avoid any mixing of line length during installation. Who is correct?
   A. Technician A
   B. Technician B
   C. Both Technician A and Technician B
   D. Neither Technician A nor Technician B

_____ **9.** Technician A says that worn gear trains will cause injection pump timing to retard because gear backlash increases. Technician B says that injection pump timing is designed to advance with gear train wear. Who is correct?
   A. Technician A
   B. Technician B
   C. Both Technician A and Technician B
   D. Neither Technician A nor Technician B

_____ **10.** Technician A says that loosening and rotating a delivery valve holder on a P-series pump is an effective and easier way to identify a cylinder misfire condition. Technician B says that rotating the delivery valve holder within the elongated slots will require pump removal and a comparator bench to recalibrate the injection pump delivery quantities. Who is correct?
   A. Technician A
   B. Technician B
   C. Both Technician A and Technician B
   D. Neither Technician A nor Technician B

Mechanical Distributor Injection Pumps

Chapter Review

The following activities have been designed to help you refresh your knowledge of this chapter. Your instructor may require you to complete some or all of these activities as a regular part of your training program. You are encouraged to complete any activity that your instructor does not assign as a way to enhance your learning.

Matching

Match the following terms with the correct description or example.

A. Control sleeve

B. Delivery valve

C. Inlet metering

D. Piezoelectric pressure transducer

E. Vane pump

_____ **1.** A close-fitting ring that slides along the axial plunger to open or close the spill port.

_____ **2.** A sensor clamped to an injection line that converts injection line pressure pulses into electrical signals. The signals are used to activate a timing light when checking or adjusting dynamic injection pump timing.

_____ **3.** A device that pressurizes fuel inside the pump housing.

_____ **4.** Device that operates as a one-way check to allow fuel to remain at relatively high pressure in the fuel injection line while ensuring that fuel pressure will drop far enough below nozzle-opening pressure to prevent secondary injections caused by reflecting fuel pulsations in the injector line.

_____ **5.** The use of a helical groove on the metering valve in an opposed plunger metering system to regulate fuel delivery to the pumping plungers.

Multiple Choice

Read each item carefully, and then select the best response.

_____ **1.** Until the early 1950s, fewer than _____ of all engines produced in North America were diesels.

    A. 5%

    B. 10%

    C. 15%

    D. 20%

_____ **2.** The first distributor pump was invented by _____.

    A. John Deere

    B. Robert Bosch

    C. Vernon Roosa

    D. Henry Ford

_____ **3.** The _____ design used by the Bosch VE pump and its licensees uses a sleeve metering system.

    A. opposed plunger

    B. axial piston

    C. radial piston

    D. Either A or C

_____ **4.** The _____ design uses pumping plungers arranged at 90° angles to the pump driveshaft, which operates inside a cam ring.

    A. opposed plunger

    B. axial piston

    C. radial piston

    D. Either A or C

_____ 5. The _____ design uses a multi-lobed rotating plate that looks like a disc with lumps, which is used to actuate the plunger.
A. axial piston
B. radial piston
C. wobble plate
D. opposed plunger

_____ 6. The most popular application of the opposed plunger distributor injection pump design is the model _____ pump, which was used by GM inV8 automobile engines and by Ford in truck engines.
A. VE
B. CAV DPA
C. DB2
D. DS

_____ 7. The fuel limiter leaf spring is accessed through the _____ of the injection pump.
A. top
B. bottom
C. side
D. inlet

_____ 8. The _____ uses a solenoid-operated piston, located under the top cover of the injection pump, to open the restriction fitting for the fuel return passageway.
A. metering regulator
B. housing pressure cold-start advance mechanism
C. delivery pump
D. governor

_____ 9. Axial pump plunger diameter will vary between engine models based on the _____ of the engine.
A. power rating
B. injection timing
C. emission requirements
D. Both A and C

_____ 10. To provide better cold operation, less smoke, and fewer misfires, VE pumps are equipped with one of several types of _____ devices.
A. KSB
B. control sleeve
C. idle speed adjustment
D. piezoelectric

True/False

If you believe the statement to be more true than false, write the letter "T" in the space provided. If you believe the statement to be more false than true, write the letter "F".

_____ 1. Farm equipment operated exclusively using diesel fuel until the 1950s.
_____ 2. Distributor pumps use a single pumping element to deliver fuel to all cylinders.
_____ 3. Distributor pumps are better for emission control than inline pumps.
_____ 4. The cam ring in a distributor pump is the equivalent of the camshaft in a multiple plunger pump.
_____ 5. Some electronic versions of the DB2 pump use three opposed plungers.
_____ 6. Fuel is pulled from the fuel tank by the internal transfer pump.
_____ 7. An automatic timing advance mechanism is incorporated in the design of the distributor injection pump.
_____ 8. Bosch VE pumps use about half the number of parts as an inline pump.
_____ 9. Distributor and inline injection pumps operate at one-quarter engine rpm.
_____ 10. On turbocharged engines, the KSB device modulates the quantity of fuel injected based on intake manifold pressure.

Fill in the Blank

Read each item carefully, and then complete the statement by filling in the missing word(s).

1. The development of distributor _____ _____ advanced diesel engine production into more widespread use.

2. The model designation for the Bosch VE pump is an abbreviation of the German word _____, which means distributor.

3. The _____ _____ pressurization design uses a single reciprocating plunger located along the pump axis to pressurize fuel for injection.

4. Regulating the amount of fuel delivered to the pumping plungers to match engine speed and load conditions is the job of the _____.

5. In an opposed plunger metering pump, two or four opposed pumping plungers housed within the _____ are used to pressurize fuel for injection.

6. The _____ _____ has lobes corresponding to the number of engine cylinders and surrounds the shoe and rollers of the rotor.

7. Filtered fuel is drawn into an opposed plunger pump by a _____ pump, an internal transfer pump located at the end of the hydraulic head.

8. In inlet metering, fuel flows from the internal transfer pump and around the rotor through a passage called the _____.

9. A _____ valve located in the end of the rotor's axial passageway operates like a one-way check valve during the discharge of fuel.

10. The use of a housing pressure _____-_____ advance mechanism compensates for the need for advanced injection timing after starting.

Labeling

Label the following diagrams with the correct terms.

1. Identify the parts of a Bosch VE pump:

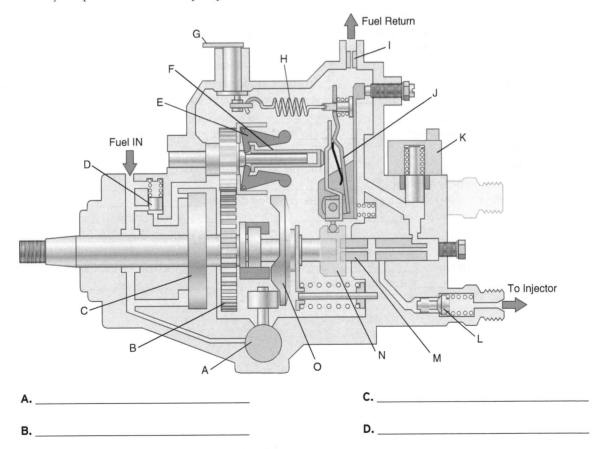

A. _____   C. _____

B. _____   D. _____

E. _____

F. _____

G. _____

H. _____

I. _____

J. _____

K. _____

L. _____

M. _____

N. _____

O. _____

Skill Drills

Test your knowledge of skill drills by filling in the correct words in the photo captions.

1. Measuring Dynamic Injection Pump Timing:

   Step 1: Attach a _____ injection line clamp pressure _____ to injection line. Make sure to _____ the line area where the clamp is attached with some _____ _____. Attach the _____ _____ for the transducer to engine _____.

   Step 2: Attach the _____ _____ of an ignition _____ _____ to the pressure transducer _____ _____. The timing light should be the _____ type used to check spark _____ _____.

   Step 3: Mark the _____ _____ top dead center (TDC) indicator to highlight _____ _____ for TDC.

   Step 4: Start the _____ and allow it to _____ until it reaches _____ temperature.

   Step 5: If required by the pressure transducer manufacturer, apply an _____ _____ factor to the timing light _____ _____. The _____ _____ is the correction factors used to account for the _____ time between the _____ induced in the line sensor by injection line _____ and the moment when the timing light _____. A common offset value is _____.

   Step 6: Operate the engine at _____ rpm or at the speed the _____ requires when _____ _____ is measured. Observe and record injection timing.

   Step 7: Bypass the _____-_____ switch with a _____ _____ to activate the cold-start _____ in the injection pump. Observe and record the injection timing.

   Step 8: Compare the _____ injection timing with the OEM's _____. If the timing is incorrect, loosen the pump _____ _____ and _____ the pump to achieve the correct timing specifications. If timing does not _____ as the engine speed increases, recommend an _____ _____ replacement or overhaul.

   Step 9: Compare the _____ _____ with and without the _____-_____ mechanisms energized. There should be a change of at least _____. If injection pump _____ does not _____ when the cold-start mechanisms are _____, recommend an injection pump _____ or _____.

2. Measuring Pump Housing Pressure:

Step 1:   Thoroughly _____ the injection pump _____ to prevent any _____ contamination of sensitive _____ _____ components.

Step 2:   On DB pumps, remove the _____ _____ cover lock _____ from the _____ of the pump.

Step 3:   Insert the purpose-made _____ into the _____ _____ of the pump and connect the adapter to a _____-_____ psi (0–1103 kPa) _____ _____.

Step 4:   Start the engine and let it _____ to purge air from the _____ _____ that may have entered when the _____ was removed. After engine speed has _____, move the _____ to the _____-_____ position.

Step 5:   Record the _____ pump housing _____. A typical specification for a DB pump is _____-_____ psi (621–827 kPa).

Step 6:   If pump housing pressure is too _____, remove the pump _____ line _____ fitting and _____ it.

Step 7:   Retest and _____ and _____ the internal pump housing _____.

Step 8:   If the pump hosing _____ is too _____, recommend a pump _____ or _____.

Step 9:   On Bosch VE pumps, the injection _____ _____ is controlled by _____ _____ pressure. Housing pressure is measured at the _____ line _____, which has an integral _____ _____.

Step 10: Insert the line pressure _____ and measure pressure there. Housing pressure _____ with _____ _____; for example, housing pressure may be _____ psi (303 kPa) at _____ rpm and _____ psi (517 kPa) at _____ rpm. Consult the OEM's specifications to compare _____ and _____ values.

3. Adjusting Static Pump-to-Engine Timing:

Static Timing in Degrees Before TDC	Plunger Travel in mm
10.0	3.25
10.5	3.35
11.0	3.45
11.5	3.55
12.0	3.65
12.5	3.7
13.0	3.8
13.5	3.9
14.0	4.0

Step 1: Position the crankshaft at _____ for cylinder _____ and mark the engine position on the front _____ _____. If the engine uses a _____ _____, locate cylinder _____ _____ using the method described in Skill Drill 19–3.

Step 2: Remove the _____ _____ from the pump's distributor head and install a purpose-made _____ _____. The dial _____ is capable of indicating movement of _____ mm with the _____ marked in increments of _____ mm. An _____ dial will measure _____ mm in one _____ with a total indicator travel of _____ mm.

Step 3: Rest the dial indicator _____ _____ on the axial pumping _____ in the pump.

Step 4: With the engine at TDC for cylinder 1, _____ the engine over _____ one _____ of a turn, or until the dial indicator needle movement stops. _____ in the dial indicator _____.

Step 5: Bar the engine over in a _____ rotation while pressing on the _____ _____ or while having an _____ precisely stop the engine at TDC. When the engine is at _____ for cylinder _____, stop and note dial indicator _____.

Step 6: Compare the _____ _____ movement with the OEM's specifications or the above _____.

Step 7: If the _____ _____ is not within the OEM's specifications, loosen the pump _____ _____ and _____ the pump housing until the dial indicator pointer matches the _____ for the correct _____ _____. For example, an engine with pump to injection timing of _____° before TDC should have a dial indicator movement of _____ mm.

Step 8: Tighten the _____ mounting _____; reinstall and reattach the _____ _____.

Step 9: Run the _____ and _____ its operation.

Step 10: When properly timed, the pump-to-engine _____ _____ used to _____ _____ the pump will be closely, if not exactly, _____. These marks are _____ into the pump housing and engine _____ _____.

Crossword Puzzle

Use the clues in the column to complete the puzzle.

Across

3. A multi-lobed rotating plate in an axial plunger injection pump used to produce a reciprocating movement of the axial plunger.

4. A probe threaded into the glow plug holes of the first cylinder that senses the light produced by a combustion event. The probe is used to help adjust injection pump timing during initial installation.

5. A mechanism that is used to advance injection timing when an engine is cold.

Down

1. A device that provides better cold operation, less smoke, and fewer misfires. It operates by moving the servo piston of the hydraulic advance mechanism.

2. A ring with lobes arranged on its internal diameter that is used to force opposing pumping plungers together to produce an injection event.

ASE-Type Questions

Read each item carefully, and then select the best response.

_____ 1. Technician A says that distributor injection pumps have not been used by on-highway vehicles since before the year 2000. Technician B says that distributor injection pumps are used on late-model, Tier 3, off-road equipment. Who is correct?
  A. Technician A
  B. Technician B
  C. Both Technician A and Technician B
  D. Neither Technician A nor Technician B

_____ 2. Technician A says that distributor pumps were first popularized by automobiles during the oil crisis of the 1970s. Technician B says that distributor injection pumps were first widely used on farm equipment. Who is correct?
  A. Technician A
  B. Technician B
  C. Both Technician A and Technician B
  D. Neither Technician A nor Technician B

_____ 3. Technician A says that vane transfer pumps are used in all distributor injection pumps. Technician B says that only Bosch VE pumps use vane pumps. Who is correct?
  A. Technician A
  B. Technician B
  C. Both Technician A and Technician B
  D. Neither Technician A nor Technician B

_____ 4. Technician A says that to advance injection timing, a cam ring is rotated in the opposite direction of rotor shaft movement in a Stanadyne DB pump. Technician B says that the cam plate is rotated by a servo piston. Who is correct?
  A. Technician A
  B. Technician B
  C. Both Technician A and Technician B
  D. Neither Technician A nor Technician B

_____ 5. When discussing the procedure to check dynamic injection pump timing, Technician A says the pump should advance when the cold-start device is activated by cold ambient temperatures. Technician B says that the timing advance is really a retarding of injection timing during cold-start operation and the timing should advance as the engine warms up. Who is correct?
  A. Technician A
  B. Technician B
  C. Both Technician A and Technician B
  D. Neither Technician A nor Technician B

_____ 6. To investigate a low-power complaint for a Stanadyne DB pump, Technician A says to first check to see if the accelerator pedal is moving the throttle to a fuel position. Technician B says a quicker way to check for low power is to move the light load advance lever with a screwdriver. Who is correct?
  A. Technician A
  B. Technician B
  C. Both Technician A and Technician B
  D. Neither Technician A nor Technician B

_____ 7. Technician A says that when installing a distributor injection pump, it is only necessary to line up the scribe marks on the pump housing and engine cover. Technician B says that it is important to remove the valve cover and check the position of cylinder 1 to ensure the pump is installed correctly. Who is correct?
  A. Technician A
  B. Technician B
  C. Both Technician A and Technician B
  D. Neither Technician A nor Technician B

_____ **8.** An engine with a VE pump has arrived and will not start. Technician A says that current supplied to the shut-off solenoid should open the fuel shut-off valve. Technician B says that the shut-off valve is normally closed and needs energizing only momentarily to shut the engine off. Who is correct?
  A. Technician A
  B. Technician B
  C. Both Technician A and Technician B
  D. Neither Technician A nor Technician B

_____ **9.** Technician A says that it would only require a single piece of dirt in the delivery valve of a VE distributor pump to prevent the engine from starting. Technician B says that more than that would be needed. Who is correct?
  A. Technician A
  B. Technician B
  C. Both Technician A and Technician B
  D. Neither Technician A nor Technician B

_____ **10.** Technician A says that mechanical distributor injection pumps use hydraulic governor to regulate engine speed and torque. Technician B says that distributor pumps use mechanical flyweights and linkage to regulate engine power output. Who is correct?
  A. Technician A
  B. Technician B
  C. Both Technician A and Technician B
  D. Neither Technician A nor Technician B

Electronic Signal Processing Principles

Chapter Review

The following activities have been designed to help you refresh your knowledge of this chapter. Your instructor may require you to complete some or all of these activities as a regular part of your training program. You are encouraged to complete any activity that your instructor does not assign as a way to enhance your learning.

Matching

Match the following terms with the correct description or example.

A. Electrically erasable programmable read-only memory (EEPROM)

B. Keep alive memory (KAM)

C. Programmable read-only memory (PROM)

D. Random access memory (RAM)

E. Read-only memory (ROM)

_____ **1.** Non-volatile memory technology that is used to store operating instructions or programming for an ECM.

_____ **2.** Memory used for permanent storage of instructions and fixed values used by the ECM that control the microprocessor.

_____ **3.** Memory that is retained by the ECM when the key is off.

_____ **4.** Memory that stores programming information and cannot be easily written over.

_____ **5.** A temporary storage place for information that needs to be quickly accessed.

Multiple Choice

Read each item carefully, and then select the best response.

_____ **1.** When engine operational problems leading to excess emissions occur, self-monitoring and self-diagnostic capabilities of electronic controls can _____.
   A. identify the problem
   B. alert the operator
   C. minimize noxious emission production
   D. All of the above

_____ **2.** A branch of information technology that uses specialized telecommunication applications for long-distance transmission of information to and from a vehicle is known as _____.
   A. tachography
   B. telematics
   C. reluctance
   D. pulse-width-modulation

_____ **3.** The control system element that collects sensor data and determines outputs based on a set of instructions or program software is known as _____.
   A. processing
   B. sensing
   C. input
   D. actuation

_____ **4.** A(n) _____ signal is electric current that is proportional to a continuously changing variable.
   A. digital
   B. analog
   C. binary
   D. pulse-width

_____ **5.** The smallest piece of digital or binary information is called a _____ and is represented by a single 0 or 1.
   A. speck
   B. byte
   C. dot
   D. bit

_____ **6.** When the voltage on a wire pair is a mirror opposite voltage when transmitting serial data it is called a _____.
   A. binary translation
   B. pulse-width-modulation
   C. differential voltage
   D. baud signal

_____ **7.** A signal that varies in "ON" and "OFF" time is called a(n) _____ signal.
   A. analog
   B. pulse-width-modulation
   C. binary
   D. differential

_____ **8.** The percentage of time a pulse-width-modulation signal is high or on, in comparison to off time is referred to as its _____.
   A. duty cycle
   B. frequency
   C. pulse width
   D. Either A or C

_____ **9.** The number of events or cycles that occur in a period, usually one second, is called _____.
   A. pulse width
   B. megahertz
   C. frequency
   D. duty cycle

_____ **10.** The CPU _____ is an oscillator inside the microprocessor that controls how fast instructions stored in memory are processed.
   A. validation switch
   B. A-D converter
   C. modulator
   D. clock

True/False

If you believe the statement to be more true than false, write the letter "T" in the space provided. If you believe the statement to be more false than true, write the letter "F".

_____ **1.** High-performance police cars were the first commercial vehicle systems transformed by electronic controls.

_____ **2.** In a few minutes with some keystrokes, a stock vehicle chassis can be reprogrammed to operate as an ambulance, an on-highway tractor, dump truck, or bus.

_____ **3.** Sensing functions collect data about operational conditions or the state of a device by measuring some value such as temperature, position, speed, or pressure.

_____ **4.** The alternating electrical current produced by a variable reluctance–type sensor would be considered a digital signal.

_____ **5.** When serial digital data is transmitted using a pair of wires, each wire will transmit a voltage pulse represented as a rectangular waveform.

_____ **6.** The term frequency refers to the number of data bits transmitted per second.

_____ **7.** The units for measuring pulse width are always expressed in units of time.

_____ **8.** Referred to as the electronic control module, a microprocessor or microcontroller is the heart of the control unit.

_____ **9.** Non-volatile memory will be lost if power to the computer is interrupted.

_____ **10.** Random access memory is both readable and writable.

Fill in the Blank

Read each item carefully, and then complete the statement by filling in the missing word(s).

1. A(n) _____ report provides details such as diagnostic fault codes, fuel consumption, idle time, and emission system performance. The report can be extracted from a vehicle's electronic control module during scheduled maintenance.

2. The use of electronic engine and vehicle _____ provides for enhanced vehicle and occupant safety and security.

3. Programmable _____ provides flexibility to engines, transmissions, and body accessories for adaptation to specific job applications.

4. The presence of _____ is communicated through the malfunction indicator lamps.

5. The _____ of a system are functions performed by electrical signals produced by the processor.

6. The signal voltage from a throttle position sensor is a type of _____ data.

7. Every number from 0 to infinity and the letters of the alphabet letters can be represented by a combination of 0s and 1s using _____ code.

8. To convert analog signals to digital binary information, special circuits, known as _____ or analog to digital converters, are used.

9. A(n) _____-_____-_____ signal is commonly used as an output signal of an electronic control module.

10. ROM, RAM, and PROM are examples of different types of computer _____.

Elements of Electronic Signal Processing Systems

Identify which division each of the following system functions belongs to.

_____ 1. Fuel injector

_____ 2. Potentiometer

_____ 3. Switch

_____ 4. RAM

_____ 5. Voltage regulator

_____ 6. Relay

_____ 7. Thermistor

_____ 8. Actuator

_____ 9. Self-diagnosis

_____ 10. Check engine light

A. Sensing

B. Processing

C. Output

Crossword Puzzle

Use the clues in the column to complete the puzzle.

Across

2. A unit of 8 bits.

3. Reprogramming or recalibrating the ECM. Information is stored in the ECM's memory.

5. A special-purpose processor with limited capabilities, designed to perform a set of specific tasks.

Down

1. A type of data storage that is lost or erased when the ignition power is switched off.

4. A unit of measure for electrical frequency measurement, in cycles per second.

ASE-Type Questions

Read each item carefully, and then select the best response.

_____ **1.** Technician A says that not a single vehicle system operates without at least some degree of electronic control. Technician B says that understanding the operating principles of electronic control systems is fundamental for choosing diagnostic strategies. Who is correct?
   A. Technician A
   B. Technician B
   C. Both Technician A and Technician B
   D. Neither Technician A nor Technician B

_____ **2.** Technician A says that diesel engines were the first commercial vehicle systems transformed by electronic controls. Technician B says that smarter engines deliver ever-increasing power from smaller displacements. Who is correct?
   A. Technician A
   B. Technician B
   C. Both Technician A and Technician B
   D. Neither Technician A nor Technician B

_____ **3.** Technician A says that telematics uses specialized telecommunication applications for long-distance transmission of information to and from a vehicle. Technician B says that telematics is not capable of transmitting information on fault codes. Who is correct?
   A. Technician A
   B. Technician B
   C. Both Technician A and Technician B
   D. Neither Technician A nor Technician B

_____ **4.** Technician A says that technicians can take advantage of programmable electronic controls. Technician B says that power and torque rise profiles are easily altered electronically. Who is correct?
   A. Technician A
   B. Technician B
   C. Both Technician A and Technician B
   D. Neither Technician A nor Technician B

_____ **5.** Technician A says that electronic control systems use a variety of sensors, wires, electrical actuators, and electronic modules moved with invisible electrical signals. Technician B says that the three major divisions of electronic control systems are sensing, processing, and output. Who is correct?
   A. Technician A
   B. Technician B
   C. Both Technician A and Technician B
   D. Neither Technician A nor Technician B

_____ **6.** Technician A says that processing refers to the control system element that collects sensor data and determines outputs based on a set of instructions or program software. Technician B says that operational algorithms are included in the software that determines the steps taken when processing electrical data. Who is correct?
   A. Technician A
   B. Technician B
   C. Both Technician A and Technician B
   D. Neither Technician A nor Technician B

_____ **7.** Technician A says that an analog signal is one type of electrical signal commonly used in electronic engine control applications. Technician B says that a tandem signal is one type of electrical signal commonly used in electronic engine control applications. Who is correct?
   A. Technician A
   B. Technician B
   C. Both Technician A and Technician B
   D. Neither Technician A nor Technician B

_____ **8.** Technician A says that, in contrast to analog signals, digital signals do not vary in voltage, frequency, or amplitude. Technician B says that the binary code does not lend itself to use in microprocessor circuits where processing large amounts of alphabetic or numerical data, represented in strings of 0s or 1s, is performed. Who is correct?
  A. Technician A
  B. Technician B
  C. Both Technician A and Technician B
  D. Neither Technician A nor Technician B

_____ **9.** Technician A says that serial data is used to transmit information from one electronic module to another. Technician B says that baud rate refers to the number of data bits transmitted per minute. Who is correct?
  A. Technician A
  B. Technician B
  C. Both Technician A and Technician B
  D. Neither Technician A nor Technician B

_____ **10.** Technician A says that a pulse-width-modulated (PWM) electrical signal is an electrical signal that shares similar characteristics with both a digital and analog signal. Technician B says that common examples of devices using PWM signals are solenoids, injectors, and light circuits. Who is correct?
  A. Technician A
  B. Technician B
  C. Both Technician A and Technician B
  D. Neither Technician A nor Technician B

Chapter Review

The following activities have been designed to help you refresh your knowledge of this chapter. Your instructor may require you to complete some or all of these activities as a regular part of your training program. You are encouraged to complete any activity that your instructor does not assign as a way to enhance your learning.

Matching

Match the following terms with the correct description or example.

A. Hall effect sensor   **D.** Rheostat

B. Passive sensor   **E.** Thermistor

C. Potentiometer

_____ **1.** A sensor that does not use a current supplied by the ECM to operate.

_____ **2.** A variable resistor with three connections—one at each end of a resistive path, and a third sliding contact that moves along the resistive pathway.

_____ **3.** A temperature-sensitive variable resistor commonly used to measure coolant, oil, fuel, and air temperatures.

_____ **4.** A sensor commonly used to measure the rotational speed of a shaft.

_____ **5.** A variable resistor constructed of a fixed input terminal and a variable output terminal, which vary current flow by passing current through a long resistive tightly coiled wire.

Multiple Choice

Read each item carefully, and then select the best response.

_____ **1.** Oxygen sensors, NO_x sensors, and variable reluctance sensors are considered _____.
   A. resistive sensors
   B. variable capacitance sensors
   C. voltage generators
   D. switches

_____ **2.** When a switch is connected between the ECM and the battery positive, the switch is known as a(n) _____.
   A. pull-up switch
   B. single throw switch
   C. pull-down switch
   D. open switch

_____ **3.** A position sensor such as the throttle position sensor is usually a _____.
   A. rheostat
   B. potentiometer
   C. thermistor
   D. Hall effect sensor

_____ **4.** Knock sensors that measure abnormal combustion signals are a common application of _____.
   A. variable capacitance pressure sensors
   B. voltage generators
   C. Wheatstone bridge sensors
   D. piezoresistive sensors

_____ 5. A _____ is an active sensor that uses the distance between two plates, or dielectric strength, inside the sensor to measure both dynamic and static pressure.
   A. variable reluctance sensor
   B. Wheatstone bridge sensor
   C. variable capacitance pressure sensor
   D. Hall effect sensor

_____ 6. A _____ is a two-wire sensor commonly used to measure rotational speed, wheel speed, vehicle speed, and engine speed.
   A. variable reluctance sensor
   B. piezoresistive sensor
   C. variable capacitance sensor
   D. potentiometer

_____ 7. What type of sensor is used to evaluate the operation of selective catalyst reduction (SCR) systems?
   A. CO_2 sensor
   B. Wide-range planar sensor
   C. Mass airflow sensor
   D. NO_X sensor

_____ 8. The _____ constantly checks for malfunctions in any engine or emission-related electrical circuit or component providing input or output signals to an ECM.
   A. functionality monitor
   B. comprehensive component monitor
   C. input/output monitor
   D. All of the above

_____ 9. To identify faults and measure signal voltage, _____ are often connected to internal pull-up resistors.
   A. thermistors
   B. planar sensors
   C. voltage generators
   D. variable reluctance sensors

_____ 10. A _____ will produce waveforms or data that can be observed by using a graphing meter.
   A. Hall effect sensor
   B. variable reluctance sensor
   C. mass airflow sensor
   D. pressure sensor

True/False

If you believe the statement to be more true than false, write the letter "T" in the space provided. If you believe the statement to be more false than true, write the letter "F".

_____ 1. A sensor will be considered active or passive depending on whether they use power supplied by the electronic control module to operate.

_____ 2. The industry-standard reference voltage value used by all manufactures is 12 volts direct current.

_____ 3. Switches are the simplest sensors of all, because they have no resistance in the closed position and infinite resistance in the open position.

_____ 4. Rheostats are three-wire variable resistance sensors that are commonly used as input devices to an ECM.

_____ 5. Three wire sensors, regardless of how they appear or what function they perform, have a common wiring configuration.

_____ 6. Hall effect throttle position sensors are more reliable than dual-path throttle position sensors because they have no moving parts.

_____ 7. The ability of a material to conduct or resist magnetic lines of force is known as capacitance.

_____ 8. Wide-band oxygen sensors are commonly used on gasoline engines operating at stoichiometric air–fuel ratios.

_____ 9. The potential for ammonia to be released to the atmosphere has led to the required use of an ammonia sensor for most engines produced since 2014.

_____ **10.** Output circuits, or output control devices, consist of display devices, serial data for network communication, and electromagnetic operator devices.

_____ **11.** Evenly spaced reluctor ring teeth are used to identify the cylinder stroke position.

_____ **12.** A functionality fault is triggered when the signal voltage of a sensor falls outside 85% of reference voltage.

_____ **13.** Rationality codes need careful pinpoint diagnostic tests to determine if a sensor is defective or some outside influence is affecting sensor data.

_____ **14.** When two resistors are connected in series, the greatest voltage drop takes place across the resistor with the lowest resistance.

_____ **15.** A broken magnet on a variable reluctance sensor will cause a low voltage reading.

Fill in the Blank

Read each item carefully, and then complete the statement by filling in the missing word(s).

1. Sensors are a type of _____ that convert physical conditions or states into electrical data.

2. The use of a(n) _____ voltage is important in processor operation, because the value of the variable resistor can be calculated by measuring voltage drop when another resistor with a known voltage input is connected in series with it.

3. In a(n) _____ temperature coefficient thermistor, the resistance decreases as the temperature increases.

4. For safety reasons, manufacturers will use an idle _____ switch to verify throttle position.

5. A(n) _____ _____ measures small changes in the resistance of tiny wires caused by stretching or contraction.

6. A(n) _____ bridge calculates the value of an unknown resistor using several other resistors of known fixed value.

7. The most common arrangement of a(n) _____ _____ sensor uses a metal interrupter ring or shutter and a permanent magnet positioned across from the sensor.

8. Diesel oxygen sensors are wide-range _____ sensors, which means they are flat rather than thimble-shaped.

9. A(n) _____ _____ sensor is a device that measures the weight of air entering the engine intake.

10. Electronic control systems have self-diagnostic capabilities to identify _____ in circuits and sensors.

11. Switch status can be determined by measuring the _____ _____ across a current-limiting resistor.

12. Three-wire circuits, whether digital or analog, passive or active, use a reference voltage, signal, and _____ wire, also referred to as ground return by some manufacturers.

13. When supplying a negative polarity or ground to a device, current is switched through a transistor called a(n) _____-_____ driver.

14. Several temperature and resistance values are supplied by the manufacturer to properly evaluate a(n) _____ when testing using an ohmmeter.

15. When performing pinpoint testing the signal voltage is always measured between the _____ return and signal wire for all sensors.

Labeling

Label the following diagrams with the correct terms.

1. Identify the parts of a Hall effect throttle position sensor:

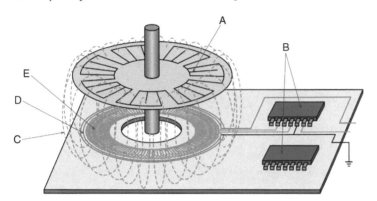

A. _____
B. _____
C. _____
D. _____
E. _____

2. Identify the parts of a silicon-based piezoresistive sensor:

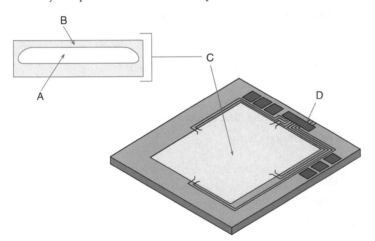

A. _____
B. _____
C. _____
D. _____

3. Identify the parts of a variable capacitance sensor:

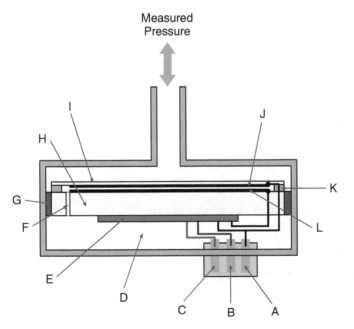

A. _____
B. _____
C. _____
D. _____
E. _____
F. _____
G. _____
H. _____
I. _____
J. _____
K. _____
L. _____

4. Identify the parts of an oxygen sensor:

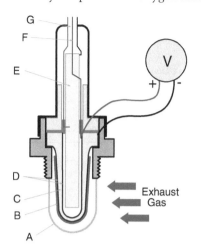

Exhaust
Gas

A. _____

B. _____

C. _____

D. _____

E. _____

F. _____

G. _____

Society of Automotive Engineers (SAE) J1939 Failure Mode Identifiers (FMI)

Match the failure mode identifier code to the correct Society of Automotive Engineers text.

Failure mode identifier code:

0. _____   A. Data valid but below normal operating range—moderately severe level

1. _____   B. Current above normal or grounded circuit

2. _____   C. Reserved for SAE assignment

3. _____   D. Abnormal rate of change

4. _____   E. Data valid but above normal operational range—most severe level

5. _____   F. Data valid but above normal operating range—least severe level

6. _____   G. Voltage above normal or shorted to high source

7. _____   H. Condition exists

8. _____   I. Abnormal frequency or pulse width or period

9. _____   J. Special instructions

10. _____   K. Data valid but below normal operational range—most severe level

11. _____   L. Bad intelligent device or component

12. _____   M. Received network data in error

13. _____   N. Current below normal or open circuit

14. _____   O. Data erratic, intermittent, or incorrect

15. _____   P. Data valid but above normal operating range—moderately severe level

16. _____   Q. Abnormal update rate

17. _____   R. Mechanical system not responding or out of adjustment

18. _____   S. Out of calibration

19. _____   T. Voltage below normal or shorted to low source

20-30. _____   U. Data valid but below normal operating range—least severe level

31. _____   V. Root cause not known

Crossword Puzzle

Use the clues in the column to complete the puzzle.

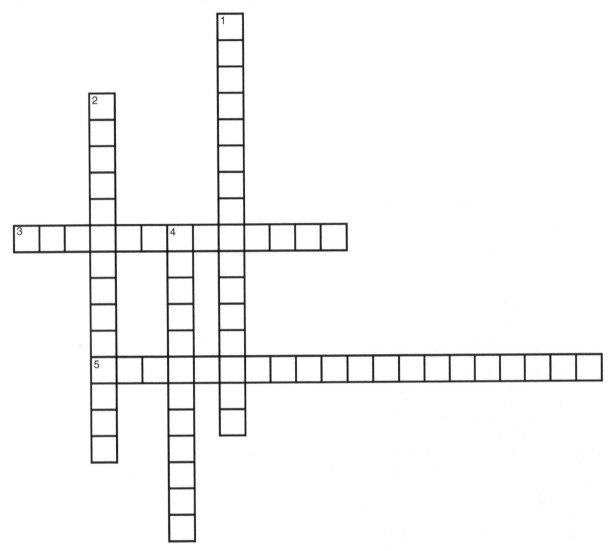

Across

3. A sensor used in selective catalyst reduction (SCR) that provides data to the ECM that is used to determine if ammonia values are out of anticipated range.

5. A circuit used for safety reasons that is used to verify throttle position.

Down

1. A precisely regulated voltage supplied by the ECM to sensors; the value is typically 5 VDC, but some manufacturers use 8 or 12 volts.

2. A switch connected between the ECM and a negative ground current potential.

4. A sensor that uses a current supplied by the ECM to operate.

ASE-Type Questions

Read each item carefully, and then select the best response.

_____ **1.** All of following are examples of a terminal connector, except:
   A. split-bolt
   B. butt
   C. eye ring
   D. push-on spade

_____ **2.** Two technicians are discussing engine management input sensors. Technician A says that switches are the simplest sensors of all, because they have no resistance in the closed position and infinite resistance in the open position. Technician B says that a zero-volt signal would present as a closed switch, while 12 volts would present as an open switch. Who is correct?
   A. Technician A
   B. Technician B
   C. Both Technician A and Technician B
   D. Neither Technician A nor Technician B

_____ **3.** Technician A says that a knock sensor measuring abnormal combustion signals is a common application of piezoresistive sensors. Technician B says that silicon-based piezoresistive sensors are very sensitive to slight pressure changes. Who is correct?
   A. Technician A
   B. Technician B
   C. Both Technician A and Technician B
   D. Neither Technician A nor Technician B

_____ **4.** A mass air flow (MAF) Hall effect sensor is being diagnosed using a graphing multimeter. Sometimes the circuit within the sensor can fail and produce a waveform unrecognizable to the ECM. Which of these is LEAST LIKELY resulting waveform?
   A. Technician A
   B. Technician B
   C. Both Technician A and Technician B
   D. Neither Technician A nor Technician B

_____ **5.** If the problem is related to temperature, vibration, or moisture, the circuit or control module can be heated, lightly tapped, or even sprayed with water to simulate the failure conditions. What measuring tool with glitch testing capabilities can identify and record the circuit fault in microseconds?
   A. Technician A
   B. Technician B
   C. Both Technician A and Technician B
   D. Neither Technician A nor Technician B

_____ **6.** Technician A says that switches are categorized as sensors whenever they provide information to an electronic control system. Technician B says that switch data may indicate a physical value such as open or closed, up or down, high or low, or it may indicate on and off. Who is correct?
   A. Technician A
   B. Technician B
   C. Both Technician A and Technician B
   D. Neither Technician A nor Technician B

_____ **7.** All of these are examples of variable reluctance sensors, except:
   A. crankshaft position
   B. camshaft position
   C. vehicle speed signal
   D. engine coolant temperature

_____ **8.** Technician A says that wide-band oxygen sensors produce a voltage proportional to a narrow oxygen level. Technician B says that oxygen sensors are used to measure air–fuel ratio in order to calibrate EGR flow rates and air–fuel ratios for exhaust after-treatment devices. Who is correct?
   A. Technician A
   B. Technician B
   C. Both Technician A and Technician B
   D. Neither Technician A nor Technician B

_____ **9.** At which of these locations is diesel exhaust fuel (DEF) added on a light-duty vehicle diesel equipped vehicle?
   A. Fitting near fuel door
   B. Fitting near the SCR (selective catalyst reduction)
   C. Directly into the fuel tank
   D. Special tank next to the fuel pump

_____ **10.** What type of engine fault checks sensor voltages and, in a few cases, current draw to determine whether the sensor or associated circuits are open or have shorts?
   A. Plausibility
   B. Out of range
   C. Functionality
   D. Rationality

Electronic Distributor Injection Pumps

Chapter Review

The following activities have been designed to help you refresh your knowledge of this chapter. Your instructor may require you to complete some or all of these activities as a regular part of your training program. You are encouraged to complete any activity that your instructor does not assign as a way to enhance your learning.

Matching

Match the following terms with the correct description or example.

A. Axial piston pressurization

B. Bosch VP-37

C. Bosch VP-44

D. Radial piston pressurization

E. Stanadyne DS-4

_____ **1.** A full-authority distributor pump that has a vane internal transfer pump common to all other distributor pumps, but, rather than a single axial piston plunger, pressurization of fuel is accomplished using radial-opposed pumping plungers.

_____ **2.** A full-authority distributor first introduced in 1994. The adaptation of electronic controls to the pump enabled the flexibility to adjust delivery quantities and timing more accurately than mechanical systems.

_____ **3.** A distributor pump design that uses opposed plunger metering. Plungers move inside a cam ring to pressurize fuel.

_____ **4.** A distributor pump design that uses a pumping plunger that reciprocates along the axis of the pump and uses a cam plate to move the plunger back and forth.

_____ **5.** An electronic pump with similar construction and operational characteristics to the mechanical VE pump.

Multiple Choice

Read each item carefully, and then select the best response.

_____ **1.** Three generations of the _____ pump were built between 1994 and 1999.
   A. Bosch VP-44
   B. GM DB-2
   C. Stanadyne DS-4
   D. Bosch VP-37

_____ **2.** Electronic control of injection provides better _____.
   A. fuel economy
   B. noise levels
   C. idle quality
   D. All of the above

_____ **3.** The Bosch VE mechanical pump uses _____ pressurization and sleeve metering principles.
   A. radial piston
   B. axial piston
   C. opposed plunger
   D. hydraulic

_____ 4. The _____ feature on electronic governors prevents rapid changes in engine speed using the electronically controlled actuator if the throttle is moved too quickly.
   A. idle speed control
   B. adaptive strategy
   C. anti-shudder
   D. closed-loop feedback

_____ 5. The most popular North American application for the _____ injection system is in the Cummins ISB engine.
   A. Bosch VP-44
   B. Stanadyne DS-4
   C. Bosch VP-37
   D. GM DB-2

_____ 6. The _____ supplies the PCM with data regarding pump speed, rotor position, cam ring position, and fuel temperature.
   A. injection timing stepper
   B. optical sensor tracking encoder
   C. fuel solenoid driver
   D. fuel pump control module

_____ 7. The stages of injection of a DS pump include all of the following **EXCEPT**:
   A. filling
   B. end of filling
   C. beginning of injection
   D. spilling

_____ 8. The DS-4 pump's crankshaft position sensor is a(n) _____ sensor, which means it measures the speed of rotation of four teeth located on the crankshaft sprocket.
   A. hall effect
   B. optical
   C. inductive
   D. harmonic

_____ 9. The _____ is an electronic actuator that moves the control sleeve adjusting shaft of the VP-37.
   A. control sleeve position sensor
   B. needle lift actuator
   C. optical sensor tracking encoder
   D. fuel quantity solenoid

_____ 10. The _____ was introduced in 1998 and used until it was replaced by the high-pressure common rail system in 2004.
   A. Stanadyne DS-6
   B. Cummins Accumulator Pump System
   C. Bosch VP-47
   D. GM DB-4

True/False

If you believe the statement to be more true than false, write the letter "T" in the space provided. If you believe the statement to be more false than true, write the letter "F".

_____ 1. Because of tighter emission standards, no distributor pumps are used on current model vehicles in North America.

_____ 2. Mechanical distributor pumps used as few as half the number of parts as inline versions, but still produced the same engine horsepower.

_____ 3. The Stanadyne DS-4 injection pump can reach peak injection pressures up to 18,000 psi (1241 bar).

_____ 4. The Stanadyne DS-4 injection pump is used on many European diesels, including Volkswagen TDI engines.

_____ **5.** With the use of an electronic governor, the fuel system can adjust idle speed metering to each individual cylinder to avoid rough and shaky engine idle.

_____ **6.** Injection control of the Bosch VP-44 is performed by two electronic processors: a fuel pump-mounted fuel pump control module and the ECM.

_____ **7.** The Stanadyne DS pump is operated by power train control modules that control both engine and transmission operation.

_____ **8.** Injection timing of the DS pump is managed by the injection timing stepper motor.

_____ **9.** Changing the fuel rate calibration resistor between the two terminals of the driver module or using a resistor of lower resistance value decreases engine power output at full load.

_____ **10.** Cummins constructed the CAPS fuel system as a modular fuel system, which enables it to be easily serviced in the field.

Fill in the Blank

Read each item carefully, and then complete the statement by filling in the missing word(s).

1. Lower injection pressures used by mechanical distributor pumps make them less favorable for reducing _____.

2. The adaptation of _____ controls to injection pumps provided flexibility to more accurately adjust delivery quantities and timing than what mechanical systems were capable of.

3. In 1998, both misfire detection and _____ _____ _____ were added to the Stanadyne DS pump.

4. The Bosch VP-37 system uses a _____ _____ sensor, which provides a reference signal to the ECM for the beginning of injection.

5. The use of _____ loops provides for more accurate metering and injection timing over the engine's entire life.

6. The Bosch VP-44 pump is capable of _____ injection using its electronically controlled high-pressure metering control valve.

7. At 1800 rpm, the pump-mounted _____ on the DS-4 switches the solenoid switches on and off approximately 7200 times a minute, which generates a significant amount of heat.

8. The _____ _____ _____ motor regulates internal pump housing fuel pressure used to retard and advance injection timing.

9. The _____ _____ operates to meter the injection quantity by controlling the end of the fuel pressurization event, just as it does in the mechanical VE pump.

10. The Cummins CAPS system uses a steel tube known as a _____ _____ to connect the injector with the high-pressure fuel lines.

Labeling

Label the following diagrams with the correct terms.

   1. Identify the components of the Bosch VP-37:

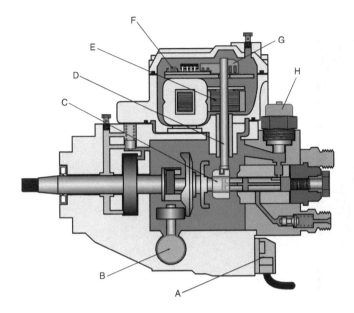

A. _____

B. _____

C. _____

D. _____

E. _____

F. _____

G. _____

H. _____

   2. Identify the components of the Bosch VP-44:

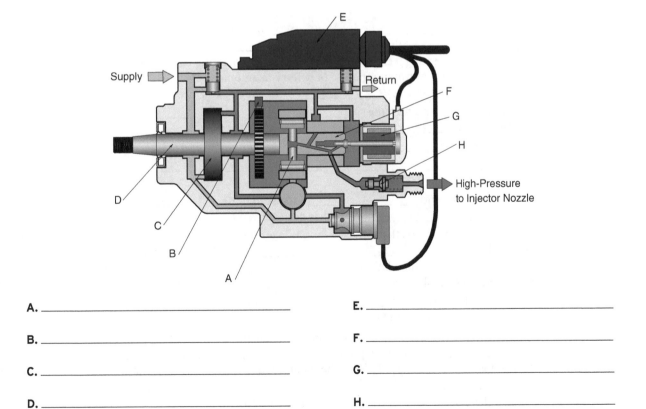

A. _____   E. _____

B. _____   F. _____

C. _____   G. _____

D. _____   H. _____

Skill Drills

Test your knowledge of skill drills by filling in the correct words in the photo captions.

    1. Performing a TDC Offset Relearn:

Step 1:   Using a suitable _____ _____ with _____ _____ _____ capabilities, clear any _____ _____. Run the engine until it reaches operating temperature. After it reaches operating temperature, the _____ _____ control monitor PCM will try to automatically _____ a new TDC offset. The revised TDC offset will _____ the previous TDC offset.

Step 2:   Shut the engine off and turn the _____ _____ to the _____ position with the engine _____ (_____).

Step 3:   Fully depress the _____ _____ for at least _____ seconds.

Step 4:   Turn the _____ _____ to the _____ position for _____ seconds.

Step 5:   Restart the engine and _____ to the scan tool's _____ menu used to verify that _____ _____ has been cleared to _____.

Step 6:   Operate the engine at less than _____ rpm and _____ the TDC offset parameter displayed on the _____ _____; it should be between _____ and _____. If the TDC offset is _____ specifications, the pump is _____ positioned to establish correct pump-to-engine _____ and relearn procedure is complete.

Step 7:   If the TDC offset position is _____ within _____, the _____ _____ needs to be _____.

Step 8:   To _____ the injection pump, loosen the injection pump _____ _____ and turn the pump _____ the _____ side of the vehicle if the offset is _____. Turn the pump to the _____ side of the vehicle if the offset is _____.

Step 9:   Recheck the TDC offset _____ displayed on the _____ to verify that the correct _____ is established.

2. Measuring Transfer Pump Fuel Pressure and Volume in a VP-44 pump:

Step 1: Inspect all _____ _____ for _____, _____, and other damage.

Step 2: Connect a fuel pressure _____ to the fuel filter pump _____ using an _____ _____.

Step 3: Start and run the engine. _____ the vehicle. Normal fuel _____ should be _____–_____ psi (97–103 kPa) at _____ road speeds. Fuel pressure should never fall below _____ psi (60 kPa), even if the engine seems to run well at that pressure.

Step 4: Snap the throttle to _____ _____ throttle while observing the _____ _____. Pressure should not fall below _____ psi (83 kPa), and should quickly return to _____–_____ psi (97–103 kPa). If the pressure falls below _____ psi (83 kPa), recommend a _____ _____ replacement and further pump pressure _____ testing.

Step 5: To measure pump volume _____ and _____, connect a _____" (91 cm) piece of clear plastic _____ to the filter _____ and route it to a fuel _____.

Step 6: Turn the _____ _____ to the _____ position. The electric _____ _____ should operate and stop after _____ seconds.

Step 7: Briefly _____ the _____ without starting the engine to supply an engine _____ signal to the _____. The electric _____ _____ should run for _____ seconds and _____.

Step 8: Observe and measure the fuel _____ from the fuel _____. Compare the _____ volume with the manufacturer's _____. The fuel should be free of any _____ _____.

Step 9: If fuel volume is _____ than the manufacturer's specification, measure the _____ _____ across the fuel _____. Compare this with OEM's specifications, which should require a _____ of less than _____ psi (34 kPa). Clean filters generally have a pressure drop of less than _____ psi (7 kPa). Excessive drop means the filter is _____. If the pressure drop is _____, but the fuel _____ is less than the OEM's specifications, measure the _____ pressure to the _____ transfer pump in _____ (centimeters) of _____ (Hg). If the restriction is _____ than the OEM's specifications (generally less than _____" [15 cm] Hg), a _____ exists between the _____ pump and the _____ _____.

Step 10: Measure the _____ between the electric _____ pump and the fuel _____ with the key _____ and engine _____. High pressure indicates a _____ fuel filter. Low pressure indicates _____ transfer pump _____ _____, which requires pump _____.

3. Inspecting and Replacing a CAPS Injector Quill Tube:

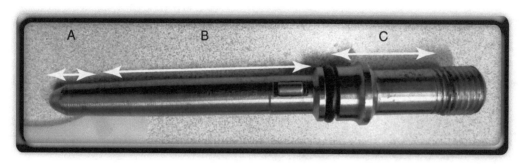

Step 1: Clean any _____ from the injector sleeve _____ and from the injector _____. Thoroughly clean the _____ if it is being reused.

Step 2: Inspect the injector sealing _____ where the _____ _____ meets the _____. An _____ seating surface, _____, etching, or _____ will produce injector _____. Clean the injector sealing area with electrical _____ cleaner. This liquid _____ quickly and is cleaner than _____ cleaner.

Step 3: Lubricate the injector sealing _____ and the injector _____ with engine _____.

Step 4: Lightly _____ and _____ the injector with by lightly _____ it with a soft-faced _____. Correctly _____ the injector's _____ _____ or alignment _____ with the _____ in the head.

Step 5: Inspect the new _____ _____. Examine it for _____ or _____ around the _____ and _____ ends of the connector. Check the tube's edge _____ for signs of _____. Clean the tube end with _____ cleaner. Install a new _____ on the tube and _____ it.

Step 6: Install the quill tube into the _____ _____ and lightly _____ the tube. Use the manufacturer's specifications for _____ to the _____ stage _____, which is measured in _____-_____ (Nm). This procedure helps _____ the injector and _____.

Step 7: Use the manufacturer's specifications to _____ _____ the _____ hold-down bolt to the _____ stage of _____.

Step 8: Tighten the quill tube to the _____ stage _____ tightening to begin to _____ the tube into the _____ _____.

Step 9: Torque the injector hold-down _____ to _____. This will _____ the injector into the _____ and _____ the injector against the sealing _____ at the bottom of the injector _____.

Step 10: Torque the _____ _____ to specifications to _____ the _____ into the injector's high-pressure _____ _____.

Step 11: Re-torque the injector _____-_____ bolt and _____ _____. Reconnect the high-pressure _____ _____ to the quill tube and _____ to the manufacturer's specifications to prevent _____ from over-torqueing the injector _____ _____ and _____ due to a _____ line _____.

Step 12: Run the engine and check for _____ running, _____, and _____ conditions. A prolonged _____ condition may require _____ the fuel return _____ when the engine is running to check for a further _____ _____ leakage.

Crossword Puzzle

Use the clues in the column to complete the puzzle.

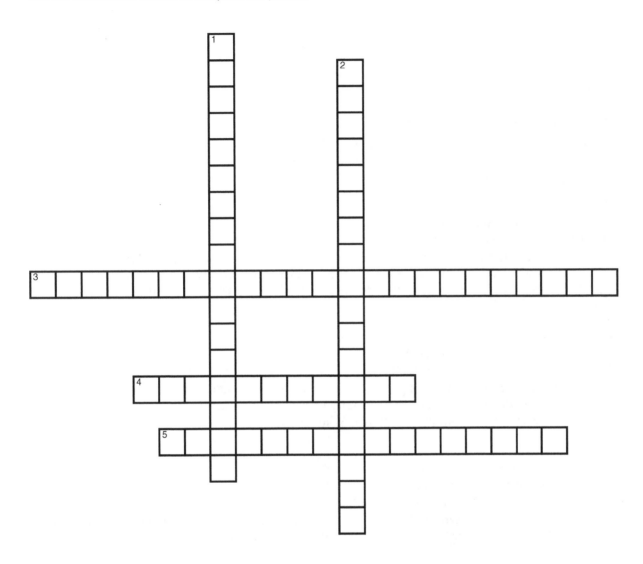

Across

3. A feature that measures the power output of each cylinder at idle using speed changes in the crankshaft velocity detected by the optical pump speed/position sensor.

4. A feature that prevents rapid changes in the engine speed using the electronically controlled actuator if the throttle is moved too quickly.

5. A sensor that provides a reference signal to the ECM for BOI by providing information about movement of the nozzle valve.

Down

1. A control module that supplies electrical signals to control the operation of the spill valve.

2. An electronic control module that contains a pair of high-current switching transistors that send electrical signals to the fuel metering control solenoid located inside the hydraulic head of the pump.

ASE-Type Questions

Read each item carefully, and then select the best response.

_____ 1. When comparing the differences between mechanical and electronic distributor injection pumps, Technician A says that electronic distributor injection pumps are full-authority systems. Technician B says that all electronic distributor injection pumps have electronic governors and are drive-by-wire fuel systems. Who is correct?
   A. Technician A
   B. Technician B
   C. Both Technician A and Technician B
   D. Neither Technician A nor Technician B

_____ 2. While determining how to add a fast idle feature for PTO operation, Technician A said that a throttle cable needs to be installed for the electronic distributor pump used by a truck. Technician B says that only a switch and some wiring need to be added. Who is correct?
   A. Technician A
   B. Technician B
   C. Both Technician A and Technician B
   D. Neither Technician A nor Technician B

_____ 3. When replacing a DS-4 injection pump, Technician A says the pump mounted driver (PMD) control module contains a resistor that needs to be transferred to the new module on the new pump. Technician B says that the new pump will have a resistor and the older resistor should not be transferred to the new pump. Who is correct?
   A. Technician A
   B. Technician B
   C. Both Technician A and Technician B
   D. Neither Technician A nor Technician B

_____ 4. The fuel temperature sensor of a DS-4 pump is continuously reading –40°F (–40°C) on a hot summer day. Technician A says the engine's fuel temperature sensor needs replacing. Technician B says it is the optical sensor tracking encoder (OSTE) that is defective. Who is correct?
   A. Technician A
   B. Technician B
   C. Both Technician A and Technician B
   D. Neither Technician A nor Technician B

_____ 5. An electronic distributor injection pump is starting poorly whenever the engine is restarted after a long run or if it has worked very hard. Technician A says the pump is likely worn out and has excessive internal leakage. Technician B says the fuel viscosity is low and causing excessive internal leakage. Who is correct?
   A. Technician A
   B. Technician B
   C. Both Technician A and Technician B
   D. Neither Technician A nor Technician B

_____ 6. Technician A says that a CAPS pump camshaft is lubricated with engine oil to support higher pump injection pressures. Technician B says the pump's camshaft is lubricated with diesel fuel like most other injection pumps. Who is correct?
   A. Technician A
   B. Technician B
   C. Both Technician A and Technician B
   D. Neither Technician A nor Technician B

_____ 7. Technician A says the nozzle lift sensor provides feedback to the electronic control module (ECM) for the precise beginning of the injection event. Technician B says the nozzle lift sensor helps reduce injection lag. Who is correct?
   A. Technician A
   B. Technician B
   C. Both Technician A and Technician B
   D. Neither Technician A nor Technician B

_____ **8.** Technician A says the VP-44 pump uses a cam ring and opposed plungers, which make it more similar in operation to the mechanical DB-2 injection pump. Technician B says that the VP-44 pump uses a cam plate and an axial pumping plunger because it is an upgraded version of the older mechanical Bosch VE pumps. Who is correct?
   A. Technician A
   B. Technician B
   C. Both Technician A and Technician B
   D. Neither Technician A nor Technician B

_____ **9.** Technician A says that a distributor injection pump rotates at the same speed as the engine camshaft. Technician B says that a distributor pump turns at the same speed as the engine crankshaft. Who is correct?
   A. Technician A
   B. Technician B
   C. Both Technician A and Technician B
   D. Neither Technician A nor Technician B

_____ **10.** Technician A says the Cummins CAPS pump is a type of common rail injection system because it can electronically adjust injection pressure at any engine speed and does not depend on high engine speed to provide the greatest injection pressure. Technician B says the CAPS system does not use a fuel rail and therefore it cannot be classified as a common rail fuel system. Who is correct?
   A. Technician A
   B. Technician B
   C. Both Technician A and Technician B
   D. Neither Technician A nor Technician B

CHAPTER 24

Electronic Unit Injectors and Unit Pumps

Chapter Review

The following activities have been designed to help you refresh your knowledge of this chapter. Your instructor may require you to complete some or all of these activities as a regular part of your training program. You are encouraged to complete any activity that your instructor does not assign as a way to enhance your learning.

Matching

Match the following terms with the correct description or example.

A. Beginning of injection period (BIP)

B. Cylinder contribution test

C. Cylinder cut-out test

D. Nozzle control valve (NCV)

E. Spill control valve (SCV)

_____ **1.** A test is used to identify misfiring or noisy cylinder.

_____ **2.** A valve that operates to change injection pressure as needed to meet operating requirements.

_____ **3.** A test that compares cylinder pressures to one another and measures the output of each cylinder.

_____ **4.** The closing of the solenoid poppet valve.

_____ **5.** A valve that allows the injector to operate like a conventional hydraulically balanced nozzle valve, like those used in common rail injectors.

Multiple Choice

Read each item carefully, and then select the best response.

_____ **1.** The Delphi E3 EUI can produce injection pressures of approximately _____.

    A. 15,000–18,000 psi (1034–1241 bar)

    B. 20,000–23,000 psi (1379–1586 bar)

    C. 27,000–32,000 psi (1862–2206 bar)

    D. 35,000–38,000 psi (2412–2620 bar)

_____ **2.** Electronic unit injectors contain between _____ spray holes.

    A. 1 and 5

    B. 4 and 8

    C. 5 and 13

    D. 6 and 10

_____ **3.** The _____ is the circular part of the camshaft that does not include the lobe.

    A. inner base circle

    B. journal

    C. outer base circle

    D. crankpin

_____ **4.** The ECM collects and processes sensor data using _____ to decide the exact injection timing and fuel quantity necessary to obtain best performance, lowest emissions, and highest fuel economy.

    A. calibration files

    B. operating algorithms

    C. fuel timing maps

    D. All of the above

_____ 5. The problem of inductive reactance in the solenoid coils is solved by using a current-shaping strategy called _____.
   A. inversion
   B. current ramping
   C. rectification
   D. inductive resistance

_____ 6. The _____ uses two independent, fast-response precision actuators to provide pilot-, post-, and split-injection events as well as ramped, low-NO_x injection profiles.
   A. Delphi N3
   B. Delphi A3
   C. Delphi E3
   D. Both A and C

_____ 7. A _____ is used by the ECM to adjust timing and fuel flow through the injector.
   A. nozzle control coil
   B. calibration code
   C. spill control coil
   D. unit pump

_____ 8. Because _____ cannot pass easily through nozzle orifices, it can accumulate below the nozzle valve, vaporize, and then cause a tip to blow off an injector.
   A. water
   B. oil
   C. coolant
   D. dirt

_____ 9. If an injector is suspected to be defective, performing a _____ can identify the bad injector.
   A. cylinder cut-out test
   B. cylinder leakage test
   C. cylinder contribution test
   D. Either A or C

_____ 10. Made from brass or stainless steel _____ transfer heat from combustion and pressurization of fuel to the engine coolant.
   A. nozzle valve tips
   B. valve bodies
   C. injector cups
   D. needle chambers

True/False

If you believe the statement to be more true than false, write the letter "T" in the space provided. If you believe the statement to be more false than true, write the letter "F".

_____ 1. EUIs currently offer the highest spray-in pressures of any fuel injection system.

_____ 2. The Delphi E3 EUI can electronically vary injection pressure over all engine speeds using a second electrically operated control valve.

_____ 3. The extremely fine spray produced by unit injectors results in one of the best combinations of fuel atomization and distribution available.

_____ 4. EUI plunger travel is not adjustable.

_____ 5. If two or more resistors are connected in series, the greatest voltage drop takes place across the resistor with the lowest resistance.

_____ 6. EUI injectors use a peak and hold strategy to energize the solenoid windings.

_____ 7. High resistance in an injector solenoid circuit generally occurs when the engine is warmed up.

_____ 8. Rate shaping is easily accomplished in EUIs using electronically controlled magnetic solenoid coils.

_____ **9.** Electronic unit pump injection systems have permitted the adaptation of high-pressure electronically controlled injection systems to engines previously using inline pump injection systems without extensive engine modifications.

_____ **10.** Electronic unit pump injection systems in operation are adjustment-free and require little maintenance except during engine overhaul or replacement due to failure.

Fill in the Blank

Read each item carefully, and then complete the statement by filling in the missing word(s).

1. The first major use of an _____ _____ _____ system was in Detroit Diesel's Series 60 (S60) engines.

2. Actuating the injectors with an overhead camshaft permits the least amount of injection _____ because there are no pushrod tubes to bend, injector lines to swell, or delivery valves to lift.

3. First-generation EUIs used a single electrically controlled poppet or _____ _____ valve that opened and closed to control the beginning and end of the injection event.

4. The injector plunger begins its downward stroke as the camshaft rotates onto the _____ base circle of the cam lobe.

5. Allowing _____ in the injector adjustment will cause the yoke and clevis to cycle back and forth with high force and ultimately break.

6. A signal type known as a _____-_____ modulated current drives the injector solenoids.

7. If injectors have different resistances, have bad connectors, or become overheated, their _____ _____ will lengthen.

8. When the poppet valve closes, it changes the strength of the solenoid's magnetic field, which in turn produces a slight change in coil resistance, or _____ _____.

9. The poppet or SCV is easily scored, worn, and damaged by the continuous abrasive action of _____.

10. Cylinder head casting irregularities and variations in sealing washer thicknesses and between injectors may produce different amounts of injector tip _____.

Labeling

Label the following diagrams with the correct terms.

1. Identify the parts of a Delphi E3 electronic unit injector:

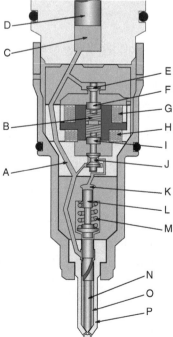

A. _____

B. _____

C. _____

D. _____

E. _____

F. _____

G. _____

H. _____

I. _____

J. _____

K. _____   **N.** _____

L. _____   **O.** _____

M. _____   **P.** _____

2. Identify the parts of an electronic unit pump fuel system:

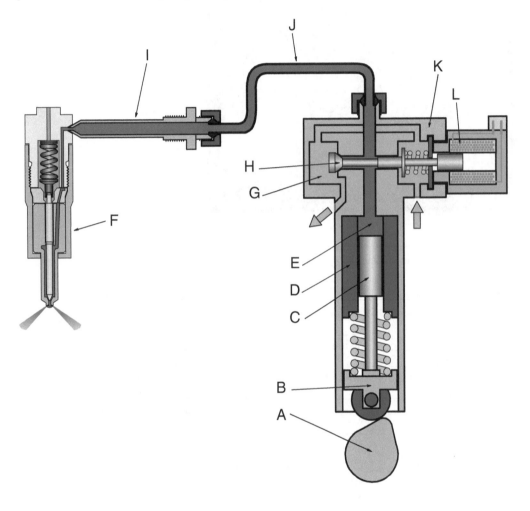

A. _____   **G.** _____

B. _____   **H.** _____

C. _____   **I.** _____

D. _____   **J.** _____

E. _____   **K.** _____

F. _____   **L.** _____

Skill Drills

Test your knowledge of skill drills by filling in the correct words in the photo captions.

1. Performing a Cylinder Cut-Out Test:

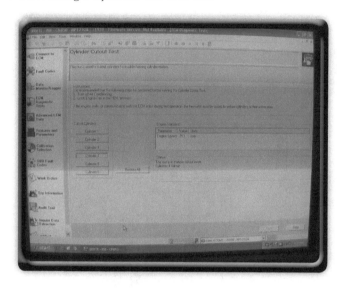

Step 1: Start the _____ and bring it to _____ temperature.

Step 2: Connect the vehicle to _____ _____ or a suitable replacement that can perform a _____-_____ test.

Step 3: Check for _____ _____; if there are any fault codes, _____ them before proceeding.

Step 4: Cylinder cut-out test _____ will be _____ if the engine _____ changes _____ the test. It is important to leave the engine fan, air compressor, air conditioning, and other sources of _____ either _____ or _____ to keep loads _____ during testing. If possible, manually switch _____ the engine fan or _____ the fan control _____. Disable the air conditioning or switch it to _____ mode. Build up vehicle _____ _____ and make sure there are no major _____.

Step 5: Navigate to _____ _____-_____ testing using the _____ menu.

Step 6: Adjust and _____ the engine at a speed above _____ for best results; _____ rpm is ideal and can be set using the _____ switch or _____ _____ switch.

Step 7: For a _____ cut-out test, select a _____ and cut it out using the _____ commands. Listen for a change in engine _____ and _____ changes when the cylinder is _____ _____. No change in speed indicates a _____ or _____ cylinder. Wait for at least _____ seconds between each cylinder cut out. Leave the cylinder cut out for at least _____ seconds when testing.

Step 8: To perform _____ cut-out tests, disable _____ cylinders for double cut outs: _____ and _____, _____ and _____, and _____ and _____. Alternatively, for _____ cut-out testing, cut out cylinders _____, _____, and _____, wait _____ seconds, and then switch the cylinders back on. Repeat for cylinders _____, _____, and _____ after resuming for _____ seconds.

Step 9:   Cylinders that are overfueling will cause the _____ amount of fueling _____ in other cylinders when the overfueling cylinder is cut out. Similarly, a cylinder that is _____ _____, or that has _____ contribution, will produce the _____ increase in fueling in the other cylinders when the _____-_____ cylinder is cut out.

Step 10: Multiple cylinder cut-out testing can be used to look for _____ variations between cylinder _____ or _____ if torque _____ is supplied by the OEM software. Problems with _____ _____ that affect multiple cylinders, or wiring harness _____ that affect cylinder _____, are more easily _____ using _____ cylinder cut-out testing.

Step 11: If a _____ injector is suspected, the injector can be _____ to another _____. If the low contribution _____ follows the _____, the problem is likely the injector. If the problem remains in the same _____ after _____ an injector, a _____ problem is indicated.

2. Measuring Injector Tip Protrusion:

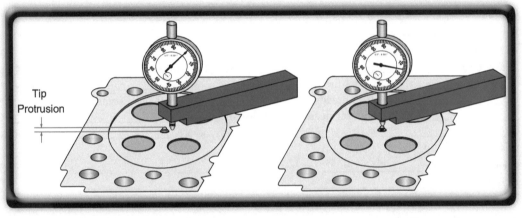

Tip Protrusion

Step 1:   Install and _____ the _____ in the injector _____.

Step 2:   Zero a dial indicator on the _____ _____ deck. The dial indicator should be mounted in a _____ _____.

Step 3:   Lift and _____ the dial indicator _____ to the _____ _____.

Step 4:   Record the height _____ and note the _____ of the _____ that the injector is in.

Step 5:   Compare the amount of _____ _____ with the OEM's _____. Minimum and maximum specifications for tip protrusion should be _____ in OEM _____ _____. If the protrusion is out of _____, the injector may be _____, or the injector _____ replaced, to bring the protrusion to _____ _____.

3. Replacing an Injector Cup:

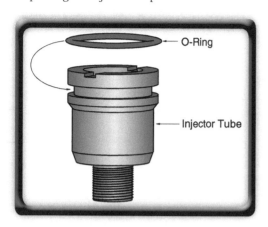

O-Ring

Injector Tube

Step 1:   Remove the _____.

Step 2:   Clean and _____ the injector cup. If the cup is _____ or _____, it
will need to be _____.

Step 3:   Drain the _____ _____.

Step 4:   Remove the _____ _____ using the tool that the OEM recommends to
_____ the cup from the _____ _____. The cup is likely to
be _____ because thread-locking _____ is used sometimes to retain the
_____ in the cylinder head. Do not use an _____ _____. Cups
often use _____-_____ threads, so a _____ turn may be required
to remove the cup.

Step 5:   Clean the injector _____ opening in the _____ _____ with a
round _____ _____.

Step 6:   Apply _____ lubricant to the sealing _____ and install it.

Step 7:   Apply high-temperature _____ _____ to the cup threads.
_____-based _____-_____ thread lubricant is ideal.

Step 8:   Torque the _____ in the _____ _____ per the OEM's
_____.

Step 9:   Refill the _____ with _____ and reinstall the _____.

Crossword Puzzle

Use the clues in the column to complete the puzzle.

Across

4. A unit injector that injects fuel directly into the combustion chamber. Timing, metering, pressurization, and distribution of fuel are all integrated into a single injector body.

5. Current induced in a coil of a solenoid's windings which opposes ECM current when initially energized; also known as inductive resistance.

Down

1. A numbered or alphanumerical value applied to the injector that provides information about unique fuel flow rates through the injector; also known as E-trim, injector code, or a fuel trim code.

2. The strategy of tracking time variations between the voltage drops for each injection.

3. The buildup of current flow through the solenoid coils during the initial energization period.

ASE-Type Questions

Read each item carefully, and then select the best response.

_____ **1.** Technician A says that EUIs are better than previous injectors because they have no injection lag caused by swelling pump lines and delivery valves. Technician B says that the use of electromagnetic solenoids by unit injectors produces injection delay. Who is correct?
  A. Technician A
  B. Technician B
  C. Both Technician A and Technician B
  D. Neither Technician A nor Technician B

_____ **2.** Technician A says that when setting unit injector adjustments during replacement, tune-up, or overhaul, the proper operating clearance should be adjusted using the rocker arm adjusting screw. Technician B says that unit injectors do not use operating clearances and only injector preload is set on the injector's adjuster spring. Who is correct?
  A. Technician A
  B. Technician B
  C. Both Technician A and Technician B
  D. Neither Technician A nor Technician B

_____ **3.** Technician A says that injection spray-in pressure from a unit injector can change with engine speed. Technician B says spray-in pressures depend only on a EUI's nozzle opening pressure. Who is correct?
  A. Technician A
  B. Technician B
  C. Both Technician A and Technician B
  D. Neither Technician A nor Technician B

_____ **4.** Technician A says that the electrical signal to a EUI injector is pulse-width modulated (PWM), but unlike other PWM signals it does not have a duty cycle. Technician B says the electrical signal is DC current. Who is correct?
  A. Technician A
  B. Technician B
  C. Both Technician A and Technician B
  D. Neither Technician A nor Technician B

_____ **5.** Technician A says that an electromagnetic solenoid limits the number of injection events of most styles of unit injectors to one main injection. Technician B says that some unit injectors are capable of having pilot injection events. Who is correct?
  A. Technician A
  B. Technician B
  C. Both Technician A and Technician B
  D. Neither Technician A nor Technician B

_____ **6.** Technician A says that secondary filters used by EUI fuel systems filter down to 2 microns. Technician B says that secondary fuel filters used by EUI fuel systems filter 10–20 microns. Who is correct?
  A. Technician A
  B. Technician B
  C. Both Technician A and Technician B
  D. Neither Technician A nor Technician B

_____ **7.** Technician A says that in the latest EUIs, the fuel control valves control injection timing and meter the correct quantity of fuel for injection. Technician B says that injection pressure and timing are controlled by the valves. Who is correct?
  A. Technician A
  B. Technician B
  C. Both Technician A and Technician B
  D. Neither Technician A nor Technician B

_____ **8.** While discussing the installation procedures for a EUI, Technician A says that the plunger travel of the injector is one of the last steps to perform during injector replacement. Technician B says that the coil resistance and available voltage should be checked after replacing the injector. Who is correct?
   A. Technician A
   B. Technician B
   C. Both Technician A and Technician B
   D. Neither Technician A nor Technician B

_____ **9.** While discussing potential reasons for a hard start and prolonged engine cranking period on a EUI fuel system, Technician A suggested air could be entering the injectors due to a poorly seating low-pressure regulator valve. Technician B suggested the complaints are likely caused by a leaking check valve in a hand primer pump. Who is correct?
   A. Technician A
   B. Technician B
   C. Both Technician A and Technician B
   D. Neither Technician A nor Technician B

_____ **10.** While discussing the potential cause of a failed injector with a seized plunger, Technician A says the failure was likely caused by water in the fuel. Technician B says the cause is likely a worn plunger and barrel assembly. Who is correct?
   A. Technician A
   B. Technician B
   C. Both Technician A and Technician B
   D. Neither Technician A nor Technician B

Cummins Unit Injection Systems

Chapter Review

The following activities have been designed to help you refresh your knowledge of this chapter. Your instructor may require you to complete some or all of these activities as a regular part of your training program. You are encouraged to complete any activity that your instructor does not assign as a way to enhance your learning.

Matching

Match the following terms with the correct description or example.

A. CELECT

B. High-pressure injection, time-pressure injection (HPI-TPI)

C. INSITE

D. Metering plunger

E. Timing plunger

_____ **1.** A unique fuel system where metering and injection timing are controlled by varying fuel pressure supplied to the injector.

_____ **2.** The upper plunger in either the CELECT injector or HPI-TPI injector.

_____ **3.** A service tool for Cummins electronic engine control systems.

_____ **4.** The first generation of full-authority electronic engine control introduced by Cummins in 1990.

_____ **5.** The lower plunger in either the CELECT injector or the HPI-TPI injector.

Multiple Choice

Read each item carefully, and then select the best response.

_____ **1.** The first unit injection system used by the Cummins Engine Company was the _____.

A. partial-authority system

B. Interact System

C. pressure time injection system

D. CELECT system

_____ **2.** The Cummins PT injection system pump receives mechanical inputs from _____.

A. the throttle pedal

B. the pump drive gear

C. a line connecting the pump to the intake manifold

D. All of the above

_____ **3.** The pump output pressure of the CELECT system is regulated to deliver fuel at a pressure of approximately _____ to a fuel rail drilled through the cylinder head.

A. 100 psi (7 bar)

B. 150 psi (10 bar)

C. 200 psi (14 bar)

D. 225 psi (16 bar)

_____ **4.** Cummins _____ system injectors were used on Cummins electronically controlled engines between 1990 and 2001.

A. CELECT

B. partial-authority

C. CELECT Plus

D. Both A and C

_____ **5.** The injectors on Cummins CELECT and CELECT Plus systems are adjusted at an engine position of approximately _____.
   A. 15° before TDC
   B. 30° after TDC
   C. 45° after TDC
   D. 30° before TDC

_____ **6.** When the accessory drive pulley and the engine front cover are aligned with the letter "B," the engine is positioned correctly to perform a valve and injector adjustment on cylinder number _____.
   A. 2
   B. 3
   C. 5
   D. Either A or C

_____ **7.** Cummins small-, medium-, and large-bore engines series B, C, L, and M built in the late 1990s all used the prefix _____.
   A. SX
   B. IS
   C. CP
   D. X

_____ **8.** Until 2009, Cummins 15L (915 cubic inch) ISX and Signature 600 used a unique fuel system called _____.
   A. high-pressure injection time-pressure injection
   B. CELECT
   C. pressure time
   D. CELECT Plus

_____ **9.** The most recent HPI-TPI injectors can spray in fuel up to _____.
   A. 15,000 (1034 bar)
   B. 25,000 (1724 bar)
   C. 33,000 psi (2275 bar)
   D. 37,000 psi (2551 bar)

_____ **10.** The _____ in the HPI-TPI injector enables a crisp end to injection.
   A. upper injector plunger
   B. trapped volume spill port
   C. lower injector plunger
   D. metering Check Valve

True/False

If you believe the statement to be more true than false, write the letter "T" in the space provided. If you believe the statement to be more false than true, write the letter "F".

_____ **1.** The partial-authority Cummins engine was the first injection system that incorporated the use of network communications.

_____ **2.** Unit injectors incorporate pressurization, timing, metering, and atomization functions into a single component.

_____ **3.** PT injectors are closed-nozzle injectors that use a spring to hold the nozzle valve on its seat.

_____ **4.** The CELECT injector uses two internal plungers: a timing plunger and a metering plunger.

_____ **5.** Both the valves and injector on Cummins CELECT and CELECT Plus systems are adjusted at the same time for an individual cylinder.

_____ **6.** The ending of the CELECT system injection event is determined electronically.

_____ **7.** The Dodge Ram ECM, built by Motorola, is constructed to specifications using different software and network communication protocols.

_____ **8.** In the high-pressure injection time-pressure injection system a cam-driven gear pump supplies pressurized fuel that is regulated by a 250-psi regulator valve integrated into the integrated fuel system module.

_____ **9.** The 250-psi regulator valve of the HPI-TPI system prevents severe damage from high fuel pressure in the event of a fuel shut-off valve failure or other blockage in the IFSM circuit.

_____ **10.** Electrically controlled solenoids control both the metering and timing of HPI-TPI injectors.

Fill in the Blank

Read each item carefully, and then complete the statement by filling in the missing word(s).

1. A _____-_____ system combines elements of a traditional mechanical system but uses an electronic governor instead of a mechanical one.

2. By varying pump output pressure the Cummins PT injection system changes the amount of _____ supplied to the injectors.

3. CELECT systems meter and time the injection event using a _____ injector.

4. Timing and metering functions for CELECT systems are performed by applying two _____-_____ modulated signals of close to 75 volts, once during upward stroke of the injector plunger and a second during the downward stroke.

5. Injector adjustment on Cummins CELECT and CELECT Plus systems is accomplished by bottoming out the _____ in the injector and then lifting them slightly.

6. CELECT injector metering ends when the ECM de-energizes the injector _____ _____, causing it to open.

7. With the _____ _____, the ECM communicates with service tools and some other vehicle controllers through the J-1939 on-board vehicle network.

8. The Cummins HPI-TPI is a _____ fuel system that uses the same components across all engine power ratings.

9. In the HPI-TPI system the _____ rail supply inlet is uncovered by the lower plunger, and allows fuel to enter the injector cup.

10. The timing fuel actuator of the HPI-TPI system opens and supplies fuel to the timing rail _____ _____.

Labeling

Label the following diagrams with the correct terms.

1. Identify the parts of a Cummins PT injector:

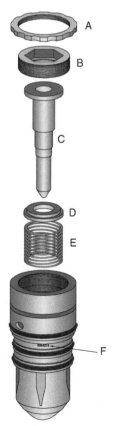

A. _____

B. _____

C. _____

D. _____

E. _____

F. _____

2. Identify the parts of a Cummins CELECT unit injector:

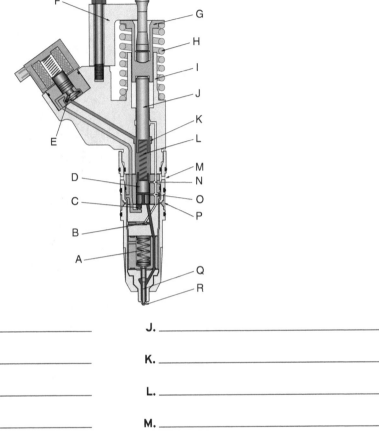

A. _____

B. _____

C. _____

D. _____

E. _____

F. _____

G. _____

H. _____

I. _____

J. _____

K. _____

L. _____

M. _____

N. _____

O. _____

P. _____

Q. _____

R. _____

3. Identify the parts of a Cummins HPI-TPI injector:

HPI-TPI Injector

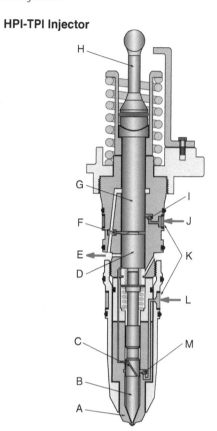

A. _____   H. _____

B. _____   I. _____

C. _____   J. _____

D. _____   K. _____

E. _____   L. _____

F. _____   M. _____

G. _____

Skill Drills

Test your knowledge of skill drills by filling in the correct words in the photo captions.

1. Checking for Air in Fuel:

Step 1: Connect a _____ _____ between the engine _____ _____ and the _____-side fuel _____-_____ line.

Step 2: Start and run the engine at _____ speed. The vacuum gauge should _____ to as much as _____" (25 cm) Hg; _____–_____" (3–15 mm) _____ is normal.

Step 3: After shutting down the engine, _____ the vacuum gauge. The gauge reading should _____ be _____ after _____–_____ minutes.

Step 4: If the gauge reading _____ to _____ after _____–_____ minutes, an inline _____ _____ can be installed to _____ the presence of _____.

Step 5: Install an inline _____ _____ that enables observation of the _____-side fuel stream entering the _____ _____.

Step 6: Start and run the engine to check for _____ in the site glass. Some small _____ passing through the glass are generally _____. Large _____ that continuously pass through the glass indicate a _____-side line _____.

Step 7: Tighten all line _____; inspect all lines for _____ or _____. Remove and inspect the fuel tank _____-_____ _____.

Crossword Puzzle

Use the clues in the column to complete the puzzle.

Across

1. A Cummins engine family prefix.

3. A full-authority electronic engine control based on CELECT that uses several additional sensors; a faster, more capable ECM; and additional programmable controls.

4. A premium ISX engine that produces the highest engine power output and has several key components built with extra durability.

Down

1. The third generation of Cummins electronics; this system could integrate with other vehicle control systems, such as the transmission, braking system, and traction control system.

2. A Cummins unit injection system used until the early 1980s.

ASE-Type Questions

Read each item carefully, and then select the best response.

_____ **1.** Technician A says that a Cummins diesel engine installed in an automobile won the Indianapolis 500 race one year. Technician B says that diesels are too slow to even qualify for a race. Who is correct?
  A. Technician A
  B. Technician B
  C. Both Technician A and Technician B
  D. Neither Technician A nor Technician B

_____ **2.** Technician A says that Cummins ISX injectors do not use a nozzle valves. Technician B says that all injectors need a nozzle valve to control fuel spray-in pressures and prevent combustion gases from entering the fuel system. Who is correct?
  A. Technician A
  B. Technician B
  C. Both Technician A and Technician B
  D. Neither Technician A nor Technician B

_____ **3.** Technician A says that it is important to use a fuel hand primer to prime an ISX or CELECT fuel system after replacing a fuel filter. Technician B says that after installing a dry fuel filter, she leaves the ignition key on for about 90 seconds to prime the filter before starting the engine. Who is correct?
  A. Technician A
  B. Technician B
  C. Both Technician A and Technician B
  D. Neither Technician A nor Technician B

_____ **4.** Technician A says that a CELECT unit injector controls timing and metering by energizing and de-energizing the injection control valve during a downward movement of the injector plunger. Technician B says that the CELECT Plus injector controls metering by energizing the injection control valve during downward plunger travel but the injector has a fixed point in plunger travel which ends injection. Who is correct?
  A. Technician A
  B. Technician B
  C. Both Technician A and Technician B
  D. Neither Technician A nor Technician B

_____ **5.** Technician A says that a CELECT injector has two electromagnetic solenoids that control timing and metering events. Technician B says that a single solenoid that is energized at least twice during a combustion cycle controls timing and metering in a CELECT system. Who is correct?
  A. Technician A
  B. Technician B
  C. Both Technician A and Technician B
  D. Neither Technician A nor Technician B

_____ **6.** Technician A says that an HPI-TPI fuel system uses a single timing solenoid to control fuel pressure to three injectors. Technician B says that a single metering solenoid controls fuel pressure to three injectors. Who is correct?
  A. Technician A
  B. Technician B
  C. Both Technician A and Technician B
  D. Neither Technician A nor Technician B

_____ **7.** Technician A says that a fuel shut-off solenoid that has a broken wire or is burnt out will prevent any fuel pressure from entering the fuel filter. Technician B says that a burnt-out fuel shut-off solenoid will cause the 380-psi (26-bar) pressure relief valve to open. Who is correct?
  A. Technician A
  B. Technician B
  C. Both Technician A and Technician B
  D. Neither Technician A nor Technician B

_____ **8.** Technician A says that the camshaft pressurizes fuel for injection in an HPI-TPI fuel system. Technician B says that a gear pump supplies highly pressurized fuel for injection. Who is correct?
   A. Technician A
   B. Technician B
   C. Both Technician A and Technician B
   D. Neither Technician A nor Technician B

_____ **9.** Technician A says that an ISX HPI-TPI fuel system needs a 2 μ final filter because it is sensitive to any abrasive dirt. Technician B says that the open nozzle design and lack of an injection control valve in the injector means this system is not as sensitive to fine abrasives as other systems. Who is correct?
   A. Technician A
   B. Technician B
   C. Both Technician A and Technician B
   D. Neither Technician A nor Technician B

_____ **10.** Technician A says that both the CELECT and HPI-TPI injectors are adjusted by bottoming out the injector plungers when the injector lobe is on its outer base circle. Technician B says that both injectors are adjusted when the injector lobe is on its outer base circle and when the engine is positioned approximately 45° after TDC. Who is correct?
   A. Technician A
   B. Technician B
   C. Both Technician A and Technician B
   D. Neither Technician A nor Technician B

HEUI Injection Systems

Chapter Review

The following activities have been designed to help you refresh your knowledge of this chapter. Your instructor may require you to complete some or all of these activities as a regular part of your training program. You are encouraged to complete any activity that your instructor does not assign as a way to enhance your learning.

Matching

Match the following terms with the correct description or example.

A. Cam-less diesel

B. Digital control valve

C. Injection control pressure regulator (ICPR)

D. Injection rate control

E. Split shot injection

_____ **1.** The valve technology that replaced the poppet valve used in the HEUI A and HEUI B designs.

_____ **2.** The control of fuel delivery volume per degree of crank angle rotation into the cylinder during an injection event.

_____ **3.** A system that uses electrohydraulic actuation of intake and exhaust valves to operate valves.

_____ **4.** An injection strategy that delivers fuel in two distinct events during one combustion cycle.

_____ **5.** An electrically operated spool valve that moves in response to the strength of a magnetic field.

Multiple Choice

Read each item carefully, and then select the best response.

_____ **1.** HEUI engines use _____ to control injection.
   A. electronic engine sensors
   B. cam lobes
   C. microprocessors
   D. Both A and C

_____ **2.** HEUIs have the capability to achieve maximum injection pressures of _____, depending on the engine model.
   A. 18,000–22,000 psi (1241–1517 bar)
   B. 23,000–28,500 psi (1586–1965 bar)
   C. 29,000–32,000 psi (1999–2206 bar)
   D. 33,000–39,000 psi (2275–2689 bar)

_____ **3.** The advantage of retarding the main injection is _____.
   A. a reduction of oxides of nitrogen emissions
   B. more fuel is in the cylinder at TDC
   C. a reduction in cylinder pressure
   D. All of the above

_____ **4.** The HEUI system used by the C7 and C9 ACERT had a Caterpillar-developed injector designated the _____ that was used until 2007.
   A. HEUI A
   B. Gen II HEUI
   C. HIB-300
   D. HEUI B

_____ **5.** The _____ injector is distinguished by its white solenoid.
   A. HEUI A
   B. HEUI B
   C. Gen II HEUI
   D. HIB-300

_____ **6.** Fuel below the amplifier piston is injected at a factor _____ times higher than oil pressure.
   A. 3 to 5
   B. 5 to 7
   C. 7 to 10
   D. 10 to 12

_____ **7.** What is the benefit to using a split shot injection strategy?
   A. Lower combustion chamber noise
   B. Lower NO$_x$ emissions
   C. Fewer particulate emissions
   D. All of the above

_____ **8.** The energization time of a Gen II HEUI injector is measured in _____.
   A. tenths of a second
   B. milliseconds
   C. microseconds
   D. nanoseconds

_____ **9.** An oil circuit that does not pass through a filter, but connects the engine's main oil gallery to the reservoir is called a(n) _____ supply.
   A. direct
   B. short-circuit
   C. indirect
   D. unfiltered

_____ **10.** The purpose of the _____ is to operate and monitor injector operation.
   A. injector drive module
   B. amplifier piston
   C. fuel injection control module
   D. Either A or C

True/False

If you believe the statement to be more true than false, write the letter "T" in the space provided. If you believe the statement to be more false than true, write the letter "F".

_____ **1.** Better control of injection rate and timing has helped diesels obtain 99% reduction in noxious emissions today compared to engines built in the early 1990s.

_____ **2.** HEUI injectors are classified as unit injectors.

_____ **3.** Unlike other types of injectors HEUI injectors are interchangeable.

_____ **4.** The Gen II HEUI injector uses digital valve technology.

_____ **5.** The Gen II HEUI uses much more energy than previous models.

_____ **6.** No electrical current is applied to the injector solenoid during the injection cycle.

_____ **7.** Gen II HEUI control valves use springs to center or return the valve to one end of the barrel in which it operates.

_____ **8.** The HIB-300 injector is capable of five different injection rate shapes and an electrically controlled pilot injection.

_____ **9.** The use of oil manifolds supplying oil through the top of the injectors eliminates the problem with O-ring leakage when oil is supplied though the cylinder head.

_____ **10.** Oil viscosity influences the operation of the HEUI systems.

Fill in the Blank

Read each item carefully, and then complete the statement by filling in the missing word(s).

1. HEUI injection systems have replaced the mechanical force produced by an injection pump or engine _____ to pressurize fuel for injection.

2. HEUI systems use the _____ force of highly pressurized lubrication oil rather than a mechanical camshaft to actuate plungers and pressurize fuel for injection.

3. With a sloped or _____ injection rate there is a more gradual buildup of fuel injected into the cylinder, which results in a gentler rise in cylinder pressure.

4. The Gen II HEUI injector uses _____ valve technology.

5. Depending on the manufacturer and engine model, the top surface area of the _____ piston is seven to ten times larger than the bottom plunger diameter.

6. The _____ cycle ends when the solenoid is de-energized.

7. A HEUI B _____ _____ injector can mechanically separate the injection event into two parts using a uniquely shaped plunger design.

8. Digital control valve technology replaced the _____ valve used in the HEUI A and B designs.

9. High-pressure oil is supplied to Gen II HEUI injectors through a high-pressure oil _____ or rail externally attached to the top of the injectors.

10. The _____ _____ _____ sensor provides closed-loop feedback to the ECM about whether the oil pressure is too low or high.

Labeling

Label the following diagrams with the correct terms.

1. Identify the parts of a HEUI B injector:

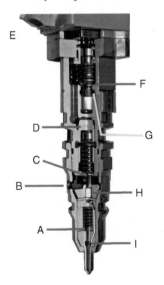

A. _____

B. _____

C. _____

D. _____

E. _____

F. _____

G. _____

H. _____

I. _____

2. Identify the parts of a Gen II HEUI injector:

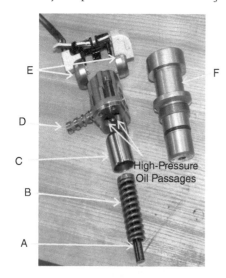

A. _____

B. _____

C. _____

D. _____

E. _____

F. _____

3. Identify the parts of a HIB-300 poppet valve:

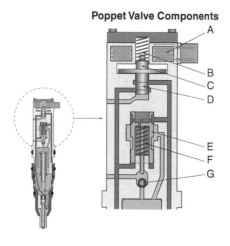

A. _____

B. _____

C. _____

D. _____

E. _____

F. _____

G. _____

4. Identify the parts of a HIB-300 nozzle valve:

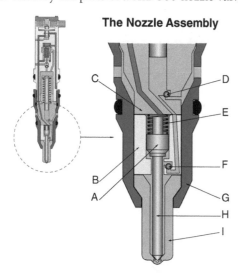

A. _____

B. _____

C. _____

D. _____

E. _____

F. _____

G. _____

H. _____

I. _____

Skill Drills

Test your knowledge of skill drills by filling in the correct words in the photo captions.

1. Performing an ICPR Test:

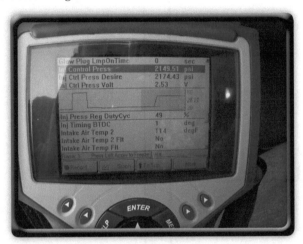

Step 1: Start and warm up the engine.

Step 2: Connect a _____ or _____ _____ to the engine. Navigate to a _____ item that displays live _____ _____ parameters.

Step 3: Locate the _____ for injection control _____ _____ and injection control _____ _____.

Step 4: Run the engine at _____ to observe and _____ injection control _____ and _____ _____.

Step 5: Run the engine at _____ _____ speed and _____ the two _____ again.

Step 6: Compare the _____ you found with the manufacturer's _____. An _____-_____ duty cycle means the system is _____, the oil is too _____, or the _____-_____ pump is worn out. There is no _____ limit to _____ _____ for an engine that is running _____.

Step 7: If the _____ pressure duty cycle is _____ average, recommend further _____ checks to identify _____ caused by defective injector _____ or worn _____.

Crossword Puzzle

Use the clues in the column to complete the puzzle.

Across

4. A piston that multiplies the force of high-pressure oil pressure and is used to pressurize fuel to injection pressure; also known as the amplifier piston.

5. A module on some first-generation and Gen II HEUIs that operates and monitors injector operation. It stores information such as engine firing order and operating and diagnostic software instructions; also known as the fuel injection control module (FICM) on later models of HEUI engines.

Down

1. A small injection event taking place 8–10° before the main injection event.

2. A hydraulic wave-dampening device that minimizes a rhythmic cackling noise at idle caused by high-pressure pump pressure waves synchronizing with injection events.

3. A valve that controls the flow of oil into and out of HEUI A and B injectors.

ASE-Type Questions

Read each item carefully, and then select the best response.

_____ **1.** Technician A says that higher levels of detergents and antifriction additives are needed by HEUI engines to maintain stable injection control oil pressure. Technician B says that antifoaming agents are more important for a smooth and efficient engine operation. Who is correct?
   A. Technician A
   B. Technician B
   C. Both Technician A and Technician B
   D. Neither Technician A nor Technician B

_____ **2.** Technician A says amplified wave attenuation (AWA) fittings in the oil manifold of some G2 HEUI engines reduce irregular combustion noise. Technician B says split shot injection reduces combustion noise. Who is correct?
   A. Technician A
   B. Technician B
   C. Both Technician A and Technician B
   D. Neither Technician A nor Technician B

_____ **3.** Technician A says an above-normal increase in the duty cycle of the PWM signal applied to the HEUI ICPR of a Cat C7 engine indicates the engine oil has thickened due to excessive soot loading. Technician B says a jumper plug in the wiring harness indicates to the engine's ECM that 10w-30 engine oil rather than 15w-40 oil is being used in the crankcase. Who is correct?
   A. Technician A
   B. Technician B
   C. Both Technician A and Technician B
   D. Neither Technician A nor Technician B

_____ **4.** Technician A says the measuring unit for the electrical signal to the injection control pressure regulator of a HEUI fuel system is reported as a percentage (%) on a scanner display of engine parameters. Technician B says the PWM signal is reported as time (in milliseconds). Who is correct?
   A. Technician A
   B. Technician B
   C. Both Technician A and Technician B
   D. Neither Technician A nor Technician B

_____ **5.** While diagnosing the cause of a hard start/prolonged cranking complaint, Technician A says that the high-pressure oil between the high-pressure pump and injectors should stay pressurized for days. Technician B says the oil pressure to the injectors should quickly drop to zero when the engine is shut off. Who is correct?
   A. Technician A
   B. Technician B
   C. Both Technician A and Technician B
   D. Neither Technician A nor Technician B

_____ **6.** While diagnosing the cause of a rough running MaxxForce DT engine, Technician A says that an incorrect injector calibration code will produce uneven cylinder contribution at idle. Technician B says that G2 injectors do not use calibration codes. Who is correct?
   A. Technician A
   B. Technician B
   C. Both Technician A and Technician B
   D. Neither Technician A nor Technician B

_____ **7.** Technician A says that it is important to remove and drain the oil reservoir for a HEUI high-pressure pump when changing engine oil so the oil does not contaminate the clean engine oil. Technician B says that it is not required or practical to drain the oil reservoir or accumulator when changing oil. Who is correct?
   A. Technician A
   B. Technician B
   C. Both Technician A and Technician B
   D. Neither Technician A nor Technician B

_____ **8.** When investigating the cause of frequent injector failures on a HEUI engine, Technician A says that a likely cause could be engine oil contaminated with dirt entering the engine through a leaking air filter. Technician B says that condition will not cause injector failure because the oil is filtered before supplying the injectors. Who is correct?
   A. Technician A
   B. Technician B
   C. Both Technician A and Technician B
   D. Neither Technician A nor Technician B

_____ **9.** While discussing the purpose of pilot or split shot injection, Technician A says HEUI injectors use it to reduce NO_x emissions. Technician B says PRIME metering is used to reduce combustion noise. Who is correct?
   A. Technician A
   B. Technician B
   C. Both Technician A and Technician B
   D. Neither Technician A nor Technician B

_____ **10.** While considering ways to increase engine power output, Technician A says that using a special injection control pressure (ICP) sensor, which reports oil pressure as lower than the actual pressure, is an effective shortcut. Technician B says that using the modified ICP sensor signal will result in less fuel injected. Who is correct?
   A. Technician A
   B. Technician B
   C. Both Technician A and Technician B
   D. Neither Technician A nor Technician B

Common Rail Fuel Systems

Chapter Review

The following activities have been designed to help you refresh your knowledge of this chapter. Your instructor may require you to complete some or all of these activities as a regular part of your training program. You are encouraged to complete any activity that your instructor does not assign as a way to enhance your learning.

Matching

Match the following terms with the correct description or example.

A. Amplified common rail (ACR)

B. Coaxial variable nozzle injector

C. Fuel mean value adaptation (FMA)

D. Pressure wave correction (PWC)

E. Zero fuel mass calibration (ZFC)

_____ 1. The process of recalibrating injectors during service to compensate for wear and deterioration.

_____ 2. A correction factor made to an injector's energization time based on changes in fuel delivery rates caused by wear and deterioration.

_____ 3. Two-stage amplification of fuel pressure inside the injector that provides improved power output with lower emissions, noise, and fuel consumption, and that produces a unique shape to the injection rate profile.

_____ 4. The process used to produce a calibration code for a common rail injector.

_____ 5. A fourth-generation injector concept from Bosch that contains a two-stage nozzle lift with two rows of spray holes.

Multiple Choice

Read each item carefully, and then select the best response.

_____ 1. High pressurization enhances the _____ of fuel in the combustion chamber.
  A. atomization
  B. volume
  C. distribution
  D. Both A and C

_____ 2. Currently, the fastest piezo CR injector can produce _____ separate injection events during one combustion cycle.
  A. 4
  B. 6
  C. 8
  D. 10

_____ 3. Which of the following is NOT one of the three main types of CR injectors?
  A. Electro-Hydraulic Solenoids
  B. Modular HEUI
  C. Piezoceramic Electric Actuators
  D. Hydraulically Amplified Common Rail

_____ **4.** Hydraulically amplified diesel injection systems are currently capable of injection pressures as high as _____.
   - **A.** 35,000 psi (2413 bar)
   - **B.** 36,500 psi (2517 bar)
   - **C.** 37,500 psi (2586 bar)
   - **D.** 40,000 psi (2758 bar)

_____ **5.** Servo actuators used by Siemens to open and close nozzle valves are _____ valves.
   - **A.** mushroom-shaped
   - **B.** spindle-shaped
   - **C.** ball
   - **D.** butterfly

_____ **6.** Bosch CR1 and CR2 injectors use a four-step _____ operation to inject fuel.
   - **A.** spring coil
   - **B.** servo-hydraulic
   - **C.** cam and plunger
   - **D.** split shot

_____ **7.** In CRS3 injectors the magnetic solenoids are replaced with a _____.
   - **A.** piezoceramic material
   - **B.** single spring armature
   - **C.** spindle-shaped control valve
   - **D.** dual spring armature

_____ **8.** The Bosch CRS3 injector incorporates a(n) _____ that carries out additional functions.
   - **A.** electromagnetic actuator
   - **B.** bypass valve
   - **C.** hydraulic coupler
   - **D.** Both A and C

_____ **9.** The CRS4 hydraulically amplified injector is capable of producing all of the following shape profiles **EXCEPT**:
   - **A.** boot
   - **B.** ramp
   - **C.** triangle
   - **D.** square

_____ **10.** To identify the source of a fuel system leak, you should measure pressure at the _____.
   - **A.** injector fuel return
   - **B.** high-pressure pump return
   - **C.** high-pressure relief valve return
   - **D.** All of the above

True/False

If you believe the statement to be more true than false, write the letter "T" in the space provided. If you believe the statement to be more false than true, write the letter "F".

_____ **1.** Injection timing in common rail injection systems is accurate to within one-tenth of a degree of crankshaft rotation.

_____ **2.** The greatest advantage CR injection offers is injection rate shaping capabilities.

_____ **3.** Though the technology is older, hydraulically amplified control of CR injectors is used on most current medium- and heavy-duty diesels.

_____ **4.** Bosch has developed four generations of CR injectors, three of which are currently in production vehicles.

_____ **5.** In Bosch's first- and second-generation CR systems, injection events are controlled by nozzle valve spring force.

_____ **6.** The difference between the CRS1 and CRS2 injectors is in the solenoid.

_____ **7.** The biggest drawback to the use of piezoelectric crystals is the high amount of inductive resistance.

_____ **8.** Third-generation Bosch injectors use as much as 250 volts to open and require electrical linesmen gloves as a safety precaution when working on some systems.

_____ **9.** With some engine control systems, the pressure regulator acts as a fuel temperature sensor.

_____ **10.** The high-pressure fuel pump is driven at one-quarter engine speed and coupled to the engine through a chain drive mechanism.

Fill in the Blank

Read each item carefully, and then complete the statement by filling in the missing word(s).

1. The term _____-_____ actuator describes the force multiplication taking place inside a CR injector.

2. Bosch CRS1 and CRS2 injectors are capable of faster response due in large part to the use of hydraulically _____ nozzle valves.

3. The injector solenoid is energized with current supplied by the fuel injector _____ _____.

4. A _____ actuator can switch fuel on and off in as little as 0.0001 second.

5. The fourth-generation CRS4 uses an internal hydraulic _____ to multiply injection pressure at a ratio of 2:1.

6. The Bosch fourth-generation concept injector CRI4-PV is a _____ variable nozzle injector.

7. High-pressure _____ _____ develop the pressure required for injection under all engine-operating conditions, including quick starting of the engine.

8. A _____ pressure control valve is used to regulate the quantity of fuel admitted into the high-pressure fuel pump.

9. The CR fuel system monitor monitors fuel system _____ to verify it is operating within an expected range.

10. Without a strategy to _____ an injector, a vehicle could pass out of compliance with emission standards and emission system durability requirements.

Labeling

Label the following diagrams with the correct terms.

1. Identify the parts of a Denso CR injector:

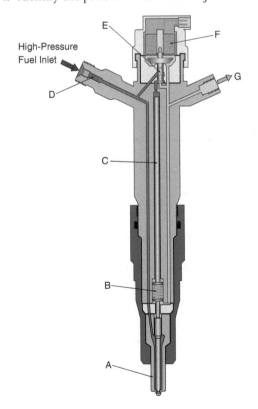

A. _____

B. _____

C. _____

D. _____

E. _____

F. _____

G. _____

2. Identify the parts of a Bosch CRS1 injector:

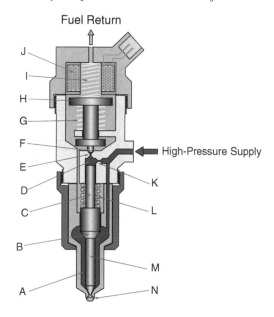

Fuel Return

High-Pressure Supply

A. _____

B. _____

C. _____

D. _____

E. _____

F. _____

G. _____

H. _____

I. _____

J. _____

K. _____

L. _____

M. _____

N. _____

3. Identify the parts of a Siemens CR injector:

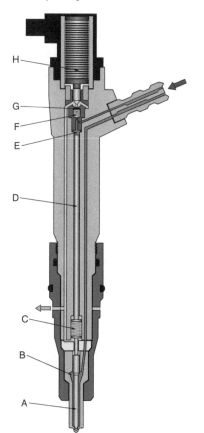

A. _____

B. _____

C. _____

D. _____

E. _____

F. _____

G. _____

H. _____

Skill Drills

Test your knowledge of skill drills by filling in the correct words in the photo captions.

1. Measuring Injector Back Leakage (Method 1):

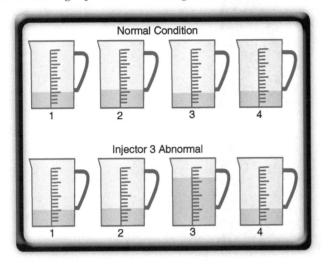

Step 1:   Remove the _____ _____ hose from each injector and install _____ _____ to _____ _____ fittings.

Step 2:   Connect the jumper tube _____ _____ hoses to a set of _____ _____.

Step 3:   Start and run the engine at _____. Measure and record the _____ of _____ accumulating in the graduated cylinders for _____ minutes.

Step 4:   Operate the engine at _____ _____ speed for _____ minutes. Measure and _____ the _____ of _____ accumulating in the graduated cylinders.

Step 5:   Compare _____ accumulations to manufacturers' _____. Generally, a _____ injector will flow _____ times the _____ return rate. No fuel return indicates a _____ injector _____. Injector _____ is recommended in _____ _____.

2. Measuring Injector Back Leakage (Method 2):

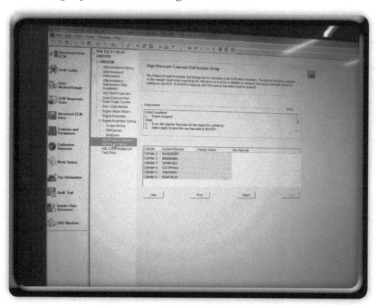

Step 1: Connect OEM software to the _____ _____ adapter and navigate to the _____ _____ diagnostic menu. Enable the fuel leakage test to _____ the _____ _____ to _____ pressure at _____. Alternatively, operate the engine at _____ idle.

Step 2: Collect and measure the _____ return from the _____ _____. If the return is _____, one or more _____ may be _____ internally due to defective _____ _____, or a _____ _____ may be leaking.

Step 3: Shut off the engine and _____ cylinder _____'s injector line at the _____ _____. Install a purpose-made _____ on the _____ fitting to _____ fuel flow.

Step 4: Start and run the engine again in the _____ _____ diagnostic mode or at _____ _____.

Step 5: Collect, measure, and record the _____ of _____ returned from the _____ _____ while the injector is _____.

Step 6: Repeat the fuel _____ and _____ procedure for each _____ in the engine.

Step 7: Compare _____ return volume. Note any _____ that had an _____-_____ drop in fuel return _____ when its fuel line was _____. This cylinder likely has a _____ injector or _____ _____. Alternatively, measure and record fuel return when _____ fuel lines are _____ and compare with _____ _____ for each _____.

3. Measuring Fuel Leakage from Other Fuel System Components:

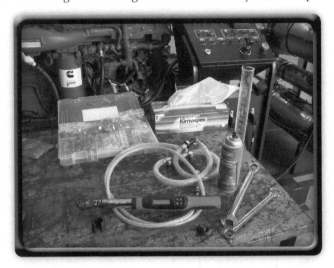

Step 1:   Verify the _____ _____ pressure remains _____ with the engine
_____. Connect a _____ or OEM _____ _____ to
the data link connector and observe the rail _____. A good system will _____
rail pressure for _____ at values close to where they were when the engine was
_____ _____. If rail pressure _____ _____ quickly or goes to less
than several _____ psi (bar) in a few _____, there is a _____-
_____ system leak.

Step 2:   Remove the _____ _____ and inspect individual _____ carefully
for evidence of _____ _____.

Step 3:   Navigate to the _____ menu of the OEM software and request a _____
_____ test. Run the engine in the _____ _____ test mode, which
_____ rail pressure to its _____ value.

Step 4:   Connect a clear plastic _____ to the function _____ or _____
_____ of the high-pressure _____. Collect and measure the _____
_____ in graduated cylinders with the engine _____ in fuel leakage
_____ _____ or at _____ idle. Record your observations.

Step 5:   Connect a clear plastic _____ to the _____ block or fuel return line for the
rail pressure _____ _____. Collect and measure the fuel _____ in
graduated cylinders with the engine running in _____ _____ test mode or at
high _____. Record your observations.

Step 6:   If an engine doesn't have individual _____ _____, but does have return
_____ through the cylinder _____, measure _____ leakage.
Connect a clear plastic hose to the function block or fuel return line for the _____
_____ from the _____ _____. Collect and measure the fuel
volume in _____ _____ with the engine _____ in fuel leakage
_____ _____ or at _____ _____. Record your
observations.

Step 7:   Compare the fuel _____ to the manufacturers' _____. Generally, a
_____ high-pressure _____ or _____ pressure _____
_____ will return _____ fuel if it is _____ _____ or
_____.

Crossword Puzzle

Use the clues in the column to complete the puzzle.

Across

4. Current induced that opposes ECM current when initially energized; also known as inductive reactance.

5. To use a small movement of an electrically operated control valve to manipulate much larger and powerful hydraulic forces.

Down

1. An actuator composed of piezoceramic discs that change shape and in turn change the balance of hydraulic forces inside the injector.

2. A strategy used by the ECM to adjust fuel delivery quantities to each cylinder to achieve consistent pressures among all cylinders. Crankshaft speed data is used to make corrections to the volume of fuel injected in each cylinder.

3. Optimizing the injection discharge curve to best match engine-operating conditions.

ASE-Type Questions

Read each item carefully, and then select the best response.

_____ 1. Technician A says that a common rail engine can vary the injection pressure, timing, and injection rate shape for each injector. Technician B says that the injection pressure is the same for all injectors in common rail engines, and injectors can perform multiple injection events during each combustion cycle. Who is correct?
   A. Technician A
   B. Technician B
   C. Both Technician A and Technician B
   D. Neither Technician A nor Technician B

_____ 2. Technician A says that servo injector actuators use a small amount of control valve movement to control larger, more powerful, and faster-acting hydraulic forces. Technician B says that control valves that use piezoelectric control valves are the only actuators capable of servo action. Who is correct?
   A. Technician A
   B. Technician B
   C. Both Technician A and Technician B
   D. Neither Technician A nor Technician B

_____ 3. Technician A says that rate shaping involves changing the amount of fuel discharged from the injector spray holes. Technician B says that rate shaping requires multiple injection events and a high-pressure fuel system with the ability to vary injection pressure. Who is correct?
   A. Technician A
   B. Technician B
   C. Both Technician A and Technician B
   D. Neither Technician A nor Technician B

_____ 4. Technician A says that dirt bypassing the filter on many common rail injectors can cause an injector to stick open and continuously fuel a cylinder. Technician B says that any dirt particles may potentially damage the injector, but would not allow an injector to full fuel or the engine to run away. Who is correct?
   A. Technician A
   B. Technician B
   C. Both Technician A and Technician B
   D. Neither Technician A nor Technician B

_____ 5. Technician A says that faster responding piezoelectric injectors are best suited for use in common rail engines. Technician B says that engine speeds of heavy-duty, on-highway engines do not require the piezoelectric injector's higher number of injection events. Who is correct?
   A. Technician A
   B. Technician B
   C. Both Technician A and Technician B
   D. Neither Technician A nor Technician B

_____ 6. Technician A says that servo-hydraulic actuators using electromagnets have better durability than piezoceramic actuators. Technician B says piezoceramic actuators are as durable, if not more durable, as servo-hydraulic injectors using electromagnets. Who is correct?
   A. Technician A
   B. Technician B
   C. Both Technician A and Technician B
   D. Neither Technician A nor Technician B

_____ 7. Technician A says that Detroit Diesel's DD series engines use fourth-generation coaxial-type injectors with two separate sets of spray holes. Technician B says that Detroit Diesel's DD series engines have less than 20,000 psi (1379 bar) of fuel pressure in the fuel rail. Who is correct?
   A. Technician A
   B. Technician B
   C. Both Technician A and Technician B
   D. Neither Technician A nor Technician B

_____ **8.** Technician A says that cylinder misfires can be detected on common rail engines by slightly cracking open the fuel line to each injector when the engine is running. Technician B says that it is important to place a shop towel over the injector when checking for misfires to prevent pressurized fuel from penetrating the skin. Who is correct?
   A. Technician A
   B. Technician B
   C. Both Technician A and Technician B
   D. Neither Technician A nor Technician B

_____ **9.** Technician A says that Detroit ACR injectors will amplify injection pressure under heavy loads as needed by the engine. Technician B says that injection amplification in the ACR injector takes place at engine speeds just above idle. Who is correct?
   A. Technician A
   B. Technician B
   C. Both Technician A and Technician B
   D. Neither Technician A nor Technician B

_____ **10.** While discussing the purpose of a second electrical control valve, which regulates fuel volume supplied to the inlet of the high-pressure pump, Technician A says the volume control valve helps improve fuel economy. Technician B says the volume control valve is needed to reduce emissions. Who is correct?
   A. Technician A
   B. Technician B
   C. Both Technician A and Technician B
   D. Neither Technician A nor Technician B

_____ **11.** While performing a back-leakage test for a first-generation Bosch common rail fuel system, the fuel volume was measured to be above specification. Technician A says the cause could be a leaking quill tube. Technician B says the cause could be one or more injectors with worn-out ball valve seats. Who is correct?
   A. Technician A
   B. Technician B
   C. Both Technician A and Technician B
   D. Neither Technician A nor Technician B

Air Induction and Exhaust Systems

Chapter Review

The following activities have been designed to help you refresh your knowledge of this chapter. Your instructor may require you to complete some or all of these activities as a regular part of your training program. You are encouraged to complete any activity that your instructor does not assign as a way to enhance your learning.

Matching

Match the following terms with the correct description or example.

A. Closed crankcase ventilation system

B. Naturally aspirated

C. Open crankcase ventilation system

D. Stoichiometric ratio

E. Tangential intake port

_____ **1.** A process of sending vapors into the air intake, such as in the case of water-methanol injection systems.

_____ **2.** An engine that uses only atmospheric pressure and not pressurized air to charge the cylinders with air.

_____ **3.** The mass of air required to completely burn all fuel in the combustion chamber so no fuel or air remains after combustion.

_____ **4.** An intake port design that admits air into the cylinder at an angle to impart more swirl, or turbulence, to charge air.

_____ **5.** A traditional ventilation system for the diesel crankcase that vents the crankcase directly to the atmosphere.

Multiple Choice

Read each item carefully, and then select the best response.

_____ **1.** A diesel engine of 350 horsepower typically requires an air intake capacity of close to _____ cubic feet per minute.
   A. 500
   B. 1000
   C. 1500
   D. 2000

_____ **2.** The best choice for detecting leaks in the negative pressure side of the air intake system is a(n)_____.
   A. soap bubble test
   B. ultrasonic test
   C. engine oil analysis
   D. UV leak test

_____ **3.** The number of oxygen molecules entering the cylinder will vary with a change in _____.
   A. atmospheric pressure
   B. ambient temperature
   C. humidity
   D. All of the above

_____ 4. Plastic or rubber tubes are frequently used for air intake construction because they _____ better than metal tubes.
   A. transfer little heat
   B. resist corrosion
   C. dampen intake noise
   D. All of the above

_____ 5. In a diesel engine, blow-by leaking past the rings consists primarily of _____.
   A. air
   B. soot
   C. oil
   D. fuel

_____ 6. A _____ regulates, or meters, the quantity of blow-by back into the engine's intake manifold.
   A. barometric pressure sensor
   B. crankcase depression regulator
   C. road draft tube
   D. centrifugal oil-coalescing device

_____ 7. The _____ sensor measures the weight of air entering the engine.
   A. mass airflow
   B. barometric pressure
   C. manifold absolute pressure
   D. All of the above

_____ 8. High amounts of intake swirl, or turbulence, is needed to reduce the formation of _____ at low- to mid-speed operating conditions.
   A. carbon monoxide
   B. hydrocarbon
   C. particulate emissions
   D. All of the above

_____ 9. As an air filter loads with more dirt, efficiency and restriction increase; this is referred to as the _____ principle.
   A. capacity
   B. positive filtration
   C. saturation
   D. effectiveness

_____ 10. When _____ is injected into the intake system, the process of vaporization absorbs heat from the intake air and reduces its temperature.
   A. water and methanol
   B. propane
   C. nitrous oxide
   D. ethyl ether

True/False

If you believe the statement to be more true than false, write the letter "T" in the space provided. If you believe the statement to be more false than true, write the letter "F".

_____ 1. Diesel engines require an excess supply of air relative to the quantity needed to completely burn fuel in the cylinders.

_____ 2. Stoichiometric ratios are measured in volume not weight.

_____ 3. A room with a 50% relative humidity at 68°F (20°C) will have less oxygen than a room with 80% relative humidity will have at the same temperature.

_____ 4. Gases escaping past piston rings can accumulate in the engine crankcase, pressurizing the engine and contaminating lube oil.

_____ 5. Oil accumulations on the compressor wheel and housing are normal when using a closed crankcase ventilation system.

_____ 6. Data from the barometric pressure sensor is used to modify fuel injection timing and fuel rates to minimize emissions.

_____ 7. Unlike gasoline-fueled engines, diesel engines are able to use a large amount of valve overlap to enhance engine breathing and performance characteristics.

_____ 8. PowerCore filters are a wall flow-type filter element that uses a synthetic web-like fiber referred to as nanofiber to cover a specially formulated cellulose material.

_____ 9. Adding oxides of nitrogen to the intake air can supply a power boost if additional fuel is burned to use up the oxygen in the cylinder.

_____ 10. Ether is suited to assist starting compression-ignition engines due to its low auto-ignition temperature and flammability.

Fill in the Blank

Read each item carefully, and then complete the statement by filling in the missing word(s).

1. The best emissions are obtained from gasoline engines operating using a _____ ratio of 14.73:1.

2. The SAE _____ _____ factors adjust calculations of power output measurements to an atmospheric pressure of 29.23 inches of mercury, a temperature of 77°F, and 0% humidity.

3. To prevent damage, the engine power needs to be _____ if temperatures exceed threshold values.

4. Excessive _____ pressure can lower crankcase pressure too much and allow dirt to be drawn into the engine through seals and gaskets.

5. The _____ pressure sensor provides data regarding ambient air pressure for altitude compensation.

6. Data from the _____ _____ _____ sensor, which is also called the intake boost pressure sensor, is used to sense engine load and adjust fuel rates.

7. An electronically controlled _____ _____ valve will, under certain conditions, restrict excessive airflow into the engine, increasing exhaust gas temperatures.

8. The use of _____-style pre-cleaner tubes pre-cleans the intake air by spinning dirt out of the airflow to prevent it from entering the filter.

9. Paper filter elements are made from compressed _____ fibers and chemically treated to resist water damage.

10. An air filter _____ _____ in the air filter housing is connected to the instrument cluster to warn the driver to service the element.

Labeling

Label the following diagrams with the correct terms.

    1. Identify the engine and exhaust components involved in the air induction system:

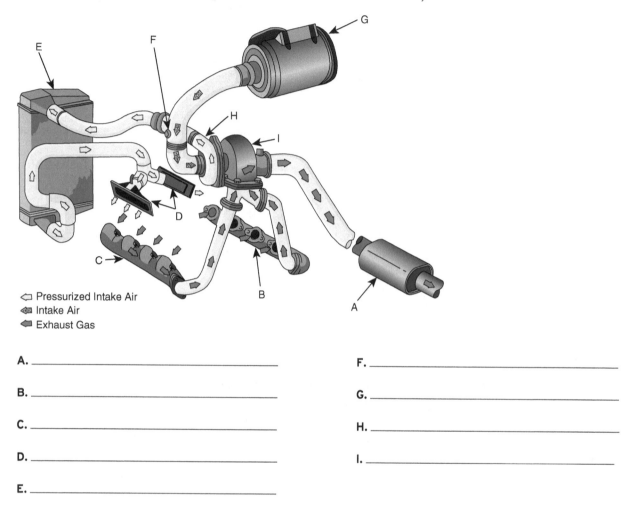

◁ Pressurized Intake Air
◁ Intake Air
◀ Exhaust Gas

A. _____   F. _____

B. _____   G. _____

C. _____   H. _____

D. _____   I. _____

E. _____

Skill Drills

Test your knowledge of skill drills by filling in the correct words in the photo captions.

1. Diagnosing High Crankcase Pressure Codes:

Step 1:   Inspect all _____ ventilation _____ for _____ or
_____.

Step 2:   If equipped, inspect the oil _____ _____ and oil drain _____
_____ for _____.

Step 3:   Check the crankcase _____ _____ for damage.

Step 4:   Remove the crankcase filter _____ and check to see the filter is properly _____.
Replace the crankcase ventilation _____. In _____ weather, the filter may
become _____ and produce high-pressure _____.

2. Measuring Air Filter Restriction:

PRESSURE CONVERSION

Unit	inH₂O	cmH₂O	inHg	cmHg	psi	kg/cm²	atm	kPa
1 inH₂O	1	2.54	0.0735	1.866	0.0361			0.248
1 inHg	13.6	34.544	1	2.54	0.491	0.0345	0.0334	3.386
1 psi	27.7	70.104	2.036	5.171	1	0.0703	0.068	6.8948
1 kg/cm²	393.73	1000.0	28.96	73.55	14.22	1	0.9678	101.28
1 atm	407.19	1033.0	29.92	75.96	14.70	1.033	1	. . . .
1 kPa	4.01	10.18	0.295	0.750	0.145	0.026	. . . .	. . . .

Step 1: Connect a _____ gauge to the _____ side of the _____
_____. A _____ gauge measures pressures in _____
of _____ _____. An electronic pressure _____ or a
_____ with long plastic lines is needed.

Step 2: Place the engine under _____ during a _____ _____ to operate
the engine at maximum _____ _____.

Step 3: Observe and record _____ _____ _____.

Step 4: Recommend air filter _____ if _____ is more than _____–_____ (30–38 cm)
of _____.

3. Pressure Testing the Air Induction System:

Step 1: Remove the _____ _____ and wrap it in a large heavy-duty plastic
_____ _____.

Step 2: Reinstall the _____ _____ into the _____ _____.

Step 3: Connect a supply of _____ _____ that is regulated to _____–
_____ psi (34–55 kPa) to the _____ system. Removing the filter
_____ _____ is an easily accessible point to pressurize the air intake
system. Higher pressure will _____ the bag and _____ the engine if an
_____ _____ is open. The engine may need to be _____ to a
position where a _____ is not on valve _____, allowing the _____
to pass through to the _____ system.

Step 4: Inspect the intake _____ and _____ for _____. Spray down the
connections between the _____ and _____ inlet with _____
_____.

Step 5: Retighten loose _____, realign _____ as necessary, and _____
any detectable _____ _____. Leaks on the _____ side of the
_____ system after the _____ are not a concern, because pressurized air will
_____ dirt out rather than _____ it in.

Crossword Puzzle

Use the clues in the column to complete the puzzle.

Across

4. Engine test standards for ambient temperature, atmospheric pressure, and humidity. Manufacturer measurements of horsepower and torque must be made using standard day factors to ensure uniformity of test results.
5. A comparison between measured cylinder volume and the volume of air actually filling a cylinder; expressed as a percentage.

Down

1. A method of cleaning up blow-by emissions by recycling crankcase emissions back into the intake manifold.
2. The tube that connects the crankcase to the atmosphere in an open crankcase ventilation system; also known as a crankcase ventilation tube.
3. The process of collecting together oil in crankcase vapors to separate it from the vapors.

ASE-Type Questions

Read each item carefully, and then select the best response.

_____ 1. Technician A says that the best practice is to replace air filters on turbocharged engines when the restriction gauge reads 20–25" (51–63 cm) of H_2O. Technician B says the filter should be replaced around 10–15" (25–38 cm) H_2O to prevent increased fuel consumption caused by a restricted air filter. Who is correct?
   A. Technician A
   B. Technician B
   C. Both Technician A and Technician B
   D. Neither Technician A nor Technician B

_____ 2. Technician A says that it is an acceptable practice to clean air filters using compressed shop air. Technician B says it is better to clean air filters by dropping or lightly tapping the filter against the shop floor. Who is correct?
   A. Technician A
   B. Technician B
   C. Both Technician A and Technician B
   D. Neither Technician A nor Technician B

_____ 3. While examining a piston crown that has vertical cracks through the edges of the piston's combustion chamber bowl, Technician A suggests the piston crown was not getting properly cooled due to low mass airflow in the combustion chamber during the valve overlap period. Technician B suggests the cracks were caused by inadequate cooling by the oil cooler nozzles. Who is correct?
   A. Technician A
   B. Technician B
   C. Both Technician A and Technician B
   D. Neither Technician A nor Technician B

_____ 4. An engine had a fault code for high crankcase pressure and its power is derated. Technician A says that the crankcase filter could have frozen when exposed to extreme cold conditions. Technician B says that a frozen filter would likely blow engine gaskets and seals rather than cause a derate condition. Who is correct?
   A. Technician A
   B. Technician B
   C. Both Technician A and Technician B
   D. Neither Technician A nor Technician B

_____ 5. Technician A says that diesel-fueled engines use more air than gasoline-fueled engines because 1 gallon (4 liters) of diesel fuel requires more air to burn than gasoline. Technician B says that a diesel engine uses more air to prevent pistons and valves from burning. Who is correct?
   A. Technician A
   B. Technician B
   C. Both Technician A and Technician B
   D. Neither Technician A nor Technician B

_____ 6. Technician A says that crankcase coalescing filters are used to minimize particulate emissions from diesel engines. Technician B says that centrifugal air–oil separators reduce engine oil consumption. Who is correct?
   A. Technician A
   B. Technician B
   C. Both Technician A and Technician B
   D. Neither Technician A nor Technician B

_____ 7. Technician A says that a crankcase depression regulator is used to prevent over-pressurization of an engine's crankcase. Technician B says that the crankcase depression regulator prevents dirt from entering the engine through seals and gaskets. Who is correct?
   A. Technician A
   B. Technician B
   C. Both Technician A and Technician B
   D. Neither Technician A nor Technician B

_____ **8.** Technician A says that a throttle plate on a late-model diesel engine helps increase the exhaust temperatures for the exhaust aftertreatment catalysts. Technician B says diesel air intake is not throttled. Who is correct?
  A. Technician A
  B. Technician B
  C. Both Technician A and Technician B
  D. Neither Technician A nor Technician B

_____ **9.** Technician A says that frequent air filter changes help maintain the cleanest quality of air that enters the engine. Technician B says that dirty filters allow cleaner air to enter the engine than clean filters. Who is correct?
  A. Technician A
  B. Technician B
  C. Both Technician A and Technician B
  D. Neither Technician A nor Technician B

_____ **10.** Technician A says that electric intake heaters are used to reduce cold-start and warm-up emissions. Technician B says that intake air heaters help to shorten the cranking time of a cold engine. Who is correct?
  A. Technician A
  B. Technician B
  C. Both Technician A and Technician B
  D. Neither Technician A nor Technician B

Fixed Geometry and Wastegated Turbochargers

Chapter Review

The following activities have been designed to help you refresh your knowledge of this chapter. Your instructor may require you to complete some or all of these activities as a regular part of your training program. You are encouraged to complete any activity that your instructor does not assign as a way to enhance your learning.

Matching

Match the following terms with the correct description or example.

A. Asymmetrical turbocharger

B. Fixed geometry turbocharger

C. Parallel turbocharger

D. Single sequential turbocharger (SST)

E. Variable geometry turbocharger (VGT)

_____ 1. A turbocharger with volutes of two different sizes.

_____ 2. A turbocharger design that uses a single turbine wheel and two compressor wheels.

_____ 3. A turbocharger without boost pressure controls.

_____ 4. The use of two turbochargers that share the exhaust energy from an engine's exhaust manifold.

_____ 5. A turbocharger with the capability of changing boost pressure independent of engine speed and load.

Multiple Choice

Read each item carefully, and then select the best response.

_____ 1. A _____ is a positive displacement-type air pump driven by the engine directly through the gear train.
   A. supercharger
   B. turbocharger
   C. rootes blower
   D. All of the above

_____ 2. Helping diesel engines develop greater power output from engines with smaller displacement has the indirect effect of reducing _____ emissions.
   A. carbon dioxide
   B. oxides of nitrogen
   C. carbon monoxide
   D. hydrocarbon

_____ 3. The term given to the turbocharger's ability to compensate for altitude change is _____.
   A. displacement
   B. normalization
   C. turbo lag
   D. barometric offset

_____ 4. The cycle of adding fuel to produce more intake boost and then adding more fuel incrementally is referred to as _____.
   A. ramping
   B. normalization
   C. spooling
   D. accumulating

_____ **5.** Compressor wheels are made out of _____.
  A. titanium alloys
  B. steel super alloys with high nickel content
  C. lightweight aluminum
  D. Either A or C

_____ **6.** A _____ turbocharger is a solution to the problems of sluggish, low-power performance and high emissions at low engine speeds.
  A. fixed geometry
  B. wastegated
  C. pulse
  D. series

_____ **7.** When the compressor output of one turbocharger is directly connected to the compressor inlet of the other, it is called _____ turbocharging.
  A. series
  B. parallel
  C. series sequential
  D. variable geometry

_____ **8.** Detroit's DD series engines use _____ turbochargers to increase exhaust backpressure from the narrower volute that supplies the EGR system with exhaust gases.
  A. series
  B. pulse
  C. asymmetrical
  D. series sequential

_____ **9.** The volume of air supplied to the engine by the turbocharger is determined by the _____.
  A. geometry of the compressor wheel
  B. housing shape
  C. compressor wheel speed
  D. All of the above

_____ **10.** When turbocharger discharge pressure is too high, it can cause an increase in _____ emissions.
  A. particulate matter
  B. hydrocarbon
  C. nitrogen oxide
  D. carbon monoxide

True/False

If you believe the statement to be more true than false, write the letter "T" in the space provided. If you believe the statement to be more false than true, write the letter "F".

_____ **1.** Boosting intake air pressure dramatically improves the volumetric efficiency of an engine by more than 300% and more than doubles its power output.

_____ **2.** Turbocharging produces louder noise emissions than naturally aspirated engines and require additional manifold components to dampen intake air noise.

_____ **3.** Turbine housings become hotter than the exhaust manifold when the engine is under load.

_____ **4.** Turbo lag is the direct result of turbocharger inertia and friction.

_____ **5.** Wastegated turbochargers can be identified by their dual inlets to the turbine housing.

_____ **6.** Series sequential turbochargers are necessary for engines equipped with high-pressure cooled exhaust gas recirculation.

_____ **7.** The compressor housing is shaped like the turbine housing but with opposite direction of gas flow.

_____ **8.** A turbine housing that is too large results in excessive exhaust backpressure producing low-power complaints and engine overheating.

_____ **9.** The center-housing rotating assembly is dynamically balanced by removing metal from the underside of the turbine and compressor.

_____ **10.** Measuring axial and radial bearing clearances is an important estimate of turbocharger service life and can pinpoint imminent failures.

Fill in the Blank

Read each item carefully, and then complete the statement by filling in the missing word(s).

1. In a turbocharger, exhaust gases drive a turbine wheel, which is connected to a _____ _____ through a common shaft.

2. Engines not equipped with superchargers have cylinders charged with air at atmospheric pressure and are classified as _____ _____.

3. Undersized exhaust pipes and mufflers, dents and numerous bends cause exhaust _____ to increase.

4. Turbochargers operate by converting _____ energy into _____ energy that in turn forces more air into the engine.

5. Because the amount of exhaust energy is low when an engine is lightly loaded, a _____ _____ turbocharger can produce little boost at low speeds.

6. Turbocharger failure will result if the _____ is seized closed or tampered with to prevent it from opening.

7. The _____ _____ is a numerical representation of the diameter of the inlet opening to the volute compared to the radius of the volute.

8. Turbocharger _____ is a condition where the turbocharger passes oil into the exhaust system.

9. Using an _____ type ball bearing as a center housing support eliminates the need for a thrust bearing because endplay is controlled by the ball and race assembly rather than a sleeve.

10. Many turbochargers use engine _____ passing through passages cast into the center housing to remove heat.

Labeling

Label the following diagrams with the correct terms.

1. Identify the components of a turbocharger:

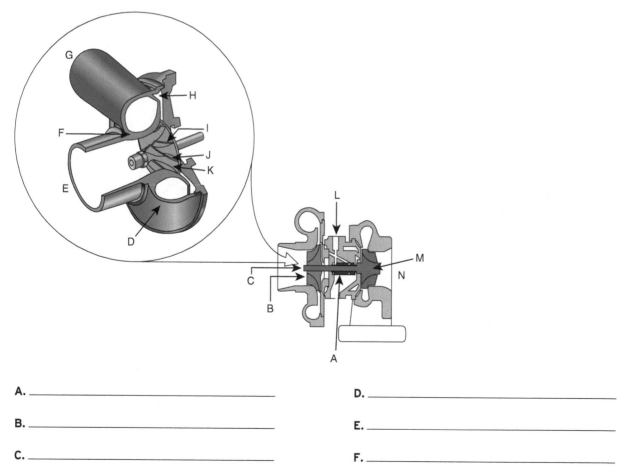

A. _____

B. _____

C. _____

D. _____

E. _____

F. _____

G. _____

H. _____

I. _____

J. _____

K. _____

L. _____

M. _____

N. _____

2. Identify the components attached to the turbine shaft:

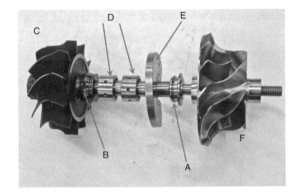

A. _____

B. _____

C. _____

D. _____

E. _____

F. _____

Skill Drills

Test your knowledge of skill drills by filling in the correct words in the photo captions.

1. Measuring Turbocharger Radial Bearing Clearance:

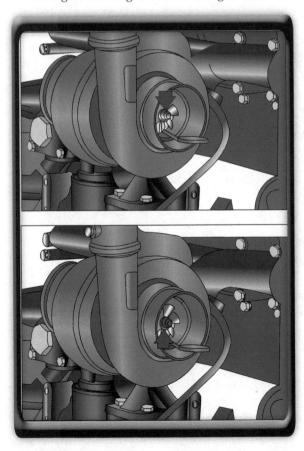

Step 1:   With the engine off, remove the intake air piping.

Step 2:   Inspect the area between the _____ _____ and _____ for evidence of contact. Make a careful _____, particularly if an operator has reported an engine _____ complaint.

Step 3:   Rotate the _____ _____; while rotating, check for any _____ or _____.

Step 4:   Grasp the compressor wheel _____ _____ between your fingers and move the wheel _____ and _____ and _____ and _____. Any contact between the compressor wheel and _____ indicates that the _____ support bearings are excessively _____ and the turbocharger should be _____.

Step 5:   If there is _____ _____ between the compressor wheel and housing, _____ the compressor wheel while applying a slight amount of _____ _____ to the wheel. Again, any _____ or _____ while rotating the wheel indicates the turbocharger should be _____ from _____. Contact in _____ _____ only may indicate the compressor _____ is _____. Loosen any _____ _____ or _____ bolts to _____ the housing and recheck.

Step 6:   To measure center support _____ _____, push down on the _____ _____ with _____ finger pressure while _____ the thickest _____ _____ that will fit between the _____ and _____. Record the _____ of the _____ _____.

Step 7:   Repeat the same procedure while _____ the compressor _____. Record the thickness of the _____ _____ inserted in the _____ _____ while the compressor wheel is lifted in the _____ direction.

Step 8:   Subtract the _____ feeler blade size from the _____ feeler blade size and _____ the results against the manufacturer's _____. Report the bearing _____ and make a service recommendation.

2. Measuring Turbocharger Axial Bearing Clearance:

Step 1:   Place a _____-base dial indicator on the _____ _____; if the turbocharger is _____ the _____, place the indicator on the turbine _____.

Step 2:   Place the dial indicator needle's _____ _____ at the _____ of the compressor wheel's _____ _____.

Step 3:   Push the _____ forward in the turbine _____ with moderate _____ pressure.

Step 4:   Zero the _____ _____.

Step 5:   Push the compressor wheel _____ or pull on the turbine _____ with moderate _____ _____.

Step 6:   Observe and record the _____ _____ movement. Compare the _____ _____ clearances with the manufacturer's specifications and make a _____ recommendation.

3. Inspecting for Turbine Seal Leakage:

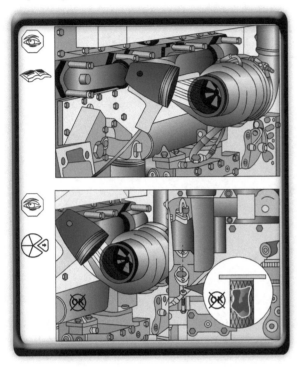

Step 1:   Inspect the exhaust manifold _____ and the area on the engine _____ below the exhaust _____. Oil leakage or _____ present at these points likely indicates _____ originating from the _____ and not the _____.

Step 2:   Add oil tracing _____, which is visible using an _____ light, to the engine _____ and run the engine to _____ temperature. Run the engine at _____ for _____–_____ minutes.

Step 3:   Allow the engine _____ to _____.

Step 4:   Remove the _____ _____ from the turbocharger and use a _____ _____ to inspect the area around the turbocharger _____. Any accumulations of bright _____- or _____-colored dye at the turbine _____ likely indicate a _____ turbocharger _____.

Step 5:   Remove the turbocharger oil _____ _____ to inspect for _____. If the engine oil _____ is not _____ and the engine has acceptable _____ _____, make a service recommendation to _____ the turbocharger.

Crossword Puzzle

Use the clues in the column to complete the puzzle.

Across

1. Emissions produced temporarily when the engine load or speed is increased, such as when accelerating or upshifting gears.
4. The housing that encloses the compressor wheel.
5. An exhaust bypass valve in the turbine housing that allows exhaust gases to bypass the turbine and directly enter the exhaust pipe, thus "wasting" some of the exhaust energy.

Down

2. An engine that pressurizes the air intake system above atmospheric pressure.
3. A delay between driver demand for power and the point when the engine responds with power proportional to driver demand.

ASE-Type Questions

Read each item carefully, and then select the best response.

_____ 1. Technician A says that all engines lose power at higher altitudes due to lower air density. Technician B says that turbocharged diesel engines are an exception and intake manifold air pressure remains close to atmospheric pressure at high altitudes. Who is correct?
  A. Technician A
  B. Technician B
  C. Both Technician A and Technician B
  D. Neither Technician A nor Technician B

_____ 2. Technician A says that turbocharging a diesel engine reduces noxious emissions because the cylinder pressure is higher. Technician B says that turbocharging lowers emissions because it provides more air to completely burn fuel in the cylinders. Who is correct?
  A. Technician A
  B. Technician B
  C. Both Technician A and Technician B
  D. Neither Technician A nor Technician B

_____ 3. Technician A says that turbocharging pressure in a diesel engine is limited by the threshold at which a diesel combustion chamber will begin to detonate rather than burn fuel in a controlled manner. Technician B says that diesel turbocharger pressures are limited by the air–fuel ratio limits of the engine combustion system. Who is correct?
  A. Technician A
  B. Technician B
  C. Both Technician A and Technician B
  D. Neither Technician A nor Technician B

_____ 4. Technician A says that fixed geometry turbochargers that lack controls are designed to provide maximum boost pressure at rated speed or peak horsepower. Technician B says that a properly matched turbocharger will need to provide maximum boost pressure at the highest cylinder pressure, which is peak torque. Who is correct?
  A. Technician A
  B. Technician B
  C. Both Technician A and Technician B
  D. Neither Technician A nor Technician B

_____ 5. Technician A says that a barometric pressure sensor on an electronically controlled diesel engine prevents fixed geometry turbocharger damage caused by overspeeding. Technician B says that wastegates provide turbocharger overspeed protection. Who is correct?
  A. Technician A
  B. Technician B
  C. Both Technician A and Technician B
  D. Neither Technician A nor Technician B

_____ 6. Technician A says that turbocharger lag is caused by the inertia of heavy compressor and turbine wheel assemblies. Technician B says turbocharger lag is caused by the slow buildup of fuel rate by the high-pressure injection system. Who is correct?
  A. Technician A
  B. Technician B
  C. Both Technician A and Technician B
  D. Neither Technician A nor Technician B

_____ 7. Technician A says wastegated turbochargers enable smaller displacement diesel engines to produce more power at low engine speeds. Technician B says wastegates prevent turbochargers from overspeeding at high speed and load conditions. Who is correct?
  A. Technician A
  B. Technician B
  C. Both Technician A and Technician B
  D. Neither Technician A nor Technician B

_____ **8.** Technician A says that an engine that uses two turbochargers will use compressor and turbine housings of two different sizes. Technician B says that an engine that uses two turbochargers will use identical turbochargers, which is referred to as a parallel turbocharged engine. Who is correct?
   A. Technician A
   B. Technician B
   C. Both Technician A and Technician B
   D. Neither Technician A nor Technician B

_____ **9.** Technician A says that if a turbocharger is disassembled and a new compressor wheel is installed, then the turbocharger will need to be balanced. Technician B says that a compressor wheel's light weight will not affect turbocharger operation one way or another. Who is correct?
   A. Technician A
   B. Technician B
   C. Both Technician A and Technician B
   D. Neither Technician A nor Technician B

_____ **10.** Technician A says that excessive wear on the thrust bearing will cause the compressor wheel to contact the compressor housing. Technician B says that only excessively worn center support bearings will allow the compressor wheel to contact the compressor housing. Who is correct?
   A. Technician A
   B. Technician B
   C. Both Technician A and Technician B
   D. Neither Technician A nor Technician B

Variable Geometry and Series Turbochargers

Chapter Review

The following activities have been designed to help you refresh your knowledge of this chapter. Your instructor may require you to complete some or all of these activities as a regular part of your training program. You are encouraged to complete any activity that your instructor does not assign as a way to enhance your learning.

Matching

Match the following terms with the correct description or example.

A. Charge air cooler (CAC)

B. Chuffing

C. High-pressure cooled EGR (HP-CEGR)

D. Turbo lag

E. Unison ring

_____ **1.** The sound a VGT turbocharger can produce when actuator response is slow.

_____ **2.** A device used by VGT turbochargers to rotate the nozzle ring vanes together simultaneously.

_____ **3.** An exhaust gas recirculation system that depends on a VGT to build exhaust backpressure.

_____ **4.** The system responsible for removing excess heat from the air charging the cylinders.

_____ **5.** A delay from the driver's demand for power from the engine to the point when the engine responds with power proportional to driver demand.

Multiple Choice

Read each item carefully, and then select the best response.

_____ **1.** Variable geometry turbochargers (VGTs) are also known as _____.

    A. variable nozzle turbochargers

    B. variable pressure turbochargers

    C. variable vane turbochargers

    D. Both A and C

_____ **2.** Adding EGR systems to most 2002 and later engines was necessary to meet lower _____ emission standards.

    A. hydrocarbon

    B. oxides of nitrogen

    C. carbon monoxide

    D. particulate matter

_____ **3.** VGTs often have a built-in safety default position, which is approximately _____.

    A. 50–60% open

    B. 75–80% closed

    C. 80–90% open

    D. 90–95% closed

_____ **4.** The _____ manufactured by Delphi combines controller area network communication with a pulse-width-modulated control of a brushless DC electric motor.

    A. Sliding Nozzle Actuator

    B. Smart Remote Actuator

    C. Magnetic Stepper Actuator

    D. Remote Controlled Actuator

_____ **5.** On some engines using _____ turbocharger actuators, an analog position sensor with a movable tip rides on the vane actuator cam and measures the vane position to provide feedback to the control module.
  A. hydraulic
  B. electronic
  C. pneumatic
  D. mechanical

_____ **6.** The heavy-duty on-board diagnostics system monitors turbo operation using a(n) _____ sensor.
  A. air pressure
  B. mass airflow
  C. speed
  D. temperature

_____ **7.** The sound referred to as chuffing is caused by a condition called _____ that is created when the turbocharger spins very fast and the engine rpm falls more quickly than the turbocharger boost pressure.
  A. turbo surge
  B. pressure drop
  C. inlet restriction
  D. aspiration

_____ **8.** A _____ test is used to inspect the actuator operation on a turbocharger with external linkage.
  A. linkage movement
  B. bounce
  C. actuator voltage
  D. throttle response

_____ **9.** A(n) _____ turbocharger can be used with a low-pressure, cooled EGR system, where the turbocharger does not increase exhaust backpressure for the system.
  A. parallel
  B. asymmetrical
  C. series
  D. compound

_____ **10.** Ford's 6.7L PowerStroke diesel uses a unique, patented _____ turbocharger design that integrates two turbochargers into a single component.
  A. single sequential
  B. parallel
  C. tangential
  D. asymmetrical

True/False

If you believe the statement to be more true than false, write the letter "T" in the space provided. If you believe the statement to be more false than true, write the letter "F".

_____ **1.** Shorter turbo lag time means fewer emissions are produced while the turbocharger spools, or speeds up.

_____ **2.** The EGR valve must remain open while turbine speed and boost pressure reach maximum limits.

_____ **3.** Holset turbochargers have an electronic actuator that is used to change the opening in the turbine housing.

_____ **4.** VGT control modules are controlled directly by the ECM.

_____ **5.** Duramax engines use oil pressure to move the vane adjustment mechanism.

_____ **6.** Many turbochargers have a Hall-effect sensor built into the center housing.

_____ **7.** Replacing motors and modules in an SRA requires the ECM to learn the actuator's new position.

_____ **8.** Turbocharger response to nozzle ring movement is an intrusive monitoring strategy that measures boost pressure and compares it with expected values while driving.

_____ **9.** If battery voltage occurs when the ignition key is switched on during an actuator voltage test the actuator is working properly.

_____ **10.** Series turbochargers use different sizes of compressor and turbine housings designated as high-pressure and low-pressure turbochargers.

Fill in the Blank

Read each item carefully, and then complete the statement by filling in the missing word(s).

1. A primary advantage of using VGTs is fast turbocharger response times with minimal _____ _____.

2. VGTs vary the opening size of the turbine housing _____ _____ that directs exhaust gas onto the turbine wheel.

3. VGTs use vanes, which are also referred to as _____, around the circumference of the turbine wheel.

4. The VGT actuator is adjusted to increase exhaust _____ as required by the EGR system.

5. Using a VGT as part of an engine's _____ strategy requires heavier housings to reduce the amount of creep, or expansion, taking place under high temperatures and pressures.

6. Holset turbochargers use a _____ nozzle ring to change the opening in the turbine housing.

7. On hydraulic actuators used on smaller displacement Navistar engines, the end of the VGT control valve has a _____ cam follower to provide positional feedback to a sensor.

8. The bearing housing of the turbocharger and the variable geometry actuator usually contains engine _____ passages.

9. Carbonized _____ in the turbine housing is the most common problem affecting actuator movement.

10. Miller cycle engines are referred to as a _____-_____ cycle because the compression stroke is divided into two phases.

Labeling

Label the following diagrams with the correct terms.

1. Identify the parts of the VGT design:

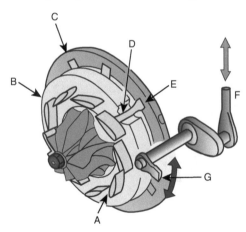

A. _____

B. _____

C. _____

D. _____

E. _____

F. _____

G. _____

2. Identify the components of a series turbocharger:

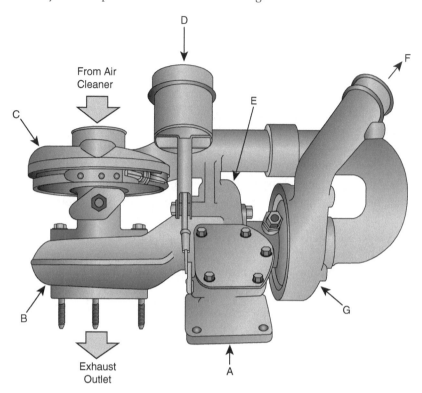

A. _____   E. _____

B. _____   F. _____

C. _____   G. _____

D. _____

Skill Drills

Test your knowledge of skill drills by filling in the correct words in the photo captions.

1. Running a Turbocharger Bounce Test:

Step 1:   Perform a _____ _____-_____ test. Observe the turbocharger _____ linkage while _____ the key switch to the _____ position. The linkage should smoothly complete a _____ _____ at KOEO. No partial or _____ movement is permissible. Several successful completions of this test indicate that the turbocharger actuator is operating satisfactorily and no further tests are required. If the turbocharger does not properly complete the linkage _____-_____ test, a linkage _____ test or _____ test is required.

Step 2:   With the key and engine _____, push the _____ linkage with _____ pressure to the opposite end of travel and _____ it. The linkage should move _____ with slight spring _____, then return to its original position. Good linkage will bounce _____ or _____ times when it returns; however, the linkage does not need to _____ when it returns to the _____ to pass this test.

Step 3:   If the linkage _____, operates erratically, _____, or does not return to its starting position, the _____ mechanism is likely the problem. This will require a turbocharger _____ or disassembly, _____, and _____ with a high-temperature _____-_____ compound. Occasionally, the turbocharger actuator _____ may be _____ and should be disconnected from the _____ to verify whether it is _____ properly when rotated to the _____ of its travel.

Step 4:   If the turbocharger passes the _____ _____ test, further _____ diagnostic checks are needed to determine the reason for the unresponsive _____.

2. Checking VPOD Output Pressure:

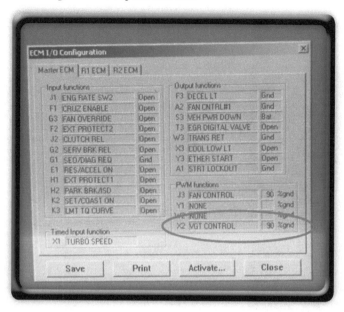

Step 1: Measure the _____ _____ entering the _____ to ensure it is within specifications. It should be near _____ air pressure.

Step 2: Listen for _____ _____ at the _____ and _____. Repair or replace _____ components.

Step 3: Disconnect the _____ _____ lines from the _____ valve and _____ actuators.

Step 4: Install pressure gauges _____ with the _____ of the EGR and VGT _____. This leaves the devices _____ while the gauges read air pressure _____.

Step 5: Using the _____ _____ software, navigate to the system _____ menu screen. Using a different setting, activate the _____ _____ #_____ and _____ _____ #_____ duty cycles while observing and recording the _____ pressure from the _____.

Step 6: Compare the _____ air supply pressures at _____% and _____% duty cycle. Compare with OEM specifications. Generally, air supply pressure at _____% duty cycle should correspond to _____ ± _____ psi (120.6 ± 14 kPa). At _____%, pressure should correspond to _____ ± _____ psi (500.6 ± 14 kPa).

Step 7: When activating the _____, both the _____ and _____ actuators must operate with _____ _____ of the _____ to their respective stops at _____% duty cycle.

Step 8: Make a service recommendation based on observations of _____ _____ and _____ _____.

ASE-Type Questions

Read each item carefully, and then select the best response.

_____   1. Technician A says that VGT engines have less turbo lag. Technician B says VGT engines have more exhaust backpressure in the exhaust pipe after the turbocharger. Who is correct?
   A. Technician A
   B. Technician B
   C. Both Technician A and Technician B
   D. Neither Technician A nor Technician B

_____   2. Technician A says that a late-model engine equipped with a compression release brake and a VGT will close the vanes to increase intake boost and exhaust backpressure during braking. Technician B says the vanes will open to reduce intake air flow during engine braking. Who is correct?
   A. Technician A
   B. Technician B
   C. Both Technician A and Technician B
   D. Neither Technician A nor Technician B

_____   3. Technician A says that VGT engines can electronically vary turbocharger boost pressure. Technician B says that boost pressure from VGTs is typically higher than boost pressure from fixed geometry turbochargers. Who is correct?
   A. Technician A
   B. Technician B
   C. Both Technician A and Technician B
   D. Neither Technician A nor Technician B

_____   4. Technician A says that without power to the VGT actuator, the actuator will typically provide a lot of boost because the vanes are as much as 95% closed. Technician B says the turbocharger will not provide very much boost because the vanes default to an open position. Who is correct?
   A. Technician A
   B. Technician B
   C. Both Technician A and Technician B
   D. Neither Technician A nor Technician B

_____   5. Technician A says the turbocharger speed sensor is used to sense and prevent a turbocharger overspeed condition. Technician B says the speed sensor is used by the HD-OBD system to detect faults with the turbocharger. Who is correct?
   A. Technician A
   B. Technician B
   C. Both Technician A and Technician B
   D. Neither Technician A nor Technician B

_____   6. Technician A says that coolant passageways through the turbocharger housing are used to keep the turbocharger bearings and other parts cooled when the engine is running. Technician B says that coolant passageways are used primarily to circulate coolant after the engine is shut off. Who is correct?
   A. Technician A
   B. Technician B
   C. Both Technician A and Technician B
   D. Neither Technician A nor Technician B

_____   7. Technician A says the operation of the VGT actuator's electric motor is inspected during a bounce test. Technician B says the motor needs to be removed and checked with an ohmmeter to determine whether it is faulty. Who is correct?
   A. Technician A
   B. Technician B
   C. Both Technician A and Technician B
   D. Neither Technician A nor Technician B

_____ **8.** While discussing series turbocharging, Technician A says the high-pressure turbocharger has a wastegate that prevents overspeeding. Technician B says the low-pressure turbocharger uses a wastegate to direct exhaust gases to the high-pressure turbocharger. Who is correct?
A. Technician A
B. Technician B
C. Both Technician A and Technician B
D. Neither Technician A nor Technician B

_____ **9.** Technician A says that series sequential turbochargers use two compressor wheels and one turbine wheel. Technician B says that series sequential turbochargers have two separate compressor and turbine housings. Who is correct?
A. Technician A
B. Technician B
C. Both Technician A and Technician B
D. Neither Technician A nor Technician B

_____ **10.** After listening to the noise made by a VGT when the key was switched on but the engine wouldn't start, Technician A said the actuator was moving to a default spring-loaded position after it was shut down in a wide-open position. Technician B says the turbocharger actuator was relearning maximum and minimum actuator sweep positions during a calibration process. Who is correct?
A. Technician A
B. Technician B
C. Both Technician A and Technician B
D. Neither Technician A nor Technician B

Exhaust Gas Recirculation

Chapter Review

The following activities have been designed to help you refresh your knowledge of this chapter. Your instructor may require you to complete some or all of these activities as a regular part of your training program. You are encouraged to complete any activity that your instructor does not assign as a way to enhance your learning.

Matching

Match the following terms with the correct description or example.

A. Delta pressure differential sensor

B. Exhaust back-pressure (EBP) sensor

C. Nitric oxide (NO)

D. Nitrogen dioxide (NO_2)

E. Wide-band heated oxygen sensor (HOS)

_____ **1.** A sensor that measures pressure in the exhaust manifold.

_____ **2.** A reddish-brown gas formed from nitric oxide and oxygen.

_____ **3.** An exhaust gas sensor that provides feedback to the ECM about EGR flow rates.

_____ **4.** An unstable, highly reactive, colorless gas.

_____ **5.** A sensor that measures the pressure drop across two points in a gas circuit.

Multiple Choice

Read each item carefully, and then select the best response.

_____ **1.** By reintroducing exhaust gas back into the cylinders, a major reduction in exhaust emissions of _____ is achieved.
   A. particulate matter
   B. oxides of nitrogen
   C. carbon monoxide
   D. carbon dioxide

_____ **2.** The most abundant type of NO_x initially produced during diesel combustion is _____.
   A. nitric oxide
   B. nitrous oxide
   C. nitrogen dioxide
   D. ozone gas

_____ **3.** The amount of heat required by a gas, solid, or liquid to produce a temperature change of 1°F within a specified time period is called _____.
   A. latent heat
   B. focused heat
   C. dynamic heat
   D. advection

_____ **4.** Cooled EGR leads to the formation of _____ in the combustion chamber after reactions take place.
   A. water condensation
   B. higher sulfuric acid levels
   C. higher nitric acid levels
   D. All of the above

_____ 5. A(n) _____ uses a metering valve and control circuits to deliver exhaust gas into the intake manifold.
   A. internal EGR
   B. low-pressure EGR
   C. external EGR
   D. high-pressure EGR

_____ 6. Too low of an EGR rate will _____.
   A. not obtain the required emission reductions
   B. starve the combustion process of adequate oxygen
   C. drive up production of carbon monoxide emissions
   D. All of the above

_____ 7. A(n) _____ draws EGR gas into the cylinders through either the turbocharger inlet or after the turbocharger between a throttle plate and intake manifold.
   A. internal EGR
   B. low-pressure EGR
   C. external EGR
   D. high-pressure EGR

_____ 8. EGR coolers send exhaust gas through a heat exchanger where its temperature can be reduced from as much as 1000°F (538°C) to approximately _____.
   A. 212°F (100°C)
   B. 425°F (218°C)
   C. 575°F (302°C)
   D. 650°F (343°C)

_____ 9. A _____ style mixer evenly blends gas into the intake stream around the circumference of the inlet of the intake manifold.
   A. venturi
   B. cyclone
   C. fluted
   D. differential

_____ 10. Measurement of the actual amount of exhaust gas delivered to and from a closed loop feedback circuit for the EGR valve is performed by _____.
   A. a mass airflow sensor
   B. a delta pressure differential sensor
   C. oxygen sensors
   D. All of the above

True/False

If you believe the statement to be more true than false, write the letter "T" in the space provided. If you believe the statement to be more false than true, write the letter "F".

_____ 1. EGR technology has been used on heavy-duty diesel engines for nearly four decades.
_____ 2. The principle behind all EGR systems is to disrupt the chemical processes that form NO_x.
_____ 3. Both high altitude and low barometric pressures will increase EGR flow.
_____ 4. EGR gas does not increase its temperature as much as air does when it absorbs the same amount of heat.
_____ 5. Engine torque and power output will fall unless other engine operating strategies and design compensate for EGR use.
_____ 6. Underhood temperatures are much lower on vehicles equipped with EGR engines.
_____ 7. EGR rates are much higher in diesel engines than in gasoline-fueled engines.
_____ 8. Detroit Diesel's DD series engines use a high-pressure EGR system with a variable geometry turbocharger.
_____ 9. EGR coolers most often fail due to the constant thermal expansion and contraction cycles caused by exhaust heat and exhaust backpressure produced by the turbocharger.
_____ 10. The EGR manual override test is used to determine if the EGR valve is sticking, stuck in one position, or not actuating the full amount of travel.

Fill in the Blank

Read each item carefully, and then complete the statement by filling in the missing word(s).

1. When NO_x breaks down in the presence of sunlight and heat, it converts to nitrogen and _____ gas, which is a primary component of smog.

2. Replacing combustion _____ with EGR gas is a strategy used by all EGR systems.

3. Injection timing may be advanced in many EGR engines to enable adequate burn time for the slower _____ speeds.

4. Heat _____ refers to the amount of heat transferred to the coolant rather than converted into mechanical force driving down the pistons.

5. Since the introduction of _____ _____ systems, which break down NO_x in the exhaust system, manufacturers have depended less on in-cylinder NO_x.

6. Symptoms of an EGR cooler leak include high _____ levels in scheduled oil samples, and white smoke with a sweet odor.

7. Some engines use the turbulence of the intake manifold and/or valve port design to _____ recirculated exhaust gas and intake charge air.

8. EGR _____ may be located on either the hot side between the exhaust manifold and cooler or the cold side between the cooler and intake manifold.

9. A _____ _____ sensor measures the weight of air entering the engine and can detect air inlet restrictions caused by a restricted air filter or intake when pressure drops below a threshold value.

10. Oxygen sensors, also called _____ sensors, are used by some manufacturers as feedback devices for EGR controls.

Labeling

Label the following diagrams with the correct terms.

1. Identify the components of an EGR system used on a Ford 6.4L PowerStroke engine:

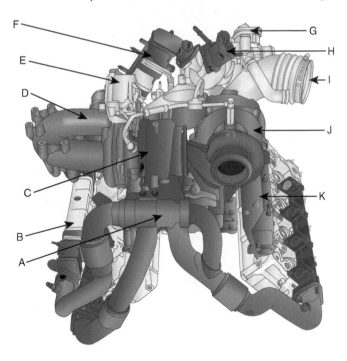

A. _____   C. _____

B. _____   D. _____

E. _____   I. _____

F. _____   J. _____

G. _____   K. _____

H. _____

2. Identify the parts of a single poppet EGR valve using a DC motor and position sensor:

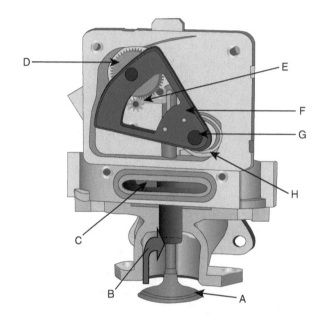

A. _____   E. _____

B. _____   F. _____

C. _____   G. _____

D. _____   H. _____

Skill Drills

Test your knowledge of skill drills by filling in the correct words in the photo captions.

1. Inspecting an EGR Cooler for Leaks:

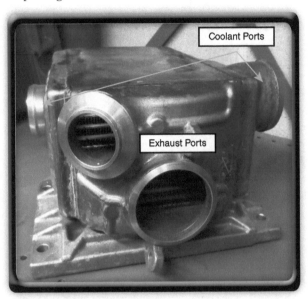

Coolant Ports

Exhaust Ports

Step 1: Pressurize the _____ system. Disconnect and remove the _____ at each end of the _____ _____.

Step 2: Visually examine the EGR cooler _____. The presence of _____ _____ liquid is an indicator of an _____ _____.

Step 3: Disconnect and remove the EGR _____ from its _____. A gooey black _____ covering the _____ indicates an EGR _____ leak.

Step 4: Inspect the EGR _____ for _____ coolant _____. White _____ indicates coolant _____ have leaked from _____ emitted by the EGR cooler.

Step 5: After _____ inspecting the engine for coolant _____ during a _____ test, the EGR cooler can be _____ and _____.

Step 6: Using purpose-made _____ _____, plug the exhaust _____ and _____ ports with purpose-made _____.

Step 7: Using shop _____ _____ regulated to _____ psi (138 kPa), pressurize the cooler _____ _____.

Step 8: Immerse the cooler in a _____ _____ or check the coolant _____ for leaking air using _____ _____. Any _____ leaks indicate a _____ EGR cooler.

2. Testing a Pressure Sensor:

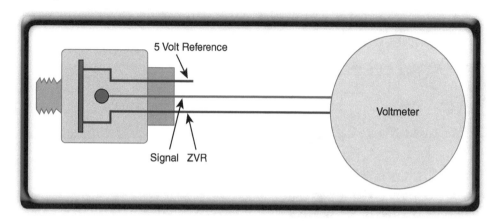

Step 1: Disconnect the _____ from the engine _____.

Step 2: Connect a _____ kilohm _____ across the _____ return and _____ _____ return (ZVR) leads of the sensor.

Step 3: Supply a regulated _____-volt _____ electrical supply to the sensor's _____ voltage (VREF) and _____ wire.

Step 4: Measure the _____ of the sensor between the _____ and _____ line. If necessary, supply a regulated _____ signal to the sensor or wave a piece of _____ past the _____ _____ sensor.

Step 5: Compare your _____ with the manufacturer's _____ and make a _____ recommendation.

3. Testing an EGR Valve:

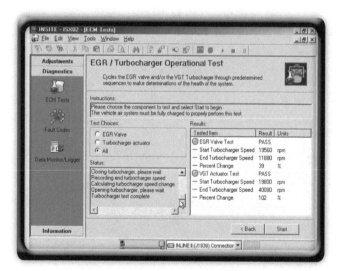

Step 1: Connect an electronic _____ _____ or _____ software to _____ the EGR valve _____ and _____.

Step 2: While monitoring the turbocharger _____, listen to the change in _____ noise when the valve is _____. The noise should _____ when the valve is _____ _____ and _____ when the valve is _____.

Step 3: Monitor the turbocharger _____.

Step 4: Open the _____ and observe the _____ in turbocharger _____. Closing the _____ should cause the turbocharger _____ to _____.

ASE-Type Questions

Read each item carefully, and then select the best response.

_____ 1. Technician A says that EGR systems lower in-cylinder NO_x formation by reducing peak cylinder pressures and temperatures. Technician B says EGR systems reduce NO_x emissions by reducing displaced air in the cylinder. Who is correct?

   A. Technician A
   B. Technician B
   C. Both Technician A and Technician B
   D. Neither Technician A nor Technician B

_____ 2. Technician A says that turbocharger boost pressures are higher in EGR engines to compensate for power loss when using EGR gas. Technician B says that higher boost pressures are used to ensure the combustion chamber receives an adequate amount of oxygen to support combustion. Who is correct?

   A. Technician A
   B. Technician B
   C. Both Technician A and Technician B
   D. Neither Technician A nor Technician B

_____ 3. Technician A says the piston stroke length in an EGR engine is often longer than in the same model engine without an EGR system. Technician B says that the longer stroke length used by some EGR model engines has nothing to do with the use of EGR, and that some EGR engines have shorter stroke length than non-EGR model engines. Who is correct?

   A. Technician A
   B. Technician B
   C. Both Technician A and Technician B
   D. Neither Technician A nor Technician B

_____ 4. Technician A says that the oil used in EGR engines has a different API designation than oil used in engines with particulate filters. Technician B says that the oil used in engines equipped with particulate filters can be used in EGR engines. Who is correct?

   A. Technician A
   B. Technician B
   C. Both Technician A and Technician B
   D. Neither Technician A nor Technician B

_____ 5. Technician A says that diesel engines using EGR systems often have longer engine break-in periods. Technician B says that the use of EGR gas introduces abrasive soot into the cylinders, which shortens the break-in period. Who is correct?

   A. Technician A
   B. Technician B
   C. Both Technician A and Technician B
   D. Neither Technician A nor Technician B

_____ 6. Technician A says that internal EGR systems use a throttle plate to draw EGR gases into the air intake flow. Technician B says that high-pressure cooled EGR systems need throttle plates to draw exhaust gases into the intake manifold. Who is correct?

   A. Technician A
   B. Technician B
   C. Both Technician A and Technician B
   D. Neither Technician A nor Technician B

_____ 7. Technician A says that diesel engines use MAF sensors to measure exhaust airflow into the cylinders. Technician B says that exhaust gas does not pass through an MAF sensor so the MAF sensors cannot measure exhaust gas flow. Who is correct?

   A. Technician A
   B. Technician B
   C. Both Technician A and Technician B
   D. Neither Technician A nor Technician B

_____ **8.** Technician A says that oxygen sensors used by diesel engines adjust air–fuel ratios. Technician B says that oxygen sensors can be used to adjust the amount of EGR gas metered into the cylinders. Who is correct?
   A. Technician A
   B. Technician B
   C. Both Technician A and Technician B
   D. Neither Technician A nor Technician B

_____ **9.** While discussing possible causes of engine coolant loss, Technician A says the EGR cooler is likely cracked and leaking. Technician B says that a cracked EGR cooler would leak coolant into the intake manifold. Who is correct?
   A. Technician A
   B. Technician B
   C. Both Technician A and Technician B
   D. Neither Technician A nor Technician B

_____ **10.** Technician A says that EGR gas containing soot is present in all EGR systems. Technician B says that Caterpillar's EGR system, called the Clean Gas Induction system, does not contain soot. Who is correct?
   A. Technician A
   B. Technician B
   C. Both Technician A and Technician B
   D. Neither Technician A nor Technician B

Charge Air Cooling

Chapter Review

The following activities have been designed to help you refresh your knowledge of this chapter. Your instructor may require you to complete some or all of these activities as a regular part of your training program. You are encouraged to complete any activity that your instructor does not assign as a way to enhance your learning.

Matching

Match the following terms with the correct description or example.

A. Air-to-air aftercooler (ATAAC)

B. Charge air cooler (CAC)

C. Heat exchanger

D. Interstage cooling

E. Jacket water aftercooler (JWAC)

_____ **1.** A system that transfers heat from coolant to the atmosphere.

_____ **2.** A system that uses engine coolant to remove heat from the pressurized intake air.

_____ **3.** A system that uses ambient air to remove heat from the pressurized intake air.

_____ **4.** The use of a liquid charge air cooler between two turbochargers connected in series.

_____ **5.** The system responsible for removing excess heat from the air charging the cylinders.

Multiple Choice

Read each item carefully, and then select the best response.

_____ **1.** When performing boost pressure tests, intake pressure must be corrected for an ambient temperature of _____.

   A. 60°F (16°C)

   B. 68°F (20°C)

   C. 72°F (22°C)

   D. 75°F (24°C)

_____ **2.** Power decreases 1% for every 10°F above _____.

   A. 60°F (16°C)

   B. 70°F (21°C)

   C. 80°F (27°C)

   D. 90°F (32°C)

_____ **3.** Denser, cooler air improves fuel economy up to _____.

   A. 5%

   B. 10%

   C. 15%

   D. 20%

_____ **4.** Still popular on marine diesel engines, _____ aftercoolers are used in series turbocharger applications, where very high boost pressures produce even hotter intake air temperatures.

   A. air-to-air

   B. engine oil

   C. jacket water

   D. forced air

_____ **5.** A properly functioning CAC has a maximum temperature differential of _____ between air intake temperature and outside air when airflow is 30 mph (48 km/h).
  A. 15°F
  B. 30°F
  C. 60°F
  D. 90°F

_____ **6.** If the side to side pressure in an ATAAC drops more than _____, check the cooler for internal restrictions and leaks.
  A. 1 psi (7 kPa)
  B. 2 psi (14 kPa)
  C. 3 psi (21 kPa)
  D. 4 psi (28 kPa)

_____ **7.** Underhood noises during heavily loaded operating conditions can be pinpointed to _____.
  A. leaking clamps and hoses
  B. improper cooler mounting
  C. a defective turbocharger
  D. All of the above

_____ **8.** Justification for the replacement of a CAC is best determined using a _____.
  A. internal restriction test
  B. pressure test
  C. external restriction test
  D. temperature differential test

_____ **9.** Cooler cores should be back-flushed with _____ after a turbocharger failure or if a core has become internally restricted.
  A. solvent
  B. coolant
  C. compressed air
  D. Both A and C

_____ **10.** To evaluate whether there is excessive internal resistance to flow because of an internal restriction, complete a _____ of the cooler.
  A. pressure test
  B. differential test
  C. pressure drop test
  D. Both A and C

True/False

If you believe the statement to be more true than false, write the letter "T" in the space provided. If you believe the statement to be more false than true, write the letter "F".

_____ **1.** A cubic foot of air, when heated, contains fewer oxygen molecules and weighs less than when it is not heated.

_____ **2.** Generally, a 1°F increase in charge-air temperature produces a 5°F increase in exhaust temperature.

_____ **3.** Prior to 1988 diesels needed to meet only a standard for exhaust opacity during a throttle snap test.

_____ **4.** When an ATAAC is used to cool air between each stage of turbocharging, it is often referred to as intercooling.

_____ **5.** During cold weather operation ATAACs require the use of a radiator cover called a winter front to maintain cab heat.

_____ **6.** ATAACs use unique connector hoses that are often color coded to differentiate the hot and cold sides of the cooler.

_____ **7.** Because CACs are pressurized and the turbocharger produces excess air, CACs can tolerate small cracks without allowing dirt into the engine intake.

_____ **8.** Lubrication oil loaded inside a cooler core does not present a problem because a diesel engine can easily run on aspirated engine oil.

_____ **9.** When conducting a pressure drop test the vehicle needs to be traveling at approximately 30 mph (48 km/h).

_____ **10.** CAC efficiency is calculated by measuring the temperature differential between the CAC's inlet and outlet.

Fill in the Blank

Read each item carefully, and then complete the statement by filling in the missing word(s).

1. When gas temperatures increase, molecules spread farther apart, so the gas loses _____.

2. Normally, _____, which makes up approximately 77% of the composition of air, remains inert and uninvolved in combustion processes.

3. Increased air density and oxygen content improves _____ quality.

4. Efficient and effective heat _____ is necessary to keep engine emissions low and prevent engine damage.

5. High intake temperatures will cause the engine to _____ power or even shut down.

6. Most ATAACs are constructed of _____ for maximum heat transfer and strength.

7. Thermal _____ can stress a CAC until it cracks.

8. After a turbo _____, flushing a cooler thoroughly is important to prevent ingestion of debris into an engine.

9. CACs can internally accumulate oil, water, debris, and even ice. The result is a loss of _____ _____ due to the internal restriction.

10. To diagnose an external restriction, a _____ _____ test identifies a loss of cooling across a cooler.

Skill Drills

Test your knowledge of skill drills by filling in the correct words in the photo captions.

1. Pressure Testing a CAC:

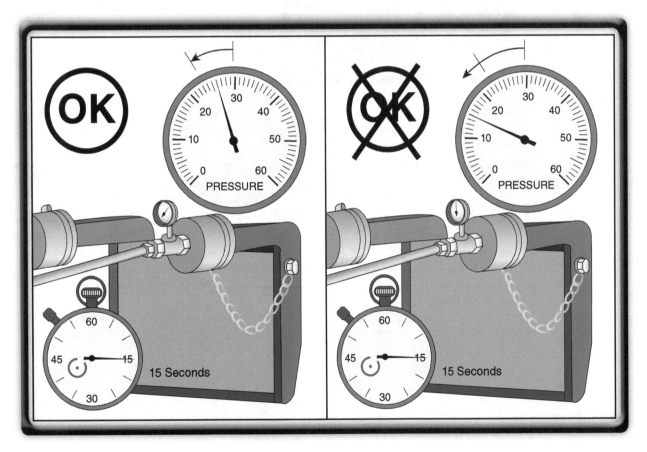

Step 1: Disconnect the CAC _____ and _____ pipes.

Step 2: Connect purpose-made _____ to the CAC pipe _____. One adapter has a _____ valve and the other has a _____-_____ fitting.

Step 3: Connect an air pressure _____ to the test adapter _____ and _____ the cooler to _____ psi (207 kPa).

Step 4: Shut off the _____ _____ supply to the regulator and _____ the number of _____ it takes for the cooler to drop _____ psi (34 kPa).

Step 5: Generally, any _____ that allows a _____ _____ of more than _____ psi (34 kPa) in _____ seconds is too large.

Step 6: Make a _____ recommendation based on manufacturer's _____ and the observed _____ it took for a _____ _____ in the _____.

2. Testing a CAC for Internal Restrictions:

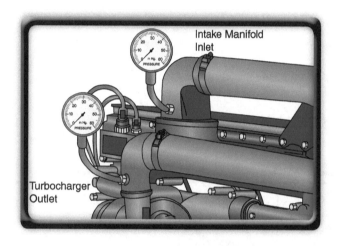

Step 1: Connect two _____-_____ pressure _____ or a pressure gauge with _____ separate, _____ inputs to the _____ _____ and turbocharger _____.

Step 2: Road test the vehicle while _____ the engine to achieve _____ boost pressures. This is done by _____ the engine at _____ _____ while the _____ is a couple of gear steps _____ where it should be.

Step 3: While the engine _____ down and the turbocharger moves through _____ _____ pressure, observe and _____ the pressure at _____ points in the _____ systems.

Step 4: Compare the _____ against the manufacturer's _____. Generally, no more than _____ inHg (15 cmHg) or _____ psi (21 kPa) of _____ drop is _____.

Step 5: Make a _____ _____ based on observations of the pressure _____ across the CAC. The CAC may require _____ or _____-_____ with _____ to clean the _____.

3. Inspecting a CAC for External Restrictions:

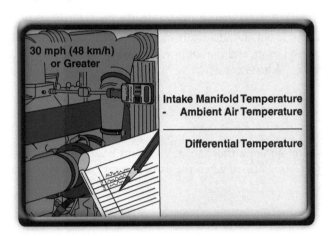

Step 1:   Measure the _____ _____.

Step 2:   Road test the vehicle and _____ the engine to produce _____
          _____ pressures. Ensure the road speed is faster than _____ mph (48 km/h) to
          obtain good _____ across the _____.

Step 3:   Monitor the intake _____ temperature sensor and _____ the intake air
          _____ in the manifold at _____ _____.

Step 4:   Subtract the intake manifold _____ _____ from _____
          temperature, and _____ that with the manufacturer's _____.

Step 5:   Based on test _____, make a _____ recommendation for _____
          the _____ or _____. Generally, the temperature _____ should not
          exceed _____°F.

ASE-Type Questions

Read each item carefully, and then select the best response.

_____ 1. Technician A says that adding a CAC to an engine will automatically increase power output. Technician B says that adding a CAC will do little to increase power, and that only additional air and fuel will increase engine power output in CAC-equipped engines. Who is correct?
   A. Technician A
   B. Technician B
   C. Both Technician A and Technician B
   D. Neither Technician A nor Technician B

_____ 2. Technician A says that, as intake air passes through the turbocharger, it absorbs heat from the turbocharger turbine housing. Technician B says that intake air is heated when the turbocharger compresses the intake air charge. Who is correct?
   A. Technician A
   B. Technician B
   C. Both Technician A and Technician B
   D. Neither Technician A nor Technician B

_____ 3. Technician A says that an externally restricted CAC can cause cracks in the piston crown of aluminum engines. Technician B says that only an internally restricted CAC can cause cracks. Who is correct?
   A. Technician A
   B. Technician B
   C. Both Technician A and Technician B
   D. Neither Technician A nor Technician B

_____ 4. While examining the dull, rounded metal edges of a turbocharger turbine wheel, Technician A says the turbine blades were likely melted due to a restricted CAC. Technician B says that the condition of the blades is normal and the CAC would have no effect on the operating condition of the turbocharger turbine wheel. Who is correct?
   A. Technician A
   B. Technician B
   C. Both Technician A and Technician B
   D. Neither Technician A nor Technician B

_____ 5. While inspecting the cracked mounting brackets of a CAC, Technician A says that chassis vibration combined with thermal cycling of the CAC was the likely cause of the bracket failure. Technician B says that the use of star lock washers and overtightening the brackets caused the failure. Who is correct?
   A. Technician A
   B. Technician B
   C. Both Technician A and Technician B
   D. Neither Technician A nor Technician B

_____ 6. After refilling the cooling system of an engine with a liquid interstage CAC, about 1 gallon (3.7 L) of coolant was left over and would not go back into the cooling system. Technician A says the cooler likely has air in it that needs to be removed before the coolant can go back in. Technician B says the engine should be put under load for a long road test to determine whether the coolant level will drop and allow the leftover coolant to refill the cooling system. Who is correct?
   A. Technician A
   B. Technician B
   C. Both Technician A and Technician B
   D. Neither Technician A nor Technician B

_____ 7. Technician A says that high intake manifold temperatures caused by the use of a winter front could result in the engine protection system derating the engine power. Technician B says that a winter front across the front radiator of a truck would not produce an engine protection fault. Who is correct?
   A. Technician A
   B. Technician B
   C. Both Technician A and Technician B
   D. Neither Technician A nor Technician B

_____ **8.** Technician A says that the CAC should always be replaced after a turbocharger failure to prevent pieces of the turbocharger and any engine oil from damaging the engine. Technician B says that the CAC needs to be removed and back-flushed with solvent after a turbocharger failure. Who is correct?
  A. Technician A
  B. Technician B
  C. Both Technician A and Technician B
  D. Neither Technician A nor Technician B

_____ **9.** While considering possible causes of an overheated cooling system, Technician A says the cause was likely a broken water pump impeller. Technician B says overheated coolant could be the result of an externally restricted CAC. Who is correct?
  A. Technician A
  B. Technician B
  C. Both Technician A and Technician B
  D. Neither Technician A nor Technician B

_____ **10.** After removing a CAC and draining close to 0.25 gallon (1 L) of oil from the cooler, Technician A says the condition is normal. Technician B says that any oil in the CAC is likely there because the turbocharger is defective. Who is correct?
  A. Technician A
  B. Technician B
  C. Both Technician A and Technician B
  D. Neither Technician A nor Technician B

33 Exhaust Aftertreatment Systems

Chapter Review

The following activities have been designed to help you refresh your knowledge of this chapter. Your instructor may require you to complete some or all of these activities as a regular part of your training program. You are encouraged to complete any activity that your instructor does not assign as a way to enhance your learning.

Matching

Match the following terms with the correct description or example.

A. Active regeneration

B. Oxidation reaction

C. Passive regeneration

D. Reduction reaction

E. Selective catalyst reduction (SCR) system

_____ **1.** A process where relatively low-temperature chemical reactions take place in the exhaust catalysts to oxidize soot into CO_2 and H_2O.

_____ **2.** An exhaust aftertreatment system that decomposes NO_x molecules using ammonia NH_3.

_____ **3.** A process in which soot is burned inside the DPF through supplemental heating of the DPF filter.

_____ **4.** Reactions that remove oxygen from NO_x molecules, converting NO_x into N_2 and O_2.

_____ **5.** Reactions that add O_2 to HCs and CO to produce H_2O, CO_2, and heat.

Multiple Choice

Read each item carefully, and then select the best response.

_____ **1.** Catalytic converters are classified according to _____.
  A. the noxious emission converted
  B. the type of catalyst material
  C. the type of chemical reaction
  D. Either A or C

_____ **2.** Because _____ converters clean up two noxious emissions, they are called two-way converters.
  A. oxidation
  B. exhaust gas recirculation
  C. select catalyst reduction
  D. All of the above

_____ **3.** The primary purpose of a _____ is to remove soot and other solid particles from diesel exhaust, rendering the exhaust completely smokeless.
  A. catalyst substrate
  B. p-trap
  C. diesel particulate filter
  D. washcoat

_____ **4.** The process of _____ regeneration can occur if the engine is operated under sufficient load to increase exhaust temperatures to 482°F (250°C) or hotter.
  A. heat-assisted
  B. passive
  C. natural
  D. active

_____ 5. During the process of _____ regeneration, the DPF is heated by adding small amounts of fuel to the exhaust stream.
   A. active
   B. assisted
   C. passive
   D. artificial

_____ 6. During regeneration exhaust temperature at the tailpipe exit can reach _____.
   A. 500°F (260°C)
   B. 750°F (399°C)
   C. 900°F (482°C)
   D. 1150°F (621°C)

_____ 7. Sintered metal foil catalyst substrate can handle 2.5 times more ash than _____ substrates.
   A. carbon fiber-based
   B. platinum-based
   C. ceramic-based
   D. Kevlar-based

_____ 8. In addition to eliminating over 90% of NO_x emissions, _____ catalysts typically convert 20–40% of particulate matter (PM) to CO_2 and H_2O.
   A. SCR
   B. oxidation
   C. EGR
   D. Both A and C

_____ 9. Another name for lean NO_x trap technology is _____.
   A. $DeNO_x$
   B. $DeSO_x$
   C. hydrocarbon-SCR
   D. Both A and C

_____ 10. NO_x sensors detect incorrect concentrations of _____ emitted by dosing injectors and other emission-related faults.
   A. DNO
   B. DAC
   C. DEF
   D. DSO

True/False

If you believe the statement to be more true than false, write the letter "T" in the space provided. If you believe the statement to be more false than true, write the letter "F".

_____ 1. Cold exhaust temperatures and excess air content in diesel exhaust are the biggest technical challenges with diesel catalysts.

_____ 2. The level of sulfur in diesel fuel reduces the temperature level at which chemical reactions in catalytic materials occur and improves the efficiency of diesel oxidation converters.

_____ 3. Active regeneration is only possible using original equipment manufacturer software, a scanner, or another electronic service tool.

_____ 4. The need for active regeneration is determined by measuring the pressure drop across the DPF filter.

_____ 5. The regeneration inhibit switch must be depressed for 5 seconds after the control module has verified safe conditions for an active regeneration are met.

_____ 6. Cordierite is more durable than silicon carbide, and capable of tolerating higher exhaust regeneration temperatures, but it is considerably more expensive.

_____ 7. The advantage of selective catalyst reduction technology is that it enables the lowest fuel consumption of existing exhaust aftertreatment technologies while improving power output, engine durability, and longevity.

_____ 8. Sometimes, the DPF is placed downstream of the SCR because this configuration can minimize the need for regeneration of the DPF.

_____ **9.** NAC aftertreatment systems are only used in heavy-duty diesels.

_____ **10.** Sulfur regeneration is a maintenance step where prolonged fuel-enriched heating of the catalyst is necessary to burn the sulfur out of an NAC.

Fill in the Blank

Read each item carefully, and then complete the statement by filling in the missing word(s).

1. Catalytic converters speed up _____ reactions of noxious exhaust emissions and change them into harmless combustion by-products.

2. Oxidation converters contain a ceramic material formed into a honey-comb-like structure called a _____.

3. Iron or copper mixed with _____ are commonly used in North American low-temperature oxidation catalysts.

4. A renewal process called _____ purges soot from the diesel particulate filter and cleans it.

5. Active stationary regeneration is also called _____ regeneration.

6. Ash is inorganic, which means it has no _____ content to burn.

7. Selective catalyst reduction is a process where liquid _____ is sprayed into the exhaust stream to destroy NO_x molecules.

8. NO_x _____ technology is a catalyst strategy for removing NO_x in the low-temperature, oxygen-rich exhaust environment of diesel engines.

9. Dodge Ram markets lean NAC technology as part of the wider range of NO_x-reducing emission systems known as _____.

10. A _____ _____ sensor measures the exhaust pressure at the DPF inlet and outlet and supplies that data to the ECM.

Labeling

Label the following diagrams with the correct terms.

1. Identify the parts of an SCR system:

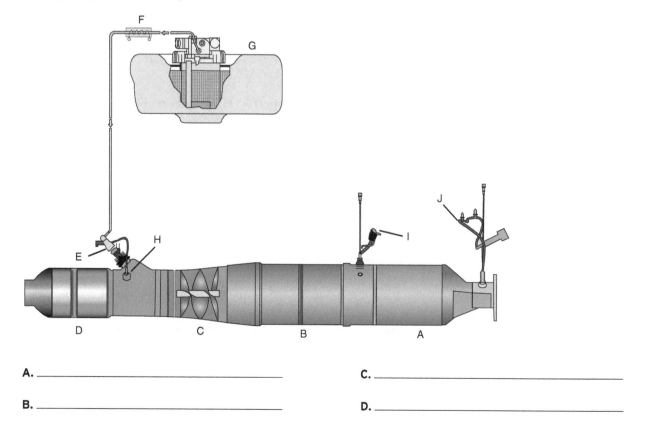

A. _____   **C.** _____

B. _____   **D.** _____

E. _____   H. _____

F. _____   I. _____

G. _____   J. _____

Skill Drills

Test your knowledge of skill drills by filling in the correct words in the photo captions.

1. Performing an Active Regeneration Procedure:

Step 1: The _____ _____ lamp must be illuminated before an _____ _____ can be performed.

Step 2: Verify that _____ conditions are met: the engine should be fully _____ _____ with a coolant temperature _____ than _____°F (85°C); the engine must be at _____ idle; the _____ cannot be _____ if the engine is in _____ idle or _____ mode.

Step 3: The aftertreatment _____ _____ must verify that the _____ regeneration can be performed _____. It will request _____ of the _____ brake, _____, and _____ start switch.

Step 4: In order for an _____ regeneration to occur, the transmission must be in _____, the _____ _____ applied, and no vehicle _____ can be sensed.

Step 5: With the engine _____, press and _____ the DPF inhibit/regeneration _____ to the _____ position for _____ seconds and _____ it. The engine speed will _____ and the _____ lamp will typically _____ _____ once the regeneration event begins.

Step 6: The regeneration will take approximately _____–_____ minutes. It is _____ when the engine returns to _____ idle and the _____ lamp remains off. The length of time the regeneration event takes depends on the amount of _____ _____ in the DPF. The aftertreatment _____ system will _____ the regeneration event when the DPF _____ and _____ temperatures are nearly the same, which means there is no longer any consumable _____ in the _____. Note: If the _____ lamp comes back on after the procedure, the regeneration has _____ and requires further _____ _____.

Step 7: To _____ or _____ an active regeneration procedure, _____ the _____ switch to the _____ position for _____ seconds and _____. An active regeneration will _____ if the key is turned to the _____ position, the vehicle is put into _____, or the parking brake is _____.

2. Performing a Forced DPF Regeneration:

Step 1: With the ignition switch _____ and the engine running, connect an electronic _____ _____ to the vehicle's _____ _____ connector.

Step 2: Check for _____ diagnostic _____ _____. On a number of engines, _____ _____ and other engine malfunctions prevent an _____ _____ from taking place. Diagnostic _____ detected _____ the _____ will often cause the event to abort.

Step 3: Warm up the engine to _____ the _____ to execute a command for _____ regeneration. Many engines need to reach a _____ temperature of _____°F (54°C) before executing commands to _____ the _____.

Step 4: Carefully _____ other instructions given by the _____ _____ or electronic service tool to meet _____ necessary _____ regeneration can begin. For example, on light-duty vehicles a _____ tank of fuel is generally required before regenerating, or the _____ must be _____. On heavier vehicles, the _____ or _____ _____ should not be _____. The transmission must be in _____, the _____ _____ applied, and no vehicle _____ should be sensed.

Step 5: If the vehicle is equipped with a regeneration _____ _____, ensure that the _____ is not in the _____ position.

Step 6: Ensure that the engine is operating at _____ _____ speed. Note whether the _____, brake, and _____ _____ switch are _____ to verify that the vehicle is in a proper _____ to _____ begin a regeneration.

Step 7: Command the _____ control system to _____. The regeneration will take approximately _____–_____ minutes. Once regeneration is complete and the engine returns to _____ _____, the _____ _____ should be switched _____. If the _____ _____ comes back on, the regeneration _____ and further _____ procedures need to be performed.

3. Replacing the DPF:

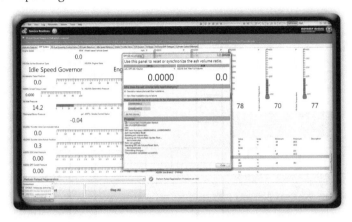

Step 1:   Disconnect and remove the _____-_____ band _____ holding the removable DPF _____ in the DPF filter _____.

Step 2:   Scrape and _____ the filter _____ surfaces of the filter _____.

Step 3:   Reinstall the _____ or _____ filter with new _____. Carefully note the _____ of _____ flow through the _____ _____ during installation.

Step 4:   Perform a _____ regeneration of the _____ or _____ filter to increase _____-_____ capacity.

Step 5:   Reset the _____ _____ according to the OEM service procedures. An example from Detroit Diesels requires a technician to _____ "Diesel Particulate Filter (DPF) _____ _____" from the _____ menu of DDl service software.

Step 6:   Follow the _____ _____ for entering the new filter _____ _____, the type of filter installed (_____ or _____), and the _____ vehicle _____.

Step 7:   Follow these installation tips:

• Use only manufacturer-recommended filter _____ procedures. Do not use cleaning _____ on filters; they do not work and are likely to _____ the filter and solidify _____ in the filter _____.

• Do not use a shop _____ in an open area to clean a filter.

• Use a _____ jack or _____ jack to help maneuver the filter from the _____ of the vehicle.

• Do not _____ clean the DPF; water will turn _____ to a _____-_____ material.

• Oil-contaminated filters are generally _____ reusable, but may be _____ through _____ in an industrial _____ to remove the _____.

• Do not _____ the filter _____ on the shop floor to remove _____.

• DPF ash must be _____ and _____ as a _____ _____.

• Make sure that filter _____ are installed in the correct _____ of _____.

Crossword Puzzle

Use the clues in the column to complete the puzzle.

Across

4. An NO_x reduction technology that mixes exhaust gas with fresh intake air.

5. A material that speeds up or slows down chemical reactions without entering the chemical reactions.

Down

1. Exhaust pressure build-up in the exhaust system. The pressure can be before or after the turbocharger.

2. An ammonia-carrying molecule that breaks down in hot exhaust gas.

3. NH_3 that escapes from the SCR catalyst and into the atmosphere.

ASE-Type Questions

Read each item carefully, and then select the best response.

_____ **1.** The SCR reservoir of a 2010 truck has been depleted for more than 10 hours of driving time and the engine power has derated. Technician A says the correct service recommendation is to fill the DEF reservoir and clear associated fault codes to return the vehicle to service and full power. Technician B says the correct procedure is to fill the DEF reservoir and prime the DEF lines to remove the derate condition. Who is correct?

    A. Technician A

    B. Technician B

    C. Both Technician A and Technician B

    D. Neither Technician A nor Technician B

_____ **2.** Technician A says diesel exhaust oxidation catalysts used by diesel engines are like those used in automobiles for the last two decades. Technician B says diesel exhaust oxidation catalysts must store noxious emissions in the substrate when the exhaust temperatures are low. Who is correct?

    A. Technician A

    B. Technician B

    C. Both Technician A and Technician B

    D. Neither Technician A nor Technician B

_____ **3.** Technician A says the problem with using automobile catalysts in the exhaust system of diesel engines is diesel engine exhaust's excess air and cool temperatures. Technician B says diesel exhaust catalysts need to be designed to withstand the higher exhaust temperatures of a diesel engine and its exhaust's lower oxygen content. Who is correct?

    A. Technician A

    B. Technician B

    C. Both Technician A and Technician B

    D. Neither Technician A nor Technician B

_____ **4.** The DPF warning light is flashing along with the red shut-down warning lamp. Technician A says the DPF filter needs to be removed and replaced. Technician B says the DPF needs an active regeneration. Who is correct?

    A. Technician A

    B. Technician B

    C. Both Technician A and Technician B

    D. Neither Technician A nor Technician B

_____ **5.** Technician A says nitric oxide is used by the DPF to convert soot to harmless emissions. Technician B says that the SCR catalysts cause nitric oxide to convert to harmless emissions. Who is correct?

    A. Technician A

    B. Technician B

    C. Both Technician A and Technician B

    D. Neither Technician A nor Technician B

_____ **6.** Technician A says that lean NO_x traps are used by only light-duty diesel engines. Technician B says that lean NO_x traps are used by light- and heavy-duty diesel engines. Who is correct?

    A. Technician A

    B. Technician B

    C. Both Technician A and Technician B

    D. Neither Technician A nor Technician B

_____ **7.** Technician A says that, without the Delta P sensor, the exhaust DPF would not regenerate because the amount of soot loading could not be properly calculated. Technician B says that the amount of soot loading is only calculated, and not measured, using the Delta P sensor. Who is correct?

    A. Technician A

    B. Technician B

    C. Both Technician A and Technician B

    D. Neither Technician A nor Technician B

_____ **8.** Technician A says that DEF is always evacuated from lines and valves after the vehicle has shut down to prevent DEF from crystalizing and plugging the SCR system. Technician B says that DEF is removed to prevent it from freezing and causing damage. Who is correct?
   A. Technician A
   B. Technician B
   C. Both Technician A and Technician B
   D. Neither Technician A nor Technician B

_____ **9.** Technician A recommends a yearly removal and cleaning of the DPF to customers. Technician B says the DPF needs to be actively regenerated at every oil change. Who is correct?
   A. Technician A
   B. Technician B
   C. Both Technician A and Technician B
   D. Neither Technician A nor Technician B

_____ **10.** After examining a broken and disintegrated DPF filter, Technician A says the filter damage was caused by water contamination. Technician B says the filter was damaged by too frequent back-to-back regenerations. Who is correct?
   A. Technician A
   B. Technician B
   C. Both Technician A and Technician B
   D. Neither Technician A nor Technician B

Exhaust Systems and Engine Retarders

Chapter Review

The following activities have been designed to help you refresh your knowledge of this chapter. Your instructor may require you to complete some or all of these activities as a regular part of your training program. You are encouraged to complete any activity that your instructor does not assign as a way to enhance your learning.

Matching

Match the following terms with the correct description or example.

A. Charging lobe

B. Decompression lobe

C. Flex pipe

D. Pyrometer

E. Resonator

_____ **1.** This device provides additional dampening and tuning of exhaust noise.

_____ **2.** A component that lifts the exhaust rocker lever near TDC to release engine compression.

_____ **3.** A temperature gauge designed to measure exhaust temperatures.

_____ **4.** A component that admits extra gas exhaust volume into the cylinder before compression.

_____ **5.** A component used between the engine pipe and the rest of the exhaust system to absorb twists and movement of pipe caused by engine torque reaction.

Multiple Choice

Read each item carefully, and then select the best response.

_____ **1.** High exhaust backpressure leads to _____.

    A. high exhaust valve temperatures

    B. excessive exhaust emissions

    C. low turbocharger speed and boost pressure

    D. All of the above

_____ **2.** Heavy-duty vehicles require a _____ exhaust system.

    A. horizontal

    B. diagonal

    C. vertical

    D. pulse-type

_____ **3.** Higher horsepower engines with high fuel and airflow rates from the turbocharger require _____ to supply enough expansion volume for exhaust gases to reduce backpressure.

    A. resonators

    B. dual exhaust stacks

    C. air coolers

    D. All of the above

_____ **4.** An EBP regulator is used to actuate a _____, which increases exhaust pressure inside a diesel engine's exhaust manifolds.

    A. butterfly valve

    B. restrictor

    C. governor

    D. solenoid

_____ **5.** To increase combustion temperatures during cranking and improve warm-up characteristics, Volvo uses an
_____, which also reduces cold start emissions.
- **A.** EBP regulator
- **B.** exhaust brake
- **C.** exhaust pressure governor
- **D.** Both A and C

_____ **6.** High quality _____ feature thermocouples that are sheathed in stainless steel and can withstand
temperatures up to 2500°F (1371°C).
- **A.** manometers
- **B.** pyrometers
- **C.** hygrometers
- **D.** anemometers

_____ **7.** To compensate for the natural loss of engine braking, aftermarket _____ can be installed on vehicles with
diesel engines to improve their braking ability.
- **A.** regenerative brakes
- **B.** hydraulic brakes
- **C.** exhaust brakes
- **D.** Either A or C

_____ **8.** Without a standard transmission and direct connection to the engine compression release braking would
require a _____ retarder.
- **A.** driveline
- **B.** turbocharger
- **C.** transmission
- **D.** Either A or C

_____ **9.** The Volvo compression release brake uses _____ bump profiles on the exhaust lobe.
- **A.** two
- **B.** three
- **C.** four
- **D.** six

_____ **10.** When 4 properly muffled trucks drive by together the resulting exhaust noise level will be ____ higher than
the noise level of a single truck.
- **A.** + 3 dBA
- **B.** + 4 dBA
- **C.** + 6 dBA
- **D.** + 12 dBA

True/False

If you believe the statement to be more true than false, write the letter "T" in the space provided. If you believe the
statement to be more false than true, write the letter "F".

_____ **1.** An engine's ability to draw a fresh air charge for combustion relies on the efficiency of its exhaust system.

_____ **2.** Vertical exhaust systems are most commonly used on light- and medium-duty diesel-powered vehicles.

_____ **3.** Single piece exhaust manifolds are more efficient at optimizing turbocharger performance than divided and
split manifold designs.

_____ **4.** Low-pressure areas at the exhaust valve stems and turbochargers tend to drag oil out of these components
and into the exhaust stream.

_____ **5.** Exhaust aftertreatment devices, such as DPFs, SCRs, and oxidation catalysts, can eliminate the need for a
muffler.

_____ **6.** A pyrometer must be placed in the exhaust stream after it exits the turbocharger.

_____ **7.** Pumping loss is energy expended by the engine when attempting to pull air around a closed throttle plate.

_____ **8.** Variable geometry turbochargers can be calibrated to operate as exhaust brakes.

_____ **9.** Pressure applied to the slave cylinder will cause the master cylinder to operate the compression release
brake.

_____ **10.** Electronically controlled brakes may require a minimum road speed and engine rpm to enable the brake.

Fill in the Blank

Read each item carefully, and then complete the statement by filling in the missing word(s).

1. Installing an _____ system that can efficiently collect and discharge combustion gas is an important element of vehicle design and improved engine performance.

2. A _____ exhaust system routes the exhaust components under the chassis and aims the outlet pipe downward toward the ground or to the rear of the vehicle.

3. Limits to acceptable backpressure in most diesels are 3" (8 cm) of mercury or 14" (36 cm) of water column as measured with a _____ _____.

4. A _____ exhaust system generally has a longer life span due to improved drainage of water and corrosive acids.

5. Exhaust _____ are divided and split between front and rear cylinder banks on four- and six-cylinder engines to prevent interference of exhaust pulses between front and rear cylinders.

6. The service life of a _____ _____ is improved if it is installed in a relaxed position.

7. Several U.S. states require _____ _____ on any vehicle traveling off road.

8. When an operator wants to speed engine warm-up, he or she can switch on the _____ _____ to promote a quicker increase to coolant temperature.

9. Regulated _____ _____ controls the operation of the butterfly valve in the exhaust brake.

10. Approximately 70% of heavy-duty vehicles produced in North America are equipped with _____ release engine brakes.

Labeling

Label the following diagrams with the correct terms.

1. Identify the components of the regulated air pressure controls for an exhaust brake:

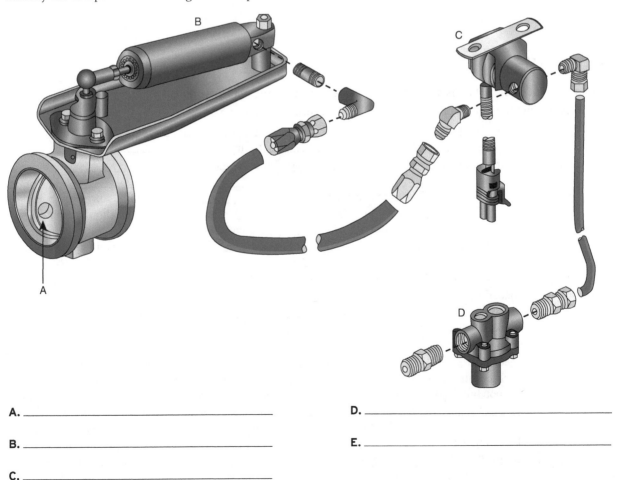

A. _____

B. _____

C. _____

D. _____

E. _____

2. Identify the parts of a fixed-orifice exhaust brake:

Fixed Orifice Exhaust Brake Operation

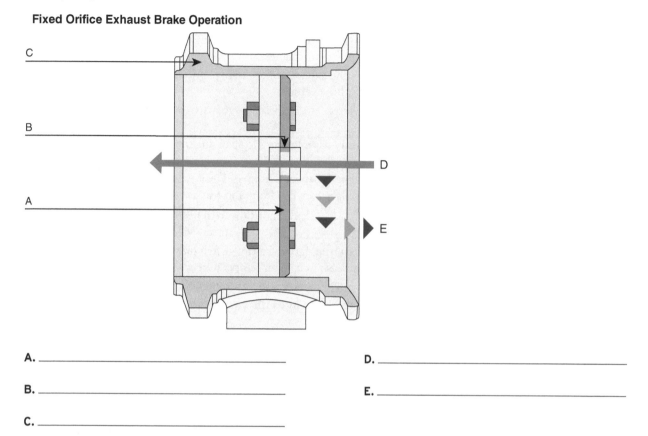

A. _____

B. _____

C. _____

D. _____

E. _____

Skill Drills

Test your knowledge of skill drills by filling in the correct words in the photo captions.

1. Adjusting the Exhaust Brake (Off-Idle Pressure Test):

Step 1: Connect a purpose-made exhaust _____-_____ gauge to a long _____ to view _____ in the _____ of the vehicle.

Step 2: With the exhaust _____ engaged and the engine at _____, measure the exhaust backpressure at the _____ _____ on the _____ _____. Consult the manufacturer's specifications for _____. Generally, a pressure below _____ psi (90 kPa) is _____. The exhaust system should be checked for _____ and the _____ system should be checked for a _____ to determine whether _____ _____ pressure is escaping through an _____ valve that is _____ _____.

Step 3: If the exhaust backpressure is more than _____ psi (172 kPa), an adjustment of the spring-loaded _____ _____ is necessary. Loosen the stop bolt _____ _____ and turn the bolt _____ to lengthen the bolt and _____ the spring tension applied to the _____ valve. Retest _____ backpressure.

Step 4: Measure _____-_____ backpressure by operating the vehicle at _____ speed on a _____ grade. Compare your observations with the manufacturer's specifications. The backpressure should not exceed the _____ backpressure recommended by the _____. Carbon buildup in variable _____ brakes will tend to _____ backpressure with _____ and _____. Off-idle backpressure is set by adjusting the air pressure _____, which will _____ or _____ off-idle exhaust backpressure. Lowering the air pressure will _____ the _____ backpressure and vice versa.

Step 5: If off-idle _____ are performed, _____ the idle pressure adjustment and _____ as necessary.

2. Adjusting a Caterpillar Compression Release Brake:

Step 1:   The compression _____ adjustment provides specifications for a _____
          engine. The _____ should be allowed to _____ before performing an
          _____ procedure.

Step 2:   All clearances between the _____ _____ and the exhaust valve
          _____ are made when the exhaust valves are _____.

Step 3:   Position the engine at _____ for cylinder _____ by installing a threaded
          _____ /_____" (9.5 mm) bolt in the _____ _____
          cover and locking the _____ at _____. The bolt hole is accessed on the
          _____ side of the engine, opposite the _____ motor. When the engine is
          at _____, remove the _____ _____ thread the bolt into the
          _____.

Step 4:   Verify the correct _____ is chosen to begin performing adjustments. Shaking the
          _____ _____ on cylinders _____ and _____
          should indicate the rocker levers are both _____ on cylinder _____ and both
          _____ on cylinder _____. The cylinder _____ slave piston can be
          adjusted.

Step 5:   Insert a _____ _____ of the correct thickness between the _____
          piston and valve _____. Tighten the adjusting screw for the _____
          _____ until you feel a light _____ on the feeler blade. Lock the valve adjustment
          screw and _____ the _____ _____ to specifications. Recheck
          the _____ between the _____ _____ and _____
          _____.

Step 6:   Complete the adjustment the _____ _____ for cylinders _____ and
          _____.

Step 7:   Remove the _____ _____ from the flywheel and _____ the
          engine _____ degrees. This position will place the piston of cylinder _____
          at the _____ at the end of its _____ stroke. Both rocker levers should be
          _____ on cylinder _____. Perform the same procedure to adjust cylinders
          _____, _____, and _____.

Step 8:   Remove the timing _____ from the _____ after all _____
          _____ adjustments have been performed and _____ the _____
          _____.

3. Adjusting Engine Brake Programmable Parameters:

Step 1: Connect the vehicle's _____ link adapter to the _____ software launched from a _____ or desktop computer cart. For example, the Caterpillar Electronic Technician _____ is used to adjust engine _____ and is available from the Cat Service Information System _____ _____.

Step 2: Navigate to the vehicle _____ menu and select the menu item for _____ _____ parameters.

Step 3: Within the cruise control parameters, select _____ mode and note the drop-down selection for _____, _____, and _____.

Step 4: Determine which _____ best suits the vehicle's operation. Highway _____, line-haul runs with _____ or _____ grades, and _____ _____ require different settings for optimal driver comfort and reduced service brake wear. Review the following application descriptions to select the most appropriate application:

- Manual mode: The engine _____ _____ brake is enabled regardless of whether the _____ _____ switch is on. The brake will _____ when the following conditions are met: the _____ switch is on, the engine speed is faster than _____ rpm, and the _____ _____ is released at _____.

- Coast mode: The _____ brake is enabled only when the _____ _____ switch is _____ and the service brake _____ is applied. When the pedal is _____, the brake _____.

- Latch mode: The engine brake is enabled only when the _____ _____ switch is _____ and the _____ brake pedal is applied. Releasing the service brake pedal does not _____ the _____ brake. The engine brake will remain _____ until another input, such as the _____ or _____ _____, is pushed, the engine speed drops below _____ rpm, or the engine brake _____ is turned _____.

Crossword Puzzle

Use the clues in the column to complete the puzzle.

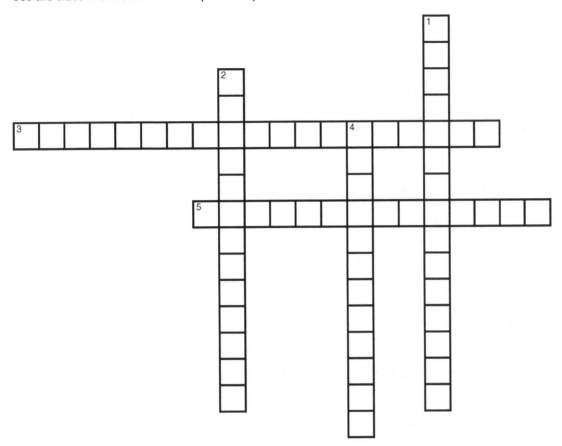

Across

3. The pressure produced in an exhaust system by restrictions to exhaust gas flow.

5. A slack u-tube device used to measure EBP using inches of water column.

Down

1. A component that collects exhaust gases from each cylinder of the cylinder head.

2. A screen covering the exhaust outlet that prevents fires by trapping large incandescent carbon particles. Exhaust gas flow pounds these particles into smaller pieces and cools them in the process.

4. An engine brake that works by placing a restriction in the exhaust system, which increases backpressure, causing the engine to exert a retarding force against the driveline.

ASE-Type Questions

Read each item carefully, and then select the best response.

_____ 1. Technician A says that the force supplying pressure to push a slave cylinder is provided by the injector camshaft lobe. Technician B says the force is often an intake valve lobe. Who is correct?
   A. Technician A
   B. Technician B
   C. Both Technician A and Technician B
   D. Neither Technician A nor Technician B

_____ 2. Technician A says installing larger diameter exhaust pipes will help improve the ability of an engine to increase intake airflow. Technician B says larger exhaust pipes will only increase engine noise. Who is correct?
   A. Technician A
   B. Technician B
   C. Both Technician A and Technician B
   D. Neither Technician A nor Technician B

_____ 3. Technician A says that vertical exhaust systems are advantageous because they have longer service life and do not allow exhaust gases to drift upward into the cab or bunk. Technician B says horizontal exhaust systems are advantageous because they are not damaged by low bridges or tree branches. Who is correct?
   A. Technician A
   B. Technician B
   C. Both Technician A and Technician B
   D. Neither Technician A nor Technician B

_____ 4. Technician A says the use of a turbocharger reduces exhaust noise and the requirement for a large amount of sound damping by the muffler. Technician B says that turbochargers can contribute to exhaust noise and require larger mufflers in the exhaust system. Who is correct?
   A. Technician A
   B. Technician B
   C. Both Technician A and Technician B
   D. Neither Technician A nor Technician B

_____ 5. Technician A says that the use of a DPF does not eliminate the need for an exhaust system muffler. Technician B says a muffler is generally not needed if a vehicle uses a DPF. Who is correct?
   A. Technician A
   B. Technician B
   C. Both Technician A and Technician B
   D. Neither Technician A nor Technician B

_____ 6. Technician A says that an exhaust backpressure governor helps reduce the amount of hydrocarbon emissions produced during idle. Technician B says any exhaust backpressure regulator or governor can be used to speed up coolant warm-up time. Who is correct?
   A. Technician A
   B. Technician B
   C. Both Technician A and Technician B
   D. Neither Technician A nor Technician B

_____ 7. Technician A says it's best to install the exhaust pyrometer in the exhaust pipe after the turbocharger, because the most accurate exhaust temperature can be recorded there. Technician B says that the most accurate exhaust temperature can be observed by installing the exhaust pyrometer in the exhaust manifold. Who is correct?
   A. Technician A
   B. Technician B
   C. Both Technician A and Technician B
   D. Neither Technician A nor Technician B

_____ **8.** Technician A and Technician B are investigating a customer complaint about an increase in turbocharger noise when the compression release brake is used. Technician A says that the louder noise is normal, because the turbocharger speed increases during engine braking. Technician B says that the louder noise is not normal, because the engine does not fuel during braking and the turbocharger should slow down. Who is correct?
   A. Technician A
   B. Technician B
   C. Both Technician A and Technician B
   D. Neither Technician A nor Technician B

_____ **9.** While considering a replacement muffler for an engine equipped with a compression release brake, Technician A says that the same muffler can be used on a vehicle with or without an engine brake. Technician B says that the muffler used on an engine with a compression release brake will generally have more sound damping properties. Who is correct?
   A. Technician A
   B. Technician B
   C. Both Technician A and Technician B
   D. Neither Technician A nor Technician B

_____ **10.** While considering the procedure to adjust the slave piston clearance on a compression release brake, Technician A says the clearance is adjusted after the intake and exhaust valves are adjusted. Technician B says slave piston clearance is adjusted after correct lash is set between the valve bridges and valve stems. Who is correct?
   A. Technician A
   B. Technician B
   C. Both Technician A and Technician B
   D. Neither Technician A nor Technician B

On-Board Diagnostics

Chapter Review

The following activities have been designed to help you refresh your knowledge of this chapter. Your instructor may require you to complete some or all of these activities as a regular part of your training program. You are encouraged to complete any activity that your instructor does not assign as a way to enhance your learning.

Matching

Match the following terms with the correct description or example.

A. Active fault

B. Fault mode identifier (FMI)

C. Historical fault

D. Incipient fault

E. Intermittent fault

_____ **1.** A fault that took place at one time but that is now corrected and no longer active.

_____ **2.** A fault that is the result of system or component deterioration.

_____ **3.** A fault that is not ongoing and can be both active and historical.

_____ **4.** The type of failure detected in the SPN, PID, or SID.

_____ **5.** A fault that is currently taking place and uninterrupted in action.

Multiple Choice

Read each item carefully, and then select the best response.

_____ **1.** The simplest, most familiar definition of _____ is the diagnostic function of electronic control systems to identify or self-diagnose system faults and report fault codes.

    A. on-board diagnostics

    B. off-board diagnostics

    C. trouble code monitoring

    D. telematics

_____ **2.** The introduction of _____ in 2007 added a level of complexity to emissions systems that required monitoring to ensure they were properly functioning.

    A. particulate filters

    B. crankcase ventilation systems

    C. exhaust gas recirculation systems

    D. All of the above

_____ **3.** A _____ diagnostic strategy compares system and component behaviors to expected patterns of operation.

    A. traditional

    B. isolation-based

    C. model-based

    D. historical

_____ **4.** An unknown and uncontrolled input acting on the system such as electromagnetic interference, fluid or gas leakage from a hydraulic or pneumatic system, or excessive mechanical friction is known as a(n) _____.

    A. disturbance

    B. incipient fault

    C. preliminary incident

    D. intermittent fault

_____ 5. Directly measuring the level of emissions using a sensor to identify a noxious emission is called _____.
   A. continuity monitoring
   B. threshold monitoring
   C. rationality monitoring
   D. functionality monitoring

_____ 6. HD-OBD legislation for diesels includes _____.
   A. standardized names and abbreviations of components and systems
   B. reading of fault codes by aftermarket electronic test equipment
   C. standardized 9-pin DLC in the driver area
   D. All of the above

_____ 7. The threshold for diesel misfire detection is _____ per 1,000 crankshaft revolutions.
   A. 2%
   B. 4%
   C. 8%
   D. 10%

_____ 8. HD-OBD requirements for the diesel EGR monitor include detecting EGR _____ before emissions exceed HD-OBD thresholds.
   A. response rate
   B. flow rate
   C. cooling system performance
   D. All of the above

_____ 9. Two common _____ system monitors are diesel particulate filter (DPF) monitoring and selective catalyst reduction (SCR) monitoring.
   A. aftertreatment
   B. EGR
   C. fuel
   D. crankcase ventilation

_____ 10. Type _____ diagnostic trouble codes are emissions-causing faults that must occur at least once on two consecutive trips before the malfunction indicator light (MIL) will illuminate.
   A. A
   B. B
   C. C
   D. D

_____ 11. Both the J-1587/1708 and the J-1939 network connections are found in the _____ DLC.
   A. 6-pin
   B. 9-pin
   C. 12-pin
   D. None of the above

_____ 12. A _____ is the first byte or character of each message that identifies which control module on the J-1587 serial communication link originated the information.
   A. message identifier
   B. system identifier
   C. parameter identifier
   D. fault mode identifier

_____ 13. The _____ is the smallest identifiable fault.
   A. system identifier
   B. fault mode identifier
   C. suspect parameter number
   D. occurrence identifier

_____ 14. Suspect parameter number, source addresses, and failure mode indicator information are part of a larger J-1939 message called the _____.
   A. proprietary identification number
   B. fault identification number
   C. subsystem identification number
   D. parameter group number

_____ **15.** Priority fault codes _____ are reserved for messages that require prompt access to the bus in order to prevent severe mechanical damage.
- **A.** 1 and 2
- **B.** 3 and 4
- **C.** 5 and 6
- **D.** 7 and 8

True/False

If you believe the statement to be more true than false, write the letter "T" in the space provided. If you believe the statement to be more false than true, write the letter "F".

_____ **1.** The legislated standards for maximum vehicle emissions levels are called on-board diagnostic standards.

_____ **2.** The HD-OBD standards have fewer standardized legal requirements and are less comprehensive than the EMD standards.

_____ **3.** All OBD standards are developed by SAE International and adopted by the EPA.

_____ **4.** An illuminated malfunction indicator light or check engine light indicates a historical fault.

_____ **5.** An HD-OBD system executes, or runs, monitors once every 24 hours of engine operation.

_____ **6.** HD-OBD legislation requires 14 mandatory major system monitors for diesel engines.

_____ **7.** All emissions systems are monitored continuously.

_____ **8.** OBD crankcase ventilation system monitoring includes detecting closed-loop feedback control.

_____ **9.** A diesel exhaust fluid quality sensor can now determine the quality of DEF fluid by measuring its density.

_____ **10.** The higher the first number is in the message, the greater importance attached to the information.

Fill in the Blank

Read each item carefully, and then complete the statement by filling in the missing word(s).

1. A(n) _____ self-diagnostic strategy focuses on specific areas of commercial vehicle control, such as the engine, anti-lock braking, traction control, and transmissions.

2. A(n) _____ is a deviation of at least one characteristic property of the system from its standard behavior.

3. Fault _____ is best accomplished using a diagnostic fault tree supplied by the manufacturer.

4. Testing the operation of individual emissions system components using an organized procedure is known as a(n) _____.

5. The _____ _____ connector is the connection point for electronic service tools used to access fault code and other information provided by chassis electronic control modules.

6. OBD _____ software identifies fault codes, ensures emissions systems are operating correctly, and regularly evaluates malfunctions in the emissions systems unique to diesel engines.

7. The _____ _____ monitor tracks electrical circuits operating power train components that can cause a measurable emissions increase during any reasonable driving conditions.

8. During _____-_____ diagnostics, the technician may monitor system operation, perform actuator tests, pinpoint electrical tests, and inspect components.

9. After a repair has been made an HD-OBD service tool displays a(n) _____ code indicating that a monitor has completed its functionality test and no fault was found.

10. The _____ _____ represents the number of times a fault combination of SPN/FMI has taken place.

Message Identifier Numbers

Match the Message Identifier Number to its correct description.

MID number:

_____	**1.** 128	**A.** Satellite
_____	**2.** 130	**B.** Instrument cluster unit
_____	**3.** 136	**C.** Collision avoidance
_____	**4.** 140	**D.** ECM
_____	**5.** 180	**E.** Off-board diagnostics
_____	**6.** 181	**F.** Transmission control unit
_____	**7.** 190	**G.** Cellular
_____	**8.** 229	**H.** ABS
_____	**9.** 231	**I.** Climate control module

Crossword Puzzle

Use the clues in the column to complete the puzzle.

Across

2. A branch of information technology that uses specialized applications for long-distance transmission of information to and from a vehicle.

4. A value or identifier of an item being reported with fault data.

5. A method of providing fault code data for a specific system that involves counting the number of flashes from a warning lamp and observing longer pauses between the light blinks.

Down

1. A fault code used by J-1587 protocols that identifies which subsystem has failed.

3. The field that designates which control module is sending the message.

ASE-Type Questions

Read each item carefully, and then select the best response.

_____ 1. Two technicians are discussing HD-OBD for trucks. Technician A says that the simplest, most familiar definition is the diagnostic function of electronic control systems to identify or self-diagnose system faults and report fault codes. Technician B says the automotive and light-duty truck version of OBD is called OBD II. Who is correct?
   A. Technician A
   B. Technician B
   C. Both Technician A and Technician B
   D. Neither Technician A nor Technician B

_____ 2. Technician A says that a fault is a deviation of at least one characteristic property of the system from its standard behavior. Technician B says that a historical fault took place at one time and can never be active again. Who is correct?
   A. Technician A
   B. Technician B
   C. Both Technician A and Technician B
   D. Neither Technician A nor Technician B

_____ 3. A(n) _____ fault is not ongoing and can be both active and historical.
   A. inactive
   B. incipient
   C. intermittent
   D. historical

_____ 4. All of following are part of the HD-OBD legislation for diesels, *except*:
   A. 9-pin diagnostic connector
   B. 6-pin diagnostic connector
   C. standardized emissions-related fault codes for all manufacturers
   D. reading of fault codes by aftermarket electronic test equipment

_____ 5. Which of these HD-OBD terms describes when the ECM stores a snapshot of the engine operating conditions present at the time the malfunction was detected?
   A. Freeze frame
   B. Diagnostic trouble code (DTC)
   C. C-type code
   D. D-type code

_____ 6. Technician A says that threshold monitoring directly measures the level of emissions using a sensor to identify a noxious emission. Technician B says that a historical fault took place at one time and can never be active again. Who is correct?
   A. Technician A
   B. Technician B
   C. Both Technician A and Technician B
   D. Neither Technician A nor Technician B

_____ 7. What kind of monitoring measures voltage drops and signal and ground return voltage from sensors or output devices to validate circuits are not open or shorted to ground and battery voltage?
   A. Intermittent
   B. Threshold
   C. Electrical circuit continuity
   D. Out of range

_____ 8. HD-OBD legislation for diesels includes all of the following features, *except*:
   A. standardized 6-pin DLC
   B. standardized emissions-related fault codes for all manufacturers
   C. reading of fault codes by aftermarket electronic test equipment
   D. standardized names and abbreviations of components and systems

_____ **9.** Which of these systems' faults is LEAST LIKELY to be detected before emissions exceed standards?
   A. Oxidation catalyst
   B. Lean NO_X (oxides of nitrogen) catalyst
   C. SCR (selective catalyst reduction) catalyst
   D. Glow plugs and intake air heaters

_____ **10.** Which part of the heavy-duty diesel HD-OBD management system stores diagnostic information?
   A. Misfire
   B. Vehicle-in vehicle-out information
   C. Freeze frame
   D. Trip

Navistar

Chapter Review

The following activities have been designed to help you refresh your knowledge of this chapter. Your instructor may require you to complete some or all of these activities as a regular part of your training program. You are encouraged to complete any activity that your instructor does not assign as a way to enhance your learning.

Matching

Match the following terms with the correct description or example.

A. MaxxForce

B. PowerStroke

C. SinterCast

_____ **1.** Navistar's name for its CGI engine block construction.

_____ **2.** A brand of diesel engines owned by Navistar.

_____ **3.** Navistar's name for its mid-bore V-block diesel engines.

Multiple Choice

Read each item carefully, and then select the best response.

_____ **1.** International Harvester introduced the first engine with a _____, it is regarded as the greatest single improvement ever made on a truck engine.
   A. wet sleeve block
   B. removable cylinder head
   C. compression ignition system
   D. turbocharger

_____ **2.** Navistar is a holding company that owns the manufacturer of all of the following **EXCEPT**?
   A. MaxxForce brand diesel engines
   B. Detroit Diesel brand diesel engines
   C. International brand commercial trucks
   D. IC Bus school and commercial buses

_____ **3.** Which of the following is an example of a Navistar Common Rail Engine?
   A. PowerStroke N-10, 10.5L
   B. VT 275, 4.5L
   C. MaxxForce DT, 7.6L
   D. All of the above

_____ **4.** Algorithms determine EGR valve positioning based on _____.
   A. EGR flow-based intake boost pressure
   B. intake manifold temperature
   C. exhaust backpressure
   D. All of the above

_____ **5.** Turbocharger vanes can often seize as a result of excessive engine _____ from idling or low-load and low-speed conditions.
   A. temperature
   B. slobber
   C. backpressure
   D. All of the above

_____ **6.** When turbochargers are arranged in a series, the air passes through a _____, which is located between the low- and high-pressure turbochargers.
   A. low-pressure charge air cooler
   B. pressure condenser
   C. interstage cooler
   D. Either A or C

_____ **7.** Navistar uses _____ to make adjustments to the EGR gas mass flow.
   A. oxygen sensors
   B. air–fuel ratio meters
   C. temperature sensors
   D. Both A and C

_____ **8.** The MaxxForce 11, 13, and 15 engines were the first to use _____ systems developed by Bosch beginning in 2007.
   A. HEUI
   B. biodiesel
   C. common rail
   D. indirect injection

_____ **9.** Navistar's version of a multiplex-controlled electrical system is called _____.
   A. MAXX
   B. Diamond Logic
   C. DAVIE
   D. STAR logic

_____ **10.** Navistar's comprehensive set of software solutions to manage fleet operations is called _____.
   A. OnCommand
   B. Fleetrack
   C. OnStar
   D. Roadmaster

True/False

If you believe the statement to be more true than false, write the letter "T" in the space provided. If you believe the statement to be more false than true, write the letter "F".

_____ **1.** Navistar partnered with International Harvester to become the first company to enter the hybrid commercial truck market.

_____ **2.** The actuator on a variable geometry turbocharger can both transmit and receive information over the vehicle's controller area network.

_____ **3.** Increasing the exhaust backpressure and opening the EGR valve will meter fewer exhaust gases into the cylinder charge.

_____ **4.** After 2006, engine crankcases were no longer permitted to be ventilated to the atmosphere.

_____ **5.** Series turbocharging increases particulate emissions, which must be filtered out of the exhaust system.

_____ **6.** MaxxForce 11 and 13 engines have no coolant passages between the engine block and the cylinder head through the cylinder head gasket.

_____ **7.** Navistar proved that the use of massive exhaust gas recirculation rates was a more efficient method than using liquid SCR to meet EPA10 emission standards.

_____ **8.** Navistar integrated valve train operation into the high-pressure oil actuation system and created the cam-less diesel in 1998.

_____ **9.** Pressurization of fuel and injection are separate functions in the common rail injection system.

_____ **10.** CAN-connected remote air solenoid modules may contain up to sixteen electric over air solenoids.

Fill in the Blank

Read each item carefully, and then complete the statement by filling in the missing word(s).

1. Navistar leads the industry in the innovative use of quiet and exceptionally strong composite _____ _____ engine blocks.

2. The _____ _____ system encompasses all the controls that regulate the air and EGR gas entering and exiting the combustion chamber of the engine.

3. At the center of the AMS system used in 2002–2006 is a _____ _____ turbocharger, which is responsible for building boost pressure and driving the exhaust gas pressure above the intake air charge pressure.

4. Properly operating actuator linkage and vanes will contact the closed position and _____ at least once, if not two or three times.

5. With _____ turbocharging, the compressor output pressure of one turbocharger feeds into the compressor inlet of another turbocharger.

6. A low-temperature EGR _____ circuit is needed to better control the temperature of EGR gas entering the cylinders.

7. In addition to using an electric heating element in the air inlet of the intake manifold, Navistar also uses a _____ _____ assist system.

8. Navistar developed the _____ system to replace the mechanical camshaft with highly pressurized lubrication oil, which is used instead of cam lobes to actuate plungers pressurizing fuel for injection.

9. A constant fuel pressure in the _____ _____ is available to all the injectors, which lends the name "common rail" to the fuel system.

10. The ESC module operates circuits such as headlights, taillights, windshield wipers, and the A/C system controls. Using _____ _____ transistors as output drivers.

Labeling

Label the following diagrams with the correct terms.

1. Identify the parts of a Navistar cold start fuel igniter:

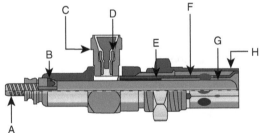

A. _____

B. _____

C. _____

D. _____

E. _____

F. _____

G. _____

H. _____

2. Identify the parts of a common rail fuel system:

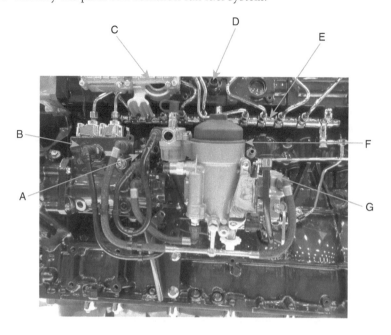

A. _____   E. _____

B. _____   F. _____

C. _____   G. _____

D. _____

Skill Drills

Test your knowledge of skill drills by filling in the correct words in the photo captions.

1. Calibrating a Navistar Oxygen Sensor:

Wide Band Oxygen Sensor

Step 1: Verify there are no oxygen sensor _____ _____ before sensor _____.
The sensor may be _____, but _____ and _____ cannot have _____.

Step 2: With the sensor removed from the _____ system, first connect the _____ sensor to the engine _____ before running the _____ sensor _____ procedure. Leave the sensor _____ the _____ system.

Step 3: From the _____ software, select "Run O_2 Sensor _____ procedure."

Step 4: Turn on the _____ switch, turn off the _____, and run the _____ procedure.

Step 5: After calibration is complete, _____ the _____ _____ in the _____ system.

2. Isolating Fuel Rail Pressure Leakage:

Step 1: Cap cylinder _____'s high-pressure line _____ with an OEM-prescribed high-pressure _____ _____.

Step 2: Disconnect the fuel _____ line from the cylinder _____ and run a clear plastic _____ to the line. Place the other end of the plastic line into a _____ _____ to measure fuel _____.

Step 3: Start the engine and operate it at _____ idle. Once fuel flow and volume are _____, measure the _____ volume for exactly _____ minute.

Step 4: Repeat the procedure for cylinders _____–_____ by continuing to _____ off one injector _____ fitting at a time until the excessive leak is _____.

Step 5: Compare the fuel return _____ to Navistar's _____. The _____ expected _____ for fuel returned for connected cylinders may resemble the following:
- Five connected injectors: _____–_____ mL
- Four connected injectors: _____–_____ mL
- Three connected injectors: _____–_____ mL
- Two connected injectors: _____–_____ mL

Step 6: If the observed results are much _____ than manufacturer's specifications, the _____ injector(s) will produce a _____ return volume when _____. When connected, return fuel volume will _____ specifications. If the fuel volume is _____ specifications, replace the _____ _____ and high-pressure connector _____ for cylinder _____.

Step 7: Replace the defective _____ (s) and _____ the system.

3. Accessing Navistar OEM DTCs:

Using the LCD Display:

Step 1:   Set the _____ _____ and turn the _____ _____ to the _____ position.

Step 2:   Press and release the _____ _____ button and the _____/ _____ button simultaneously. If no active _____ are logged, the instrument cluster LCD _____ will display "_____ _____."

Step 3:   If the _____ detects an _____ fault, the _____ CEL light will remain on.

Step 4:   Switch off the _____ _____ to end the instrument cluster's _____ mode.

Using Blink Codes (Flashing SEL and CEL Lights):

Step 1:   Set the _____ _____ and turn the ignition key to the _____ position.

Step 2:   Press and release the _____ _____ and the _____/_____ buttons simultaneously _____ within _____ seconds.

Step 3:   If _____ are detected, the standard key-_____, engine-_____ (KOEO) test will run to _____ system outputs, and codes will begin to _____. The _____ SEL light will flash or _____ once to indicate the _____ of _____ DTCs. Then, the _____ CEL light will flash or blink _____ indicating an _____ DTC code.

Step 4:   Count the yellow _____ flashes/blinks in _____. After each _____ of the _____-digit _____ _____ is flashed, a short _____ will occur. For example, two _____ and a _____ would indicate the number _____. Two _____ and a pause, _____ flashes and a pause, and _____ flash and a pause would indicate DTC _____.

Step 5:   When more than _____ DTC is stored, the red _____ light will _____ once more following the _____ CEL flashes to indicate the _____ of another _____ _____.

Step 6:   After all DTCs have been _____ or _____, the red _____ lamp will flash _____ times to indicate the _____ of _____.

Step 7:   To _____ the _____ transmission, again push _____ cruise control buttons simultaneously _____ and the _____ will _____ the stored DTCs.

Clearing Inactive DTCs:

Step 1:   Set the parking _____ and turn the _____ key to the _____ position.

Step 2:   Press and _____ the _____ _____ button and the _____/ _____ button simultaneously.

Step 3:   While _____ _____ both the _____ buttons, _____ and _____ the accelerator pedal _____ times within _____ seconds.

Step 4:   Release _____ cruise _____.

Step 5:   Ensure that the _____ codes are _____. (If no active _____s are present, the red _____ light should flash _____.)

ASE-Type Questions

Read each item carefully, and then select the best response.

_____ 1. Technician A says Navistar has made PowerStroke engines for Ford since the early 1980s and continues to this day. Technician B says that Ford currently designs and manufactures its PowerStroke engines. Who is correct?

   A. Technician A
   B. Technician B
   C. Both Technician A and Technician B
   D. Neither Technician A nor Technician B

_____ 2. Technician A says that, like all other medium- and heavy-duty diesel manufacturers, Navistar engines use liquid SCR aftertreatment systems. Technician B says that Navistar is the exception and relies on other NO$_x$ reduction strategies to eliminate the need for liquid SCR aftertreatment systems. Who is correct?

   A. Technician A
   B. Technician B
   C. Both Technician A and Technician B
   D. Neither Technician A nor Technician B

_____ 3. Technician A says that Navistar uses electric intake preheaters. Technician B says that Navistar uses a flame-type intake heater that sprays diesel fuel into the intake manifold, where it is ignited by an electric glow plug. Who is correct?

   A. Technician A
   B. Technician B
   C. Both Technician A and Technician B
   D. Neither Technician A nor Technician B

_____ 4. Technician A says that the engine-mounted air control valve (ACV) regulates the operation of the turbochargers and the EGR valve. Technician B says the ACV regulates the operation of the exhaust back-pressure valve (EBPV) and the coolant control valves. Who is correct?

   A. Technician A
   B. Technician B
   C. Both Technician A and Technician B
   D. Neither Technician A nor Technician B

_____ 5. Technician A says that coolant leaking from the cylinder head gasket on MaxxForce 11 and 13 engines is likely due to a poor seal between the gasket and cylinder head. Technician B says that no coolant can leak from the head gasket of those engines. Who is correct?

   A. Technician A
   B. Technician B
   C. Both Technician A and Technician B
   D. Neither Technician A nor Technician B

_____ 6. Technician A says that, after 2012, Navistar engines used an aftertreatment system control module (ACM) to regulate the SCR system on its vehicles. Technician B says Navistar has always used an ACM to control the operation of the aftertreatment DPF. Who is correct?

   A. Technician A
   B. Technician B
   C. Both Technician A and Technician B
   D. Neither Technician A nor Technician B

_____ 7. Technician A says that Navistar engines have used Bosch high-pressure common rail injectors since 2007. Technician B says the Bosch common rail injectors only began to replace HEUI injectors beginning in late 2010. Who is correct?

   A. Technician A
   B. Technician B
   C. Both Technician A and Technician B
   D. Neither Technician A nor Technician B

_____ **8.** Technician A says Navistar Sure Lock technology refers to the use of split fracture main bearing caps and rods. Technician B says only connecting rod bearing caps are split fracture split. Who is correct?
   A. Technician A
   B. Technician B
   C. Both Technician A and Technician B
   D. Neither Technician A nor Technician B

_____ **9.** Technician A says that chassis air devices are switched through air control solenoids. Technician B says the electrical system controller (ESC) module regulates the operation of the power divider lock and air suspension system. Who is correct?
   A. Technician A
   B. Technician B
   C. Both Technician A and Technician B
   D. Neither Technician A nor Technician B

_____ **10.** While considering how to add a set of aftermarket fog lights to a late-model Navistar chassis, Technician A says the dash switch can be connected using ServiceMaxx software. Technician B says that Diamond Logic Builder is the software needed to install the fog lights. Who is correct?
   A. Technician A
   B. Technician B
   C. Both Technician A and Technician B
   D. Neither Technician A nor Technician B

Detroit Diesel

Chapter Review

The following activities have been designed to help you refresh your knowledge of this chapter. Your instructor may require you to complete some or all of these activities as a regular part of your training program. You are encouraged to complete any activity that your instructor does not assign as a way to enhance your learning.

Matching

Match the following terms with the correct description or example.

A. Amplified common rail (ACR)

B. Axial power turbine (APT)

C. E3 EUI

D. Synchronous reference sensor (SRS)

E. Timing reference sensor (TRS)

_____ **1.** A high-pressure injection system that multiplies the fuel rail pressure inside the injector.

_____ **2.** A type of electronically controlled unit injector containing a nozzle control valve and spill control valve.

_____ **3.** Detroit Diesel's term for a crankshaft position sensor.

_____ **4.** Detroit Diesel's term for a camshaft position sensor.

_____ **5.** A device located after the turbocharger that uses a turbine wheel to capture exhaust energy and convert it into usable engine power.

Multiple Choice

Read each item carefully, and then select the best response.

_____ **1.** Versions of the Detroit Diesel _____ were produced as alternative fuel engines and could operate on compressed or liquid natural gas fuel.

    A. S50

    B. S60

    C. S60H

    D. S70

_____ **2.** The first-generation Detroit Diesel electronic unit injector, designated N2, used a _____ to regulate the beginning and end of injection.

    A. hydraulically balanced nozzle valve

    B. poppet-type control valve

    C. rocker lever

    D. spiral control valve

_____ **3.** The _____ stage of the Detroit Diesel N2 electronic unit injector begins when the injector plunger begins to move downward as the injector lobe lifts the injector rocker lever.

    A. fill

    B. spill

    C. injection

    D. pressure relief

_____ **4.** The Detroit Diesel N3 used a _____ type nozzle control valve that enabled the use of pilot injection.
   A. ball
   B. poppet
   C. butterfly
   D. spindle

_____ **5.** To prevent O-ring damage during N3 injector installation, Detroit Diesel recommends using a thin coat of clean _____.
   A. transmission fluid
   B. engine oil
   C. ethylene glycol
   D. Any of the above

_____ **6.** The Delphi E3 electronic unit injector was developed to meet _____ emission standards.
   A. EPA05
   B. EPA07
   C. EPA09
   D. EPA10

_____ **7.** The Detroit Diesel DD series engines, which includes the DD13, DD15, and DD16, has close to a _____ parts commonality
   A. 75%
   B. 80%
   C. 90%
   D. 95%

_____ **8.** The _____ electronic engine control system for the DD15 uses an engine-mounted MCM and a common power train controller located inside the cab.
   A. DDEC III
   B. DDEC IV
   C. DDEC V
   D. DDEC VI

_____ **9.** The ACR injector can produce a _____ shaped injection discharge curve that is best used for reducing NO_x at moderate engine speeds.
   A. boot
   B. ramped
   C. square
   D. diamond

_____ **10.** Detroit Diesel uses a telematics communications package called _____ to exchange information between a vehicle chassis and a central dispatch, which monitors the operation of the vehicle.
   A. OnStar
   B. DAVIE
   C. Virtual Technician
   D. Fleet Watch

True/False

If you believe the statement to be more true than false, write the letter "T" in the space provided. If you believe the statement to be more false than true, write the letter "F".

_____ **1.** By flipping around the camshaft, and reversing the direction of rotation for the coolant, fuel, and oil pumps, a modular engine could be made to turn clockwise or counterclockwise.

_____ **2.** Currently, DDEC IV is used on engines that meet Greenhouse Gas 2014 emissions standards.

_____ **3.** Detroit Diesel engines were the first electronic diesels to use crankshaft and camshaft position sensors to calculate injection timing and measure injection quantity.

_____ **4.** Three different types of electronic unit injectors are used by Detroit Diesel in addition to the amplified common rail system used in its latest engines.

_____ **5.** Detroit Diesel N2 electronic unit injectors use a six-digit fuel injector calibration code to correct inconsistent delivery volume.

_____ **6.** Detroit Diesel S50 and S60 engines do not have any external indicator for TDC of cylinder 1 or 6.

_____ **7.** Delphi's E3 EUI has a dual control valve that enables high-speed, ultra-high-pressure operation with rate shaped injection events.

_____ **8.** Detroit Diesel DD series engines use a unique Bosch hydraulically balanced high-pressure injection system that multiplies the fuel rail pressure inside the injectors.

_____ **9.** Bosch's hydraulically amplified direct injector is capable of five injection events per combustion cycle and two-stage pressure amplification, which doubles the injection pressure supplied by a fuel rail.

_____ **10.** The GHG14 aftertreatment device is an air actuated dosing system used on DD series engines.

Fill in the Blank

Read each item carefully, and then complete the statement by filling in the missing word(s).

1. The Detroit Diesel S50 engine is a four-cylinder version of the S60 model with an added _____ _____ to minimize torsional vibrations.

2. When the Detroit Diesel engine is initially cranked for starting, the _____ _____ sensor detects cylinder 1's position using a specially marked reluctance wheel attached to the crankshaft.

3. On S50 and S60 Detroit Diesels that use N2 injectors, the valves and injectors have a unique adjustment procedure that uses _____ _____ as a reference point to correctly position the engine and select the appropriate valve and injector to adjust.

4. The additional control valve in the E3 compact injector package is a _____ _____ valve that regulates the injection pressure available at the nozzle tip.

5. Backpressure for the EGR system of a Detroit Diesel DD series engine is provided by an _____ turbocharger.

6. Detroit Diesel added an _____ control module in 2010, which processes sensor data and controls the outputs of the DPF and the selective catalytic reduction system.

7. In the _____-_____ module, fuel leaves the low-pressure pump and returns to the filter module and into a water separator.

8. The _____ control valve meters the fuel supplied to the high-pressure pump.

9. Under ideal conditions, the _____ _____ turbine on the DD15 can convert exhaust energy that is normally wasted into as much as 50 hp and transfer the power to the engine's rear-mounted gear train.

10. A four-light bar segment indicates the _____ _____ fluid level in 25% increments.

Labeling

Label the following diagrams with the correct terms.

1. Identify the rocker levers and injector adjustments on an S50/S60 engine:

A. _____

B. _____

C. _____

D. _____

2. Identify the internal parts of an N3 electronic unit injector:

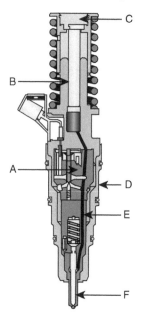

A. _____

B. _____

C. _____

D. _____

E. _____

F. _____

3. Identify the internal components of the ACR injector:

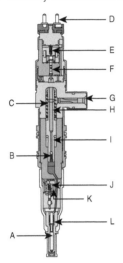

A. _____

B. _____

C. _____

D. _____

E. _____

F. _____

G. _____

H. _____

I. _____

J. _____

K. _____

L. _____

4. Identify the parts of a Parker-Racor fuel module:

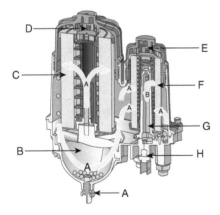

A. _____

B. _____

C. _____

D. _____

E. _____

F. _____

G. _____

H. _____

Skill Drills

Test your knowledge of skill drills by filling in the correct words in the photo captions.

1. Adjusting Valves and Injectors on an S60 Engine:

Step 1: Bar the engine over in the correct _____ of _____. Most engines turn _____ when viewed from the _____ and _____ when viewed from the _____.

Step 2: Rotate the engine until a _____ of _____ on _____ is identified.

Step 3: Adjust the _____ and _____ valves on the _____ cylinder of the _____ cylinder (see Table 37-2 to find the correct companion cylinder). The _____ are adjusted by _____ an adjusting screw and inserting a _____ _____ of the _____ thickness between the _____ _____ and _____ _____.

Step 4: While the engine remains in the _____ _____, adjust the _____ in the cylinder that is _____ in the _____ _____.

Step 5: Use the correct _____ tool height _____ to adjust _____ travel. A small _____ beside the injector spring locates the _____ tool. A _____ on the _____ should sweep across the _____ of the _____ to remove an _____ film. Loosen and turn the injector adjusting screw to obtain the correct _____ height.

2. Adjusting Valves and Brakes on DD Series Engines:

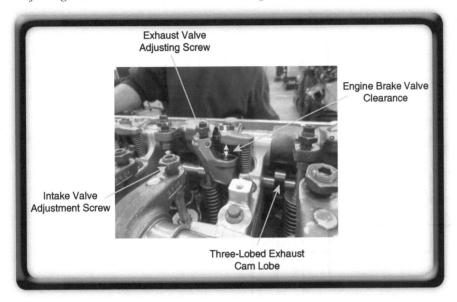

Step 1:   Steam clean the _____ and _____ _____ the ignition _____ for safety.

Step 2:   Remove any components that would interfere with removing the _____ _____, such as the air cleaner _____ and turbocharger _____ _____. Refer to the OEM's procedures.

Step 3:   After removing the _____ cover, _____ the engine over until cylinder _____ is at _____ at the end of _____ stroke. Shake the _____ levers on cylinders _____ and _____ to _____. Cylinder _____ should have two _____ levers while _____ should have two _____ levers.

Step 4:   Using a _____ gauge, adjust the intake valve _____ clearances on the _____ rocker levers for cylinders _____, _____, and _____ to the manufacturer's specifications. The intake _____ are all on one side of the _____ and driven by a separate _____ from the _____ and _____ _____ camshaft. The specifications can be found on the engine's emission _____. A typical specification is _____" (0.4 mm). All the adjusting screws in _____ contact with the exhaust and intake _____.

Step 5:   Adjust the valve _____ clearances on the exhaust _____ levers for cylinders _____, _____, and _____.

Step 6:   Bar the engine over _____ degrees and _____ the _____ by adjusting the _____ valve _____ on cylinders _____, _____, and _____. The exhaust valve _____ can be adjusted on cylinders _____, _____, and _____.

Step 7:   Adjust the engine brake rocker lever _____ after each exhaust valve _____ has been set. This is done by _____ the _____ until the cylinder to be adjusted has reached its _____ intake valve _____. By observing the _____ _____ of the rocker lever _____, the engine can be properly _____ to adjust the engine brake adjusting _____.

Step 8:   When the engine brake _____ _____ begins to make contact with the _____ valve, set the _____ using the engine brake rocker arm adjusting _____. The _____ is set between the _____ piston and the exhaust valve rocker _____. A typical clearance is _____" (4.1 mm).

Step 9:   Adjust the brake lash _____ in the cylinder _____ of the engine _____ _____: 1, 5, 3, 6, 2, and 4.

Step 10: Torque the _____ _____ valve adjusting _____ to specifications and _____ the engine.

Crossword Puzzle

Use the clues in the column to complete the puzzle.

Across

2. Any mechanical device used to pressurize the intake air above atmospheric pressure. Superchargers include roots blowers and turbochargers.

4. An engine that turns counterclockwise when viewed from the flywheel.

5. A general term used to describe any fuel circuit or component that supplies or transports fuel from the engine to the fuel tank.

Down

1. A tool used by technicians that is used to adjust the plunger travel of a unit injector for Detroit Diesel N2 injectors.

3. A high-volume positive displacement air pump used to pressurize intake air for Detroit Diesel two-stroke cycle diesels.

ASE-Type Questions

Read each item carefully, and then select the best response.

_____ 1. Technician A and Technician B are discussing the change in combustion noise above idle speed from a DD series engine with an ACR fuel system. Technician A says removing the pilot injection caused the noise change. Technician B says switching to fuel pressure amplification mode caused it. Who is correct?
   A. Technician A
   B. Technician B
   C. Both Technician A and Technician B
   D. Neither Technician A nor Technician B

_____ 2. Technician A says that the rail pressure in a DD series engine can exceed 30,000 psi (2068 bar). Technician B says it will not rise above 20,000 psi (1379 bar). Who is correct?
   A. Technician A
   B. Technician B
   C. Both Technician A and Technician B
   D. Neither Technician A nor Technician B

_____ 3. Technician A says that settings for engine idle speed and other programmable parameters are stored in the common power train controller. Technician B says that engine control data and outputs are processed in the motor control module (MCM). Who is correct?
   A. Technician A
   B. Technician B
   C. Both Technician A and Technician B
   D. Neither Technician A nor Technician B

_____ 4. Technician A says the ACR injector has two fuel return circuits from the injector. Technician B says only a high-pressure fuel line and a single return circuit connect the injector to the engine's fuel circuits. Who is correct?
   A. Technician A
   B. Technician B
   C. Both Technician A and Technician B
   D. Neither Technician A nor Technician B

_____ 5. Technician A says that the best injection rate for producing power from an ACR injector is produced by energizing the ACV at the same time as the NCV. Technician B says that energizing the NCV after the ACV produces a square-shaped injection rate. Who is correct?
   A. Technician A
   B. Technician B
   C. Both Technician A and Technician B
   D. Neither Technician A nor Technician B

_____ 6. While examining a camshaft failure in the high-pressure pump of a DD15 engine, Technician A says it was likely caused by a failure of the two-stage valve to close. Technician B says it was likely caused by the failure of the two-stage valve to open. Who is correct?
   A. Technician A
   B. Technician B
   C. Both Technician A and Technician B
   D. Neither Technician A nor Technician B

_____ 7. While discussing the efficiency of the DD16 engine, Technician A says the axial power turbine (APT) converts normally wasted exhaust energy to mechanical energy over all speed and load ranges. Technician B says that the DD15, not the DD16, uses an APT. Who is correct?
   A. Technician A
   B. Technician B
   C. Both Technician A and Technician B
   D. Neither Technician A nor Technician B

_____ **8.** To diagnose an engine fault code, Technician A says to use Detroit's Diagnostic Data Link (DDL) software. Technician B says Virtual Technician is the only software that can be used on late-model engines. Who is correct?
   A. Technician A
   B. Technician B
   C. Both Technician A and Technician B
   D. Neither Technician A nor Technician B

_____ **9.** Technician A says that a green light glowing on the water-in-fuel module of a DD13 engine indicates that fuel filter restriction was within the acceptable range. Technician B says that a red light indicates the secondary filter needs replacement. Who is correct?
   A. Technician A
   B. Technician B
   C. Both Technician A and Technician B
   D. Neither Technician A nor Technician B

_____ **10.** Technician A says that 2016 DD series GHG engines use an electromagnetic clutch on the engine's water pump. Technician B says that the diesel exhaust fluid (DEF) used by the SCR system is pressurized with an air-operated pump in Detroit's GHG engines. Who is correct?
   A. Technician A
   B. Technician B
   C. Both Technician A and Technician B
   D. Neither Technician A nor Technician B

Caterpillar

Chapter Review

The following activities have been designed to help you refresh your knowledge of this chapter. Your instructor may require you to complete some or all of these activities as a regular part of your training program. You are encouraged to complete any activity that your instructor does not assign as a way to enhance your learning.

Matching

Match the following terms with the correct description or example.

A. Advanced Combustion Emissions Reduction Technology (ACERT)

B. Caterpillar Regeneration System (CRS)

C. Full load setting (FLS)

D. Full torque setting (FTS)

E. Miller combustion cycle

_____ **1.** A calibration number used to determine the maximum amount of fuel injected at peak torque.

_____ **2.** A calibration number used to determine the maximum amount of fuel injected at rated speed.

_____ **3.** Caterpillar's marketing name given to its exhaust particulate filter system.

_____ **4.** A modified four-stroke engine operating cycle that varies the closing of the intake valve.

_____ **5.** A name given to a wide variety of Caterpillar's emissions reduction technologies.

Multiple Choice

Read each item carefully, and then select the best response.

_____ **1.** Caterpillar was the first company in the industry to introduce _____.
  A. turbocharging
  B. dual overhead cam engines
  C. hydraulic engine retarders
  D. All of the above

_____ **2.** What name does Caterpillar use to identify its exhaust gas recirculation system?
  A. Environmental system
  B. Clean gas induction system
  C. Emission reduction system
  D. Combustion trapping system

_____ **3.** The 140-pin _____ ECM was introduced for ACERT engines and was used until the last 2009 on-highway engines were produced.
  A. PEEC II
  B. ADEM III
  C. ADEM 4
  D. PEEC III

_____ **4.** Every flash file contains a unique _____ that corresponds to the horsepower rating, engine family, and the emission certification of the flash file.
  A. E-trim code
  B. personality module code
  C. Cat EUI number
  D. ADEM II code

_____ 5. Caterpillar's _____ can be used as a web-based system or as DVDs to access all of its product information, service bulletins, and service manuals.
   A. Service Information System
   B. Diagnostic Analysis System
   C. Virtual Technician
   D. Executive Management System

_____ 6. The _____ is a fueling parameter used by Caterpillar that corresponds to a point on an electronic torque rise curve or fuel map.
   A. full load setting
   B. fuel consumption rate
   C. full torque setting
   D. Both A and C

_____ 7. To meet the 2004 EPA emissions requirements, Caterpillar introduced what they referred to as _____.
   A. Advanced Combustion Emissions Reduction Technology (ACERT)
   B. Caterpillar Electronic Technician (Cat ET)
   C. Advanced Diesel Engine Management (ADEM)
   D. Hydraulically Amplified Direct Injection (HADI)

_____ 8. The _____ is not used at idle or during low load conditions because there is inadequate heat in low-pressure boost conditions, and cooling system temperature could drop and cause the engine to overcool.
   A. air-to-air-charge air cooler
   B. turbo induction cooler
   C. jacket water pre-cooler
   D. cooled exhaust gas recirculation system

_____ 9. To meet EPA07 NO_x requirements, Caterpillar ACERT engine technology added a _____.
   A. diesel particulate filter
   B. variable intake valve actuator
   C. cooled exhaust gas recirculation system
   D. Both A and C

_____ 10. All CT series trucks come equipped with a standard telematics system called _____.
   A. Fleet Watch
   B. Product Link
   C. OnStar
   D. DAVIE

True/False

If you believe the statement to be more true than false, write the letter "T" in the space provided. If you believe the statement to be more false than true, write the letter "F".

_____ 1. Caterpillar's first diesel engine, the D9900, weighed 5175 lbs., and produced only 89 horsepower at 700 rpm.

_____ 2. Caterpillar uses a balancing shaft dampening system on the cam gear to provide torsional vibration control.

_____ 3. The H1B-300 injector is capable of five different injection rate shapes and an electrically controlled pilot injection.

_____ 4. Continental's dual-servo actuated common rail injector design is the first of its kind that can produce three different injection rate shapes.

_____ 5. Unlike other common rail systems, Caterpillar's normally open common rail pump actuators will allow fuel to drain from the rail within a minute of engine shutdown.

_____ 6. Caterpillar requires technicians to record two numbers when replacing an injector or ECM: an injector E-trim number and the injector personality code.

_____ 7. Caterpillar's ACERT engines center around their common rail fuel system and asymmetrical turbocharger.

_____ **8.** When using variable intake valve actuation, the Miller cycle does not work during low-speed, low-load operation.

_____ **9.** During series turbocharging the output from the low-pressure turbocharger passes into the inlet of the high-pressure turbocharger compressor housing in order to multiply maximum boost pressure.

_____ **10.** Caterpillar sensors have a much longer bounce period to detect a fault and will not log a code for 30 seconds after a fault has occurred.

Fill in the Blank

Read each item carefully, and then complete the statement by filling in the missing word(s).

1. In 2004, Caterpillar introduced series turbocharging and variable valve timing to heavy-duty engines, which enabled the use of a _____ combustion cycle.

2. The use of a _____ _____ next to the liner flanges makes the liner less sensitive to height variations that lead to combustion and coolant leaks.

3. Electronic unit injectors are located in a stainless steel injector sleeve to prevent _____ erosion from the cooling system.

4. Caterpillar's C9.3, C6.6, and C4.4 engines are built using the Caterpillar _____ _____ fuel system designed by Continental, a major supplier to the automotive industry.

5. Two _____ _____ can be removed from the bell housing to insert a timing pin to lock cylinder 1 at TDC and another plug to insert a pinion tool to rotate the engine.

6. Continental's direct drive _____ injector uses more than 300 thin ceramic wafers to mechanically actuate the pressure control valve regulating nozzle movement.

7. Cat ET is the _____ used to perform Caterpillar electronic service or diagnostics.

8. The _____ _____ control limit, which is reported in cubic millimeters, refers to the maximum quantity of fuel that can be injected for a given engine speed and load condition.

9. The first ACERT engines in 2004 used series turbocharging along with _____ _____ valve actuation.

10. On 2004 ACERT engines, Caterpillar used an _____ converter similar to the technology used by spark ignition gasoline fueled engines.

Labeling

Label the following diagrams with the correct terms.

1. Identify the components of a Caterpillar mechanically actuated electronically controlled unit injector (MEUI):

A. _____

B. _____

C. _____

D. _____

E. _____

F. _____

G. _____

2. Identify the parts of Caterpillar's common rail injector:

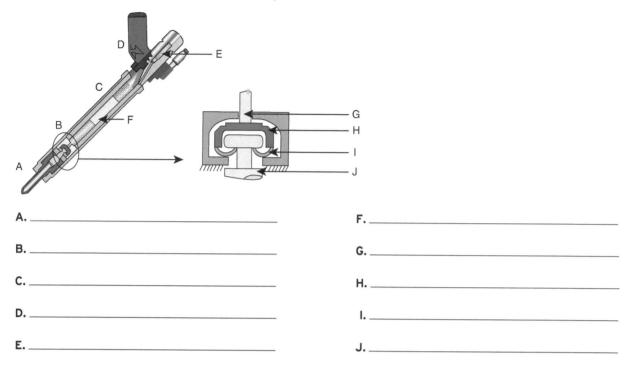

A. _____

B. _____

C. _____

D. _____

E. _____

F. _____

G. _____

H. _____

I. _____

J. _____

Skill Drills

Test your knowledge of skill drills by filling in the correct words in the photo captions.

1. Exchanging Injectors:

Step 1: Record the injector _____ _____ and the injector _____
_____ for each injector.

Step 2: Click on Service Software Files in _____ _____ _____.

Step 3: Enter the _____ number for the _____ in the _____ field.

Step 4: Download the _____ _____ _____ to the PC. Repeat this
procedure for each _____ as required.

Step 5: Connect _____ _____ to the _____ _____
connector (DLC).

Step 6:   Select the following _____ _____ on Cat ET:

- _____
- _____
- _____ _____ Calibration·

Step 7:   Select the appropriate _____.

Step 8:   Click the _____ button.

Step 9:   Select the appropriate injector _____ _____ from the _____.

Step 10:   Click the _____ button.

Step 11:   If you are _____ by Cat ET, enter the injector _____ _____ into the field. Note: The injector _____ _____ and the injector confirmation code are located on the _____. Cat ET may require the _____ of injector confirmation _____ during this process. Cat ET will _____ you for the _____ if necessary.

Step 12:   Click the _____ button. The injector _____ _____ is loaded into the _____.

Step 13:   Repeat the procedure for _____ _____ as required.

2. Programming a Flash File:

Step 1:   Obtain the _____ _____ for the new _____ _____. Note: If you do not have the flash file's _____ _____, use the Flash File _____ _____ on the Service Technician _____ (STW). Alternatively, use the Flash Software Files feature on _____ _____ _____. You must have the _____ serial number in order to search for the _____ file's _____ number.

Step 2:   Connect _____ _____ to the _____.

Step 3:   Turn the ignition key _____ and engine _____. Do not _____ the engine.

Step 4:   Select _____ from the _____ menu on Cat ET. Note: If WinFlash will not communicate with the _____, refer to _____ without a _____ _____.

Step 5:   Select the _____ ECM under the _____ _____s.

Step 6:   Click the _____ button in order to select the _____ _____ of the flash file that will be _____ or _____ into the _____.

Step 7:   When the correct _____ _____ is selected, click the _____ button.

Step 8:   Verify that the file _____ match the _____. If the file _____ do not _____ the application, _____ for the _____ flash file.

Step 9: When the correct _____ _____ is selected, click the _____ _____ button. Cat ET will indicate when flash _____ has been successfully _____.

Step 10: Start the _____ and check for proper _____.

Step 11: Access the _____ screen under the _____ menu in order to determine the _____ that require programming. Look under the _____ column. All of the parameters should have a _____ of _____ or more. If a parameter has a tattletale of _____, adjust that _____.

3. Viewing Caterpillar Proprietary Diagnostic Codes:

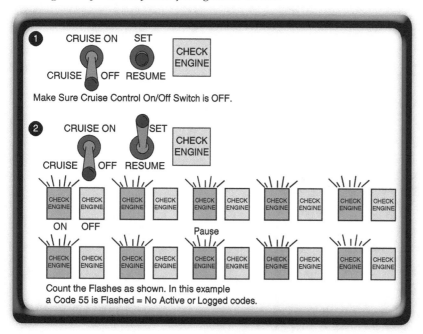

Step 1: Make sure the _____ _____ switch is set to the _____ position.

Step 2: Hold the cruise _____/_____ switch to the _____ or _____ position. Release the switch when the _____ _____ begins to _____.

Step 3: Count the number of _____. Short _____ between flashes indicate a _____ of _____. Long pauses _____ codes.

Step 4: A flash code of _____ indicates there are no _____ or _____ fault codes.

Crossword Puzzle

Use the clues in the column to complete the puzzle.

Across

3. A plate located between the engine block deck and cylinder head used on high-horsepower Caterpillar engines. The plate reduces stress transmitted to the cylinder liners.
5. Refers to the location of an engine camshaft near the engine block deck. High-mounted camshafts enable the use of shorter, less heavy pushrods.

Down

1. A patented camshaft gear design used for dampening torsional vibration transmission to the camshaft.
2. The process of uploading a new engine calibration file. A calibration file contains unique set of data or look-up tables needed by engine operating algorithms to control a particular engine model.
4. The marketing name given by Caterpillar to describe the injector calibration code assigned to Caterpillar injectors.

ASE-Type Questions

Read each item carefully, and then select the best response.

_____ 1. Technician A says Caterpillar engines use the variable intake valve actuator (VIVA) to vary the length of the compression stroke to increase engine efficiency. Technician B says the VIVA varies the beginning of the intake stroke to reduce parasitic power loss. Who is correct?

    A. Technician A

    B. Technician B

    C. Both Technician A and Technician B

    D. Neither Technician A nor Technician B

_____ 2. Technician A says Caterpillar series turbocharged engines cool intake air charges using two air-to-air charge air coolers. Technician B says a liquid and an air charge air cooler are used. Who is correct?

    A. Technician A

    B. Technician B

    C. Both Technician A and Technician B

    D. Neither Technician A nor Technician B

_____ 3. Technician A says Miller cycle engines delay the closing of the intake valve for the longest time when an engine is idling. Technician B says that the compression stroke becomes shorter as turbocharger boost pressure increases. Who is correct?

    A. Technician A

    B. Technician B

    C. Both Technician A and Technician B

    D. Neither Technician A nor Technician B

_____ 4. Technician A says that oil supply to the VIVA is electronically controlled. Technician B says the oil to the ACERT series turbochargers is electronically controlled to vary boost pressure. Who is correct?

    A. Technician A

    B. Technician B

    C. Both Technician A and Technician B

    D. Neither Technician A nor Technician B

_____ 5. Technician A says that oil supply to the VIVA is electronically controlled. Technician B says the oil to the ACERT series turbochargers is electronically controlled to vary boost pressure. Who is correct?

    A. Technician A

    B. Technician B

    C. Both Technician A and Technician B

    D. Neither Technician A nor Technician B

_____ 6. Technician A says Caterpillar sources exhaust gas for recirculation from an EGR valve located on the exhaust manifold. Technician B says exhaust gas is sourced from briefly opening the exhaust valve during the engine's intake stroke. Who is correct?

    A. Technician A

    B. Technician B

    C. Both Technician A and Technician B

    D. Neither Technician A nor Technician B

_____ 7. Technician A says supplemental heating of the particulate filter for Caterpillar's exhaust aftertreatment system is performed by the fuel injectors using a post-combustion injection event. Technician B says a fuel dosing valve located after the turbochargers is used to provide fuel for supplemental heating of the DPF. Who is correct?

    A. Technician A

    B. Technician B

    C. Both Technician A and Technician B

    D. Neither Technician A nor Technician B

_____ **8.** Technician A says that an oxidation converter is used to produce flameless combustion of fuel for supplemental heating of the particulate filter. Technician B says a spark plug ignites fuel in the exhaust system used to heat the particulate filter. Who is correct?
  A. Technician A
  B. Technician B
  C. Both Technician A and Technician B
  D. Neither Technician A nor Technician B

_____ **9.** Technician A says diagnosing fault codes on Caterpillar engines can be performed using Product Link. Technician B says Cat Electronic Technician (Cat ET) should be used. Who is correct?
  A. Technician A
  B. Technician B
  C. Both Technician A and Technician B
  D. Neither Technician A nor Technician B

_____ **10.** Technician A and Technician B are considering how to upload an injector calibration code in an excavator machine located on a job site. Technician A says a calibration file can be uploaded from a DVD. Technician B says the calibration file can be obtained through Cat Service Information System (SIS) software, which has Cat ET as a component. Who is correct?
  A. Technician A
  B. Technician B
  C. Both Technician A and Technician B
  D. Neither Technician A nor Technician B

Volvo–Mack and PACCAR

Chapter Review

The following activities have been designed to help you refresh your knowledge of this chapter. Your instructor may require you to complete some or all of these activities as a regular part of your training program. You are encouraged to complete any activity that your instructor does not assign as a way to enhance your learning.

Matching

Match the following terms with the correct description or example.

A. 7th injector

B. Econovance variable injection timing system

C. Gear fast run slow

D. High torque rise engine

E. Multi-torque

_____ **1.** An engine with the capability of changing its torque rise based on operating conditions.

_____ **2.** Volvo–Mack's name for a hydrocarbon dosing valve that sprays diesel fuel into the exhaust system after the turbocharger.

_____ **3.** An engine that has a sharp increase in torque as engine rpm drops from cruising speed when under heavy loads.

_____ **4.** A fuel-efficient operating strategy used to take advantage of a diesel engine's low rpm torque.

_____ **5.** A partial authority fuel system used by Mack trucks.

Multiple Choice

Read each item carefully, and then select the best response.

_____ **1.** Kenworth and Peterbilt are part of _____, a global producer of premium medium- and heavy-duty trucks.
   A. Mac Trucks Inc.
   B. The Volvo Group
   C. PACCAR, Inc.
   D. Delphi International

_____ **2.** In 2000, Volvo's _____ system was upgraded to include J-1934 on-board network communication capabilities.
   A. DAVIE
   B. VECTRO
   C. PACE
   D. VIVA

_____ **3.** Volvo's current diagnostic software is called _____.
   A. Premium Tech Tool
   B. Volvo Electronic Technician
   C. Virtual Technician
   D. Volvo Computer-Aided Diagnostics Systems

_____ **4.** Mack engines used in low-speed vocational operations, rather than in on-highway trucks, were called _____ engines.
   A. MackForce
   B. VMAC
   C. Econodyne
   D. PowerStroke

_____ **5.** The _____ system introduced in 1994 included 30 programmable operating features such as trip-recording functions, PTO operation, idle shutdown, and emergency shutdown features.
   A. VMAC
   B. VMAC II
   C. VMAC III
   D. VMAC IV

_____ **6.** The Mack _____ emission reduction strategy relied on the use of high-pressure cooled exhaust gas recirculation technology.
   A. ASET AC
   B. ASET AD
   C. ASET AF
   D. ASET AI

_____ **7.** The _____ injector is used across all Mack MP engines, the Volvo D12-C, and 2007 and later D-series engines.
   A. Delphi E3
   B. CR14
   C. MEUI
   D. HPI-TPI

_____ **8.** The Volvo–Mack _____ enables communication between modules to control a variety of engine, vehicle, and cab functions.
   A. engine controlled area network
   B. vehicle electronic control unit
   C. vehicle controlled area network
   D. aftertreatment control area network

_____ **9.** Volvo D12 engine uses an exhaust pressure governor to _____.
   A. speed engine warm-up
   B. operate as an exhaust brake
   C. apply exhaust system backpressure during idle EGR
   D. All of the above

_____ **10.** The earliest EGR system used by Volvo on the D12-C engine was called the _____ system.
   A. internal EGR
   B. V-pulse I-EGR
   C. high-pressure cooled EGR
   D. clean gas induction EGR

_____ **11.** The normal DPF catalyst filter element expected cleaning or replacement interval on a Volvo–Mack engine is _____.
   A. 100,000 miles
   B. 200,000 miles
   C. 250,000 miles
   D. 300,000 miles

_____ **12.** Accidentally adding diesel fuel to the DEF reservoir may result in _____.
   A. aftertreatment SCR system damage
   B. damaged injectors
   C. exhaust system corrosion between the turbocharger and DPF
   D. All of the above

_____ **13.** The cylinder block and cylinder head of PACCAR's MX engines are made out of _____.
   A. cast iron
   B. aluminum alloy
   C. compacted graphite iron
   D. carbon steel

_____ **14.** PACCAR uses a service diagnostic tool called _____.
   A. DAVIE
   B. Roadmaster diagnostics
   C. OnCommand
   D. Virtual Technician

_____ **15.** PACCAR's engine idle shutdown timer can be adjusted to reset the countdown to engine shutdown based on the _____.
- **A.** accelerator pedal
- **B.** parking brake
- **C.** engine load
- **D.** All of the above

True/False

If you believe the statement to be more true than false, write the letter "T" in the space provided. If you believe the statement to be more false than true, write the letter "F".

_____ **1.** Mack's and Volvo's engine systems and features share the same names and acronyms.

_____ **2.** Volvo's V-pulse EGR system used only in vocational trucks and industrial engines used a variable geometry turbocharger to increase exhaust backpressure.

_____ **3.** Together all the Volvo D-series engines share a 94% parts commonality in design and function.

_____ **4.** A chrome-plated bulldog hood ornament indicates that the entire truck is made of Mack components.

_____ **5.** Newer Mack Power engines have multi-torque capabilities, which Mack and Volvo call the Eco-Torque Performance feature.

_____ **6.** Mass-based variable torque is an engine governor control function that automatically adjusts engine torque output to match vehicle weight.

_____ **7.** There are four different identification markings on the E3 injector electrical connector.

_____ **8.** Diesel engines do not warm up when idling and, in fact, will cool from operating temperatures when idling.

_____ **9.** There is an adjustment screw on the exhaust valve bridge used to easily adjust exhaust valve clearances.

_____ **10.** Operation of the I-EGR system is based on meeting low NO_x requirements under various engine operating conditions.

_____ **11.** EGR cooler efficiency is evaluated by comparing cooler outlet temperature with exhaust and engine coolant temperature.

_____ **12.** The Volvo MP7 with a vertical back of cab (VBOC) is designed to meet EPA10 emissions standards and requires a spark-assisted DPF system.

_____ **13.** A failure of the system NO_x sensors to identify a proper drop in NO_x readings in the aftertreatment system will trigger a DEF Tank Level Sensor fault.

_____ **14.** PACCAR currently ranks second in the United States and third globally in the number of heavy vehicles produced, behind only Daimler AG in the U.S. market.

_____ **15.** A speed density measurement system and oxygen sensor is used to adjust and monitor EGR flow on the latest MX-13 engine.

Fill in the Blank

Read each item carefully, and then complete the statement by filling in the missing word(s).

1. The overhead camshafts on all Volvo engines have a _____ torsional dampener to improve valve timing.

2. The dual solenoid Delphi E3 injector used in Volvo's D-series engines used _____-_____-_____ injection with up to 35,000 psi (2413 bar) injection pressures and the ability to perform multiple injection events.

3. Mack's line of high _____ _____ engines, marketed first as Maxidyne engines, operated in a range of 1050–1700 rpm, at first using an unconventional large stepped five-speed transmission.

4. To meet standards for the first big reduction in engine emissions, Mack developed a _____-_____ electronically controlled injection pump-line-nozzle fuel system.

5. The current-controlled _____ _____ fuel system used two injection phases—essentially, a pilot and main injection event.

6. The _____ _____ is entered into ECM memory using the parameter programming feature in Premium Tech Tool.

7. All MP and Volvo engines use a _____ _____ pressure fuel system configuration.

8. Volvo–Mack engines have two fuel system _____ _____: one on the fuel filter and the other on the cylinder head.

9. On engines with the Volvo _____ _____, the camshaft has two additional smaller lobes: an induction or intake lobe and decompression lobe.

10. The exhaust _____ _____ on an engine with a compression brake are larger because they contain a check valve, pressure-limiting valve, and plunger at the valve bridge end of the rocker lever.

11. Intake manifold _____ and possibly some engine damage can take place when moisture-laden exhaust gases are allowed to condense in the intake manifold.

12. When an _____ regeneration of the DPF is required, supplemental heating by the oxidation converter of the DPF takes place by dosing the exhaust gases with fuel.

13. The PACCAR MX engine uses _____ _____ technology for the main bearing caps and connecting rods.

14. The PACCAR MX uses two _____ _____ to supply the fuel volume and injection pressure to the injectors.

15. Every PACCAR MX fuel injector is calibrated during production to compensate for any production tolerances and an injector _____ _____ is etched on the surface of the electrical connector for the injector.

Labeling

Label the following diagrams with the correct terms.

1. Identify the parts of a Bosch unit pump:

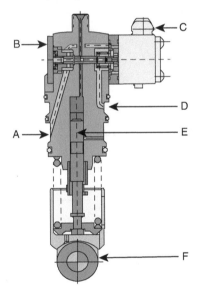

A. _____

B. _____

C. _____

D. _____

E. _____

F. _____

2. Identify the components of a Volvo–Mack compact DPF:

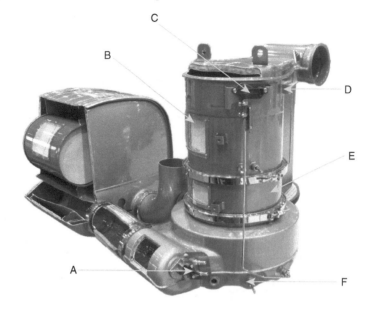

A. _____   D. _____

B. _____   E. _____

C. _____   F. _____

3. Identify the parts of a Volvo–Mack SCR:

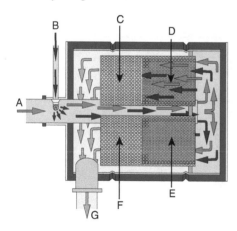

A. _____

B. _____

C. _____

D. _____

E. _____

F. _____

G. _____

4. Identify the components of a UHPCR fuel rail:

A. _____

B. _____

C. _____

D. _____

E. _____

Skill Drills

Test your knowledge of skill drills by filling in the correct words in the photo captions.

1. Bleeding a Volvo–Mack Fuel System:

Step 1:   Clean around the _____ _____ on the fuel filter _____ and cylinder _____.

Step 2:   Connect a plastic _____ to the _____ _____ housing bleeder screw. Open the bleeder screw and _____ the _____ _____ until _____ fuel runs out of the _____. Tighten the _____ _____ while _____ is still running out.

Step 3:   Attach the bleeder _____ to the rear _____ _____ bleeder screw and _____ any _____ using the same techniques in Step 2. Move to the _____ of the cylinder _____ and _____ that screw the same way.

Step 4:   Start the _____ and allow it to run at _____ _____, or with the _____ engaged, for about _____ minutes to remove _____ from the _____. Recheck the _____ system for _____.

2. Draining the Charge Air Cooler:

Step 1: Remove the _____ _____ from the bottom of the _____.

Step 2: Drain the cooler _____ and _____ into a _____.

Step 3: Start the engine and _____ the engine to _____ _____ for _____ minute to push any remaining _____ and _____ out the cooler.

Step 4: Reinstall the _____ _____.

3. Adjusting for Engine Idle Shutdown:

Step 1: Open _____ _____ _____ (PEP), which is a North American _____ application used for making changes or _____ engine _____.

Step 2: Select Engine Idle _____ _____ (EIST) from the list of _____ parameters.

Step 3: Select _____ _____ and _____ the new setting within the _____-_____ parameter _____.

Crossword Puzzle

Use the clues in the column to complete the puzzle.

Across

3. The reduction of power output by 25% or more in response to an emission-related engine fault code or an engine protection fault code.

4. An acronym for Volvo electronic control system for engine electronics.

Down

1. A steel plate attached to the oil pan rails to minimize vibration and torsional movement of the crankcase in high-horsepower engines.

2. The engine rpm where cylinder pressures are highest.

3. Service and diagnostic software used by PACCAR. It is an acronym for DAF Vehicle Investigation Tool. In North America, DAVIE refers to Diagnostic Analysis for Vehicle Interface Equipment.

ASE-Type Questions

Read each item carefully, and then select the best response.

_____ 1. Technician A says that the Volvo exhaust backpressure governor (EPG) is used to reduce hydrocarbon emissions during cold start and warm-up conditions. Technician B says the EPG is used to speed up engine warm-up and maintain the engine operating temperature in cold conditions. Who is correct?
   A. Technician A
   B. Technician B
   C. Both Technician A and Technician B
   D. Neither Technician A nor Technician B

_____ 2. Technician A says that Volvo's engine brake system uses a compression release strategy to increase engine reading force. Technician B says that the EPG is used as an engine braking device. Who is correct?
   A. Technician A
   B. Technician B
   C. Both Technician A and Technician B
   D. Neither Technician A nor Technician B

_____ 3. Technician A says that the exhaust valves on Volvo D12-C engines are adjusted with shims. Technician B says the intake valves have an adjusting screw and are adjusted using a feeler blade. Who is correct?
   A. Technician A
   B. Technician B
   C. Both Technician A and Technician B
   D. Neither Technician A nor Technician B

_____ 4. Technician A says that late-model Volvo and Mack engines use throttle plates in the intake system to help increase exhaust system temperatures. Technician B says that late-model Volvo and Mack engines recirculate air from the turbocharger outlet and back into the intake system to increase exhaust temperatures. Who is correct?
   A. Technician A
   B. Technician B
   C. Both Technician A and Technician B
   D. Neither Technician A nor Technician B

_____ 5. Technician A says an SCR reservoir contaminated with diesel fuel will result in irreversible damage to the SCR catalysts. Technician B says the DEF dosing valve will plug with crystalized DEF. Who is correct?
   A. Technician A
   B. Technician B
   C. Both Technician A and Technician B
   D. Neither Technician A nor Technician B

_____ 6. Technician A says that PACCAR MX engines use two-speed electromagnetic clutches on the water pump's drive shafts. Technician B says the engine-mounted air compressor uses electromagnetic clutches to load and unload the compressor. Who is correct?
   A. Technician A
   B. Technician B
   C. Both Technician A and Technician B
   D. Neither Technician A nor Technician B

_____ 7. Technician A says that PACCAR MX engines with common rail have two electrically controlled valves to regulate fuel rail pressure. Technician B says both electrically operated valves used to regulate rail pressure are located on the unit pumps. Who is correct?
   A. Technician A
   B. Technician B
   C. Both Technician A and Technician B
   D. Neither Technician A nor Technician B

_____ **8.** Technician A says that late-model Volvo and Mack engines use hydraulically controlled EGR valves. Technician B says the valves are air actuated. Who is correct?

    A. Technician A

    B. Technician B

    C. Both Technician A and Technician B

    D. Neither Technician A nor Technician B

_____ **9.** Technician A says that Mack engines used electronically controlled unit pumps. Technician B says that PACCAR MX engines used electronically controlled unit pumps. Who is correct?

    A. Technician A

    B. Technician B

    C. Both Technician A and Technician B

    D. Neither Technician A nor Technician B

_____ **10.** Technician A says that a chassis air supply will flow through the SCR DEF dosing valve on late-model Volvo and Mack engines. Technician B says that only DEF flows through the DEF dosing valve. Who is correct?

    A. Technician A

    B. Technician B

    C. Both Technician A and Technician B

    D. Neither Technician A nor Technician B

CHAPTER 40

Commercial Vehicle Batteries

Chapter Review

The following activities have been designed to help you refresh your knowledge of this chapter. Your instructor may require you to complete some or all of these activities as a regular part of your training program. You are encouraged to complete any activity that your instructor does not assign as a way to enhance your learning.

Matching

Match the following terms with the correct description or example.

A. Amp-hour

B. Cold cranking amps (CCA)

C. Cranking amps (CA)

D. Electrical capacity

E. Reserve capacity

_____ **1.** A measurement of the load, in amps, that a battery can deliver for 30 seconds while maintaining a voltage of 1.2 volts per cell or higher at 32°F (–0°C).

_____ **2.** The time, in minutes, that a new, fully charged battery at 80°F (26.7°C) will supply a constant load of 25 amps without its voltage dropping below 10.5 volts for a 12-volt battery.

_____ **3.** A measurement of the load, in amps, that a battery can deliver for 30 seconds while maintaining a voltage of 1.2 volts per cell or higher at 0°F (–18°C).

_____ **4.** The amount of electrical current a lead acid battery can supply.

_____ **5.** A measure of how much amperage a battery can continually supply over a 20-hour period without the battery voltage falling below 10.5 volts.

Multiple Choice

Read each item carefully, and then select the best response.

_____ **1.** Water containing _____ would be considered an electrolyte.

  A. salt

  B. acids

  C. alkaline solutions

  D. All of the above

_____ **2.** The first battery was built by _____, who alternately stacked copper and zinc plates separated with a piece of saltwater-soaked cardboard.

  A. Galvani

  B. Tesla

  C. Volta

  D. Joule

_____ **3.** Batteries used for cranking purposes have unique construction features and are commonly called _____.

  A. starting, lighting, and ignition (SLI) batteries

  B. absorbed glass mat (AGM) batteries

  C. valve-regulated lead acid (VRLA) batteries

  D. recombinant batteries

_____ **4.** Current demands on the battery when the ignition is switched off are called _____.
  A. key-off electrical loads
  B. stray currents
  C. parasitic draw
  D. Either A or C

_____ **5.** Rechargeable batteries used for propulsion in hybrid electric vehicles are called _____.
  A. deep cycle batteries
  B. traction batteries
  C. recombinant batteries
  D. valve-regulated lead acid (VRLA) batteries

_____ **6.** The electrodes and electrolyte of a lead acid battery cell produce _____ volts.
  A. 2.1
  B. 3.2
  C. 6
  D. 12

_____ **7.** A squeeze bulb and float type _____ is an instrument used to measure the density or the specific gravity of batteries.
  A. hygrometer
  B. dielectric tester
  C. hydrometer
  D. refractometer

_____ **8.** A specific gravity reading of 1.155 and an open circuit voltage of 12.06 would indicate that the battery was at a _____ state of charge.
  A. 25%
  B. 50%
  C. 75%
  D. 100%

_____ **9.** Battery Council International group numbers are established according to _____.
  A. physical case size
  B. terminal type
  C. terminal placement
  D. All of the above

_____ **10.** Automotive battery capacity is rated by _____.
  A. cranking amps (CA)
  B. cold cranking amps (CCA)
  C. reserve capacity
  D. All of the above

True/False

If you believe the statement to be more true than false, write the letter "T" in the space provided. If you believe the statement to be more false than true, write the letter "F".

_____ **1.** Primary batteries are the most practical for use in automotive applications because they can be used over and over again.

_____ **2.** Tap water will not conduct current.

_____ **3.** Lead acid batteries are the most common battery used in the transportation industry.

_____ **4.** Flooded lead acid batteries refer to battery cell construction where the electrodes are made from thin lead (Pb) plates submersed in liquid electrolyte.

_____ **5.** Plates are connected together in series to increase the amperage or capacity of a battery.

_____ **6.** The primary difference between deep cycle batteries and SLI batteries is the thickness of the plates.

_____ **7.** During charging and discharging, the specific gravity of the electrolyte changes.

_____ **8.** The common battery capacity ratings used by North American manufacturers are established by the International Electrotechnical Commission.

_____ **9.** In cold weather, battery power drops drastically because the electrolyte thickens and cold temperatures slow chemical activity inside the battery.

_____ **10.** The only way galvanic reaction will stop in a battery is if the electrical load is removed.

Fill in the Blank

Read each item carefully, and then complete the statement by filling in the missing word(s).

1. The single direction electrons flow during discharge means a battery is a source of _____ current.

2. In a _____ battery, chemical reactions are not reversible, and the battery cannot be recharged.

3. Corrosion is one example of a _____ reaction.

4. A(n) _____ consists of two dissimilar metals: an insulator material separating the metals and an electrolyte, which is an electrically conductive solution.

5. A(n) _____ _____ battery is used to deliver a lower, steady level of power for a much longer period of time than an SLI-type battery.

6. Connecting cells together in _____ allows batteries to be produced in a variety of output voltage.

7. To prevent the battery positive and negative plate from touching and short circuiting, _____ plates are placed between each plate in every cell.

8. Lead acid battery _____ is a mixture of 36% sulfuric acid and 64% water.

9. A battery's internal _____ determines how quickly a battery can be charged or discharged.

10. Introduced in the middle 1970s, no- and low-maintenance batteries reduce or eliminate the _____ content in grids.

Labeling

Label the following diagrams with the correct terms.

1. Identify the components of a wet cell battery:

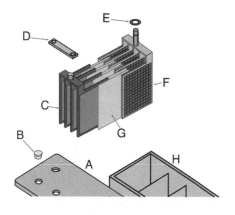

A. _____

B. _____

C. _____

D. _____

E. _____

F. _____

G. _____

H. _____

2. Identify the various types of battery terminals with their correct identification:

1. _____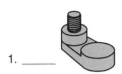

2. _____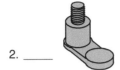

3. _____

4. _____

5. _____

6. _____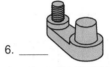

7. _____

8. _____

9. _____

A. Universal terminal (UT)

B. Low profile terminal (LPT)

C. Stud terminal (ST)

D. Wingnut terminal (WNT)

E. Automotive post and stud terminal (DT)

F. Dual wingnut terminal (DWNT)

G. High profile terminal (HPT)

H. L-terminal (LT)

I. Automotive post terminal (AP)

Crossword Puzzle

Use the clues in the column to complete the puzzle.

Across

3. An electrically conductive solution.

4. A chemical reaction that produces electricity when two dissimilar metals are placed in an electrolyte.

5. A situation that occurs when overcharging or rapid charging causes some gas to escape from the battery.

Down

1. The use of electricity to break down water into hydrogen and oxygen gases.

2. A chemical reaction that results in the soft sulfate turning to a hardened crystalline form that cannot be driven from the plates in the battery.

ASE-Type Questions

Read each item carefully, and then select the best response.

_____ 1. Technician A says that hybrid electric vehicles are not commonplace in urban transit but are likely to be in the future. Technician B says that commercial equipment, particularly diesel-powered equipment, will use multiple batteries connected in series or parallel to produce adequate starting current. Who is correct?
   A. Technician A
   B. Technician B
   C. Both Technician A and Technician B
   D. Neither Technician A nor Technician B

_____ 2. Technician A says that a spiral cell (Optima battery) is not considered a sealed lead acid (SLA) battery. Technician B says that an absorbed glass mat (AGM) battery is not considered a sealed lead acid (SLA) battery. Who is correct?
   A. Technician A
   B. Technician B
   C. Both Technician A and Technician B
   D. Neither Technician A nor Technician B

_____ 3. Technician A says that a fully charged 12-volt battery is 12.00 volts. Technician B says that connecting cells together in series allow batteries to be produced in a variety of output voltage. Who is correct?
   A. Technician A
   B. Technician B
   C. Both Technician A and Technician B
   D. Neither Technician A nor Technician B

_____ 4. Technician A says that the primary difference between deep cycle batteries and SLI is the thickness of the plates. Technician B says that deeply discharging SLI batteries dramatically shortens their service life. Who is correct?
   A. Technician A
   B. Technician B
   C. Both Technician A and Technician B
   D. Neither Technician A nor Technician B

_____ 5. Technician A says that lead acid battery electrolyte is a mixture of 64% sulfuric acid and 36% water. Technician B says that sulfuric acid has a specific gravity of 1.835, which means it is much heavier than water. Who is correct?
   A. Technician A
   B. Technician B
   C. Both Technician A and Technician B
   D. Neither Technician A nor Technician B

_____ 6. Technician A says that the battery case is usually made of polypropylene. Technician B says that ribbing and irregular features on the outside of the case add to the appearance of the battery and make it sturdy. Who is correct?
   A. Technician A
   B. Technician B
   C. Both Technician A and Technician B
   D. Neither Technician A nor Technician B

_____ 7. Technician A says that battery plates are made of two different compositions of lead that is fabricated from paste and bonded to lead-alloy grids. Technician B says that the negative plate uses lead peroxide (PbO_2) and the positive plate uses lead (Pb). Who is correct?
   A. Technician A
   B. Technician B
   C. Both Technician A and Technician B
   D. Neither Technician A nor Technician B

_____ **8.** Technician A says that both soft and hard sulfate can be driven from the plates, bringing the battery back into service. Technician B says that the latest innovation to lead acid battery technology incorporates black-carbon graphite foam into the plate paste to prevent sulfation damage. Who is correct?
   A. Technician A
   B. Technician B
   C. Both Technician A and Technician B
   D. Neither Technician A nor Technician B

_____ **9.** Technician A says that during charging and discharging, water in the electrolyte is broken apart into its constituent hydrogen and oxygen in a process called electrolysis. Technician B says if battery electrolyte is too low, the plates dry out, and the increased acid concentration of electrolyte permanently damages the grids. Who is correct?
   A. Technician A
   B. Technician B
   C. Both Technician A and Technician B
   D. Neither Technician A nor Technician B

_____ **10.** Technician A says that the latest and most advanced commercial vehicle battery technology are absorbed glass mat (AGM) batteries. Technician B says that the AGM battery can deliver more cranking amperage and absorb up to 10% more charging current than conventional lead acid. Who is correct?
   A. Technician A
   B. Technician B
   C. Both Technician A and Technician B
   D. Neither Technician A nor Technician B

Advanced Battery Technologies

Chapter Review

The following activities have been designed to help you refresh your knowledge of this chapter. Your instructor may require you to complete some or all of these activities as a regular part of your training program. You are encouraged to complete any activity that your instructor does not assign as a way to enhance your learning.

Matching

Match the following terms with the correct description or example.

A. Absorbed glass mat (AGM) battery

B. Gel cell battery

C. Lithium–ion (Li-ion) battery

D. Nickel–metal hydride (NiMH) battery

E. Spiral-wound cell battery

_____ **1.** A type of battery that does not use a galvanic reaction and in which a gel, salt, or solid material replaces the electrolyte solution.

_____ **2.** A type of lead acid battery that uses a thin fiberglass plate to absorb the electrolyte.

_____ **3.** A type of AGM battery in which the positive and negative electrodes are coiled into a tight spiral cell with an absorbent micro-glass mat placed between the plates.

_____ **4.** A type of battery to which silica has been added to the electrolyte solution to turn the solution to a gel-like consistency.

_____ **5.** A battery in which metal hydroxide forms the negative electrode and nickel oxide forms the positive electrode.

Multiple Choice

Read each item carefully, and then select the best response.

_____ **1.** The ability to convert charging current into storage capacity is known as _____.
  A. energy density
  B. deep cycling
  C. energy efficiency
  D. life span

_____ **2.** What type of batteries are used in consumer electronics and are also the preferred battery chemistry for hybrid drive vehicles?
  A. Lead acid
  B. Nickel–metal hydride (NiMH)
  C. Lithium–ion
  D. Nickel–cadmium (NiCad)

_____ **3.** Which type of battery chemistry produces the highest amount of voltage per cell?
  A. Lithium–ion
  B. Nickel–metal hydride (NiMH)
  C. Lead acid
  D. Ultra capacitors

_____ **4.** Which type of battery is used primarily in laptops, cell phones, and other consumer electronic devices?
  A. Nickel–cadmium (NiCad)
  B. Lithium–ion
  C. Spiral-wound
  D. Absorbed glass mat

_____ **5.** One lithium cell can replace _____ NiCad or NiMH cells, which have a cell voltage of only 1.2 volts.
  A. two
  B. three
  C. four
  D. five

_____ **6.** What is the advantage to using valve-regulated lead acid batteries?
  A. No need to add distilled water
  B. The fastest recharge possible
  C. No corrosive gas in battery compartment
  D. All of the above

_____ **7.** The battery case of a(n) _____ battery is pressurized constantly to between 1–4 psi (6.9–27.6 kPa).
  A. lead acid
  B. lithium–ion
  C. absorbed glass mat
  D. nickel–cadmium (NiCad)

_____ **8.** A deep cycle spiral cell battery will have a _____ top cover.
  A. blue
  B. red
  C. yellow
  D. green

_____ **9.** A(n) _____ is used to assist batteries for the first 1.5 seconds during cranking to supply an additional 2,000 amps of current to supplement the starter batteries.
  A. smart charger
  B. split charge relay
  C. ultra capacitor
  D. battery isolator

_____ **10.** A(n) _____ will sense battery voltage and drive a higher charge rate into weaker batteries and less current into stronger batteries.
  A. equalizer
  B. isolator
  C. balancer
  D. Either A or C

True/False

If you believe the statement to be more true than false, write the letter "T" in the space provided. If you believe the statement to be more false than true, write the letter "F".

_____ **1.** Energy efficiency is expressed in watt-hour per kilogram (Wh/kg) and watt-hour per liter (Wh/l).

_____ **2.** Nickel–metal hydride batteries provide twice the energy storage of lead acid batteries by weight, but only half the power output.

_____ **3.** Lithium-ion batteries are identical in construction as disposable lithium batteries.

_____ **4.** Cold temperatures slow down the nongalvanic reactions in lithium-ion batteries.

_____ **5.** Lithium-ion batteries cost eight times more than conventional lead acid batteries for each kilowatt of power produced per hour.

_____ **6.** There are two common types of valve-regulated lead acid batteries—absorbed glass mat and gel.

_____ **7.** Absorbed glass mat batteries can charge up to 10 times the rate of conventional lead acid batteries.

_____ **8.** The deeper the discharge between charges, the shorter the life cycle of the battery.

_____ **9.** Ultra capacitors are not worn out by continuous charge and discharge cycles.

_____ **10.** Battery equalizers enable charging of an auxiliary battery by the vehicle charging system and electrical separation of the auxiliary battery from the starting circuit when the engine shuts down.

Fill in the Blank

Read each item carefully, and then complete the statement by filling in the missing word(s).

1. The _____ _____ of a battery is measured by the number of charge/discharge cycles as a function of depth of discharge.

2. Lithium-ion batteries have low internal _____ and can discharge their current four times faster when compared to lead acid batteries.

3. _____ _____ _____ batteries eliminate water loss through a process called oxygen recombination.

4. Absorbed glass mat cells are extremely sensitive to damage from overcharging and should be charged using a(n) _____ charger.

5. A(n) _____-_____ cell battery is an absorbed glass mat battery in every way except that the electrodes for each cell are not made of rectangular plates.

6. In the mid-1960s, spill-proof batteries were introduced using _____ cells.

7. A(n) _____ _____ is capable of supplying large bursts of energy and quickly recharging, which makes them ideal for use in modern vehicles.

8. Components of the battery _____ system include battery isolators, low-voltage disconnects, battery balancers and equalizers, and battery monitors.

9. Devices that monitor battery voltage and disconnect noncritical electrical loads when the battery voltage level falls below a preset threshold value are called low-voltage _____.

10. Hybrid commercial vehicles use battery _____ to collect battery data for display to the operator and service technician.

Labeling

Label the following diagrams with the correct terms.

1. Identify the components of a flooded absorbed glass mat battery:

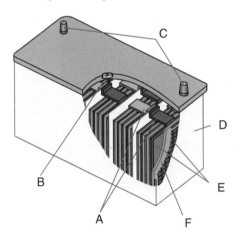

A. _____

B. _____

C. _____

D. _____

E. _____

F. _____

2. Identify the components of a spiral cell battery:

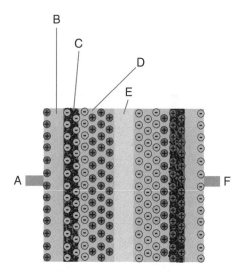

A. _____

B. _____

C. _____

D. _____

E. _____

3. Identify the components of a fully charged ultra capacitor:

A. _____

B. _____

C. _____

D. _____

E. _____

F. _____

Crossword Puzzle

Use the clues in the column to complete the puzzle.

Across

3. A system designed to separate the main starting battery and the auxiliary battery. Also called a battery isolator system.

4. A new generation of high-capacity and high-energy density capacitors.

5. A system of electrical devices used to manage battery performance.

Down

1. A battery charger with microprocessor-controlled charging rates and times.

2. Devices designed to adjust battery voltage to compensate for unequal charges in multiple batteries. Also called battery equalizers.

ASE-Type Questions

Read each item carefully, and then select the best response.

_____ 1. Technician A says that the demand for advanced battery technology in commercial vehicles is growing. Technician B says that, not only do the increasing popular hybrid electric vehicles require advanced batteries, heavy-duty commercial vehicles also have a greater need for electrical storage capacity to run accessories. Who is correct?

   A. Technician A
   B. Technician B
   C. Both Technician A and Technician B
   D. Neither Technician A nor Technician B

_____ 2. Technician A says that nickel–metal hydride (NiMH) is one type of battery used in commercial vehicles. Technician B says that lithium and lead acid batteries are also used in commercial vehicles. Who is correct?

   A. Technician A
   B. Technician B
   C. Both Technician A and Technician B
   D. Neither Technician A nor Technician B

_____ 3. Technician A says that lithium–ion cells maintain a constant voltage for over 90% of their discharge curve as compared to conventional lead acid batteries maintaining voltage until only 60% discharged. Technician B says that once charged, lithium–ion batteries self-discharge at very low rate. Who is correct?

   A. Technician A
   B. Technician B
   C. Both Technician A and Technician B
   D. Neither Technician A nor Technician B

_____ 4. Technician A says that one disadvantage of current lithium–ion battery technology is cost. Technician B says that lithium–ion batteries cost four times more than conventional lead acid batteries for each kilowatt of power produced per hour. Who is correct?

   A. Technician A
   B. Technician B
   C. Both Technician A and Technician B
   D. Neither Technician A nor Technician B

_____ 5. Technician A says that a VRLA battery has the highest cranking amps—even at low temperature. Technician B says that a VRLA battery has triple the life of traditional lead acid batteries. Who is correct?

   A. Technician A
   B. Technician B
   C. Both Technician A and Technician B
   D. Neither Technician A nor Technician B

_____ 6. Technician A says that no vents are used on AGM batteries. Technician B says that AGM batteries will be damaged if charged at greater than 13.2 volts. Who is correct?

   A. Technician A
   B. Technician B
   C. Both Technician A and Technician B
   D. Neither Technician A nor Technician B

_____ 7. Technician A says that a smart charger is a battery charger in which microprocessors control charging rates and times. Technician B says that AGM state of charge can be tested with a battery hydrometer. Who is correct?

   A. Technician A
   B. Technician B
   C. Both Technician A and Technician B
   D. Neither Technician A nor Technician B

_____ **8.** Technician A says that ultra capacitors supplement increases to starter torque and speed. Technician B says that ultra capacitors are currently used to assist batteries for the first 3.5 seconds during cranking, during which time they can supply an additional 1,000 amps of current to supplement the starter batteries. Who is correct?

A. Technician A

B. Technician B

C. Both Technician A and Technician B

D. Neither Technician A nor Technician B

_____ **9.** Technician A says that battery management systems (BMS) are designed to protect the cells or the battery from damage. Technician B says that battery management systems (BMS) are designed to prolong the life of the battery. Who is correct?

A. Technician A

B. Technician B

C. Both Technician A and Technician B

D. Neither Technician A nor Technician B

_____ **10.** Technician A says that battery balancers attempt to adjust battery voltage to compensate for unequal charges in multiple batteries. Technician B says that equalizers are found in many commercial applications using 24-volt charging systems, including transit and tour buses, private coaches, and off-highway equipment. Who is correct?

A. Technician A

B. Technician B

C. Both Technician A and Technician B

D. Neither Technician A nor Technician B

Servicing Commercial Vehicle Batteries

Chapter Review

The following activities have been designed to help you refresh your knowledge of this chapter. Your instructor may require you to complete some or all of these activities as a regular part of your training program. You are encouraged to complete any activity that your instructor does not assign as a way to enhance your learning.

Matching

Match the following terms with the correct description or example.

A. Constant-current charger

B. Constant-voltage charger

C. Intelligent charger

D. Taper-current charger

E. Trickle charger

_____ **1.** A direct current (DC) power that is a step-down transformer with a rectifier to provide the DC voltage to charge.

_____ **2.** A battery charger that charges at a low amperage rate.

_____ **3.** A battery charger that applies either constant voltage or constant amperage to the battery through a manually adjusted current selection switch.

_____ **4.** A battery charger that automatically varies the voltage applied to the battery to maintain a constant amperage flow into the battery.

_____ **5.** A battery charger that varies its output according to the sensed condition of the battery it is charging.

Multiple Choice

Read each item carefully, and then select the best response.

_____ **1.** Any voltage exceeding _____ volts between the negative battery post and the top of the battery indicates that the battery is leaking current due to excessive dirt or grime.

A. 0.25

B. 0.3

C. 0.4

D. 0.5

_____ **2.** Never wear _____ when working on or near batteries, as they may provide an accidental short-circuit path for high currents.

A. neck chains

B. watches

C. rings

D. Any of the above

_____ **3.** Subjecting a battery to prolonged undercharge conditions can cause _____.

A. oxidation

B. sulfation

C. grid corrosion

D. shedding

_____ **4.** A condition called _____ takes place primarily in the positive grid and is accelerated by overcharging and high temperatures.
  A. grid corrosion
  B. sulfation
  C. shedding
  D. calcification

_____ **5.** A fully charged battery should have an open-circuit voltage of _____ volts.
  A. 2.1
  B. 6.25
  C. 12.65
  D. 24

_____ **6.** The state of charge is best evaluated by measuring the density of electrolyte in each cell using a _____.
  A. refractometer
  B. spectrometer
  C. bulb-type hydrometer
  D. Either A or C

_____ **7.** If a battery has an open circuit voltage of 12.24 and a specific gravity reading of 1.190 it would indicate that the battery has a _____ state of charge.
  A. 100%
  B. 75%
  C. 50%
  D. 25%

_____ **8.** A _____ test performs a measurement of the amount of active plate surface area available for chemical reaction.
  A. state of charge
  B. conductance
  C. discharge
  D. load

_____ **9.** A(n) _____ charger can be left connected indefinitely without overcharging since it can maintain a float charge.
  A. intelligent
  B. pulsed
  C. trickle
  D. taper-current

_____ **10.** The voltage threshold of a low-voltage disconnect systems is normally set between _____.
  A. 2.1 and 2.3 volts
  B. 6.2 and 6.4 volts
  C. 12.2 and 12.4 volts
  D. 24.2 and 24.4 volts

True/False

If you believe the statement to be more true than false, write the letter "T" in the space provided. If you believe the statement to be more false than true, write the letter "F".

_____ **1.** To clean dirt and grime from the top of a battery you should use a mixture of diluted ammonia and baking soda.

_____ **2.** An explosive gas mixture consisting of hydrogen and oxygen is produced during the charging and discharging of a battery.

_____ **3.** To minimize self-discharge, batteries are best stored in cool, dry places.

_____ **4.** Although voltage and electrolyte readings may be satisfactory, contaminants even in one cell will cause the battery to self-discharge quickly.

_____ **5.** The readings from a refractometer must be corrected for electrolyte temperature.

_____ **6.** All manufacturers require the use of a state of charge test in order for warranty coverage to be considered.

———— **7.** The most sophisticated testers today can identify not only the type and condition of a battery, but also the manufacturer and other battery details.

———— **8.** If a battery fails a load test after it has had its state of charge properly qualified, the battery should be recharged and tested again.

———— **9.** Vehicle computer systems require a small amount of power to maintain the computer memory while the vehicle is off.

———— **10.** The recycling of batteries is mandatory.

Fill in the Blank

Read each item carefully, and then complete the statement by filling in the missing word(s).

1. A(n) _____ drain of battery current should be no more than 0.5 amps of current.

2. Always wear _____ clothing such as rubber gloves and goggles or full-face shields when handling batteries.

3. Always remove the _____ or ground terminal first when disconnecting battery cables.

4. A three-minute battery charge test can be used to verify a diagnosis of _____.

5. Excessive _____ can cause open circuits in the internal battery connections and "shed" or shake loose plate material, which settles to the bottom of the battery case.

6. Batteries should be given a _____ inspection before proceeding with any other significant tests.

7. A(n) _____ _____ _____ test will tell you how charged or discharged a battery is, not how much capacity it has.

8. The _____ _____ of electrolyte indicates the state cell charge.

9. A(n) _____ test determines the ability of a battery to deliver cranking amperage and is based on the battery CCA rating.

10. Batteries connected in _____ are connected side by side, with positive connected to positive and negative to negative.

Skill Drills

Test your knowledge of skill drills by filling in the correct words in the photo captions.

1. Performing a Battery State of Charge Test:

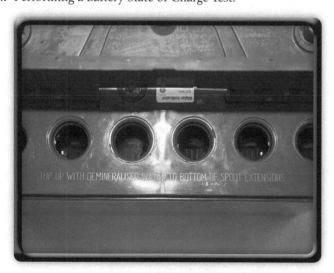

Step 1: If the battery is not a _____ unit, it will have individual or combined removable _____ on top. Remove them and look inside to check the level of the _____. If the level is below the tops of the _____ and their _____ inside, add _____ water or water with a low _____ content until it covers them. Be careful

not to overfill the cells; they could "boil" over when charging. If water is added, the battery will need to be _____ to ensure the newly added water mixes with the electrolyte before measuring the _____ _____.

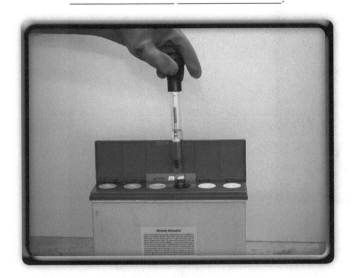

Step 2:   Using a _____ designed for battery testing, draw some of the electrolyte into the tester and look at the float inside it. A scale indicates the battery's relative _____ of _____ by measuring how high the float sits in relation to the _____ level. A very _____ overall reading (1.150 or below) indicates a low state of charge. A _____ overall reading (about 1.280) indicates a high state of charge. The reading from each _____ should be the same. If the variation between the highest and lowest cell exceed 0.050, the battery is _____ and should be _____. Be sure to consult temperature _____ _____ if the battery electrolyte temperature is not at or around 80°F (27°C).

Step 3:   Using the _____, place one or two _____ of electrolyte on the specimen window and lower the cover plate. Make sure the liquid completely _____ the _____ window. If not, add another drop of electrolyte:

- Look into the _____ with the refractometer under a bright _____.
- Read the scale for _____ _____. The point where the _____ area meets the _____ area is the reading. Compare the _____ with the values given in step 2.

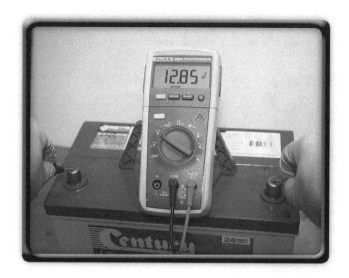

Step 4: For open circuit _____ testing with a _____, perform the following actions:
   a. With the engine not running, select the "_____ _____" position on your _____ and attach the _____ to the battery terminals (red to _____, black to _____).
   b. With all vehicle _____ switched _____ and the battery near 80°F (27°C), the voltage reading should be _____ volts if the battery is fully charged. This may be slightly lower at _____ temperatures.

2. Conductance Testing a Battery:

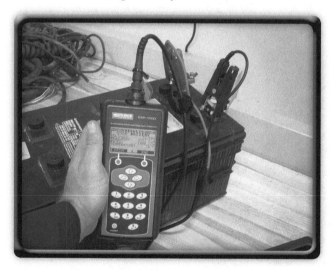

Step 1: Consult manufacturers' procedures and guidelines for the _____ being tested and _____ being used.

Step 2: Isolate batteries if they are _____ in a _____ so that they can be individually tested.

Step 3: Identify the type of _____, _____, and _____ for input into the test unit.

Step 4: Save information and _____ as required into the _____ _____.

Step 5: _____ the _____.

Step 6: Analyze the result by _____ them to manufacturer _____.

Step 7: Print or record _____ of the _____ _____. Repeat steps if _____ batteries are to be _____.

3. Load Testing a Battery:

Step 1: With the tester controls _____ and the _____ _____ turned to the off position, connect the tester _____ to the battery. Observe the correct _____ and be sure the _____ fully contact the battery _____.

Step 2: Place the inductive _____ _____ around either the _____ or the _____ tester _____ in the correct orientation.

Step 3: Verify that the battery's _____ _____ _____ is more than _____% before beginning the test. Also measure the battery's _____ to make any correction to the cut-off _____ threshold.

Step 4: If you are using an automatic _____ _____, enter the battery's _____ and select "test" or "start." If you are using a _____ load tester, calculate the _____ _____, which is _____ of the CCA. Turn the _____ _____ or press the "_____" button.

Step 5: Maintain _____ _____ of 1/2 the CCA rating for _____ seconds while watching the _____. At the end of the _____-second test load, read the voltmeter and immediately turn the control knob _____. At room temperature, the voltage must be _____ volts or higher at the end of the _____-second load. If the battery is _____ than room temperature, correct the battery failure _____ _____ against temperature. Close to 1/10 volt lower is allowed for every _____°F (12°C) below _____°F (21°C). Using the results from the test, determine any necessary action.

4. Jump-Starting Commercial Vehicles:

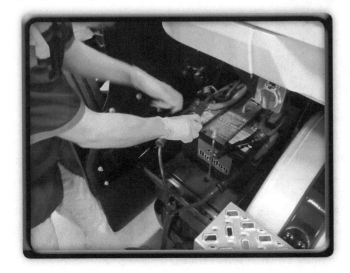

Step 1: Position the _____ battery close enough to the _____ battery that it is within comfortable range of your _____ _____. If the charged battery is in another vehicle, make sure the two vehicles are not _____.

Step 2: Always connect the leads in this order:

- First, connect the _____ jumper lead to the _____ terminal of the _____ battery in the vehicle you are trying to start. The _____ terminal is the one with the _____ sign.
- Next, connect the other end of this lead to the _____ _____ of the _____ battery.
- Then connect the _____ jumper lead to the _____ terminal of the _____ battery. The _____ terminal is the one with the _____ sign.
- Connect the other end of the _____ lead to a good _____ on the _____ of the vehicle with the _____ battery, and as far away as possible from the battery.
- DO NOT connect the lead to the _____ terminal of the _____ battery itself; doing so may cause a dangerous _____.

Step 3: Try to _____ the vehicle with the discharged battery. If the _____ battery does not have enough _____ or the jumper cables are too _____ in diameter to do this, _____ the _____ in the booster vehicle and allow it to partially _____ the discharged battery for several _____. Try starting the first vehicle again with the booster vehicle's engine _____.

Step 4: Disconnect the leads in the _____ _____ of connecting them. Remove the _____ lead from the chassis _____ away from the battery. Then disconnect the _____ lead from the _____ _____. Next remove the _____ lead from the booster battery, and lastly, disconnect the other _____ end from the battery in the vehicle you have just _____. If the _____ _____ is working correctly and the battery is in good condition, the battery will be _____ while the engine is running. Note, a deeply _____ set of batteries can cause the _____ to charge at an excessively high rate for too long and _____ the alternator.

5. Measuring Parasitic Draw on a Battery:

Step 1: Research the _____ _____ specifications in the appropriate service information for the vehicle you are diagnosing. Typically this is between _____ amps and _____ amps (_____–_____ milliamps).

Step 2: Connect the low-current _____ around (or insert the ammeter in _____ with) the _____ battery cable and _____ the parasitic draw. Compare the parasitic draw with _____.

Step 3: Disconnect the circuit fuses _____ at a time to determine the _____ of excessive parasitic _____ draw. Determine any necessary actions.

Crossword Puzzle

Use the clues in the column to complete the puzzle.

Across

3. A battery test that subjects the battery to a high rate of discharge, and the voltage is then measured after a set time to see how well the battery creates that current flow.

5. A battery charger that sends current into the battery in pulses of one-second cycles; used to recover sulfated batteries.

Down

1. A type of battery test that determines the battery's ability to conduct current.

2. A device that claps around a conductor to measure current flow. It is often used in conjunction with a digital volt-ohm meter (DVOM).

4. A process that reduces the plate surface area and therefore reduces capacity. This process may also produce short–circuits between the bottom of positive and negative plates.

ASE-Type Questions

Read each item carefully, and then select the best response.

_____ 1. Technician A says that batteries should be the starting point when diagnosing complaints such as hard starting, slow cranking, or no start. Technician B says that dirt on top of the battery does not cause premature self-discharge of the battery. Who is correct?
  A. Technician A
  B. Technician B
  C. Both Technician A and Technician B
  D. Neither Technician A nor Technician B

_____ 2. Technician A says you should never create a low-resistance connection or short across the battery terminals. Technician B says to always wear protective clothing such as rubber gloves and goggles or full-face shields when handling batteries. Who is correct?
  A. Technician A
  B. Technician B
  C. Both Technician A and Technician B
  D. Neither Technician A nor Technician B

_____ 3. Technician A says that a low electrolyte level is a common reason for sulfation. Technician B says that high ambient temperature is a common reason for sulfation. Who is correct?
  A. Technician A
  B. Technician B
  C. Both Technician A and Technician B
  D. Neither Technician A nor Technician B

_____ 4. Technician A says that batteries may slowly fail over time through due to the loss of a cell or open circuits within the internal connections. Technician B says that batteries may slowly fail over time through the gradual loss of capacity caused by plate deterioration. Who is correct?
  A. Technician A
  B. Technician B
  C. Both Technician A and Technician B
  D. Neither Technician A nor Technician B

_____ 5. Technician A says that, if electrolyte is lost due to spillage, then the battery should be topped up with electrolyte. Technician B says that, if electrolyte level is lost through evaporation, then tap water should be added. Who is correct?
  A. Technician A
  B. Technician B
  C. Both Technician A and Technician B
  D. Neither Technician A nor Technician B

_____ 6. Technician A says to always coat battery terminals with chassis grease to prevent corrosion. Technician B says that all slide mechanisms on battery trays should work properly. Who is correct?
  A. Technician A
  B. Technician B
  C. Both Technician A and Technician B
  D. Neither Technician A nor Technician B

_____ 7. Technician A says that a fully charged battery should have an open-circuit voltage of 12.25 volts. Technician B says that, if the battery has been recently charged, a light load applied to the battery for a few minutes will remove a surface charge. Who is correct?
  A. Technician A
  B. Technician B
  C. Both Technician A and Technician B
  D. Neither Technician A nor Technician B

_____ **8.** Technician A says that a conductance test determines the battery's ability to conduct current. Technician B says that batteries must be fully charged to test battery conductance. Who is correct?

    A. Technician A

    B. Technician B

    C. Both Technician A and Technician B

    D. Neither Technician A nor Technician B

_____ **9.** Technician A says that the load test determines the ability of a battery to deliver cranking amperage and is based on the battery CCA rating. Technician B says that a battery must be at least 95% charged to perform a capacity test, so SOC must be first evaluated before proceeding. Who is correct?

    A. Technician A

    B. Technician B

    C. Both Technician A and Technician B

    D. Neither Technician A nor Technician B

_____ **10.** Technician A says that all modern vehicles have a small amount of current draw when the ignition is turned off. Technician B says that this charge is used to run some of the vehicle systems, such as various modules making up the onboard vehicle network. Who is correct?

    A. Technician A

    B. Technician B

    C. Both Technician A and Technician B

    D. Neither Technician A nor Technician B

43 Heavy-Duty Starting Systems and Circuits

Chapter Review

The following activities have been designed to help you refresh your knowledge of this chapter. Your instructor may require you to complete some or all of these activities as a regular part of your training program. You are encouraged to complete any activity that your instructor does not assign as a way to enhance your learning.

Matching

Match the following terms with the correct description or example.

A. Automatic disengagement lockout (ADLO)
B. Counter-electromotive force (CEMF)
C. Overcrank protection (OCP) thermostat
D. Planetary gear reduction drive
E. Reduction gear drive

_____ **1.** A device that monitors the temperature of the motor and opens a relay circuit to interrupt the current to the solenoid if prolonged cranking causes the motor temperature to exceed a safe threshold.

_____ **2.** A type of gear reduction system in which a planetary gear set reduces the starter profile to multiply motor torque to the pinion gear.

_____ **3.** An electromagnetic force produced by the spinning magnetic field of the armature, which induces current in the opposite direction of battery current through the motor.

_____ **4.** A starter motor drive system in which the motor multiplies torque to the starter pinion gear by using an extra gear between the armature and the starter drive mechanism.

_____ **5.** A device that prevents the starter motor from operating if the engine is running.

Multiple Choice

Read each item carefully, and then select the best response.

_____ **1.** A _____ type of electric starter can be identified by an offset drive housing to the motor housing.
    A. direct drive
    B. reduction gear drive
    C. planetary gear reduction drive
    D. pneumatic

_____ **2.** Often used as blower motors, _____ -type DC motors develop less torque but maintain a constant speed.
    A. shunt
    B. compound
    C. stepper
    D. series

_____ **3.** What type DC motors are used in instrument clusters' gauges, turbochargers, and EGR actuators where high precision movement is required?
    A. Series
    B. Compound
    C. Stepper
    D. Shunt

_____ **4.** Low-voltage burn-out can be prevented by using _____.
    A. ultra-capacitors
    B. correctly sized battery cables
    C. overcrank protection switches
    D. All of the above

_____ **5.** A(n) _____ winding is made of heavy, flat, copper strips.
   A. shunt motor
   B. armature
   C. commutator
   D. field coil

_____ **6.** It is the role of the _____ to switch the direction of current flow through each armature coil as the armature rotates.
   A. commutator
   B. pole shoes
   C. field coil
   D. starter housing

_____ **7.** The pinion drive gear is attached to a roller-type _____ that is splined to the starter armature.
   A. one-way clutch
   B. two-way clutch
   C. overrunning clutch
   D. Either A or C

_____ **8.** Pinion clearance is adjusted using _____.
   A. an eccentric shift fork pin
   B. shims
   C. a screw or nut on the solenoid core
   D. Any of the above

_____ **9.** The automatic disengagement lockout relay contacts are connected in _____ with the starter motor control circuit.
   A. series
   B. parallel
   C. series-parallel
   D. None of the above

_____ **10.** Intermittent starter operation or starter operation that resumes after it is tapped with a hammer may indicate _____.
   A. a damaged armature
   B. worn bushings or bearings
   C. worn brushes
   D. damaged field coils

True/False

If you believe the statement to be more true than false, write the letter "T" in the space provided. If you believe the statement to be more false than true, write the letter "F".

_____ **1.** Adding more batteries increases the amount of amperage available for cranking, but the system voltage remains the same.

_____ **2.** Gear reduction starters can reduce starter weight by more than 50%.

_____ **3.** Like magnetic poles attract one another and unlike poles repel one another.

_____ **4.** The compound and stepper motor are the two most common types of DC motors found in the automotive industry.

_____ **5.** Battery current and counter-electromotive force current both flow through a motor at the same time but in opposite directions.

_____ **6.** Starters will use any combination of voltage and amperage to produce the necessary output power.

_____ **7.** Field coils are connected in parallel with the armature windings through the starter brushes.

_____ **8.** Safety switches can be located in either of two places in the control circuit—interrupting either the ground or battery positive of the starter relay.

_____ **9.** Ignition switches normally have five separate positions.

_____ **10.** Slow-crank and no-crank conditions can be caused by both electrical and mechanical faults.

Fill in the Blank

Read each item carefully, and then complete the statement by filling in the missing word(s).

1. To supply more cranking amperage in a 12-volt system, batteries are connected in _____.
2. The only gear torque multiplication in a _____ drive starter is between the pinion gear and the ring gear.
3. A(n) _____, or air starting system, consists of a geared air motor, starting valve, and a pressure tank.
4. Heavy-duty starter motors use _____ in their field and armature windings.
5. Most starter motors are _____ -wound motors because they develop the greatest amount of torque at zero rpm.
6. The _____ assembly presses onto the armature shaft.
7. A(n) _____ is an electromagnet that is used to perform work and has mechanical action.
8. The _____ _____ circuit allows the operator to use a small amount of battery current provided by the ignition switch to control the flow of a large amount of current in the starting circuit.
9. Series-parallel electrical systems, or _____ _____ as it is generally called, use two, four, or six 12-volt batteries connected in series through an equalizer to supply most of the vehicle's electrical systems.
10. Testing starter motor _____ draw is the best indicator of overall cranking system performance.

Labeling

Label the following diagrams with the correct terms.

1. Identify the components of a direct drive starter motor:

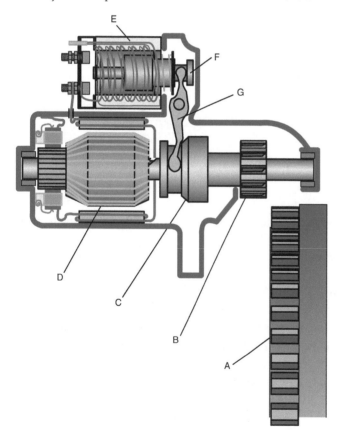

A. _____

B. _____

C. _____

D. _____

E. _____

F. _____

G. _____

2. Identify the components of a typical planetary gear reduction drive starter motor:

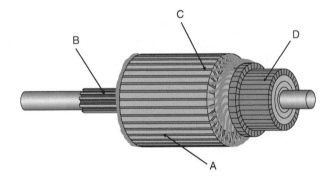

A. _____

B. _____

C. _____

D. _____

3. Identify the features of an armature:

A. _____

B. _____

C. _____

D. _____

4. Identify the components of a simple single-loop motor:

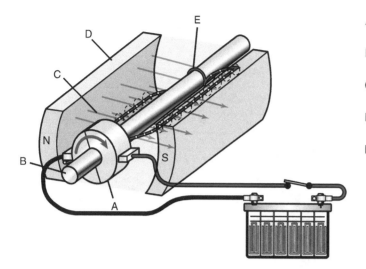

A. _____

B. _____

C. _____

D. _____

E. _____

5. Identify the components of a starter drive one-way clutch:

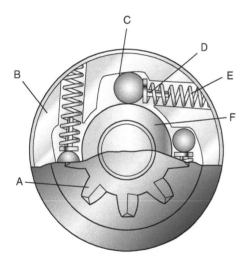

A. _____

B. _____

C. _____

D. _____

E. _____

F. _____

Skill Drills

Test your knowledge of skill drills by filling in the correct words in the photo captions.

1. Testing Starter Draw:

Step 1: Research the specifications for the starter draw test. Place an inductive type _____ _____ over either the positive or negative cable. It doesn't matter which starter cable is measured, as it is a _____ circuit, so _____ will be the same at any point in the circuit.

Step 2: Connect the AVR voltmeter leads to the _____ or at the _____.

Step 3: Make sure all of the appropriate wires are _____ the clamp and the clamp is completely _____.

Step 4: Disable the engine from starting by removing a _____ from the engine _____ or disabling the _____ system shut-off _____.

Step 5: With the engine disabled, _____ the engine and record the _____ and _____ as soon as the _____ stabilize.

Step 6: Compare the readings with the _____ and determine any necessary actions.

2. Testing Starter Circuit Voltage Drop:

Step 1: Set the DVOM to _____. Connect the _____ lead to the _____ battery post and the _____ lead to the positive _____ _____ on the starting motor.

Step 2: Crank the engine and read the maximum _____ _____ for the _____ side of the circuit. Connect the _____ lead to the _____ battery post and the _____ lead to the _____ terminal or starting motor _____ _____. Crank the engine and read the voltage drop.

Step 3: If the voltage drop is more than _____ volts on either side of the circuit, use the voltmeter and wiring diagram to _____ the voltage drop. Conduct further _____ _____ tests across individual components and cables. Determine any necessary actions.

3. Inspecting and Testing the Starter Control Circuit:

Step 1: Use a _____ to measure _____ between the solenoid control circuit terminal on the solenoid (R) terminal and the _____ of the starter while the engine is _____.

Step 2: If the voltage is less than _____ volts, measure the voltage drop between the _____ terminal and the _____.

Step 3: If the voltage drop is less than _____ volts, measure the voltage drop on the _____ side of the _____ control circuit.

Step 4: If the voltage drop is higher than _____ volts on either side of the circuit, use the _____ _____ to guide you in isolating the _____ _____ on that side of the circuit. Continue conducting voltage drop tests across individual components and cables.

Step 5: If the _____ _____ are within specifications on both sides of the circuit, the _____ of the solenoid pull-in and hold-in _____ will need to be _____. If out of specifications, the solenoid or _____ _____ and solenoid will need to be _____.

4. Inspecting and Testing Relays and Solenoids:

Step 1:   To test a relay, measure the _____ of the relay _____ and compare with specifications . If the relay is out of specifications, _____ it.

Step 2:   Use a relay _____ to mount the relay on top of the relay _____ so you can check the _____ _____ wiring and perform _____ _____ tests on the contacts.

Step 3:   Activate the relay while measuring the _____ across the relay _____. If it is near _____ voltage, the control circuit wiring is _____.

Step 4:   Measure the voltage across the _____ with the relay not activated. This should read near _____ _____ if both sides of the _____ circuit are OK. If not, perform _____ _____ tests on each side of the switch circuit.

Step 5:   Activate the relay while measuring the _____ _____ across the _____. If it is more than _____ volts, the relay will need to be _____.

Step 6:   To test a starter solenoid, measure the _____ _____ across the solenoid _____ _____ with the key in the _____ position. If it is more than _____ volts, replace the solenoid or starter assembly.

Step 7:   If the solenoid does not _____ with the key in the _____ position, remove the electrical connection for the _____ _____ at the solenoid.

Step 8:   Use a _____ _____ to apply battery voltage to the control circuit terminal on the solenoid and see if the solenoid _____. If it does, then there is likely a _____ in the control circuit wiring. If the solenoid still does not click (and the circuit is grounded), then the solenoid _____ or starter _____ are likely worn (sometimes _____ on the starter while the key is turned to the crank position will free up the brushes enough that the pull-in winding can operate). Determine any necessary actions.

5. Removing and Replacing a Starter Motor and Inspecting the Ring Gear or Flex Plate:

Step 1:   Locate and follow the appropriate procedure in the _____ _____.

Step 2:   Disconnect the battery _____ and electrical connections to the _____ _____.

Step 3:   Loosen the _____ _____, leaving them in place until you are ready to remove the _____ _____.

Step 4:   Remove the _____ _____ by supporting its weight while the _____ _____ are removed. You may need _____ to support the weight of the starter while this step is being conducted.

Step 5:   Examine the starter _____ for any wear to the drive _____.

Step 6:   Using a work light, inspect the _____ _____ or flex plate _____ for damage. Slowly turn the engine over while checking the _____ _____ or _____ _____, ensuring the circumference is inspected. In difficult-to-see locations, an engine _____ may provide assistance. Report any damage to the ring gear.

Step 7:   Reinstall the _____ _____ by _____ the steps used in steps 1 through 4 above.

Crossword Puzzle

Use the clues in the column to complete the puzzle.

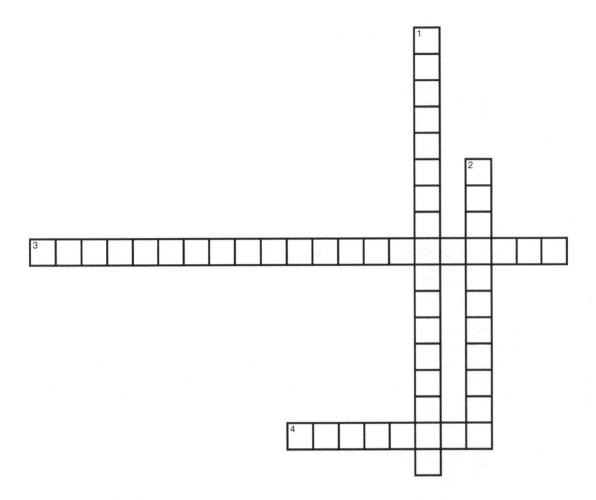

Across

3. A relay connected to the alternator that detects alternating current only when the alternator is charging.

4. The only rotating component of the starter; has three main components: the shaft, windings, and the commutator.

Down

1. A damaging condition for starter motors in which excess current flows through the starter, causing the motor to burn out prematurely.

2. A starter motor drive system in which the motor armature directly engages the flywheel through a pinion gear.

ASE-Type Questions

Read each item carefully, and then select the best response.

_____ **1.** Technician A says that dozens of electric motors are found in heavy vehicles operating a variety of devices from electric seats, fuel and coolant pumps, fan blower motors, and even instrument gauges. Technician B says that the largest of all these electric motors is the starter motor. Who is correct?
   A. Technician A
   B. Technician B
   C. Both Technician A and Technician B
   D. Neither Technician A nor Technician B

_____ **2.** Technician A says that all electric motors operate using principles of magnetic attraction and repulsion. Technician B says that because like magnetic poles attract one another and unlike poles repel, it is possible to arrange magnetic poles within the motor to be continuously in a state repulsion and attraction. Who is correct?
   A. Technician A
   B. Technician B
   C. Both Technician A and Technician B
   D. Neither Technician A nor Technician B

_____ **3.** Technician A says that the series and shunt motor are the two most common types of motor found in the automotive industry. Technician B says that series motors are called "series" because the field and armature windings are connected in series. Who is correct?
   A. Technician A
   B. Technician B
   C. Both Technician A and Technician B
   D. Neither Technician A nor Technician B

_____ **4.** Technician A says that series-wound motors also are self-limiting in speed due to the development of a counter-electromotive force (CEMF). Technician B says that CEMF is produced by the spinning magnetic field of the armature, which induces current in the same direction of battery current through the motor. Who is correct?
   A. Technician A
   B. Technician B
   C. Both Technician A and Technician B
   D. Neither Technician A nor Technician B

_____ **5.** Technician A says that cranking an engine with low battery voltage causes one of the most damaging conditions for a starter. Technician B says that low-voltage burn-out occurs when excess amperage flows through the starter, causing the motor to burn out prematurely. Who is correct?
   A. Technician A
   B. Technician B
   C. Both Technician A and Technician B
   D. Neither Technician A nor Technician B

_____ **6.** Technician A says that the starter housing, or frame, encloses and supports the internal starter components, protecting them and intensifying the magnetic fields produced in the field coils. Technician B says that in the starter housing field coils and their pole shoes are securely attached to the inside of the iron housing. Who is correct?
   A. Technician A
   B. Technician B
   C. Both Technician A and Technician B
   D. Neither Technician A nor Technician B

_____ **7.** Technician A says that different from the thin wire used in shunt motors, armature windings are made of heavy, flat, copper strips that can handle the heavy current flow of the series motor. Technician B says that in a four-brush motor, each half of a coil is wound at 60 degrees to each other. Who is correct?
   A. Technician A
   B. Technician B
   C. Both Technician A and Technician B
   D. Neither Technician A nor Technician B

_____ **8.** Technician A says that solenoid on the starter motor generates the high current flow required by the starter motor on and off. Technician B says that the solenoid on the starter motor engages the starter drive with the pinion gear. Who is correct?
A. Technician A
B. Technician B
C. Both Technician A and Technician B
D. Neither Technician A nor Technician B

_____ **9.** Technician A says that the starter drive transmits the rotational force from the starter armature to the engine via the ring gear that is mounted on the engine flywheel or torque converter. Technician B says that in the past gear reduction starters were used but that today, direct-drive starters have replaced them. Who is correct?
A. Technician A
B. Technician B
C. Both Technician A and Technician B
D. Neither Technician A nor Technician B

_____ **10.** Technician A says that some starter motors are equipped with an overcrank protection (OCP) thermostat. Technician B says that the thermostat monitors the temperature of the motor. Who is correct?
A. Technician A
B. Technician B
C. Both Technician A and Technician B
D. Neither Technician A nor Technician B

Charging Systems

Chapter Review

The following activities have been designed to help you refresh your knowledge of this chapter. Your instructor may require you to complete some or all of these activities as a regular part of your training program. You are encouraged to complete any activity that your instructor does not assign as a way to enhance your learning.

Matching

Match the following terms with the correct description or example.

A. Alternator ripple

B. Delta windings

C. Load-dumping

D. Rectification

E. Wye windings

_____ **1.** A process of converting alternating current (AC) into direct current (DC).

_____ **2.** The top of the waveform.

_____ **3.** Stator windings in which one end of each phase winding is taken to a central point where the ends are connected together.

_____ **4.** A feature that allows temporary suppression of high-voltage spikes.

_____ **5.** Stator windings in which the windings are connected in the shape of a triangle.

Multiple Choice

Read each item carefully, and then select the best response.

_____ **1.** The development of low-cost solid-state _____ in the 1950s made the use of alternating current "generators" (alternators) possible.

   A. batteries

   B. rectifiers

   C. solenoids

   D. capacitors

_____ **2.** The alternator converts mechanical energy into electrical energy by _____.

   A. electromagnetic induction

   B. rectification

   C. kinetic unification

   D. recombination

_____ **3.** The amount of current produced from an alternator is proportional to _____.

   A. the strength of the magnetic field in the rotor

   B. the speed at which the magnetic field rotates

   C. the angle between the magnetic field and conductors in the stator

   D. All of the above

_____ **4.** The two halves of the rotor's soft iron core are arranged into _____.

   A. claws

   B. rings

   C. pole pieces

   D. Either A or C

_____ **5.** The _____ is made of loops of coiled wire wrapped around a slotted metal alternator frame.
   A. stator
   B. rectifier
   C. rotor
   D. regulator

_____ **6.** A _____ - wound alternator is best adapted to supply higher amperage output to charge multiple batteries and the heavy electrical loads found in trucks and buses.
   A. Wye
   B. Delta
   C. Delta-Wye
   D. Wye-Delta

_____ **7.** A minimum of _____ diodes is required to completely rectify all three phases of alternating current into DC current.
   A. 3
   B. 6
   C. 9
   D. 12

_____ **8.** A(n) _____ voltage regulator regulates the field current by controlling the resistance through to ground.
   A. "A" type
   B. "B" type
   C. isolated field type
   D. All of the above

_____ **9.** Charging at voltages above 15 volts (12-volt system) and 31 volts (24-volt system) will cause _____.
   A. bulb and LED failure
   B. batteries to gas excessively
   C. battery plates to shed grid material
   D. All of the above

_____ **10.** Connecting alternators in _____ requires the output of each to be properly balanced so one will not work harder than the other and wear out.
   A. series
   B. parallel
   C. Wye
   D. Delta

True/False

If you believe the statement to be more true than false, write the letter "T" in the space provided. If you believe the statement to be more false than true, write the letter "F".

_____ **1.** The 12-volt electrical system load for a late model highway tractor averages 45 amps of current.

_____ **2.** DC generators are much more efficient at producing current than alternators.

_____ **3.** Alternators will produce current when rotated in either direction.

_____ **4.** Maximum amperage output of an alternator is limited by the speed at which an alternator rotates.

_____ **5.** Most heavy-duty alternators typically contain between four and six claws.

_____ **6.** Residually magnetized rotors will begin to induce current in the stator windings when the alternator starts rotating without any current passing through the rotor coil.

_____ **7.** Combination Wye and Delta stators are commonly found in heavy-duty alternators.

_____ **8.** Capacitors can be used to smooth alternator AC ripple and prevent electromagnetic interference (EMI).

_____ **9.** Larger 24-volt alternators, such as the Delco 50DN used by buses, circulate engine coolant through the alternator to remove heat from the rectifier and stator windings.

_____ **10.** Alternators that require external excitation will have an ignition excite or "I" connection.

Fill in the Blank

Read each item carefully, and then complete the statement by filling in the missing word(s).

1. In a(n) _____, the magnetic field is created by the rotor, which rotates within the stationary stator windings to generate electricity.

2. The voltage _____ circuit maintains optimal battery state of charge by sensing and maintaining a required charging system output voltage.

3. Several pairs of diodes, referred to as the _____ bridge, have the job of converting AC current to usable DC current.

4. The _____ contains a spinning electromagnet that induces current flow in the stator winding, which is made up of numerous coils of wire.

5. Regulated current to the alternator rotor is supplied through a pair of graphite _____ sliding against slip rings on the rotor shaft.

6. A(n) _____ - _____ alternator does not use a circuit connected to the ignition switch to switch on the voltage regulator and supply current to the rotor.

7. Each stator winding will produce one of three _____ of AC current.

8. A(n) _____ voltage regulator uses a pulse-width-modulated signal to control the magnetic field strength.

9. Voltage regulation for 12-volt systems will establish a maximum charging voltage, known as the _____ _____.

10. A(n) _____ _____ _____ pulley uses an internal spring and clutch system that allows it to rotate freely in one direction and provide limited, springlike movement in the other direction.

Labeling

Label the following diagrams with the correct terms.

1. Identify the parts of an alternator:

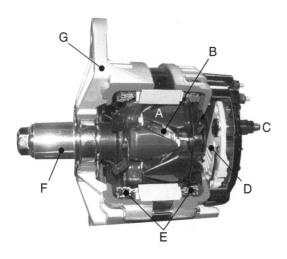

A. _____

B. _____

C. _____

D. _____

E. _____

F. _____

G. _____

Skill Drills

Test your knowledge of skill drills by filling in the correct words in the photo captions.

1. Performing a Charging System Output Test:

Step 1: Connect a charging system _____ to the battery with the _____ lead to the _____ post, the _____ lead to the _____ post, and the _____ _____ around the alternator _____ wire.

Step 2: Start the engine, turn off all _____, and measure the regulated voltage at around _____ rpm. The regulated voltage is the _____ voltage the system achieves once the battery is relatively _____, as evidenced by the _____ reading less than about _____-_____ amps when the amps clamp is around the alternator output cable. Typical regulated voltage specifications are wider than they used to be due to the ability of the _____ to adjust the _____ _____ for a wide range of conditions.

Step 3: Operate the engine at about _____ rpm and either manually or automatically load down the battery to _____ volts or _____ volts for a _____-volt system. Measure the alternator _____ output. This reading should be compared against the alternator's _____ output. Normally, the maximum output should be within _____% of the alternator's rated capacity. A _____ alternator may have slightly lower results.

2. Testing Charging Circuit Voltage Drop:

Step 1: Set the _____ up to measure _____, and select min/max if available. Connect the _____ probe of the _____ to the _____ terminal of the alternator and the _____ probe to the _____ post of the _____. The _____ probe goes on the _____ battery post because, in this case, the alternator output terminal is higher _____ than the positive battery terminal. For the meter to read correctly, the leads need to be connected as listed.

Step 2: Start the engine and _____ _____ as many electrical _____ as possible or use an external _____ _____ _____ to load the battery. Read the maximum _____ _____ for the output circuit.

Step 3: Move the leads to measure the voltage drop on the _____ circuit by placing the _____ probe on the alternator _____ and the _____ probe on the _____ terminal of the battery. With the engine running and the circuit still _____, read the maximum _____ _____ for the ground circuit.

Step 4: If the measurements are _____, check each _____ of the circuit for excessive voltage drops by slowly bringing the _____ closer together on each _____ of the circuit. Determine any necessary actions.

3. Inspecting, Repairing, or Replacing Connectors and Wires of Charging Circuits:

Step 1: Locate and follow the appropriate _____ and _____ _____ in the service manual.

Step 2: Move the vehicle into the shop, apply the _____ _____, and _____ the vehicle wheels. Observe _____ and _____ procedures.

Step 3: If the vehicle has a _____ transmission, place it in "_____." If it has an _____ transmission, place it in "_____" or "_____."

Step 4: Trace the _____ _____ from the _____ to the _____ and around the _____ _____.

Step 5: Check the _____ and _____ for wear, damage, or _____.

Step 6: Disconnect the battery _____ cable if repairs are necessary.

Step 7: Repair damaged areas with replacement _____ or _____. Ensure all harnesses are _____ to prevent _____ or damage from _____.

Step 8: Reconnect all harness _____ and _____ all connections.

Step 9: Reconnect the battery _____ cable.

Step 10: Check repair by _____ _____ and running the vehicle.

Step 11: Clean the _____ _____ and return _____ and _____ to their proper storage.

4. Removing, Inspecting, and Replacing an Alternator:

Step 1: Locate and follow the appropriate procedure in the _____ _____.

Step 2: Move the vehicle into the _____, apply the _____ _____, and _____ the vehicle wheels. Observe _____ and _____ procedures.

Step 3: If the vehicle has a _____ transmission, place it in "_____." If it has an _____ transmission, place it in "_____" or "_____."

Step 4: Disconnect the _____ from the _____.

Step 5: Disconnect _____ at the connector on the _____. Make a _____ of the location and any special insulating _____.

Step 6: Loosen _____.

Step 7: Slide the _____ off the _____.

Step 8: Lift the _____ out of vehicle.

Step 9: Place a new _____ onto the _____.

Step 10: Hand screw the _____ without tightening; connect _____ first if needed.

Step 11: After checking the condition of the _____ and _____ it if needed, slip the _____ on each _____ and _____ properly.

Step 12: If required, adjust belt _____ using belt _____ _____.

Step 13: Tighten the _____.

Step 14: Reconnect the _____.

Step 15: _____ the vehicle and _____ that the alternator is _____.

Step 16: _____ the work area and return _____ and _____ to their proper _____.

5. Overhauling an Alternator:

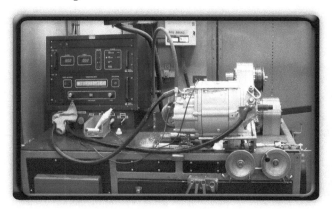

Step 1:   Locate and _____ the appropriate _____ in the service manual.

Step 2:   Check to see if the _____ need to be removed first. If so, remove the _____ _____ or _____.

Step 3:   Remove the through _____ holding the _____ together.

Step 4:   _____ the _____ apart.

Step 5:   Disassemble the component parts from the _____. Take note of the placement of _____ _____.

Step 6:   Clean, _____, and _____ all component parts. Use specialized _____ where necessary; for example, _____ tester, _____ tester, and _____.

Step 7:   Replace any _____ components. If the _____ _____ assembly requires replacement, ensure the new _____ _____ is machined on the _____.

Step 8:   Reassemble component parts into the _____.

Step 9:   Reassemble the alternator _____. Ensure the _____ are retained using a _____ _____ to prevent damage to them.

Step 10: Test the alternator in the alternator _____ _____. Ensure the _____ _____ circuit is working and test for maximum _____ output and _____ regulation.

Step 11: Clean the _____ _____ and return tools and materials to their proper _____.

Crossword Puzzle

Use the clues in the column to complete the puzzle.

Across

3. The small amount of magnetism left on the rotor after it is initially magnetized by the coil windings' magnetic field.

5. Making the alternator produce maximum amperage output.

Down

1. The practice of connecting alternators in parallel to provide higher charging voltage at idle with more available amperage.

2. A pattern produced by voltage fluctuations from the alternator that create differences between the peak voltage of an AC sine wave and the minimum voltage found in the trough between sine waves.

4. The voltage reference point the alternator uses for regulation of the output.

ASE-Type Questions

Read each item carefully, and then select the best response.

_____ 1. Technician A says that today, the average 12-volt electrical system for a late-model highway tractor add up to 150 amps at peak with an 84-amp average. Technician B says that both DC generators and alternators produce electricity by relative movement of conductors in a magnetic field. Who is correct?
  A. Technician A
  B. Technician B
  C. Both Technician A and Technician B
  D. Neither Technician A nor Technician B

_____ 2. Technician A says that alternators have more moving parts as compared to generators. Technician B says that alternators can produce power at engine idle speeds; generators cannot. Who is correct?
  A. Technician A
  B. Technician B
  C. Both Technician A and Technician B
  D. Neither Technician A nor Technician B

_____ 3. Technician A says that the two most important parts in an alternator used to produce electrical current are the rotor and stator winding. Technician B says that the rotor contains a spinning electromagnet that induces current flow in the stator winding, which is made up of numerous coils of wire. Who is correct?
  A. Technician A
  B. Technician B
  C. Both Technician A and Technician B
  D. Neither Technician A nor Technician B

_____ 4. Technician A says that the rotor is a rotating electromagnet that provides the magnetic field to induce voltage and current in the stator. Technician B says that the direct-gear drive mechanism is used in most cases but that a pulley drive may also be employed. Who is correct?
  A. Technician A
  B. Technician B
  C. Both Technician A and Technician B
  D. Neither Technician A nor Technician B

_____ 5. Technician A says that regulated current to the alternator rotor is supplied through a pair of graphite brushes sliding against slip rings on the rotor shaft. Technician B says that heavy-duty springs help the brushes maintain contact with the slip rings. Who is correct?
  A. Technician A
  B. Technician B
  C. Both Technician A and Technician B
  D. Neither Technician A nor Technician B

_____ 6. Technician A says that vehicles fitted with self-exciting alternators may require the engine rpm to be briefly increased after every start-up to initiate charging. Technician B says that using self-exciting alternators eliminates the need for a separate circuit from the key switch to the alternator and simplifies chassis wiring. Who is correct?
  A. Technician A
  B. Technician B
  C. Both Technician A and Technician B
  D. Neither Technician A nor Technician B

_____ 7. Technician A says that the stator is mounted between two end housings, and it holds the stator windings stationary so that the rotating magnetic field cuts through the stator windings, inducing an electric current in the windings. Technician B says that to smooth the pulsating current flow, there are three distinct layers of windings offset 60 degrees in each layer from one another. Who is correct?
  A. Technician A
  B. Technician B
  C. Both Technician A and Technician B
  D. Neither Technician A nor Technician B

_____ **8.** Technician A says that stators are normally serviced in a repair facility. Technician B says that stators can be visually checked during rebuilding for burnt, cut, or nicked winding laminations. Who is correct?

A. Technician A

B. Technician B

C. Both Technician A and Technician B

D. Neither Technician A nor Technician B

_____ **9.** Technician A says that alternators produce alternating current, which is acceptable for operating many electrical devices. Technician B says that converting the AC current to usable DC current is referred to as modulation. Who is correct?

A. Technician A

B. Technician B

C. Both Technician A and Technician B

D. Neither Technician A nor Technician B

_____ **10.** Technician A says that voltage regulators are first classified as either external or internal. Technician B says that the majority of late-model alternators have external regulators. Who is correct?

A. Technician A

B. Technician B

C. Both Technician A and Technician B

D. Neither Technician A nor Technician B

Electrical Wiring and Circuit Diagrams

Chapter Review

The following activities have been designed to help you refresh your knowledge of this chapter. Your instructor may require you to complete some or all of these activities as a regular part of your training program. You are encouraged to complete any activity that your instructor does not assign as a way to enhance your learning.

Matching

Match the following terms with the correct description or example.

A. Deutsche Institute Norm (DIN) diagram

B. Isometric diagram

C. Map diagram

D. Schematic diagram

E. Valley Forge (VF) diagram

_____ **1.** A wiring diagram that shows the entire vehicle wiring circuit using pictorial symbols.

_____ **2.** A wiring diagram used to locate a component within a system and which shows the outline of a vehicle or piece of equipment where the component can be found.

_____ **3.** A schematic wiring diagram that uses SAE-type symbols.

_____ **4.** A line drawing that explains how a system works by using symbols and connecting lines.

_____ **5.** A schematic wiring diagram on which symbols, terminal connection numbers, line symbols, and operational status of items such as switches and relays are defined by a specific standard.

Multiple Choice

Read each item carefully, and then select the best response.

_____ **1.** Ohm's law predicts voltage drop using the formula _____.

    A. V_{drop} = Amperage + Voltage

    B. V_{drop} = Resistance × Voltage

    C. V_{drop} = Amperage × Resistance

    D. V_{drop} = Resistance + Amperage

_____ **2.** The _____ system is more than a hundred years old and measures wire gauge in numbers from 0000 to 50.

    A. American wire gage

    B. weights and measures

    C. metric gauge

    D. Both A and C

_____ **3.** Using the AWG system, a 60' length of wire used in a 24-volt system to carry 14.0 amps of current would need to be a size _____ wire.

    A. 10

    B. 12

    C. 14

    D. 16

_____ **4.** The _____ standard specifies the dimensions, test methods, and performance requirements for single-core primary wire intended for use in road vehicle applications.

    A. SAE J1128

    B. SAE J1926

    C. ISO 6722

    D. Both A and C

_____ **5.** Type _____ wire is an extra thin primary wire that has a cross-linked polyethylene jacket that is resistant to oil, grease, gasoline, and acids.
   A. GPT
   B. SXL
   C. TXL
   D. GXL

_____ **6.** Chassis wiring often uses numerical codes to identify _____.
   A. which circuit the wire belongs to
   B. which harness the wire belongs in
   C. the wire gauge and color
   D. All of the above

_____ **7.** The compact _____ connector is considered a premium connector and used when reliability of the connection is of utmost importance.
   A. Deutsch
   B. Weather Pack
   C. Metri-Pack
   D. Bosch/AMP

_____ **8.** Wires should be joined together by bending each into a double-J bend, then twisting to form a _____ splice.
   A. Brummel
   B. Western Union
   C. pigtail
   D. butt

_____ **9.** A(n) _____ shows the power source at the top of the page and the ground points at the bottom.
   A. pictorial diagram
   B. isometric diagram
   C. Deutsche Institute Norm (DIN) diagram
   D. All of the above

_____ **10.** In a DIN diagram, a wire identified using the abbreviation "ge" would be _____ in color.
   A. green
   B. yellow
   C. black
   D. red

True/False

If you believe the statement to be more true than false, write the letter "T" in the space provided. If you believe the statement to be more false than true, write the letter "F".

_____ **1.** Smaller wires become more resistant and heat up as amperage increases.

_____ **2.** Both wire classification systems measure both the wire and the insulator when determining the total diameter of a wire.

_____ **3.** The International Organization for Standardization has designed a color code system that is followed by all manufacturers.

_____ **4.** Multi-stranded wire is better at conducting higher amounts of current with less resistance because it has more surface area to conduct electron flow.

_____ **5.** Connector housings have male and female sides and are usually shaped so that they can be connected in only one way.

_____ **6.** The wires on Metri-Pack connectors must be soldered before being seated in the connector.

_____ **7.** One of the greatest enemies to wiring is water.

_____ **8.** Color codes are used to designate wire gauge to use for shrink crimp connectors.

_____ **9.** Schematic diagrams are used to show internal circuitry.

_____ **10.** Arrangement of the components and circuit paths on a current track diagram usually correspond to their physical locations on the vehicle.

Fill in the Blank

Read each item carefully, and then complete the statement by filling in the missing word(s).

1. Longer circuits and higher amperage require a larger _____ of wire.
2. In most wiring diagrams, metric-sized wire is specified in _____ rather than metric gauge diameter.
3. A(n) _____ wiring harness is often used for a rear taillight wiring harness that includes a separate wire for stop, turn, reverse, and tail lights.
4. The simplest wiring connector is a _____ _____ that uses small studs to which ring or spade type connectors are attached and secured with machine screws.
5. A(n) _____ -_____-_____ terminal is inserted into the back of the connector cavity to seat after the terminal is crimped to the wire.
6. The male pin end of a Weather Pack connector is called the _____ while the female socket end is called the _____.
7. Once inside a wire, _____ will move into the smallest openings and spaces through adhesion.
8. If a connection is not _____, wiring can move within the connection, leading to arcing and resistance, which ultimately causes connection failure.
9. A(n) _____ diagram may start on one page and continue onto several more, mapping out individual circuits with a separate diagram.
10. Pin _____ are generally labeled on the plastic hard-shell connector housing and/or the corresponding component.

Labeling

Label the following diagrams with the correct terms.

1. Identify the components of a typical harness connector:

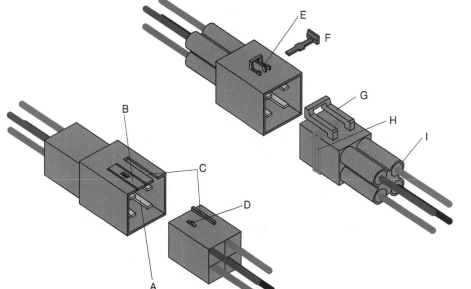

A. _____

B. _____

C. _____

D. _____

E. _____

F. _____

G. _____

H. _____

I. _____

2. Identify the components of a Weather Pack push-to-seat connector:

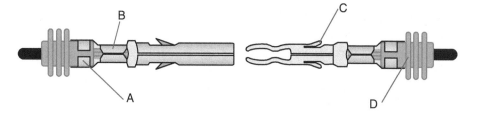

A. _____

B. _____

C. _____

D. _____

Deutsche Institute Norm (DIN) Symbols

Match the definitions to the correct DIN symbol.

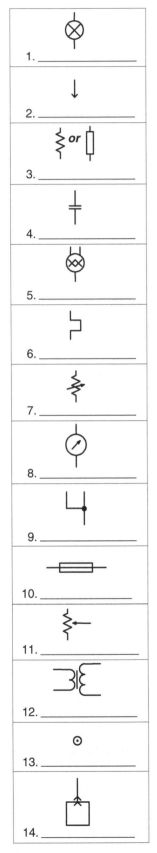

A. Ignition coil

B. Potentiometer (pressure or temp)

C. Transistors

D. Permanent magnet (one-speed motor)

E. Male connector

F. Diodes

G. Circuit breaker

H. Inductive sensor

I. Ground

J. Resistor to heating element

K. Female connector

L. Removable connection

M. Hall sensor

N. Component case directly grounded

O. Lamp

P. Distributed splice

Q. Bifilament lamp

R. Permanent magnet (two-speed motor)

S. Air mass sensor

T. Potentiometer (outside influence)

U. Connector attached to component

V. Connector attached to pigtail

W. Fuse

X. Solenoid valve, injector, cold start valve

Y. Piezoelectric sensor

Z. Capacitor

AA. Connector

BB. Gauge

Crossword Puzzle

Use the clues in the column to complete the puzzle.

Across

3. An environmentally sealed push-to-seat electrical connection system supplied in one- to six-pin configurations.

5. A pull-to-seat electrical connector with flat terminals instead of round.

Down

1. A compact, environmentally sealed electrical connector that uses solid, round metal pins and hollow female sockets.

2. The movement of water through wiring due to its adhesive and cohesive properties.

4. Another name for a DIN diagram.

ASE-Type Questions

Read each item carefully, and then select the best response.

_____ **1.** Technician A says that wires and wiring harnesses are the arteries of the vehicle's electrical system, and as such they need to be kept in good condition, free of any damage or corrosion. Technician B says that they carry the electrical power and signals through the vehicle to control virtually all of the systems on a vehicle. Who is correct?

    A. Technician A

    B. Technician B

    C. Both Technician A and Technician B

    D. Neither Technician A nor Technician B

_____ **2.** Technician A says the insulation is designed to protect the wire and prevent leakage of the current flow so that it can get to its intended destination. Technician B says aluminum is typically used because it offers low electrical resistance and remains flexible even after years of use. Who is correct?

    A. Technician A

    B. Technician B

    C. Both Technician A and Technician B

    D. Neither Technician A nor Technician B

_____ **3.** Technician A says selecting a wire gauge that is too large increases the amount of current flowing into the wiring harnesses. Technician B says the resistance of a wire affects how much current it can carry. Who is correct?

    A. Technician A

    B. Technician B

    C. Both Technician A and Technician B

    D. Neither Technician A nor Technician B

_____ **4.** Technician A says that terminals installed to wire ends provide low-current termination to wires. Technician B says that terminals allow voltage to be conducted from the end of one wire to the end of another wire. Who is correct?

    A. Technician A

    B. Technician B

    C. Both Technician A and Technician B

    D. Neither Technician A nor Technician B

_____ **5.** Technician A says a common mistake while soldering is trying to apply the solder directly to the tip of the soldering iron while the iron is heating up the wires. Technician B says it will not melt the solder leading to a cold joint. Who is correct?

    A. Technician A

    B. Technician B

    C. Both Technician A and Technician B

    D. Neither Technician A nor Technician B

_____ **6.** Technician A says linear diagrams are a variation of the map diagram. Technician B says symbols for components are always pictorial. Who is correct?

    A. Technician A

    B. Technician B

    C. Both Technician A and Technician B

    D. Neither Technician A nor Technician B

_____ **7.** Technician A says DIN schematic diagrams are also called power source track wiring diagrams because they show the power source at the top of the page and the ground points at the bottom. Technician B says newer DIN standards do indicate on which side of the vehicle a component may be located. Who is correct?

    A. Technician A

    B. Technician B

    C. Both Technician A and Technician B

    D. Neither Technician A nor Technician B

_____ **8.** Technician A says knowing the standards for wiring colors makes the job of reading and interpreting schematics easier. Technician B says some colors and terminal designations for wiring are used across a number of standards. Who is correct?
  A. Technician A
  B. Technician B
  C. Both Technician A and Technician B
  D. Neither Technician A nor Technician B

_____ **9.** Technician A says wiring diagrams also indicate the wire gauge used (shown in mm^2), designating the cross sectional area of the wire. Technician B says because standards exist for the maximum permissible voltage drop across a circuit, wire gauge is critical. Who is correct?
  A. Technician A
  B. Technician B
  C. Both Technician A and Technician B
  D. Neither Technician A nor Technician B

_____ **10.** Technician A says wiring diagrams tell the user where pin numbers for wires could terminate. Technician B says knowing where the wires terminate intensifies the diagnostic procedure. Who is correct?
  A. Technician A
  B. Technician B
  C. Both Technician A and Technician B
  D. Neither Technician A nor Technician B

Hybrid Drive Systems and Series-Type Hybrid Drives

Chapter Review

The following activities have been designed to help you refresh your knowledge of this chapter. Your instructor may require you to complete some or all of these activities as a regular part of your training program. You are encouraged to complete any activity that your instructor does not assign as a way to enhance your learning.

Matching

Match the following terms with the correct description or example.

A. Electric vehicle (EV)
B. Hybrid electric vehicle (HEV)
C. Parallel drive
D. Series drive
E. Series-parallel drive

_____ **1.** A vehicle in which both the engine and electric motor work together, blending motor and engine torque, to propel the vehicle.

_____ **2.** A type of vehicle that combines an internal combustion engine with an electric propulsion system.

_____ **3.** A vehicle in which only an electric traction motor supplies torque to propel the vehicle.

_____ **4.** A vehicle in which only electric motors are used to move a vehicle.

_____ **5.** A more complex system enabling an engine only, an electric motor only, and a combined engine-motor operation.

Multiple Choice

Read each item carefully, and then select the best response.

_____ **1.** Hybrid propulsion systems use a _____ engine assisted by an electric motor to accelerate the vehicle.
   A. natural gas
   B. diesel
   C. reciprocating
   D. Any of the above

_____ **2.** Studies have shown that approximately _____ of energy used to accelerate a city bus is quickly dissipated into heat by frequent braking.
   A. 35%
   B. 50%
   C. 65%
   D. 75%

_____ **3.** All of the following are advantages to using a hybrid drive train, *except*:
   A. Smoother acceleration
   B. Lower purchase cost
   C. Increased brake life
   D. Quieter vehicle operation

_____ **4.** What type of hybrid drive configuration is also called a power-split configuration?
   A. Series drive
   B. Parallel drive
   C. Series-parallel drive
   D. Plug-in hybrid

_____ **5.** A _____ system works best in frequent stop-and-go service conditions.
   A. conventional
   B. series drive
   C. parallel drive
   D. series-parallel drive

_____ **6.** Shock hazard to the human body is a function of the _____.
   A. type of current
   B. skin resistance
   C. voltage
   D. All of the above

_____ **7.** Class _____ lineman gloves are recommended for use on high voltage hybrid circuits and offer protection from 1,500 to 5,000 volts.
   A. 0
   B. 1
   C. 2
   D. 3

_____ **8.** Connected directly to the flywheel of the engine is the _____, which converts mechanical energy produced by the engine into electrical current for the propulsion system.
   A. intuitive drive system
   B. propulsion control system
   C. alternating current traction generator
   D. energy storage system

_____ **9.** During _____, the vehicle is powered only—or almost only—by the energy stored in the battery.
   A. charge-sustaining mode
   B. charge-depleting operating mode
   C. intuitive operating mode
   D. Both A and C

_____ **10.** A(n)_____ type current inverter is used in the HybriDrive system.
   A. DC-to-AC
   B. resolver
   C. AC-to-DC
   D. Both A and C

True/False

If you believe the statement to be more true than false, write the letter "T" in the space provided. If you believe the statement to be more false than true, write the letter "F".

_____ **1.** Vehicles operating under long-haul highway conditions are best suited to hybrid use.

_____ **2.** A series system requires a larger electric motor and battery pack, but a smaller internal combustion engine than a parallel system.

_____ **3.** Hydraulic launch assist systems are a series-parallel hybrid system.

_____ **4.** In HLA performance mode, energy stored in the accumulator during braking is used only to initially accelerate the vehicle.

_____ **5.** Under the right conditions, 5 milliamps of AC current can be dangerous, and 500 milliamps can be lethal.

_____ **6.** When working on the battery storage system, two persons are required in case one person is harmed or becomes incapable of removing themselves from a live electrical circuit.

_____ **7.** A Class B fire extinguisher is recommended for any fire that involves a hybrid vehicle.

_____ **8.** In charge-sustaining mode, the batteries' state of charge may rise and fall slightly.

_____ **9.** The brake pressure signal on HybriDrive regenerative brakes can be adjusted using a scale of 1 to 10.

_____ **10.** With the engine test switch in the test position, only the alternating current traction motor responds to the throttle pedal.

Fill in the Blank

Read each item carefully, and then complete the statement by filling in the missing word(s).

1. A feature called _____ braking uses generators to recover energy during braking.
2. A(n) _____-_____ hybrid electric vehicle contains a battery storage system that uses an external source to recharge the battery when the vehicle is not in operation.
3. The _____ _____ _____ system uses hydraulic regenerative braking to capture braking energy and help launch the vehicle during acceleration.
4. In HLA _____ mode, both the engine and accumulator will provide driveline torque until the accumulator empties.
5. Disconnecting and _____ any residual current in EV components is imperative before performing any service work.
6. Many buses using the BAE _____ system are coupled to a Cummins diesel engine to obtain the highest fuel efficiency with the lowest emissions.
7. The _____ _____ system module is the system element controlling the operation of the entire HybriDrive System.
8. To maximize acceleration energy, the _____ _____ system supplies current to the ACTM when current demand exceeds availability from the ACTG.
9. A(n) _____ _____ _____ located in the battery compartments enables technicians to disconnect the power circuit for maintenance or emergencies.
10. An optional regenerative braking _____ switch is located near the driver for use during slippery road conditions.

Labeling

Label the following diagrams with the correct terms.

1. Identify the components of a series hybrid power train configuration:

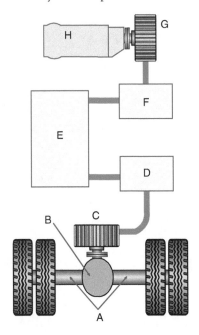

A. _____

B. _____

C. _____

D. _____

E. _____

F. _____

G. _____

H. _____

2. Identify the components of a parallel-drive hybrid configuration:

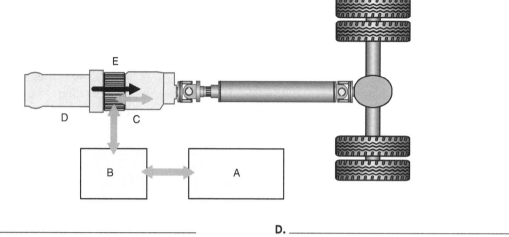

A. _____   D. _____

B. _____   E. _____

C. _____

Crossword Puzzle

Use the clues in the column to complete the puzzle.

Across

3. A special sensor that measures the rotor position and speed for the PCS to properly manage the motor operation by reducing current flow and shutting down the system as needed.

4. A motor that functions as an electrical generator in a hybrid drive system.

Down

1. An electric motor that provides propulsion to a vehicle.

2. A device that changes the shape of electrical current waves.

ASE-Type Questions

Read each item carefully, and then select the best response.

_____ 1. Technician A says that a hybrid electrical vehicle is one that has an electrical motor to drive the vehicle only and an engine to charge the vehicle batteries when necessary. Technician B says that the type of a hybrid that Technician A is describing is known as a series hybrid. Who is correct?
   A. Technician A
   B. Technician B
   C. Both Technician A and Technician B
   D. Neither Technician A nor Technician B

_____ 2. Technician A says that a parallel-drive hybrid is one in which both the engine and the electric motor combine to drive the vehicle at all times. Technician B says that series-parallel drive hybrid can use the engine, the electric motor, or both together to drive the vehicle. Who is correct?
   A. Technician A
   B. Technician B
   C. Both Technician A and Technician B
   D. Neither Technician A nor Technician B

_____ 3. Technician A says that not all hybrid drive vehicles are electric. Technician B says that hybrid drive electrical systems can be serviced in the same way as regular vehicle electrical systems. Who is correct?
   A. Technician A
   B. Technician B
   C. Both Technician A and Technician B
   D. Neither Technician A nor Technician B

_____ 4. Technician A says that electrical hybrid drive systems require an electrical storage system. Technician B says that most electrical hybrid drive systems use regenerative braking. Who is correct?
   A. Technician A
   B. Technician B
   C. Both Technician A and Technician B
   D. Neither Technician A nor Technician B

_____ 5. Technician A says that regenerative braking means that the foundation brakes can regenerate themselves after they wear. Technician B says that foundation brakes last longer when regenerative braking is used. Who is correct?
   A. Technician A
   B. Technician B
   C. Both Technician A and Technician B
   D. Neither Technician A nor Technician B

_____ 6. Technician A says that the original BAE HybriDrive system is a series hybrid. Technician B says that the original BAE HybriDrive system has two electric traction motors. Who is correct?
   A. Technician A
   B. Technician B
   C. Both Technician A and Technician B
   D. Neither Technician A nor Technician B

_____ 7. Technician A says that lead–acid batteries are used to store electricity on the latest hybrid drive systems. Technician B says that the BAE Gen 2 HybriDrive system uses nickel–metal hydride batteries as a power storage system. Who is correct?
   A. Technician A
   B. Technician B
   C. Both Technician A and Technician B
   D. Neither Technician A nor Technician B

_____ 8. Technician A says that electrical hybrid drive systems use a very high voltage traction motor to propel the vehicle. Technician B says that electrical hybrid drive systems require high voltage disconnect systems to shut off the high voltage for service. Who is correct?
   A. Technician A
   B. Technician B
   C. Both Technician A and Technician B
   D. Neither Technician A nor Technician B

_____ **9.** Technician A says that AC current is used to power the traction motor in BAE HybriDrive systems. Technician B says the nickel–metal hydride batteries in the BAE Gen 2 HybriDrive systems are AC batteries. Who is correct?

A. Technician A

B. Technician B

C. Both Technician A and Technician B

D. Neither Technician A nor Technician B

_____ **10.** Technician A says that, when a hybrid drive vehicle is brought into the shop for service, the high voltage system should be locked out. Technician B says that, when a hybrid vehicle must be towed, both axles should be removed so that the driveshaft does not rotate or damage the hybrid drive components. Who is correct?

A. Technician A

B. Technician B

C. Both Technician A and Technician B

D. Neither Technician A nor Technician B

Allison EV Drive Hybrid Systems

Chapter Review

The following activities have been designed to help you refresh your knowledge of this chapter. Your instructor may require you to complete some or all of these activities as a regular part of your training program. You are encouraged to complete any activity that your instructor does not assign as a way to enhance your learning.

Matching

Match the following terms with the correct description or example.

A. Compound split operation
B. Dual-mode hybrid drive train
C. EP 40/50 system
D. High-voltage interlock loop (HVIL)
E. Smart electrification

_____ **1.** A hybrid system that combines both mechanical and electrical propulsion systems.
_____ **2.** Blending torque from the motors and engine together.
_____ **3.** A device that prevents access to potentially hazardous energized electrical circuits.
_____ **4.** A feature that enables the EP 40/50 system's motors to switch over to generating mode to produce as much as 300 amps at 24 volts at idle.
_____ **5.** Models of Allison's electric propulsion system. Also known as Allison's electrically variable (EV) drive.

Multiple Choice

Read each item carefully, and then select the best response.

_____ **1.** The Allison H-EP 40/50s offers a feature referred to as _____ that uses a highly efficient solid-state DC-to-DC converter eliminating the need for a traditional belt-driven alternator.
   A. energy storage
   B. smart electrification
   C. dual power inversion
   D. battery boost control

_____ **2.** Most of the EP system operation is directly controlled by the _____, which collects input signals to determine electrical outputs controlling the EV transmission operation.
   A. vehicle control module
   B. hybrid control module
   C. transmission control module
   D. dual power inverter module

_____ **3.** Which of the following is an **output** of the transmission control module?
   A. Transmission output speed
   B. Remote shutdown
   C. Accelerator interlock
   D. Engine brake enable

_____ **4.** Which of the following is an **input** of the vehicle control module?
   A. Dash indicator lamp control
   B. Reverse warning
   C. Propulsion system inhibits
   D. Brake pressure sensor

_____ **5.** Two parallel-connected battery subpacks form a _____ having approximately 312 volts DC.
   A. tub
   B. substring
   C. module
   D. group

_____ **6.** The _____ is a DC-AC and AC-DC electronic wave inverter used to power the EP drive propulsion system and charge the batteries in the energy storage system.
   A. dual power inverter module
   B. vehicle control module
   C. high-voltage interlock loop
   D. transmission control module

_____ **7.** In the dual power inverter module's _____ state, both high-side and low-side relays are closed, allowing 85% of total ESS voltage to reach the DPIM.
   A. initial
   B. pre-charge
   C. operational
   D. post-charge

_____ **8.** The _____ consists of a 12V relay control circuit routed in series to switches on cover plates located on all hybrid components where potential electrical hazards exist.
   A. insulated gate bipolar transistor
   B. high-voltage interlock loop
   C. vehicle control module
   D. dual power inverter module

_____ **9.** The EP control maintains _____ operation until the vehicle's speed is under 20 or 25 mph (32 to 40 kph).
   A. Mode 1
   B. Mode 2
   C. Mode 3
   D. dual mode

_____ **10.** What is the advantage to using the Meritor dual-mode hybrid drive train?
   A. Fuel efficiency
   B. The electrification of accessories
   C. Smaller engines
   D. All of the above

True/False

If you believe the statement to be more true than false, write the letter "T" in the space provided. If you believe the statement to be more false than true, write the letter "F".

_____ **1.** A parallel drive hybrid allows you to choose between engine only, electric motor only, or combined engine-motor operation.

_____ **2.** The Allison EP system has adjustable acceleration rates to balance fuel economy with performance.

_____ **3.** The transmission control module and vehicle control module are identical looking modules that perform very different functions.

_____ **4.** Energy storage system batteries remain fully charged at all times.

_____ **5.** One advantage of using NiMH batteries is their ability to be charged and discharged repeatedly without a shortened life cycle.

_____ **6.** In the pre-charge state of the dual power inverter module all battery relays are open, and no current flows into or out of the ESS.

_____ **7.** An open high-voltage interlock loop circuit detected during forward or reverse operation will log a fault code and result in an active system shutdown.

_____ **8.** At speeds in excess of 48 mph (77 kph), the dual-mode hybrid drive train transitions to an all-electric power system, supplemented occasionally by the diesel engine.

_____ **9.** A stop system warning light indicates the propulsion system will shut down with a 30-second warning period.

_____ **10.** Four separate hydraulic filters are located in the EP drive transmission.

Fill in the Blank

Read each item carefully, and then complete the statement by filling in the missing word(s).

1. When decelerating, the EP system uses _____ braking to recover braking energy.

2. The EV drive transmission unit provides a pathway for transmitting electric motor or engine torque (or a blend of both) using three _____ gear sets.

3. The TCM and VCM both communicate over the SAEJ-1939 _____ network with other control modules.

4. Induction of a magnetic field in a(n) _____ motor is caused by the change in current flow in the stator winding.

5. Electrical energy to charge the _____ _____ _____ is generated by both drive motors during regenerative braking and from Motor A in mode one when not in use for propulsion.

6. The energy storage system battery _____ contains 240 nickel–metal hydride modules weighing under 1,000 lbs (455 kg) operating at a voltage range of 432–780 VDC.

7. A specialized field effect transistor called a(n) _____ _____ bipolar transistor inverts DC current to three-phase, variable-frequency, and variable-voltage AC current.

8. Meritor produces a(n) _____-_____ hybrid drive train specifically designed for line haul trucks.

9. Allison EP systems use a(n) _____ fault detection monitor to identify high voltage circuit shorts to the vehicle chassis.

10. A(n) _____ system warning light alerts the operator that an EP system fault has occurred but does not lead to a system derate or shut-down.

Labeling

Label the following diagrams with the correct terms.

1. Identify the standard modules of an Allison EV transmission:

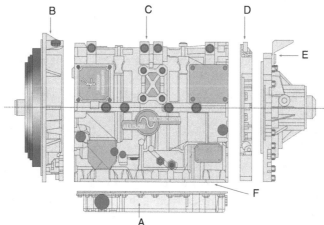

A. _____

B. _____

C. _____

D. _____

E. _____

F. _____

Crossword Puzzle

Use the clues in the column to complete the puzzle.

Across

2. A motor in which the magnetic field in the rotor is induced by induction of the magnetic field in the stationary stator.

4. PC-based service software for Allison's EP system.

5. In split-mode operation, the mode that is for low-speed operation.

Down

1. A system that stores and distributes electrical current to the various components of a hybrid drive system.

3. An electric motor that provides propulsion to a vehicle.

ASE-Type Questions

Read each item carefully, and then select the best response.

_____ 1. Technician A says that the Allison EP drive hybrid systems are series-parallel systems. Technician B says that the Allison EP drive can operate as a parallel system if required. Who is correct?
  A. Technician A
  B. Technician B
  C. Both Technician A and Technician B
  D. Neither Technician A nor Technician B

_____ 2. Technician A says that the Allison EV drive transmission has one electric traction motor. Technician B says that the Allison EV drive has three planetary gear sets. Who is correct?
  A. Technician A
  B. Technician B
  C. Both Technician A and Technician B
  D. Neither Technician A nor Technician B

_____ 3. Technician A says that the battery modules used in the Allison EP system contain 40 cells of 1.2 volts each. Technician B says that the energy storage system has 40 battery modules. Who is correct?
  A. Technician A
  B. Technician B
  C. Both Technician A and Technician B
  D. Neither Technician A nor Technician B

_____ 4. Technician A says that traction motors used in the Allison EP hybrid system use DC voltage. Technician B says that the Allison EP hybrid energy storage system operates at a voltage range of 480 to 780 VDC. Who is correct?
  A. Technician A
  B. Technician B
  C. Both Technician A and Technician B
  D. Neither Technician A nor Technician B

_____ 5. Technician A says that the DPIM converts AC to DC. Technician B says that the DPIM converts DC to AC. Who is correct?
  A. Technician A
  B. Technician B
  C. Both Technician A and Technician B
  D. Neither Technician A nor Technician B

_____ 6. Technician A says that the Allison EP hybrid system has two modes of operation—Mode 1 and Mode 2. Technician B says that, in the Allison EP system, Mode 2 is for low-speed operation. Who is correct?
  A. Technician A
  B. Technician B
  C. Both Technician A and Technician B
  D. Neither Technician A nor Technician B

_____ 7. Technician A says that the Allison EV drive transmission has six forward ratios. Technician B says that the Allison EV drive transmission has five hydraulic clutches. Who is correct?
  A. Technician A
  B. Technician B
  C. Both Technician A and Technician B
  D. Neither Technician A nor Technician B

_____ 8. Technician A says that Allison EP hybrid systems are capable of logging fault codes when a problem occurs. Technician B says that Allison EP hybrid system fault codes are two-digit main codes followed by a second two-digit sub code. Who is correct?
  A. Technician A
  B. Technician B
  C. Both Technician A and Technician B
  D. Neither Technician A nor Technician B

_____ **9.** Technician A says that the Allison EP 40 and 50 save more fuel when compared to the BAE HybriDrive system. Technician B says that the late-model Allison transmission EV drive can generate electricity at idle. Who is correct?
A. Technician A
B. Technician B
C. Both Technician A and Technician B
D. Neither Technician A nor Technician B

_____ **10.** Technician A says that the Allison EP hybrid system uses information from up to 12 microprocessors to function. Technician B system the TCM is the most important microprocessor for the EV drive operation. Who is correct?
A. Technician A
B. Technician B
C. Both Technician A and Technician B
D. Neither Technician A nor Technician B

Alternative Fuel Properties and Characteristics

Chapter Review

The following activities have been designed to help you refresh your knowledge of this chapter. Your instructor may require you to complete some or all of these activities as a regular part of your training program. You are encouraged to complete any activity that your instructor does not assign as a way to enhance your learning.

Matching

Match the following terms with the correct description or example.

A. Dimethyl ether (DME)

B. Fischer-Tropsch fuels

C. Pyrolysis

D. Wet-spark ignition system

E. Wobbe index (WI)

_____ 1. A chemical process in which biomass feedstock is heated in the absence of air to gasify the material at temperatures of 842–1112°F (450–600°C).

_____ 2. A measure of gas quality made by comparing the heating value of a gas to its density or specific gravity.

_____ 3. An engine that ignites natural gas using a pilot injection of diesel fuel.

_____ 4. A methanol-like renewable fuel, which is a gas at room temperature and requires pressurization to stay in liquid form.

_____ 5. A category of biofuels made from substances including coal, plastic, and natural gas.

Multiple Choice

Read each item carefully, and then select the best response.

_____ 1. The _____ requires increasing amounts of fuel from renewable sources to be blended with gasoline and diesel fuel every year until 2022.
A. Renewable Fuel Standard
B. Vehicle Emission Performance Standard
C. Low Carbon Fuel Standard
D. Diesel Exhaust Emission Standard

_____ 2. The term _____ refers to whether a vehicle or fuel, and its production and associated processes, can be maintained over the long-term.
A. longevity
B. durability
C. sustainability
D. feasibility

_____ 3. Which of the following is an example of fuel with limited range capability?
A. Gasoline
B. Diesel fuel
C. Natural gas
D. Ethanol

_____ **4.** Which type of fuel can be made from everything from wood and sawdust to garbage, agricultural waste, and manure?
  A. E-diesel
  B. Biomass-based fuel
  C. Cellulosic biodiesel
  D. Fischer-Tropsch fuels

_____ **5.** Oil derived from _____ can be produced from a smaller land mass than any other biofuel.
  A. cellulose
  B. ethanol
  C. garbage
  D. algae

_____ **6.** Currently, _____ is only burned in industrial boilers and furnaces as a replacement for heavy petroleum furnace fuel.
  A. wood pyrolysis liquid
  B. Fischer-Tropsch fuel
  C. Cellulosic biodiesel
  D. Propane

_____ **7.** In a dual fuel engine diesel fuel is substituted with up to 85% _____.
  A. ethanol
  B. natural gas
  C. biomass
  D. Fischer-Tropsch fuel

_____ **8.** The index that measures the knock resistance of gaseous fuels is called the _____ number.
  A. methane
  B. cetane
  C. octane
  D. Wobbe

_____ **9.** Methane is a very light fuel gas due to its high _____ content.
  A. oxygen
  B. hydrogen
  C. nitrogen
  D. ethane

_____ **10.** To be practical as a transportation fuel, natural gas must be _____ to reduce the size of fuel storage tanks.
  A. compressed
  B. emulsified
  C. liquefied
  D. Either A or C

True/False

If you believe the statement to be more true than false, write the letter "T" in the space provided. If you believe the statement to be more false than true, write the letter "F".

_____ **1.** With the use of aftertreatment systems engines powered by natural gas can almost match the exhaust emissions of current diesel-fueled engines.

_____ **2.** Most biofuels can only be used in engines that have extensive modifications to their design and construction.

_____ **3.** Fuel made from 100% biological sources is referred to as B100 and it is an entirely renewable fuel.

_____ **4.** The disadvantage to Dimethyl ether is that it has a low cetane value, which causes high levels of particulate matter formation and oxides of nitrogen emissions.

_____ **5.** The chemical structure of propane and natural gas are practically identical.

_____ **6.** Diesel engines are especially simple to convert or modify for natural gas operation.

_____ **7.** In its pure state, natural gas is odorless, colorless, tasteless, and does not usually contain any toxic substances.

_____ **8.** Natural gas fuel has a very low ignition temperature.

_____ **9.** Natural gas contains about 20% of the energy content of diesel fuel.

_____ **10.** Vehicles fueled with natural gas should not be parked in underground, commercial, or residential parking facilities.

Fill in the Blank

Read each item carefully, and then complete the statement by filling in the missing word(s).

1. The _____ _____ Fuel Standard aims to reduce transportation energy consumption by 10% by 2020 compared to a 2010 baseline.

2. Power _____ is the power output per cubic inch (or cubic centimeter) of an engine over its entire operating range.

3. Conventional _____ is any fuel derived from plant material or animal fats.

4. _____ biodiesel is derived from non-food based feedstock, like wood.

5. E-diesel is a fuel made from combining petroleum-based diesel fuel and _____, an alcohol made from plant sugars.

6. Reacting hydrogen and oxygen in a _____ _____ produces only heat and water vapor with no noxious emissions.

7. Propane is extracted in small quantities from _____ _____, which makes it more difficult to produce large supplies for widespread transportation consumption.

8. The upper and lower range of flammability of any fuel is assigned as a _____ of air in an air–fuel mixture within which the mixture can burn.

9. Compressed natural gas is sold on a _____ Gallon Equivalent basis to ensure that the customer is receiving equivalent energy value.

10. Finer grains sand and dust are removed from natural gas by running it through a _____, which is a tank partially filled with oil.

Labeling

Label the following diagrams with the correct terms.

1. Identify the components of a Cummins natural gas spark-ignition engine:

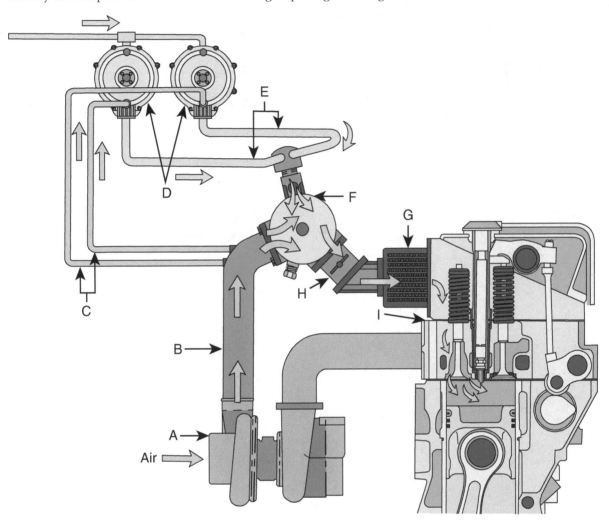

A. _____

B. _____

C. _____

D. _____

E. _____

F. _____

G. _____

H. _____

I. _____

2. Identify the parts of an LNG container:

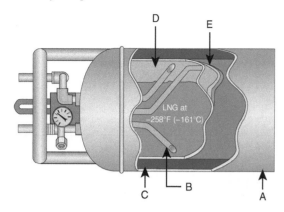

A. _____

B. _____

C. _____

D. _____

E. _____

Crossword Puzzle

Use the clues in the column to complete the puzzle.

Across

4. A process where mechanical pressure is used to mix a fuel with water or another liquid.
5. A gaseous fuel odorant that has a skunk-like or rotten egg–like smell. Mercaptan is added in very small concentrations to help detect any gaseous fuel leaks.

Down

1. The primary constituent of natural gas. Methane's chemical formula is CH_4.
2. A gaseous fuel that is heavier than air. It has the chemical formula C_6H_8. It is also referred to as liquid petroleum fuel (LPG).
3. A vacuum-sealed, bottle-like storage container for LNG that is pressurized to approximately 100 psi (689 kPa). Dewars are fabricated with an inner shell surrounded by super insulating vacuum space enclosed in an outer shell.

ASE-Type Questions

Read each item carefully, and then select the best response.

_____ 1. Technician A says using alternative fuels instead of petroleum-based diesel fuel is not practical, and the public will eventually lose any interest in using alternative fuels. Technician B says that the use of alternative fuels will increase because legislation requires increased usage, and alternative fuels are needed to minimize the impact of global warming. Who is correct?
   A. Technician A
   B. Technician B
   C. Both Technician A and Technician B
   D. Neither Technician A nor Technician B

_____ 2. Technician A says the type of fuel burned has no impact on global warming because all fuels emit CO_2 when burned, which forms greenhouse gases. Technician B says there are low-carbon fuels that can help reduce the amount of greenhouse gases in the atmosphere. Who is correct?
   A. Technician A
   B. Technician B
   C. Both Technician A and Technician B
   D. Neither Technician A nor Technician B

_____ 3. Technician A says that the use of alternative fuels, hybrid-electric vehicles, and other "green" transportation choices is only done to promote a positive social image and is not practical. Technician B says that using alternative fuels achieves significant reductions in noxious emissions from diesel engines in comparison to using petroleum-based diesel fuel. Who is correct?
   A. Technician A
   B. Technician B
   C. Both Technician A and Technician B
   D. Neither Technician A nor Technician B

_____ 4. Technician A says that little or no modifications need to be made to a diesel engine to convert it to dual fuel use, which would enable it to burn natural gas. Technician B says that, to convert a diesel engine to dual fuel use, pistons and cylinder heads need to be replaced and ignition systems added. Who is correct?
   A. Technician A
   B. Technician B
   C. Both Technician A and Technician B
   D. Neither Technician A nor Technician B

_____ 5. Technician A says that using the Fischer-Tropsch reaction to make synthetic diesel fuel is simpler and less expensive than the process used to make bio-oil. Technician B says that wood converted to fuel through fast pyrolysis promises to be one of the least expensive and simplest fuels to produce. Who is correct?
   A. Technician A
   B. Technician B
   C. Both Technician A and Technician B
   D. Neither Technician A nor Technician B

_____ 6. Technician A says that research is being performed to make improvements to the quality of WPL, enabling it to become commercially viable for use in diesel engines. Technician B says that research is being performed to identify changes in engine construction and operation needed to enable the commercial use of WPL for diesel engines. Who is correct?
   A. Technician A
   B. Technician B
   C. Both Technician A and Technician B
   D. Neither Technician A nor Technician B

_____ 7. Technician A says that fuel tanks for DME fuel need to be pressurized to keep the fuel in a liquid state in on-board storage systems. Technician B says that, in comparison to storing petroleum-based diesel fuel, storage space can be reduced by half in tanks containing liquid DME. Who is correct?
   A. Technician A
   B. Technician B
   C. Both Technician A and Technician B
   D. Neither Technician A nor Technician B

_____ **8.** Technician A says that natural gas leaks can be detected by the smell of mercaptan, which smells like rotten cabbage, because mercaptan accompanies leaks of natural gas. Technician B says that natural gas is odorless. Who is correct?
  A. Technician A
  B. Technician B
  C. Both Technician A and Technician B
  D. Neither Technician A nor Technician B

_____ **9.** Technician A says that natural gas is safer than diesel fuel because it is lighter than air and will dissipate quickly into the atmosphere if it leaks. Technician B says that natural gas will ignite in very low concentrations compared to diesel fuel. Who is correct?
  A. Technician A
  B. Technician B
  C. Both Technician A and Technician B
  D. Neither Technician A nor Technician B

_____ **10.** Technician A says that comparisons between fuel economy when using compressed natural gas and diesel fuel are not possible. Technician B says that a comparison can be done, but only if a vehicle uses liquid natural gas. Who is correct?
  A. Technician A
  B. Technician B
  C. Both Technician A and Technician B
  D. Neither Technician A nor Technician B

Natural Gas Combustion Systems

Chapter Review

The following activities have been designed to help you refresh your knowledge of this chapter. Your instructor may require you to complete some or all of these activities as a regular part of your training program. You are encouraged to complete any activity that your instructor does not assign as a way to enhance your learning.

Matching

Match the following terms with the correct description or example.

A. Bernoulli effect

B. Cryogenic

C. Detonation

D. Lean burn combustion

E. Lower flammability limit (LFL)

_____ **1.** A gas that is converted to a liquid and maintained as a liquid at a very low temperature.

_____ **2.** An air–fuel mixture that uses more air than fuel.

_____ **3.** The creation of a low-pressure area by the increased velocity of air (or a fluid).

_____ **4.** An abnormal combustion event where an air–fuel mixture ignites before the spark plug fires.

_____ **5.** The minimum concentration of fuel in air that will support combustion.

Multiple Choice

Read each item carefully, and then select the best response.

_____ **1.** When converting or modifying a heavy-duty diesel engine to run on natural gas it can often remain unchanged with the exception of the _____.
   A. gas mixing and delivery system
   B. turbocharger
   C. air handling system
   D. electronic controls

_____ **2.** Natural gas requires a compression ratio of _____ to achieve the cylinder temperature needed for ignition.
   A. 16:1
   B. 23:1
   C. 38:1
   D. 42:1

_____ **3.** Natural gas engines require a methane index number of at least _____ to resist combustion knock.
   A. 80
   B. 90
   C. 100
   D. 120

_____ **4.** A _____ engine can transition back and forth between natural gas and diesel fuel.
   A. dual-fuel
   B. liquid-ignition
   C. wet-spark
   D. direct injection

_____ 5. The difference between the voltage required to produce a spark across the spark plug gap needed to ignite the fuel and the additional voltage that can be delivered to the spark plugs is called _____.
   A. ignition voltage
   B. flash point
   C. reserve voltage
   D. capacitance

_____ 6. Natural gas has a stoichiometric ratio of _____.
   A. 2:1
   B. 7.5:1
   C. 17.5:1
   D. 20:1.5

_____ 7. When natural gas is metered into the intake air flow and mixed in the intake manifold with air entering the cylinders, the process is called _____.
   A. blending
   B. fumigation
   C. aspiration
   D. stoichiometric combustion

_____ 8. The HPDI developed by Cummins Westport, Inc., enables engines to operate on up to _____ natural gas.
   A. 65%
   B. 75%
   C. 85%
   D. 95%

_____ 9. For low-floor buses, compressed natural gas cylinders are located _____.
   A. on the rooftop
   B. at the rear of the bus
   C. beneath the driver's area
   D. on the sides of the chassis

_____ 10. A _____ compressed natural gas cylinder is constructed of a metal liner reinforced with glass or carbon fiber composite wrap around the entire tank.
   A. Type 1
   B. Type 2
   C. Type 3
   D. Type 4

True/False

If you believe the statement to be more true than false, write the letter "T" in the space provided. If you believe the statement to be more false than true, write the letter "F".

_____ 1. An engine that combusts both diesel and natural gas together in the cylinder is referred to as a hybrid-diesel engine.

_____ 2. Cummins Westport Inc. developed a unique HPDI injector that injects both diesel fuel and natural gas into the cylinder through a single injector.

_____ 3. Spark plugs used in natural gas engines have electrodes and ground straps that have platinum pads, which not only reduces firing voltage, but also makes the plugs last longer.

_____ 4. More air can enter the cylinder with gaseous fuels than with liquid fuels, which increases the amount of power a cylinder can produce from gaseous fuel relative to an injection of liquid diesel fuel.

_____ 5. Until the Environmental Protection Agency 07 emission standards were introduced, lean burn combustion dominated natural gas combustion systems.

_____ 6. Caterpillar and Cummins offer add-on systems to convert large generators and other industrial engines to natural gas by substituting up to 70% of diesel fuel with natural gas.

_____ 7. A second-generation injector introduced in 2012 for use in the ISL-G engine uses a dual control valve, one for natural gas and another for diesel fuel.

_____ **8.** Liquid natural gas trucks have a very short range making them suitable only for transit, utilities, and local or regional freight operations.

_____ **9.** Type 2 compressed natural gas cylinders are also called hoop wrapped cylinders.

_____ **10.** In service and fueling stations where LNG is found, mercaptan, a gaseous fuel odorant that has a skunk-like or rotten egg–like smell is required because LNG has no odor to warn of leaks.

Fill in the Blank

Read each item carefully, and then complete the statement by filling in the missing word(s).

1. Natural gas has a much lower _____ content compared to other fuels.

2. An engine that uses a pilot injection of diesel fuel to initiate natural gas combustion is often called a _____-_____ ignition system.

3. Because natural gas has an _____-_____ temperature of 1100–1200°F it can be highly compressed without the risk of detonation.

4. With _____ _____ combustion, which uses more air than fuel, fuel molecules are spaced farther apart.

5. Spark plug boots, cables, and other insulators are uniquely designed to withstand higher _____ and insulator breakdown caused by the higher firing voltage of natural gas engines.

6. The _____ _____ valve, which meters gas into the intake air, is connected to a diaphragm and moves on and off its seat in response to diaphragm movement.

7. Liquefied natural gas is stored in _____.

8. Compressed natural gas _____ must meet a variety of test standards to ensure they are not easily damaged and will not burst easily.

9. Thermally activated _____ _____ devices have a fusible material that melts at a predetermined temperature and opens a path for natural gas to release into the atmosphere.

10. All _____ _____ used by natural gas vehicles must conform to ASTM International standard A-13.

Labeling

Label the following diagrams with the correct terms.

1. Identify the parts of an integrated fuel module for a stoichiometric EGR spark-ignited natural gas engine:

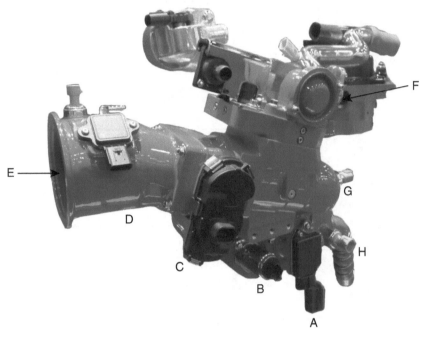

A. _____	**E.** _____
B. _____	**F.** _____
C. _____	**G.** _____
D. _____	**H.** _____

2. Identify the components of a stainless steel tube fitting:

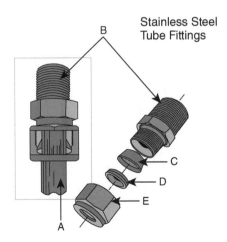

Stainless Steel
Tube Fittings

A. _____
B. _____
C. _____
D. _____
E. _____

3. Identify the parts of a high-pressure fueling receptacle:

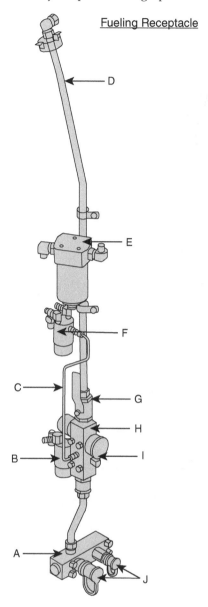

Fueling Receptacle

A. _____

B. _____

C. _____

D. _____

E. _____

F. _____

G. _____

H. _____

I. _____

J. _____

Skill Drills

Test your knowledge of skill drills by filling in the correct words in the photo captions.

1. Replacing the Coalescing Fuel Filter:

Step 1:   Shut _____ the _____.

Step 2:   Open the fuel cylinder _____ _____ on the _____ of the vehicle.

Step 3:   Turn off the manual _____-_____ valves at the _____ of each _____.

Step 4:   Start the _____ from the engine _____ using the engine ignition and _____ _____ controls and _____ the vehicle until the engine _____ because of fuel _____.

Step 5:   Check that the _____ _____ at the fuel _____ compartment reads _____ psi (0 kPa). If the system is still _____, go to Step 6.

Step 6:   Place the _____ switch on the _____ ignition and _____ _____ to the _____ position to _____ the engine from _____ during Step 7.

Step 7:   Place the _____ switch on the engine _____ to the _____ position and _____ to _____ the starting system. Residual _____ _____ from the fuel _____ will now flow to the engine's air–fuel _____, but there will be no engine _____ because the ignition _____ was turned _____ in Step 6.

Step 8:   Check the _____ _____ in the _____ _____ compartment to _____ that the fuel _____ is at _____ psi (0 kPa); if not, repeat Steps _____-_____.

Step 9:   Replace the _____ fuel _____.

Crossword Puzzle

Use the clues in the column to complete the puzzle.

Across

3. A measurement of the knock resistance of gaseous fuels that do not contain octane molecules; similar to the measurement of octane.

5. The temperature at which a fuel will ignite when heated.

Down

1. An engine capable of combusting two different types of fuel, such as natural gas and diesel fuel.

2. A combustion noise created by an abnormally sharp increase in cylinder pressure. Knock is usually caused by detonation or preignition of fuel in the cylinder by an atypical ignition source, such as a piece of hot carbon or hot spark plug insulator.

4. A device used on natural gas engines to meter the correct amount of natural gas into the intake air.

ASE-Type Questions

Read each item carefully, and then select the best response.

_____ 1. Technician A says liquid natural gas storage is better for long-distance freight hauling. Technician B says CNG storage is better for long-distance freight hauling because it is lighter and can haul more freight. Who is correct?
   A. Technician A
   B. Technician B
   C. Both Technician A and Technician B
   D. Neither Technician A nor Technician B

_____ 2. Technician A says that lean burn combustion systems are used to prevent excessive cylinder temperatures in natural gas engines. Technician B says that EGR gas, rather than excess air, is used to lower cylinder temperatures. Who is correct?
   A. Technician A
   B. Technician B
   C. Both Technician A and Technician B
   D. Neither Technician A nor Technician B

_____ 3. Technician A says that very lean air–fuel ratios near 30:1 produce very low NO_x emissions from natural gas engines. Technician B says burning natural gas at a 17.5:1 stoichiometric ratio produces the lowest engine emissions. Who is correct?
   A. Technician A
   B. Technician B
   C. Both Technician A and Technician B
   D. Neither Technician A nor Technician B

_____ 4. Technician A says that natural gas engines have limited power output due to the lower energy density of natural gas. Technician B says that, in natural gas engines, less fuel enters the cylinders as a gas than a liquid, which limits power output. Who is correct?
   A. Technician A
   B. Technician B
   C. Both Technician A and Technician B
   D. Neither Technician A nor Technician B

_____ 5. Technician A says that the likelihood of a cylinder misfire increases under load because cylinder turbulence increases the resistance of the spark plug air gap. Technician B says turbocharging increases spark plug gap resistance. Who is correct?
   A. Technician A
   B. Technician B
   C. Both Technician A and Technician B
   D. Neither Technician A nor Technician B

_____ 6. Technician A says that lean burn combustion conditions increase the firing voltage required to ignite natural gas in the cylinders. Technician B says platinum pads on spark plugs reduce firing voltage. Who is correct?
   A. Technician A
   B. Technician B
   C. Both Technician A and Technician B
   D. Neither Technician A nor Technician B

_____ 7. Technician A says that retrofitting an engine to use both diesel fuel and natural gas requires replacement of the cylinder head and pistons. Technician B says that in addition to those changes, a gas control valve installed in the air intake is one of the few major engine modifications. Who is correct?
   A. Technician A
   B. Technician B
   C. Both Technician A and Technician B
   D. Neither Technician A nor Technician B

_____ **8.** Technician A says that the latest natural gas engines require particulate filters to meet emission standards. Technician B says that natural gas engines only require three-way catalytic converters. Who is correct?
   A. Technician A
   B. Technician B
   C. Both Technician A and Technician B
   D. Neither Technician A nor Technician B

_____ **9.** Technician A says that LNG storage tanks are pressurized to more than 3000 psi (207 bar). Technician B says that gas at that high pressure requires at least two stages of pressure regulation to lower the pressure and supply the volume the engine can use. Who is correct?
   A. Technician A
   B. Technician B
   C. Both Technician A and Technician B
   D. Neither Technician A nor Technician B

_____ **10.** Technician A says that natural gas engines can only be supplied by a certified manufacturer. Technician B says that diesel engines can have conversion kits, which enables them to operate on both diesel and natural gas. Who is correct?
   A. Technician A
   B. Technician B
   C. Both Technician A and Technician B
   D. Neither Technician A nor Technician B